NEWSPAPER EXTRACTS FROM "THE HOOSIER STATE"

Newport
Vermillion County
Indiana

January 4, 1888 to December 25, 1889

Abstracted by
Carolyn Schwab

HERITAGE BOOKS
2008

HERITAGE BOOKS
AN IMPRINT OF HERITAGE BOOKS, INC.

Books, CDs, and more—Worldwide

For our listing of thousands of titles see our website
at
www.HeritageBooks.com

Published 2008 by
HERITAGE BOOKS, INC.
Publishing Division
100 Railroad Ave. #104
Westminster, Maryland 21157

Copyright © 2008 Carolyn Schwab

Other Heritage Books by Carolyn Schwab and the Marin County Genealogical Society:

Newspaper Extracts from Sausalito News, *Sausalito, Marin County, California, February 12, 1885 to December 26, 1890*
Newspaper Extracts from The Marin Journal, *San Rafael, Marin County, California, January 6, 1881 to December 25, 1884*
Newspaper Extracts from The Marin Journal, *San Rafael, Marin County, California, January 1, 1885 to December 27, 1888*
Newspaper Extracts from The Marin Journal, Marin County Tocsin
San Rafael, Marin County, California, January 3, 1889 to December 27, 1890
Newspaper Extracts from The Marin Journal, Marin County Tocsin
San Rafael, Marin County, California, January 1, 1891 to December 31,1892
Newspaper Extracts from The Marin Journal, Marin County Tocsin
San Rafael, Marin County, California, January 5, 1893 to December 27, 1894

Other Heritage Books by Carolyn Schwab:

The Hoosier State Newspapers, 1880-1881
Newspaper Extracts from "The Hoosier State", Newport, Vermillion County, Indiana, January 2, 1868 to December 25, 1873
Newspaper Extracts from "The Hoosier State", Newport, Vermillion County, Indiana, January 1, 1874 to December 30, 1875
Newspaper Extracts from "The Hoosier State", Newport, Vermillion County, Indiana, January 6, 1876 to December 27, 1877
Newspaper Extracts from "The Hoosier State", Newport, Vermillion County, Indiana, January 3, 1878 to December 31, 1879
Newspaper Extracts from "The Hoosier State", Newport, Vermillion County, Indiana, January 7, 1880 to December 28, 1881
Newspaper Extracts from "The Hoosier State", Newport, Vermillion County, Indiana, January 4, 1882 to December 27, 1882; January 3, 1883 to April 4, 1883; April 11, 1883 to April 1, 1885 Unavailable; April 8, 1885 to December 30, 1885
Newspaper Extracts from "The Hoosier State", Newport, Vermillion County, Indiana, January 6, 1886 to December 28, 1887
Newspaper Extracts from "The Hoosier State", Newport, Vermillion County, Indiana, January 4, 1888 to December 25, 1889
Newspaper Extracts from "The Hoosier State", Newport, Vermillion County, Indiana, January 1, 1890 to December 30, 1891

All rights reserved. No part of this book may be reproduced or transmitted in any form or by any means, electronic or mechanical, including photocopying, recording or by any information storage and retrieval system without written permission from the author, except for the inclusion of brief quotations in a review.

International Standard Book Number
Paperbound: 978-0-7884-4674-0
Clothbound: 978-0-7884-7219-0

Table of Contents

1888..1
1889..83
Name Index..211

One of the earliest newspapers for Vermillion County, Indiana was the Hoosier State. It was bought by Samuel Brenton Davis from Henry D. Washburn in 1868. It was published weekly. The early issues contained practically no local news, their space given to politics and world news. Only rarely was a death given or a marriage and then in the shortest possible manner. The retail advertising was almost entirely of Terre Haute stores. The style of the newspaper gradually changed and in the 1870's, local births, marriages, deaths, and business happenings began to appear. In addition to the abundance of names and relationships, news articles tell us a lot about the customs, lifestyles, and priorities of the times. Voter lists, orphan records, list of unclaimed letters, teacher and student lists, real estate transfers, and court happenings are among the items covered.   In the 1880's, several correspondents from the local towns sent in local news.

Not only did the newspaper contain information for Vermillion County, but the surrounding counties – Warren, Fountain, Parke, and Vigo – can also be found as well. Since Vermillion County, Indiana, and Vermilion County, Illinois are right next to each other, be sure to check that county also. Quite often, families would visit or send letters from where they came from or where they moved to. The early newspapers are a gold mine to the genealogist. They contain information that you cannot find anywhere but in the local newspaper.

The early newspapers contain information that is very useful to the genealogist. Sometimes you can find early births and deaths that were never recorded. It was not required by law to report these until after 1882. They were not too complete or very reliable. Other information is also found here. I hope what I have found is very useful to you in writing a story about your family.

NEWPORT HOOSIER STATE 1888

Wednesday, January 4, 1888

A Bad Accident
On last Monday night, while Col. L.R. WHIPPLE, of Eugene, and another gentleman, who were engaged in a friendly scuffle in BRUCE SIMPSON's saloon, Col. WHIPPLE met with an accident that will probably make a cripple of him for life. In falling, he wrenched his leg, breaking the large bone in two places, at the ankle joint and about three inches above, and the small bone of the leg about three inches above the ankle joint. He suffered intensely during the night, but was resting easily yesterday morning. The Col. has our warmest sympathy in his sad misfortune.

Eaten by the Hogs
SARAH G. EWING, aged 62 years, living four miles from Shelbyville, IN, was found dead in her barnyard yesterday morning by her grandson, FRANK EDWARDS. Her body was horribly mangled by the hogs, who had pulled her down the night before when she went to milk and killed her. One leg and her face were eaten off. Her grandson and his wife were away during the evening, and finding her absent on their return, supposed she had gone to her son and made no search for her.
Vincennes Commercial

Dana News
Mr. JAMES VAN ALLEN, of Utica, OH, brother of Mrs. JACOB WHITLOCK is visiting here this week. It is the first time in 20 years that brother and sister have seen each other.

Clinton Items
Mrs. PATTON, wife of BARNEY PATTON, died last Saturday morning of consumption. The funeral was held Sunday afternoon.

Something surely must be wrong in the glorious climate of the west from the way the boys are returning. O.S. STOKESBERRY returned Monday.

SAM MYERS seems to be the object of a remarkable series of bereavements. Some three months ago his sister, Mrs. BILLY BRIGHT died after a short illness. Tuesday of last week his son died of pneumonia. The next day his wife followed her boy, and on Thursday they were both buried together. On Sunday his mother died of lung fever.

A Mr. BUTTS, brother to A.L. BUTTS, died last Saturday, of Bright's disease. Mr. BUTTS had been a sufferer from this dread malady for 15 years, and during that time he was hardly ever able to perform any labor. He leaves a devoted wife and several children to mourn his loss. The funeral services were conducted from the house Sunday.

Bono
Miss ALMA JENKS, who is attending school at Greencastle, was home on a visit last week.

Born to Mr. and Mrs. JOHN BEARD, a dishwasher. She arrived last week.

Miss AMERICA INGRAM, of Illiana, was the guest of Mr. AUSTIN, Sunday last.

CHARLES BROWN is the happy father of a bouncing boy. He came to this country December 29th.

HOSFORD & BELLS	WHITESIDE
Clothing, Boots, & Shoes	Dentist
Eugene, IN	Paris, IL

S.B. DAVIS
Proprietor, Hoosier State
Newport, IN

NIXON & CATES
Agricultural Implements
Cayuga, IN

J.P. & E.H. DUNLAP
Real Estate Agents
Abstract & Loan Office
Newport, IN

H. CONLEY
J.C. SAWYER
Attorneys at Law
Newport, IN

J.C. JACKSON
Dry Goods, Groceries
Hillsdale, IN

FRED RUSH
County Surveyor
Dana, IN

L.H. AIKMAN
Short Horn Cattle
Dana, IN

H.D. PIXLEY & Co.
Clothing, Hats
Terre Haute, IN

Local News

Mrs. BELL THORNTON was elected Superintendent of the U.B. Sabbath School on Sunday last.

STEVE CLARK and Miss BELLE SWAIM, of Eugene, were united in wedlock on last Thursday evening, Esq. THOMPSON, of Cayuga, performing the marriage rites.

Roll of Honor of Primary Grade of Perrysville School Ending December 24, 1887
Pupils neither tardy nor absent:
    WILLIE HATHAWAY, JOE MITCHELL, GRACE MITCHELL, HARRY LOWE,
    LIZZIE SHAW, JOHN KELSH, and RUTH BENEFIEL
        I.M. MAFFETT, Teacher

The newly elected officers of the Odd Fellows Lodge, of this place, were installed at the regular meeting of the lodge last night. The following is a list of officers:

W.P. HENSON	Noble Grand
R.A. PARRETT	Vice Grand
J.R. SWAIN	Secretary
THOMAS CUSHMAN	Permanent Secretary
M.G. RHOADS	Treasurer
H.H. CONLEY	Trustee
R.W. STEPHENS	Trustee
JOHN RICHARDSON	Trustee

Z.P. THORNTON, landlord of the Newport Hotel, went out to Ridge Farm, IL, on last Saturday, and visited his brother over Sunday.

JOHN R. STAHL and PORTER MILLIKIN, of Eugene, took in the State Teacher's Association at Indianapolis last week. They were the only representatives from this county.

Miss ALLIE KOONSE, teacher at No. 3, returned from Lafayette on last Monday night, where she had been spending the holidays with her parents and numerous young friends.

Miss CLARA MYERS, a student in the freshman class of the Illinois University at Urbana, who has been spending the holidays at home, returned to her school on last Monday morning. While here she received a report from the regent of the school, giving her standing during the term just closed, which is marked No. 1 in all her studies.

Agents for the Hoosier
    JOHN CADE   Gessie

SMITH RABB, and Postmistress	Perrysville
HOSFORD & BELL	Eugene
Dr. E.A. FLAUGHER	Cayuga
ED VANSICKLE, Postmaster	Hillsdale
J.C. JACKSON	Hillsdale
GEORGE W. EDWARDS, Postmaster	Clinton
J.R. FINNELL	Jonestown
F.N. AUSTIN	Bono
J.E. BILSLAND	Dana
FRANK LANGSTON	Summit Grove

Personal Mention
Mrs. PIPER, of Illinois, is here visiting her daughter, Mrs. JOE HANN.

Senator SEARS took ALICE CHUNN, aged 14, to the Soldiers' Orphans Home, at Knightstown, this State, on Monday last.

FRANK BETSON has returned home from the Terre Haute Normal to stay, on account of his failing eyesight.

Notice of Settlement of Estate
    Estate of GEORGE W. HINES, deceased
    December 9, 1887
                          A.R. HOPKINS, Clerk

Notice of Settlement of Estate
    Estate of SOLOMON STULTZ, deceased
    December 22, 1887
                          A.R. HOPKINS, Clerk

Dissolution Notice
    COFFIN Bros.
    M.W. COFFIN retiring
    W.T. COFFIN will take full control
    December 26, 1887
                          M.W. COFFIN
                          W.T. COFFIN

PEARL PIERCE, who has been confined to a bed of affliction for a long time, is still in a precarious condition, and it is doubtful if he recovers. He first took down with typhoid fever, and then took a relapse, and is now suffering from dropsy and hemorrhage of the bowels.

J.W. McCONNELL, who is now running a photograph gallery at Montezuma, was up here last Friday to make out papers to get a pension by special act of Congress. The old gentleman is now past 71 years of age, and is not able to earn a living at his profession, and is deserving of support by the government.

Wednesday, January 11, 1888

Dana News
After a long sickness, at his home, one and a half miles east of Dana, on Thursday last, December 29th, the spirit of MAURICE FITZGERALD took its flight in his 69th year. The remains were taken to Greencastle for burial on the Friday night train. J.W. REDMAN, the popular undertaker, accompanied the friends.

There is a little rumor on the breeze to the effect that JOHN CRANE is to be wedded in the very near future, and has already procured his license.

Perrysville Items
ARCHIE McCONNELL, of this place, formally of Dana and Newport, came to town one evening in flying colors, as he said, to learn the tinner's trade. He studied that for quite awhile, but found that it would be a long and tedious job, but a good trade when well learned. He next tried farming south of town, but heard that the soil was more fertile on the Mound Prairie. He farmed there awhile, but found that farming was too much for his frail body, and he is now starting to learn the carpenter's trade. We do not think he will continue long as that as no one likes "kittens" but old maids. Whether he will go back and try and finish the tinner's trade, or try something else, we are at a loss to say, but hope that he will find something that suits him after while.

Clinton Items
Just as we went to press last week, a rumor reached us that JAMES L. WISHARD had died at Terre Haute. The report proved too true. The poor fellow had been driving streetcars and working about the tracks and the exposure proved too much for him. He was taken ill with pneumonia and died in a few days. The remains were taken charge of by the G.A.R. boys of Terre Haute and placed on the train and brought to this city. Here the local Post took them and carried them to Spangler's Cemetery where the St. Bernice Post of which JIM was a member, performed the burial ceremony. JIM was also a member of the M.E. Church and was a very hard working man. He was an ex-union soldier, having served his country in the 62nd IL Vol. He was born in Helt Township, October 20, 1842. He leaves a wife and 7 children.

Mr. ISAAC H. STRAIN, of this city, and Miss ADDIE A. LEWIS, of Helt township, were married Sunday at the residence of the bride's father, east of Toronto; Rev. J.H. RUMISEL officiating. As stated in our last issue, they will make their home in this city. The Argus extends to them its hearty congratulations and earnestly wishes them a happy and prosperous journey through life.

The two literary societies of the Newport High School will give a joint entertainment, at the Opera House on next Saturday evening. The following will participate:
JENNIE McKNIGHT, ALBERT WHEELER, ERNEST DARBY, QUINCY MYERS, EDNA BROWN, ANNA RICHARDSON, THOMAS HARLAN, ORA DAVIS, MORREY SWAIN, CLAUDE SEARS, JOHN HARRISON, ETTA McCONNELL, BERTIE STEPHENS, ELLA RICHARDSON, VARA PATRICK, LOU CADY, CHARLEY THORNTON, MAGGIE HOPKINS, LOU BRINDLEY, PAUL RHOADS, WILLIE RICHARDSON

CHARLEY WILTERMOOD received his commission as Postmaster on Thursday last, and took formal possession of the office on Monday last. He now writes P.M. after his name.

Home News
L.J. PLACE bought 120 acres of land from ALEXANDER DUNLAP, lying west of the old fairground, one day last week, at $33 per acre.

WILLIAM F. THORNTON, foreman of this office, has a new catnip swigger at his house. It arrived here on the 2:20 train last Monday afternoon, and is of the piano thumping gender.

JOHN L. EGGLESTON bought 80 acres of coal and timberland, at the Horse Shoe, known as the SIDWELL land, a few days ago, for $1140. It is said to be a valuable tract of land.

BEULAH GROVES, daughter of JOHN B. GROVES of this township, is down with lung fever.

The wife of PERRY ASTON, of Garden City, KS, died one day last week. Mr. ASTON was a former resident of this place.

M.B. DAVIS, a brother to the editor of this paper, who went out to Nebraska 2 or 3 years ago to seek his fortune, has bought a half interest in the Beatrice, Nebraska Republican. He has been doing the editorial work on the paper for over a year. It is a weekly, and about the same size as the Hoosier.

Married at the residence of the bride's mother, on January 1, 1888, STEPHEN A.D. THOMAS and BERTHA J. RANDALL. The marriage ceremony was performed by Rev. J.S. BROWN. There were several friends present and all seemed to enjoy themselves. Mr. THOMAS is a very nice young man, of a good family, and we hope his lady is equally as good.

Obituary
The wife of MARTIN PETTY, who resided south of town, on the Clinton road, died on Thursday last of lung fever, after a week's illness, aged about 65 years. Her funeral took place the next day at the Presbyterian Church, Rev. VAN ALLEN preaching the discourse, after which her remains were interred in the Thomas Cemetery.

At a regular meeting to the Rebekah Lodge, at this place, on last Saturday night, the following newly elected officers were installed for the ensuing term:

Mrs. M. LYTLE	Noble Grand
Mrs. ED AIKMAN	Vice Grand
MATTHEW LYTLE	Secretary
Miss ZULA HOPKINS	Treasurer
W.P. HENSON	Conductor
D.S. HOPKINS	Warden
LEWIS SHEPARD	R.S.N.G.
ED AIKMAN	L.S.N.G.
Mrs. D.S. HOPKINS	I.G.

A successfully year is the motto of the M.E. Sunday School which recently elected the following active and efficient corps of officers for the ensuing year:

ABEL SEXTON	Superintendent
J.P. HENSON	Assistant
ANNA RICHARDSON	Secretary
VARA PATRICK	Treasurer
D.R. GRAY	Chorister
ELLA PARRETT	Organist
ZULA HOPKINS	Assistant
BELLE HARRISON	Librarian
BERTIE STEPHENS	Librarian

Personal Mention
GEORGE LEWELLEN, of Ohio, is here visiting his sister, Mrs. THOMAS BRINDLEY.

Sheriff's Sale on Decree
 State of Indiana vs. THOMAS W. STEPHENS & ALICE M. STEPHENS
 $854.93
 Sale on Saturday, February 4, 1888 at courthouse
  4 acres off W end of N ½ SE ¼ Sec 7 T 18 N R 9 W
  11.77 acres off N end of NE ¼ Sec 21 T 18 N R 10 W
  10 acres in SW corner of N ½ SW ¼ Sec 7 T 18 N R 9 W
  In all 25.77 acres
 M.G. RHOADS, attorney for plaintiff
 January 11, 1888
          JOHN A. DARBY, Sheriff

Wednesday, January 18, 1888

Hillsdale News
JOSEPH FLYNN, formerly of Hillsdale, and who recently married a young lady of Paris, IL, is here visiting his brother PATRICK FLYNN.

OLIVER WHITSON, who has been very sick with typhoid fever for 4 or 5 weeks, has taken a relapse and is in rather a precarious condition.

Bono
Grandmother SMITH is on the sick list. She is one of the oldest women in the community. If she should live until the 29th of this month, she would be 87 years old.

It is rumored that DEWIE KERNS will soon start to school at Purdue University.

Bono will soon be inhabited by a new doctor. His name is Mr. PATTERSON, and he hails from Cayuga. We hope he is a good one.

Notice to Non-Residents
    CHARLES W. WARD & OSCAR B. GIBSON vs. WILLIAM L. SHEWARD &
    CHARLES C. SHEWARD
    Complaint #2981
    WARD & GIBSON – attorneys for plaintiff
    CHARLES C. SHEWARD is not a resident of State of Indiana
    Must appear before 2nd Monday in March
    Filed January 16, 1888
                                   A.R. HOPKINS, Clerk

Notice to Non-Residents
    LEWIS SKINNER vs. EMALINE SANDERS, EZRA SANDERS, her husband, &
    Advance Thresher Co. of Battle Creek, MI
    Foreclosure of Mortgage
    Advance Thresher Co. is not a resident of State of Indiana
    Must appear before 2nd Monday in March
    JOHN B. MARTIN, attorney for plaintiff
                                   A.R. HOPKINS, Clerk

Clinton Items (from the Argus)
It is rumored that Mr. ED MALLORY, of Veedersburg, and Miss CLARA SMITH were united in marriage at the residence of the bride's on North High Street, today (Thursday).

Dana News
MARK RUSH, late of this township, but now of Thomasville, GA, is visiting friends and relatives here. He reports all well pleased with their southern home.

Personal Mention
Mrs. ALICE WELHAUS, of Streator, IL, is here visiting her brother, JOHN HASTY and family.

GEORGE HEAPS and wife, of Farmersburg, Sullivan County, were up here last week visiting RILEY WHITNEY and family.

AMANDA MARRIS, of Fairmount, KS, FRANK TURNER's foster mother, was here visiting him several days last week.

Married
On Tuesday night of last week, Esq. SAMUEL C. HOLLINGSWORTH made two souls happy, by uniting in wedlock THOMAS CORBRIDGE and Mrs. ARMANTA CARICO, both of Opedee.

OMAR McMASTERS, a young unmarried man of Montezuma, was found drowned in Sugar Creek, a short distance east of here, on Monday last. He had been missing since Thursday last, and was discovered by a searching party.

Frozen to Death
It is rumored that JAMES BROCK, living near Highland was found in his bed on Wednesday morning frozen to death. We are informed that Mr. BROCK was subject to fits and it is supposed that during the night he took a fit and while in convulsions threw the cover off the bed and froze before he regained consciousness.
Montezuma Reporter

MORRIS HUGHES, at one time the most influential man in Parke County, was taken by authorities to the county infirmary yesterday morning. For several years Mr. HUGHES' mind has been affected, and he has been a great burden to his family and friends, and during the cold weather it was impossible to keep him in the house, and it was feared he would wander off and be frozen. It was thought best to take him to the infirmary.
Montezuma Reporter

Sister EMMA CUMBY, wife of HENRY CUMBY, died in Danville, IL, January 8, 1888, aged about 21 years. Her remains and the remains of her infant child were brought to the Gessie Chapel, where the funeral was preached to a crowded house. She leaves behind a husband and a darling little boy, about 2 years old, and a host of friends who sadly mourn her departure. The funeral was preached by J.S. BROWN of Gessie, IN.

Delinquent Tax List for Vermillion County for 1886

Highland Township

NAME	SECTION	TWP	RANGE	ACRES	TAX
LEE, WILLIAM, estate	19	18	10	47.85	26.71
STEPHENS, THOMAS W.	21	18	10	11.70	
STEPHENS, THOMAS W.	7	18	9	10	
STEPHENS, THOMAS W.	7	18	9	40	
STEPHENS, THOMAS W.	7	18	9	20	
STEPHENS, THOMAS W.	7	18	9	4	
STEPHENS, THOMAS W.	21	18	10	112	224.44

Eugene Township

NAME	SECTION	TWP	RANGE	ACRES	TAX
GREER, ANNA E.	28	18	10	10	8.12
McCLELLAN, WILLIAM	19	17	10	20	5.02
PETTY, ANN	18	17	9	40	40.28
PETTY, MALINDA	9	17	9	69	
PETTY, MALINDA	9	17	9	20	147.70
SIMS, LEWIS & ELIZABETH	8	17	9	7.15	14.50

Vermillion Township

NAME	SECTION	TWP	RANGE	ACRES	TAX
BROWN, DAVID	34	17	9	2	5.08
McCLELLAN, WILLIAM	30	17	10	6	
McCLELLAN, WILLIAM	30	17	10	7	
McCLELLAN, WILLIAM	30	17	10	6	18.66

| MILLER, STEPHEN | 2 | 16 | 9 | .50 | 12.08 |

Helt Township

NAME	SECTION	TWP	RANGE	ACRES	TAX
COMPTON, CATHERINE	34	16	9	8	
COMPTON, CATHERINE	34	16	9	10	37.50
MALONE, SAMUEL G.	36	16	10	73	89.55

Clinton Township

NAME	SECTION	TWP	RANGE	ACRES	TAX
BOZARTH, JAMES M.	33	14	10	9	3.26
HELT, THOMAS	34	14	9	50.25	
HELT, THOMAS	33	14	9	20	
HELT, THOMAS	33	14	9	1	31.73
HICKLAN, EMMA	8	14	9	4	10.53
LEE, MARTHA E.	28	14	10	60	22.99
POTTER, PRISCILLA	5	14	9	20	27.47
PIERCE, HARRISON	5	14	9	1	9.14
TAYLOR, SAMUEL N.	33	14	9	20	13.33

Town Lots in Perrysville

NAME	LOTS	TAX
CROCKET, ALLEN S.	G & C Addition, In lot 13	12.10
GASAWAY, MARY A.	Out lot 5	10.50

Town Lots in Eugene

NAME	LOTS	TAX
JOHNSON, WILLIAM H.	In lot 91	
JOHNSON, WILLIAM H.	G's addition North ½, In lot 6	7.10

Town Lots in Eugene Junction

NAME	LOTS	TAX
BOLLIS, DANIEL W.	In lot 37 & 38	9.99
MILLIKIN, W.S.	G & McK's addition, In lot 65 & 66	
MILLIKIN, W.S.	G & McK's addition, In lot 67 & 68	13.87
WAGGONER, HENRY	In lot 39 & 40	4.48

Town Lots in Clinton

NAME	LOTS	TAX
AYERS, CHARITY	Morey's addition In lot 9, Block 1	12.99
CANADAY, WILLIAM A.	South ½ In lot 2, Block 18	
CANADAY, WILLIAM A.	19 feet south side In lot 4, Block 18	
CANADAY, WILLIAM A.	In lot 3, Block 18	32.04
COFFEEN, HENRY A.	60x159 feet in Out lot 6	14.14
CHASE, MARGARET	Bellus addition north ½, In lot 6	10.16
DUFFER, ELIZABETH	47 feet south side, In lot 4, Block 18	
DUFFER, ELIZABETH	In lot 5, Block 18	18.13
MARTIN, FRANK E.	Part of In lot 6 & 7 & 10, Block 14	15.45
PATTON, RACHEL J.	In lot 2 & 3, Block 31	183.39
VAUGHN, JAMES	Bellus' addition In lot 1	
VAUGHN, JAMES	Bellus' addition North ½, In lot 4, Block 30	18.80

Town Lots in Dana

NAME	LOTS	TAX

KEYES, C.F.	In lot 7 & 8, Block 12	
KEYES, C.F.	In lot 11 & 12, Block 4	11.95
LANGSTON, MINERVA	In lot 22, Block 11	4.08

Wednesday, January 25, 1888

Death
MORRIS HUGHES, at one time a wealthy and prominent citizen of Montezuma, died on Tuesday last a comparatively poor citizen. His funeral, which occurred on Friday, was very largely attended by a host of warm friends. He had been in poor health for a long time, and had recently lost his mind.

Death
After a protracted illness, lasting about 6 months, Mrs. STEPHEN MILLIKIN, of Eugene, died at three o'clock on last Saturday morning, aged 75 years last July. The deceased was formerly a resident of Helt Township, where she and her late husband were well and favorably known. She leaves two sons and two daughters. Her funeral took place on last Sunday afternoon, Rev. R.B. VAN ALLEN, of the U.B. Church, holding short services at the house, after which her remains were laid to rest in the Eugene Cemetery.

Obituary
The estimable wife of Uncle ROBERT WRIGHT, of this place, died at 10 o'clock on last Friday night, January 20, 1888. She was born in Mercer County, KY, February 12, 1805, and had she lived till the 12th of next month, she would have been 83 years old. She never attached herself to any church, but was a true Christian lady in every particular, and respected and loved by all her acquaintances. She leaves a husband, two daughters, and a son. One daughter resides in Parke County and the other in Kansas. Her son WILLIAM P. WRIGHT is a resident of this place. Her funeral took place on Monday last, her remains being taken to the Linebarger Cemetery, in Parke County, for interment.

Death
Mrs. HARRIET TURPENING, mother of Senator R.B. and JACOB SEARS, died shortly after 5 o'clock on last Sunday evening, after a long and protracted illness, aged about 69 years. She had been married twice. Her first husband was GEORGE H. SEARS, who died while Treasurer of this county, in 1854 or 1855. In early life the deceased was a member of the M.E. Church, and afterwards united with the U.B. Church, but owing to poor health for many years, she had not been able to attend services, but always tried to live a true Christian life. For the last three months, she had been making her home with her son, Senator SEARS, where she was kindly cared for and everything done that was possible to alleviate her sufferings. Her funeral took place yesterday morning at 10 o'clock from the residence of her son, Rev. R.S MARTIN, pastor of the M.E. Church, and Rev. R.B. VAN ALLEN, pastor of the U.B. Church, holding joint services, after which her remains were followed by the relatives and a large number of friends to the Thomas Cemetery, where they were gently laid in the tomb to moulder back to mother dust.

Home News
DICK CHURCH, of Helt township, how has a jack full on queens. The last arrival made his appearance on the 5th of this month.

CHARLEY AYRES has worked for SMITH RABB, shoemaker, of Perrysville, for 35 years without intermission, in the same room, on the same bench, and mostly with the same tools.

JOHN W. COLEMAN, father of M.G. COLEMAN, who was principal of the Newport schools last winter, died at Cincinnati on the 13th of this month, aged 61 years. His remains were brought to Danville, IL, for burial.

Pastor R.S. MARTIN, of the M.E. Church, closed his arrival here on last Friday night. The following is a list of those who united with the church:

>Mrs. S.A. SWAIN, Mrs. MADIE RHOADS, D.R. GRAY, E.O. GRAY, J.R. SWAIN, Mrs. ELIZABETH CAIN, ETTIE FUNKHOUSER, HATTIE HANUM, MINNIE R. LYTLE, LUCY R. STOKES, CHARLES R. GRAY, Mrs. ROBERT PARRETT, SUSIE STOKES, FRED CAIN, ESSIE PORTER, D.Y. FUNKHOUSER, HARRIET WHEELER, LEONARD WHEELER, OLLIE BLUNK, M.S. SWAIN, JOHN SOLLARS, FREDERICK DUZAN, ALLIE V. KOONSE, CARRIE CROSS, MATTHEW LYTLE, BELLE DUZAN, REN M. DAVIS, ANNIE HARRISON, Mrs. N. SOLLARS, MINA HOLLINGSWORTH, BESSIE FUNKHOUSER, DELLA SOLLARS, WILLIAM SOLLARS, W.P. ASTON, ELIZABETH FUNKHOUSER.

MARTIN L. WRIGHT has been appointed administrator of the estate of PETER L. WRIGHT, deceased.

BOB ADAMS has purchased of JOHN PEELER, of Dana, the building known as the old railroad saloon, for which he paid $1200. He will apply for liquor license at the March term of Commissioner's court.

A large silver steel bell with tolling hammer and other appliances has recently been presented to, and set up in Vermillion Memorial M.E. Church south of town. It was a present from Mr. and Mrs. JAMES HARLAN. Services will be held in that church every night this week by the Pastor, Rev. R.S. MARTIN.

The occasion of unusual interest occurred at the residence of Mr. and Mrs. JOHN KERDOLFF of their sister AMANDA KERDOLFF to County Recorder MELVILLE B. CARTER, both well known and favorites in social circles. At exactly 7:30 p.m., the happy couple entered the beautiful parlor preceded by Rev. R.S. MARTIN of the M.E. Church. After a wedding trip to Ohio, the happy couple will return to live in Newport.

Dana News

The newly elected officers of the Dana Building and Loan Association are:

J.W. JARVIS	President
Dr. T.C. HOOD	Vice President
E.M. EELS	Secretary
T.S. HOOD	Treasurer
J.P. YORK	Solicitor

Wednesday, February 1, 1888

Obituary

PAUL DAVIS, son of C.S. and MARY DAVIS, died of congestion of the brain, at Salina, KS, on Saturday, January 28, 1888, at about 6:30 p.m., and was brought back here yesterday afternoon for burial. The deceased was only sick 5 or 6 hours, and was not considered dangerously ill until a very short time before the darling little boy breathed his last. He would have been 20 months old the 12th of this month, had he lived. He was the only son, and idolized by the father and mother. The sudden loss of this dear little boy was a terrible shock, and it seems hard for them to reconcile themselves to the loss of one who was so dear to them. In their sad bereavement they have the full sympathy of their many warm personal friends of Newport, their old home for many years. The remains, accompanied by the parents and their two little daughters, and RICHARD HAWKINS, arrived here on the 3:35 train yesterday afternoon. The funeral will take place today at 10:00 a.m., the pastor, Rev. R.S. MARTIN, preaching the funeral discourse, after which the body of little PAUL DAVIS will be taken to the Thomas Cemetery, and laid away in the tomb by kind friends to moulder back to mother dust.

Elopement

For several months, OLIVER P. GRUBB, of this place, has been sweet on Miss SUSIE BELL, daughter of the widow of JAMES A. BELL. Her good mother did not want her daughter to marry, but objections in case of true love availeth nothing. On last Monday night, while her mother and the rest of the family were eating supper, Miss SUSIE gave them the slip, and met her lover down in town, who had a sleigh to speed her away. He was armed with the necessary legal document to make them one. They went to Vermillion Chapel, where Rev. R.S. MARTIN was holding a meeting. They then followed him back to his residence, where he joined them in holy wedlock.

Clinton Items (from the Argus)
JIM ROBERTS will try California for his health.

Mrs. TOM WANTLING, living near Hazel Bluff farm, died Wednesday night of consumption. Four small children are left motherless.

JOHN ENGLISH, a brother of Mrs. WALRAVEN, and a resident of the western part of this township, died suddenly last Saturday. He hauled coal the day before and was apparently in sound health. The interment took place in Edgar County.

Highland
CHESTER LAKE was fooling with a pistol one day last week, when it exploded and shot him through the palm of his hand.

D.B. DINSMORE and H. OSBORN dissolved partnership last Friday, DINSMORE retiring from business on account of bad health.

Home News
Mrs. SANDERS, of Perrysville, mother in law of DAVE HOLD, died on last Monday night. She was quite an old lady.

The next wedding in Newport will probably be SCOTT AIKMAN and Miss MARY CHIPPS.

We hear it reported that Miss MATTIE LAMB, of Alvin, IL, a former resident of this place, was united in wedlock one day last week to a Mr. GEORGE FORD of that city.

JOHN SELF, residing 4 miles south of town, who has been confined to his bed for nearly two months, is reported to be gradually growing worse, and there is now very little hope entertained of his recovery.

The stockholders of the Vermillion County Fair Association, of Eugene, have elected the following officers and directors for the ensuing year:

JAMES MALONE	President
H.D. SPRAGUE	Vice President
J.S. GROENDYKE	Secretary
M.G. HOSFORD	Assistant Secretary
G.L. WATSON	Treasurer

Directors
JAMES ARRASMITH, H.C. RANDOLPH, L.H. AIKMAN, Dr. KINDERMAN, S.K. TODD, SAMUEL GROENDYKE, G.D. WITTENBURG, H.O. PETERS, L. ROACH, J.H. ILES, SAMUEL BOWERS

Personal Mention
CHARLES RALSTON, of Dana, is now father of a big boy baby, which arrived on Sunday last.

Mrs. MINNA C. MAY, wife of Lieutenant W.T. MAY, who has charge of the military department at De Pauw University, is in town visiting her cousin, Mrs. C.W. WARD.

A Short Honeymoon
On Tuesday, January 19, 1888, Esq. SAMUEL C. HOLLINGSWORTH united in wedlock Mr. THOMAS CORBRIDGE, of Parke County, aged 58, to Mrs. AMANTA CARICO, of Opedee, aged 63 years. Everything went along smoothly for two weeks, the old lady taking her new hubby to her home and feeding him on provisions earned by her own labor. When the provisions ran low, she asked him to replenish the supply. He turned his pockets inside out to show her that he had nothing. The old lady then read him the riot act, and told him if he could not support her, then get out. He left on Tuesday and went back to Parke County.

Notice of Administration
    Estate of PETER L. WRIGHT, deceased
    January 21, 1888
                                      MARTIN L. WRIGHT, Administrator

Petition to Sell Real Estate
    Estate of JOHN F. STEWART, deceased
    WILLIAM B. HOOD, Administrator vs. LIDA B. HOLLINGSWORTH, JAMES STEWART, MARY STEWART, ED STEWART, FRANK STEWART
    Personal funds insufficient to pay debts
    CONLEY & SAWYER, attorneys
                                      A.R. HOPKINS, Clerk

Application for liquor licenses
    ROBERT ADAMS – Dana
    EDMOND EDMONDS Jr. – Eugene

Wednesday, January 8, 1888

    Obituary
Grandma MILLIKIN, who died at Eugene on the 21st of January, 1888, was a kind mother and neighbor, and very kind to the poor, always ready to lend a helping hand to the needy. She was not a member of any church, but held to the Presbyterian faith. The writer, who officiated at her burial, was well acquainted with her, having known her for over 20 years, and lived a near neighbor to her for some 12 or 15 years. She suffered for many years with nervous chills, and finally passed away from the world of life to the world beyond. Her chief desire in her last sickness was to live to remain and care for her two single children, HATTIE and WILLIE MILLIKIN. She seemed to think they could not get along without her. She clung to life so much, she said to her physician she would undergo any treatment if he could do her any good. During her illness, she was kindly taken care of by her children, HATTIE, WILLIE, and SCOTT, who attended to every want. She leaves 4 children – 2 boys and 2 girls – Mrs. ISAAC PORTER of Danville, IL, Miss HATTIE, W.S. and O.W. MILLIKIN, and quite a number of grandchildren, among whom are the children of JOSEPH BURNS of Montezuma.
                                        Rev. R.B. VAN ALLEN

TOM UNDERWOOD, of Lafayette, an old and respected citizen, a prominent Odd Fellow, and an intimate friend of the late SCHUYLER COLFAX, died suddenly in Chicago on Monday last.

Montezuma Items
ABE LEATHERMAN, of Highland, is very low with typhoid pneumonia.

Dana News
CARL TEMPLE has bought a restaurant in Chrisman, IL, and will move there this week.

On Monday morning, WILLIAM SHORTER, a hard working coal miner of Clinton died, aged about 45. He leaves a wife and three children.

Mr. MILT HAYS has bought the McCLURE property in the west part of town where Prof. RUSH lives.

FRED TAYLOR left here Tuesday to supercede HARRY AIKMAN as financial manager of the Wilcox Piper Comedy Co. They are giving a week's entertainment at Newman, IL.

Home News
A small child of A.J. CONNER, of Perrysville, died suddenly on Friday last, and was taken to Montezuma on Saturday for interment.

MATT JACKSON, who resides ½ mile east of Cedar Corner, this township, is happy from center to circumference. It is a boy and arrived on Friday last.

WILSON HASTY has received a position in the railroad yards at Streater, IL, and left for there on last Sunday night. He will move his family about the first of April.

The funeral of little PAUL DAVIS (infant child of C.S. and MARY DAVIS) on Wednesday last at the M.E. Church, was very largely attended. The services were opened by singing, and prayer by Rev. JOHN W. PARRETT, after which the pastor, Rev. R.S. MARTIN, preached a discourse.

Through the influence of Senator SEARS, Miss LAURA McCONNELL, of this place, has been given a position as governess at the Soldier's Orphan's Home, of Knightstown, this State. She will leave for her field of labor on Monday next. She is a most estimable lady, and we are glad to know she has been favored with so important a position.

Card of Thanks
We desire to thank our many kind friends of Newport for their assistance, words of comfort and sympathy in the bereavement of our only little boy, PAUL WILFRED DAVIS.
            C.S. and M.A. DAVIS

Afflicted Family
Perrysville – Again and for the third time the home of Mr. and Mrs. A.J. CONNER has been visited by the sad messenger of death, taking from them their darling baby – little ALMA JOSEPHINE CONNER – aged six months and ten days.

From Terre Haute Express
Mr. and Mrs. JAMES WHITE, of Helt's Prairie, Vermillion County, celebrated their 57th wedding anniversary at their home last Friday. Mr. WHITE was born in Roane County, Tennessee, in 1805; came to Knox County, this state in 1815; from there to Fountain County and then to Vermillion County in 1823. He was a Democrat until the passage of the Kansas-Nebraska bill when he left that party and became a Republican. Physically, the old gentleman is feeble, but his mind is little impaired. He is regarded as one of the best informed old men in this part of the country. Mrs. WHITE was born in Pennsylvania in 1811 and at 6 years, removed with her parents to Covington, IN, where she and Mr. WHITE were married. They have 6 sons (all Republicans), and one daughter living, 21 grand, and 5 great grandchildren. By industry and economy they have prospered and are able to leave to each child a good home.

Rev. COLLON D. JAMES, of the Illinois Conference of the M.E. Church, died at Bonita, KS, on the 31st of January, 1888, aged 83 years. The deceased had been in the ministry over 50 years, and presiding elder during a portion of the time. He leaves 10 children, and a host of relatives in Helt township, where he is well known, to mourn his death.

Personal Mention
ANUL SYKES and wife are going over to Wayne County, this State, in about 3 weeks, to live with their rich Uncle, JOSEPH LAMB.

Mrs. DIANA EDWARDS, of Economy, Wayne County, this State, is here visiting her sister, Mrs. ELIAS LAMB.

Attorney JOE DAVIS, law partner of Judge JUMP, of Terre Haute, came up here last Saturday and spent Sunday with his sister, Mrs. C.W. WARD.

Mrs. STEPHEN S. COLLETT returned from Charlestown, WV, on last Thursday evening, where she has been visiting her daughter, Mrs. ADAM B. LITTLEPAGE, for the last 4 months. Mr. LITTLEPAGE's lame foot is no better, and he is still compelled to move about on crutches. His wife, who was dangerously ill at the time Mrs. COLLETT left here, is now in good health.

Application for liquor license
    DANIEL L. SOLLARS – Eugene

Wednesday, February 15, 1888

Memorial
ERNEST WHITE, son of WILLIAM WHITE and wife, died February 5th, 1888, aged 21 years, one month, and 6 days. He had been sick only a short time, and the family was not expecting his death. Notwithstanding his short stay on earth, he made his mark on the world. The world was made better by his having lived in it. He possessed a very keen interest, far beyond the average grade, and unlike many others, he strove to improve his talents. He was a kind hearted young man, and his heart was filled with love for all who knew him, and will be sadly missed by all the community in which he lived, and most of all by the kind family of which he was a member. His funeral was preached by the writer at the Mound Chapel on Monday, at 11:00 o'clock.
                        Rev. J.S. BROWN, Gessie, IN

Dana News
A.M. FOLGER has bought the CARL TEMPLE property in the west part of town.

Mr. WILLIAM INGRAM, living 4 ½ miles southwest of Dana, aged about 60, an old farmer, died last Thursday. The casket was furnished by undertaker REDMAN.

Mrs. W.A. DUNCAN, who came here several weeks ago to have her brother, Dr. T.C. HOOD remove a tumor from her side, is entirely cured, and left for home at Oskaloosa, IA, Tuesday.

Sheriff's Sale on Decree
    JAMES N. MITCHELL vs. JAMES C. STUTLER
    $226.30
    Sale to be held Saturday, March 3, 1888 at courthouse at 10 a.m.
        Lots 33 & 34, town of Gessie
    CONLEY & SAWYER, attorneys for plaintiff
    February 8, 1888
                        JOHN A. DARBY, Sheriff

Home News
The widow of the late JOHN R. WHITCOMB, of Clinton, died on last Thursday night.

JAMES WISE, son of DAN WISE, residing 2 miles southwest of town, died of brain fever at 10 o'clock on last Monday night, after a two weeks illness. He was about 18 years of age, and was a bright and industrious young man.

AUSTEY F. HARPER, of Eugene, and ELIAS G. SHAW, of Highland township, have been granted pensions.

We see by the Danville, Il News, that H.C. HANNAH, of that city, has just been granted a pension.

LEWIS BUTLER, of Vermilion County, IL, a son of JOHN BUTLER of this township, has been granted a pension. His arrears amount to $540. He was a member of the 149 Regiment of this State.

AMOS FLESHMAN, of Highland township, ex-Commissioner of this county, received a telegram on Saturday last, stating that his brother, JOHN W. FLESHMAN, who resides at Watson, IL, 70 miles west of Terre Haute, was lying dangerously ill, and not expected to recover. Mr. FLESHMAN left on Monday to visit his brother.

New Recruits
Rev. R.S. MARTIN, pastor of the M.E. Church at this place, closed a successful revival meeting at Vermillion Chapel on last Thursday. The following is a list of those who untied with the church:
W.B. GOSNELL, STELLA GOSNELL, EMMA CLEARWATERS, MILTON HOLLINGSWORTH, ANDREW POORE, MARY E. CLEARWATERS, ALLIE WISE, LIZZIE HOLLINGSWORTH, WILLIAM V. CLARK, SANTA CLARK, WILLIAM RAGSDALE, GLEN CLEARWATERS, GEORGE DOUGLASS, ELIAS WILSON, JOHN HUGHES, SOPHIA NICHOLS, AUGUSTUS MILLER, SARAH MILLER, MOLLIE RUSSELL, JONATHAN MERRIMAN, A.E. RUSSELL, ERNEST SPELLMAN, NELLIE POTTS, GEORGE LEACH, CLARA SPELLMAN, BELLE DOUGLASS, GEORGE W. ASBURY, ELLA POTTS, CLARI GUILLIAMS, A.C. LOVE, HETTIE CLEARWATERS, LUCY BRINDLEY.

Notice to Non-Residents
JOSEPH HANSON vs. PLATT Z. ANDERSON & JENNIE A. ANDERSON
Complaint No. 2992
PLATT Z. ANDERSON is not a resident of Indiana
Must appear before 2nd Monday in March
WILTERMOOD & STRAIN, attorneys for plaintiff
Dated January 21, 1888
            A.R. HOPKINS, Clerk

Personal Mention
WILLIAM GLEASON, agent of the C. & E.I. Railway, at Eugene, was called to Montezuma on Friday last by the death of his mother.

H.H. HOSFORD, CHARLEY ALEXANDER, and FRANK LAFFERTY, of Eugene, left yesterday evening for National City, California, where they intend to locate and seek employment.

Miss ALLIE KOONSE, teacher at Premium No. 3, left for her home at Lafayette, on last Friday, in answer to a telegram that her father is sick. Miss ELLA CADY is teaching in her place during her absence.

Wednesday, February 22, 1888

Bono
OSCAR KERNS, who went to the sweet sunny south to make his fortune, has returned home.

The Bono school paper that is read every Friday, is improving. The last paper was edited by LOCHIE SMITH. The next one will be edited by STEPHEN JENKS.

Gessie
THOMAS GOUTY has bought and moved on the old SHAW farm.

Dana News
Mr. WILLIAM SWINDELL, of Highland, has bought two lots of S.E. KAUFMAN, and anticipates building in the spring.

Born to MOOD CARPENTER and wife last Monday night, twins, a boy and a girl. Dr. O.M. KEYS was in attendance at the nativity.

Among the old people in the neighborhood that are quite sick are Uncle JOE STAATS, Uncle JOHN BILSLAND and Uncle SAM AIKMAN. We hope to hear soon of their recovery.

Clinton Items from the Argus
Miss ANNA FULTON, of Charleston, IL, is a guest of her cousin, Miss SARAH DOWNING.

Dr. HARRY SHEPHERD, of Hartford, KS, arrived in the city Wednesday night on a visit to his mother.

BENJAMIN HARRISON celebrated his 83rd birthday at his residence 3 miles west of Clinton, Wednesday, February 8th. Squire HARRISON was born in Rockingham County, VA, February 8, 1805. He was married to JANE A. BRIGHT in 1827. They moved from Virginia in 1832 to Vermillion County, built a little cabin on the land now owned by JIM PAYNE and DAVE WRIGHT. He served as Justice of the Peace for about 40 years. He was a Democrat until the war, and from that time he has been a staunch Republican. He is the father of 13 children, 7 of whom are still living, 5 sons and 2 daughters. He has 39 grandchildren and 11 great grandchildren, and the heart was made glad by their presence.

Death
Miss EVA NORRIS, daughter of LEWIS NORRIS, of this township, died of consumption on Friday last, after an illness of 10 or 12 weeks. She was 19 or 20 years of age, and a most estimable lady. She had a host of young friends who lament her sad death. Her funeral took place on Saturday last, and was very largely attended. Her remains were interred in the Vermillion Chapel Cemetery.

Death
The wife of JOHN JOHNSON, residing 1 ½ miles north of Perrysville, on the Covington road, died on Saturday last, and was buried on Sunday. The deceased was a lady who stood high among her acquaintances, and was loved and respected by everybody. She was the stepmother of Prof. RANKIN's wife, of this place. She leaves a husband and 5 or 6 children, and many friends to mourn her death.

Obituary
Mrs. MARY G. METZGER, of Perrysville, who was about 80 years of age, died at about 7 o'clock last Sunday morning, after an illness of more than a year. Some 13 or 14 months ago she was stricken down with paralysis, and had been an invalid ever since. She was among the early settlers of this county, and was a noble old lady. Her husband, Uncle JONAS METZGER, died a number of years ago. The good mother's remains were interred in the Hicks Cemetery, west of town, at 1 o'clock on last Monday afternoon.

Obituary
Montezuma – Entered into rest at Montezuma, on February 14th, ALLIE CONNER, aged only 13 days over 22 years. None in Montezuma appeared to bid fairer for long life than ALLIE, but after only five hours of sickness she was called home. We say home for she was a true Christian, and universally beloved by a large crowd of friends. Funeral services were conducted by Rev. J.C. KEMP and were very largely attended.

Death
Uncle JOHN BILSLAND was born in Ohio in 1808, and had he lived till next September, he would have been 80 years of age. He moved to this county in 1856, and settled near Bono, Helt township, where he resided up to the day of his death. Uncle JOHN, as he was familiarly known to most of the leading businessmen in this county, was strictly honest in all his dealings, and highly respected by all his neighbors. His funeral took place on Thursday, February 16, 1888, and was very largely attended, many not being able to gain admission to the church at Bono, where the funeral discourse was preached by Rev. W.A. SMITH, pastor of the M.E. Church. The remains were taken charge of by the members of the Masonic Fraternity, who performed the last sad rites.

Notice of Final Settlement of Estate
    Estate of PETER STREETMOCKER, deceased
    To be held March 12, 1888
    Filed February 17, 1888
                        A.R. HOPKINS, Clerk

Wednesday, February 29, 1888

JOHN HANNA, formerly editor and proprietor of the Crawfordsville Review, died of consumption on Tuesday of last week. He was a very popular gentleman, and his funeral was largely attended.

Clinton Items
WILLIAM WRIGHT, a well known and popular citizen of this township, is slowly dying with a peculiar malady, supposed by some to be consumption. He has lost so much flesh that he is nothing but a skeleton, and is gradually growing weaker day by day.

News reached this city last week from FRANK BORGMAN, that WILL HAVENS, who left here two or three years ago to work in the lumber of Arkansas, was recently cut in two and instantly killed by the cars at Memphis, TN. He was identified by the coroner who held the inquest by papers found on his person. He leaves a wife and four children, all living in this city.

Hillsdale Items
HARRY JONES, the youngest son of JOSEPH JONES, living two miles north of Highland is dangerously sick of typhoid pneumonia.

Home News
The pension of D.Y. FUNKHOUSER, of this place, has been increased.

DAVE DEVINS, who moved from this township to Owen County, nearly two years ago, has moved back here.

Miss CORA WHITE, daughter of ROBERT WHITE, is dangerously ill with typhoid fever. She first had the measles, which was followed by the fever.

JAMES B. PERRIN, of Bismark, MO, wishes us to state that he will be back in time to assess Eugene township.

Matrimony
On last Sunday, February 26th, at 4 o'clock p.m. at the bride's residence, Miss NANNIE WRIGHT and Mr. NELSON JONES, of IL, were united in wedlock by Rev. G. WILEY, pastor of the U.B. Church. There were about 25 guests invited, of which there were only about one half present on account of bad roads and disagreeable weather.

Crazy Again
DUNK ANDERSON, of Perrysville, who was brought home from the insane asylum last summer, and pronounced cured, was taken back there again yesterday by Sheriff DARBY, for treatment. He is as crazy as a loon. Sheriff DARBY was accompanied by attorney O.B. GIBSON.

Personal Mention
Mrs. JAMES LAWSON, of Danville, IL, is visiting her brother-in-law, W.V. CLARK, of Helt township.

Miss KATE HEGARTY of Terre Haute, and Miss KATE GILLESPIE of Springfield, MO, were here several days last week visiting their uncle, MAURICE HEGARTY, and family.

Mrs. P.W. GRUBB is out at Cherry Point, IL, attending the bedside of her sick sister, Miss MALISSA DE HAVEN. Mr. GRUBB went out there on last Monday morning.

Quaker Hill News
R.B. FOSTER, our pioneer prohibitionist, has returned home from Marshall, IL, where he has been visiting his brother.

Wednesday, March 7, 1888

Quaker Hill News
JOHN LONG, son of WILLIAM LONG, died February 21st. His funeral was largely attended. He was a devoted Christian and loved by all his associates.

Clinton Items
S.E. WISHARD, of this city, has just received a pension of $350 back pay and $9 per month for the balance of his lifetime. This comes at a time, for Mr. WISHARD is becoming too old to follow the hard trade he has worked at heretofore, viz., house moving.

Here and There
Mrs. INGRAM and Miss GEORGIE MAGLOSSEN were united in wedlock, February 29, 1888. They will not see their wedding day again for four years. They have our best wishes.

Dana News
An infant of WILLIAM FRENCH, died last Sunday.

Mr. J.F. PEELER has bought Mrs. NICHOLS' property, which A.J. RALPH now occupies.

Mrs. A.J. RALPH returned Friday, from a visit at Indianapolis, and her daughter, Mrs. IDA PURCELL, came home with her.

Home News
As soon as C.S. DAVIS succeeds in selling his mattress factory at Salina, KS, he will move his household goods back here, and become a resident of Newport once more.

Mrs. EMMA BALES, mother of CALE BALES, of Helt Township, has been granted a pension on the death of her husband, who was a soldier in the War of 1812. She is now nearly 90 years of age. She cannot live long to enjoy the benefits of a generous government.

WILLIAM DARNALL, of Dana, was in town on Thursday last. He informed us that he had leased the JOHN BILSLAND farm, west of Bono, where he would move in a few days.

TAYLOR VANNEST, of Clinton, who has been trying for a pension for a long time, is happy. He has been placed on the pension rolls, and will get a big haul on his first draw, as his pension will date back to his discharge. We are glad to here of TAYLOR's success.

The happiest old soul we have seen for a long time was Uncle JOHN HASTY on Thursday last. On that day he received notice from his attorney at Washington that he had been granted a re-rating on his pension, which will give the old gentleman about $1,436 arrears. We know of no solider who needs it worse. He is now unable to do any work, and as he still owes some off his little home, the amount will pay off his indebtedness and leave him enough, with his pension of $24 per month to keep him comfortably during the few remaining years he will remain here below.

Rev. BOB VAN ALLEN, pastor of the U.B. Church here, has received notice that his pension claim, which was filed in 1878, has been granted. He gets $4 per month from June 1865 to December 28, 1888, and $8 per month from that date. His first draw will amount to over $1100.

RILEY WHITNEY has moved his stock of dry goods down to Terre Haute, where he intends to locate and become a citizen of that beautiful city. His gentlemanly clerk, MORTON HOLLINGSWORTH accompanied him, but still retains this place as his home.

Married at the home of Mr. MARK HARDIN in Highland, on the evening of February 29th, Mr. JAMES INGRAM and Miss GEORGIA McLAUGHLIN, the Rev. MATER officiating.

Opedee Sick List
Mrs. CHARLEY WILTERMOOD, Mrs. CHARLEY INGRAM, JOHN THOMAS, Mrs. SQUIRE YOUNG, and Mrs. DICK WIMSETT.

Married, by the Rev. IRA MATER, at his residence in Hillsdale, on the 3rd instant, Mr. JOHN H. JOHNSON and Miss MARY A. UNDERWOOD, all of this county. They go immediately to their home in Illinois, followed by the good wishes of their many friends.

Obituary
Mrs. RACHEL BROWN, mother of E.B. BROWN, of this place, died at her home, 3 miles east of Howard, Parke County, on February 25th, 1888, and was buried on the day following at the Tangler Cemetery. The deceased was born in Randolph County, North Carolina, in September 1816, and had she lived until next September, she would have been 72 years of age. She had been a resident of Parke County since 1828, and was a noble old lady. She had been a faithful member of the Cumberland Presbyterian Church for 40 years, and died as she lived, a true Christian. There are 6 children – 4 boys and 2 girls – and many friends to mourn the loss of this aged mother.

Personal Mention
A.V. HOLMES, of Williamsport, a former resident of this place, has been granted an increase of pension.

Mrs. NANCY WATSON and her daughter, Miss ELLA WATSON, of Streator, IL, are visiting Mrs. PAT FLYNN, of Hillsdale, who is a relative.

Obituary
Perrysville – The infant son of OWEN and JOSIE DICKASON was born on the 9th of July last, and after a brilliant life of but a few brief months, the last few weeks of which were fraught with much suffering from disease of lungs and brain. During the last night watch of February 19th, while tearful friends and tearless angels together clustered around the little sufferer and alike watched the final struggle between parting life and approaching death for the supremacy, little BURTON JAY DICKASON closed his eyelids down in dreamless placidness to open them again with the lurid dawning of a sublimer day. The burial services were conducted at the house by Rev. BOND, assisted by Rev. WILEY, pastors of the M.E. and U.B. Churches. The sacred ashes were deposited in the cemetery on the hill, in the earthen coffin, in which God rocks.

R.H. NIXON received a telegram on last Monday, stating that his uncle, ROBERT NIXON, of Oswego, KS, was bad sick, and that he had better come immediately. Mr. NIXON and his daughter IDA NIXON left on the afternoon train for the bedside of his sick uncle, who is now 82 years of age.

Montezuma Items
ED VANSICKLE, express agent at Hillsdale, while helping load a barrel of beans in the car last Monday, got the forefinger of his right hand cut off.

Public Sale
 Saturday, March 17, 1888
 All my household furniture, 200 pounds of bacon and lard, one milk cow, and 4 sheep, also corn in the crib
         ROBERT WRIGHT

Notice of Settlement of Estate
 Estate of JOE SABIN, deceased
 Filed February 23, 1888
         A.R. HOPKINS, Clerk

Sheriff's Sale on Execution
 Saturday, March 24, 1888
  Lot 1 and N ½ Lot 2, Block 18, Town of Clinton
 Taken as property of JOHN COOPER at the suit of SARAH J. COOPER
 Filed February 29, 1888
         JOHN A. DARBY, Sheriff

Administrator's Sale
 Thursday, March 22, 1888
 Estate of JOHN BILSLAND, deceased
  Personal property, several work horses, fine brood mares and colts, several milk cows and calves, stock cattle, 2 wagons, double carriage, single carriage, harnesses, farming implements, hay, corn, wheat, and other articles
 Sale to be held at late residence in Helt Township
         JOHN E. BILSLAND, Administrator

Notice of Final Settlement of Estate
 Estate of SOLOMON JONES, deceased
 Filed March 5, 1888
         A.R. HOPKINS, Clerk

Wednesday, March 14, 1888

Dana News
Miss CELIA JACKSON is quite sick at her sister's, Mrs. WILLIAM H. DARNALL's. It is feared that she will have an attack of lung fever.

Mr. DOUGLAS HARPER and Miss LILY JAMES took a little jaunt to Terre Haute last week and came home as man and wife. Both live near Tennessee Valley.

Clinton Items
D.C. JOHNSON starts for Baxter Springs, KS, next Wednesday.

TAYLOR VANNEST, formerly of this place, now of Coal Bluff, has just been granted a pension. He receives $2200 back pension and $24 a month. Cause – deafness.

Dr. J.H. BOGART has sold his entire lumberyard to W.L. MOREY and will hereafter devote his attention exclusively to the practice of Medicine.

JIM ROBERTS has reached Oregon where he is visiting his brother. He is slightly improved in health and is expected home about April 1st.

Capt. JOHN L. LINDSEY, an old veteran of this township, was very agreeably surprised Monday morning when he received notice from the pension department that he had been re-rated, and was entitled to $1307 back pension, which had been granted for the balance of his lifetime.

Funeral
Danville – The funeral services of Mrs. MARY L. BINES took place from the residence of H.K. GREGORY, corner of Harrison and Jackson Streets, Tuesday at 10 o'clock a.m., a large number of friends being present, conducted by Rev. C.H. LITTLE, assisted by G.W. BATES, pastor of the M.E. Church at Ridge Farm.
Biography
MARY L. BINES was born near Wheeling, VA, October 2, 1815. Her maiden name was MARY L. PORTER. She was married to JOHN BINES June 6, 1839. They moved west in 1842 to Vermilion County, IL, and have lived ever since – nearly 46 years – within a radius of 20 miles. Her husband died September 8, 1868. She has but one brother living, WILLIAM I. PORTER, one half sister, Mrs. SOUTHARD, of Crawfordsville, who was also at the funeral. Her nephew, WILLIAM M. BINES, and niece, Mrs. ANNA M. GREGORY, came to Illinois in 1863, and were taken by their uncle JOHN and MARY to their home, where the nephew, WILLIAM M. BINES, has resided ever since. Losing his parents as WILLIAM did when so young as to scarcely remember anything, and living with his aunt MARY so long – nearly 25 years – he feels that in her death he has lost almost his real mother. And this is but the voice of every member of the family. The remains were interred in Springhill Cemetery.

List of letters in Newport Post office
    CORA WILSON   SAM SMITH
    THOMAS CARROLL   J. TOMPKINS

Home News
Mr. JACOB MYERS, residing north of Dana, is gaining considerable notoriety as a first class auctioneer. They say he is hard to beat.

WARD FARRINGTON, who recently moved into Aunt JANE FORD's residence, southwest of Hillsdale, was made happy on the 4th instant, by the arrival of a fine boy.

Death
The wife of GIL MACK, of Highland Township, died at 4 o'clock on last Friday afternoon, from cancer of the stomach, after an illness of one year. The deceased was about 50 years of age, and a most estimable lady. She had been a member of the U.B. Church for 12 years, and died believing she would be given a home beyond the grave. The funeral took place on Sunday; her remains being buried in the Hicks Cemetery.

Married
JOHN TOLER, of Danville, IL, aged 28, and Mrs. J.B. HARPER, of Clinton, aged 32, were united in wedlock on Tuesday last at the Clerk's office, by Rev. R.B. VAN ALLEN, pastor of the U.B. Church.

Miss CORA HAWKINS will leave for Terre Haute the last of this month or the first of next, to take music. She will take both vocal and instrumental. Miss CORA is a fine musician, and if she keeps on, she will soon be the finest in Newport.

Married
Our young friend, JESSE EDMONDS, of Eugene, was united in wedlock to Miss ALICE PINEGAR, of this place, on last Sunday evening. The ceremony took place at the residence of A.C. BROKAW, and was performed by Rev. R.B. VAN ALLEN, pastor of the U.B. Church. They left on the 11 o'clock train Monday for their home in Eugene.

Married
At 6 o'clock last Sunday evening, March 11th, at the residence of Mrs. HENRY HASTY, of Eugene, IN, Mr. MAHLON HASTY, of our county, and Miss ALICE ROWLAND of Mitchell, IN, were united in matrimony by Rev. R.S. MARTIN, of the M.E. Church. The bride and groom will continue to reside in our county, among their friends, of whom they both have many.

Double Wedding
On Thursday night of last week, two couples were united in marriage at the residence of the two bride's parents, Mr. and Mrs. PERRY OVERPECK, who live at the lower edge of Helt's Prairie. Two brothers by the name of WILBERT and FRANK SKIDMORE were united in marriage to two sisters by the name of ELLA and MAGGIE OVERPECK. A few of their friends were present at the wedding. The ceremony was performed by Rev. W.A. SMITH. WILBERT SKIDMORE and his wife ELLA will live with his father-in-law. FRANK SKIDMORE and wife will live on his father's farm, which is situated near Camargo, IL. JOHN SKIDMORE, father of the boys that were married last Thursday night, is a brother to JOE SKIDMORE, of Summit Grove.

Personal Mention
Mrs. Dr. E.T. SPOTSWOOD of Terre Haute, was in town over Sunday visiting her daughter, Mrs. HARRY B. RHOADS.

ALBERT REEDER, who left Clinton township for the Indian Territory about 3 years ago, has been back here on a visit for the last two months, but left for the great west again on last Wednesday, after paying his brother-in-law, FRANK BRINDLEY a short visit, who resides near here.

Quaker Hill News
Quite a pleasant little surprise took place at W.S. FOWLER's, on last Sabbath. His good wife anxious to make his 54th anniversary a pleasant occasion, slyly prepared dinner and invited some of their friends to partake of their hospitalities, and to assist in the surprise. When Mr. FOWLER returned home from church, he found his house crowded with good things.

Died
On last Sabbath, Uncle JESSE COONSE, in his 76th year. He was a faithful Christian from his childhood. His example and influence in life will live through eternity.

Wednesday, March 21, 1888

Death
Mr. HENRY YOUNG, who resided halfway between here and Opedee, died at 5 o'clock on last Thursday evening, aged 52 years. He was only sick four days. He was afflicted with heart disease, and had a slight attack of pneumonia, which soon terminated his existence. Mr. YOUNG was born in Parke County, and enlisted from that county, serving his country honestly and faithfully. He had been a resident of this township for 5 or 6 years, and was respected by his neighbors and acquaintances. For many years he had been a member of the M.E. Church. His funeral took place on last Thursday afternoon, a short and appropriate sermon being preached at Wimsett Schoolhouse by Rev. R.B. VAN ALLEN, pastor of the U.B. Church, after which his remains were taken charge of by Shiloh Post, G.A.R. of this place, and interred with military honors. Peace to the old veteran's ashes.

Murder
A murder was committed about 3 miles northeast of Eugene, at about 7:30 p.m. on last Sunday evening. A tramp, whose name was ALFRED HARRY KRITZENGER, with residence unknown, called upon STEVE BROWN late in the evening and wanted to stay all night. Mr. BROWN refused and sent him on his way. After traveling down to the road and asking another neighbor for lodging, and being refused, he went back to Mr. BROWN's. Without any warning, Mr. BROWN shot him with a shotgun. The tramp fell over dead. The lifeless remains of the tramp were taken to Eugene, where Coroner BRINDLEY was summoned on last Monday to hold an inquest.

ALFRED HARRY KRITZENGER was 5 feet 10 inches high, weighed 170 pounds, complexion dark, black hair, and whiskers all over his face. A small scar on his nose had been recently made. He had on a knit wool jacket, two pair of breeches, the outer pair being made of cotton. He was supposed to be between 32 and 35 years of age. He had in his pocket a promissory note for $115, given in 1875, and signed by KRITZENGER & FROST as securities.

The remains were buried yesterday at Eugene, by the Township Trustee.

Dana News
Hon. CLAUDE MATTHEWS and wife of Clinton have gone to Texas to look after a large land estate belonging to them there.

Died
On March 7, 1888, Mr. BENJAMIN MILES, died at his home four miles south of Armiesburg. The deceased was for a number of years a resident of Helt Township, and living near Staat's Schoolhouse where ALBERT FONCANNON now lives. He was a brother-in-law to Uncle JOHN STAATS having married MARY E. BORIN, who died a few years since and was buried in Pisgah Cemetery. Two daughters also repose there. Rev. H.L. GRIMES delivered the funeral discourse.

Stricken With Paralysis
At about 5 o'clock, on last Sunday morning, Uncle JOHNNY MAST, of Dana, was stricken down with paralysis while building a fire. He fell like he had been shot down. He was entirely speechless and helpless, not being able to move hand or foot. Physicians were immediately called in, and pronounced it a bad case of paralysis. All medicine given him had to be by hypodermic injection, the patient not being able to swallow anything. Late in the afternoon of the same day he was able to recognize his friends. The physicians say he may recover, but they have little hope of a favorable result.

Vermillion Chapel Items
Mrs. SLATER, who resides with her daughter, Mrs. WILLIAM REED, while getting wood, fell and bruised her shoulder, but not dangerously.

Sale of Real Estate
    Estate of JAMES GRIFFITH, deceased
    Bids to be received by Tuesday, April 10, 1888
        Lots 1, 2, 3, 4, 5, 6, 7, 8, 9, 10
        Out Lots 26, 27, & 28
        All lots situated in Perrysville
    Filed March 12, 1888
                      WILLIAM P. SMITH, Executor

Home News
GRANT DAVIS, of Dana, is going to get married on Sunday next to Miss ELLA FLANDERS, of this township.

OLIVER P. LAYMAN, a deaf mute of Parke County, wants the contract of putting new bottoms in all your old chairs. He is a first-class workman, and deserving of your patronage. He is honest, industrious, and charges reasonable prices for his work.

Obituary
The infant child of JOHN R. STAHL, of Eugene, died at 11 a.m. on Sunday last, aged about 12 months. This is the second child they have lost in the last three or four months – their two youngest. Both were bright and lovely little children, and their deaths are a sad and terrible blow to the heartbroken parents.

Personal Mention
PETER NEWPORT has moved to Lawrence County, Arkansas.

ELHANAN STEVENS, of Perrysville, is going out to Washington Territory in a few weeks to visit his son.

TOM AIKMAN, of Mason City, Nebraska, a former citizen of this county, was back here on a visit. He is a brother of Prof. E. AIKMAN, of the Newport High School.

Anniversary
Friday, March 16th, was a gay day at Uncle SAM and Aunt MATILDA JAMES', it being their 40th anniversary of wedded life. Their children and grandchildren came home, bringing baskets well filled with the good things of earth for the table. They also surprised their good old father and mother with many nice presents. Six children – 5 boys and one girl – all married, with 14 grand-children – 7 boys and 7 girls – counting the old folks, makes 28 in the family, and they were all there.

Wednesday, March 28, 1888

Jail
On Monday last, Deputy Prosecutor SCOTT AIKMAN, of this place, had a warrant issued by Esq. THOMPSON, of Cayuga, for the arrest of STEPHEN BROWN for the murder of ALFRED H. KRITZENGER. On Tuesday afternoon of last week, Mr. L. DILLMAN, uncle of the murdered tramp, arrived in Eugene, in answer to a telegram announcing the murder of his nephew. He immediately identified the body, and had them taken to the undertaker's, where they were prepared for shipment to his late home, near Oskaloosa, Clay County, IL. Mr. DILLMAN says his nephew left home last September to seek work. He was a young man about 25 years old. He had $50 in his pocket when he left home. He was of good character, and an honorable young man.

Quaker Hill News
Mrs. E.R. PUGH has returned home from Bloomingdale, where she has been attending the bedside of her sister, Mrs. J. TRIMBLE, who was down with the measles.

Mrs. WISHARD, of Clinton, has been visiting her daughter, Mrs. R.S. NELSON.

Cayuga Gaslight
POLK HOOD, who has been living at Dalles, OR, will start on his return to his old home at Eugene about the first of April.

Married
On last Wednesday evening at the residence of Mr. JOHN BRINDLEY, ROSA LANDERS and GRANT DAVIS were united in wedlock by the Rev. R.S. MARTIN. After the wedding, the young couple went to Dana, where they intend to live.

Gessie
JAMES C. STATLER, merchant at this place for the past 8 years, put all his goods and household affairs in a car and shipped them together with himself and family to Johnsonville, IN. Johnsonville is on the Wabash Road, east of Stateline City.

DAN KING, one of the RR hands here, has been promoted to section boss on a section on the Grape Creek division, near Tuscola, IL. He will soon move his family over to his new work.

JOHN RICHARDSON, a former hand on the RR at this place, has been given a section on Grape Creek division, and moved to Westville.

Died
DAVID HENRY GOUTY, proprietor of an extensive feed yard at Danville, died Friday night after a few days illness with pneumonia. His mother, Mrs. KATIE GOUTY, together with numerous relatives, live at this place. He was buried at Danville Sunday.

Dana News
Miss MATTIE FILLINGER, of Helt's Prairie, spent Saturday and Sunday with her sister, Mrs. S.E. KAUFMAN.

CHARLES LEE, who has been engaged in the butcher business here has sold out and gone back to Parke County.

Home News
On Saturday last, Uncle JOHN HASTY received his voucher from the pension agency to sign for back pension, which he gets on a re-rating. The exact amount is $1169.90. He is happy.

Death
QUINCE HARRIS, of Eugene, lost a child by death on Tuesday of last week, aged 19 months. The funeral took place on Wednesday, Rev. R.B. VAN ALLEN, pastor of the U.B. Church, preaching the funeral discourse.

Death
JAMES BENNETT, of Terre Haute, a former resident of this township, and a son of WILLIAM C. BENNETT of this place, died on Sunday last, of lung fever, after an illness of only a few days. He has resided in Terre Haute for the last 7 or 8 years, and worked in the rolling hills. Two of his little children are lying at the point of death. His remains will be brought up here for interment, which will take place at the Thomas Cemetery sometime today. He was about 30 or 32 years of age, and leaves a wife and 4 children. His wife was a sister of AARON SIDEBOTTOM, residing 5 miles west of here.

Married
FREEMAN SANKEY, of Vigo County, aged 33, and Miss DELLA NEWLIN, of the same county, aged 23, were married at the hotel, in this place, on Thursday last, Rev. R.B. VAN ALLEN, pastor of the U.B. Church, performing the ceremony.

Married
GEORGE E. SHIRK, a son of DAVID SHIRK, of Parke County, and a student in Normal College, this place, and Miss MARY CLAYPOOL, the 27 year old daughter of Hon. H.R. CLAYPOOL, of this place, skipped over to Danville, IL, on Monday last, and were united in marriage by Rev. HIRAM WOOD.
Covington People's Paper

Mixed Relationship
MAHLON HASTY, of Eugene, married Miss ROWLAND, who is the sister of his stepmother, and also first cousin to his mother. Accordingly, young HASTY is his father's brother-in-law, and is also his cousin. His stepmother is his sister-in-law. Being married to his stepmother's sister, his wife is then his step aunt, therefore he is his own uncle. His sister is his niece, etc.
Danville Commercial

Graduates from the County Schools
Clinton Township, District No. 2 – J.W. BROOKBANK, teacher
> CARRIE SALYARDS, MAGGIE BAILEY, LULA DUGGER, WILLIAM S. DUGGER

Helt Township, District 11 – R.E. WHITLOCK, teacher
> STERLING KERR, ROSALIE BOREN, ROY HUEY, HORACE G. DERBY

Helt Township, District No. 6 – G.W. STURM, teacher
> EMMA V. AIKMAN, MAMIE JENKS

Helt Township, District No. 14 – EFFIE BALES, teacher
> MYRTLE BALES

Helt Township, District No. 15 – JAMES T. HUNTER, teacher
> EVA STOKESBERRY

Helt Township, District No. 21 – HATTON JAMES, teacher
> ELSIE ANDREWS

Dana Township, FRED RUSH, Principal
> WILLIAM FINNEY, BELLE BURTON, FRED HUNT, CHARLES PETERS, BERTHA WRIGHT

Vermillion Township, No. 10 – E.E. DAVIS, Principal
> MEDIA WALTHALL, LUCY HAWORTH, LAURA NELSON, MYRA HAWORTH, CLIFFIE WHITE

Vermillion Township, No. 14 – WILLIAM COFFIN, teacher
> MARY ALDRIDGE

Eugene Township, No. 3 – JOHN R. STAHL, Principal
> LEONARD CAMPBELL, ANNA BROWN, MARY HOWMINSKI

Eugene Township, No. 11 – CORA LACEY, teacher
> GOULD G. RHEUBY

Highland Township, No. 6 – C.S. FLANDERS, Principal
> MARY McCORMACK, SUSAN SMITH, GEORGE C. HICKS, BERTHA J. LACEY

Highland Township, No. 10 – WILLIAM S. NEEL, teacher
> LEWIS WEBSTER

GEORGE W. DEALAND, Co. Supt.

Died
At his home in Raymond, IL, of pneumonia, Mr. JAMES D. HUNT, died on March 10, 1888. He leaves a wife and five children as well as a large number of relatives and friends to mourn his loss. He was a kind father, a loving husband, and was highly respected by all who knew him. The subject of this sketch formerly lived in Clinton, and will be remembered as the boy who first enlisted in Co. A, 71st IN Volunteers, Capt. DOWDY's Company – and afterwards in Co. G, 7th IN Cavalry.

Wednesday, April 4, 1888

A steamer will leave this morning for a voyage up Salt River. The vessel is officered by JIMMIE SAWYER, Captain; JIMMY CHIPPS, Pilot; FRANK BURROUGHS, 1st Mate; BUCK FORTNER, 2nd Mate; DICK WIMSETT, Coal Heaver; MARION BUSH, General Roustabout.

Dana News
Miss MARY McCULLOUGH, of St. Bernice, is visiting Miss CARRIE BALES. She and her sister are soon going to Pennsylvania to make their future home.

Joint Items
FRANCES RICE tried examination for teachers' license Friday and Saturday of last week. Success to you young FRANCIE.

WELLS & PEER	S. BOWERS
Groceries, Glassware, Boots, etc.	The Riverside Flouring Mills
Dana, IN	Eugene, IN

Obituary
OSCAR F. NEVINS died March 13th, 1888, aged 52 years and 11 days. His disease was lung fever. He was a Christian and belonged to the Cumberland Presbyterian Church. He leaves a wife and 8 children to mourn his loss. The youngest is a sweet little babe 6 months old.

Death
Mrs. WEBER died in this city Tuesday night, at the residence of CHARLES P. WALKER, with whom she has made her home for some time. She was Mrs. WALKER's grandmother, and had reached the extreme age of 93 years. The remains were taken to Logansport for interment, Wednesday.

Home News
Mrs. MALINDA CUMMINS, of Danville, IL, was down here last week visiting her sister, Mrs. JOHN EARLEY, who resides southwest of town.

E.E. NEEL, who taught at No. 9 this last winter, left for the Normal School at Danville, IN, yesterday morning.

CHARLEY BERRY, of the Waynetown Boomble Bee, has bought a half interest in the Crawfordsville Review. He paid $3500. CHARLEY is a splendid squib writer. We wish him success.

The remains of JAMES BENNETT and his two children, who died of lung fever at Terre Haute a few days ago, were brought up here yesterday afternoon and interred in the Thomas Cemetery.

Sheriff's Sale on Decree
    State of Indiana vs. DAVID S. HOPKINS, ANN J. HOPKINS, ROSE MANNING, JOHN MANNING, LULA WRIGHT, WILLIAM P. WRIGHT
    $832.04
    Sale to be held Saturday, April 28, 1888 at courthouse
        W ½ SE ¼ Sec 34 T 17 N R 9 – 80 acres
    Filed April 1, 1888
    RHOADS & AIKMAN, attorneys for plaintiff
                          JOHN A. DARBY, Sheriff

Wednesday, April 11, 1888

Death
The old soldiers of this county are beginning to drop off like the leaves of Autumn. On the 16th of last month the subject of this notice attended the funeral of HENRY YOUNG, an old Union soldier who was buried at Opedee with military honors. JACOB DOWDELL was one of the eight who fired three volleys over the grave, after the lifeless body had been lowered to its last resting place in token of respect and honor to the dead comrade. Yesterday the same honors were paid him by the men who wore the blue during the late war. Mr. DOWDELL had been in poor health for a long time, but was able to get around. He took to his bed one week ago last Monday evening, and at 5 minutes before 10 o'clock on last Sunday night his spirit had taken its flight. In 1861 he enlisted in Company K 97 Regiment, IN Volunteers, and served till the close or the war. He was 45 years of age on the 15th of last month. His remains were taken over to Lodi yesterday morning and interred in the Miller Cemetery, near that village.

Here and There
BILL RUSSELL has got a big boy.

Died
At Eugene, Saturday, March 31, 1888, Mrs. SARAH JOHNSON, aged 71 years. Mrs. JOHNSON was one of the pioneers of Eugene, and was a most excellent lady. She leaves five children, W.H. JOHNSON, of Lafayette; J.C. JOHNSON, somewhere in the west; Mrs. MARGARET DUNGAN; Mrs. SARAH YOUNG; and Miss ANN JOHNSON.

WILLIAM O. WASHBURN, of Terre Haute, IN, has been submitted to the bar at that place.

The steamer "Check" left for the headwaters of Salt River early Tuesday morning. The officers and crew are: WILS BELL, Captain; JIM MALONE, Pilot; CHARLEY THOMAS, 1st clerk; DAVE DUNCAN, mud clerk; BEN LANG, 1st mate; Col. T.W. BELL, 2nd mate; WILLIAM BELL, coal heaver; DAN SOLLARS, routabout; BILLY FULTZ, BILLY MILLIKIN, BILLY HOSFORD, and JESSE EDMONDS, deck hands. JOHN R. STAHL is to be 2nd cook.

Vermillion Township
Mrs. BARBARA WALKER, of Clinton, visited her sister Mrs. HARDESTY CLEARWATERS, last week.

Home News
ROBERT J. HOLTZ, of Eugene, has been appointed administrator of his father's estate.

HARRY WHITCOMB, of Clinton, has been appointed administrator of the estate of MARY S. WHITCOMB.

It is rumored that OMER LUNGER, of Eugene, and Miss MARIA DUGAN, of this place, will shortly be joined together in holy wedlock.

LEWIS L. BISHOP, of Eugene, has been granted a pension in the death of his son, who died while serving Uncle SAM in the army.

TOM THOMAS, of Opedee, has been granted a pension on account of disability contracted in the service, while serving Uncle SAM as a soldier.

PARIS THOMAS has bought S.H. DALLAS' residence, and Mr. DALLAS has leased J.C. SAWYER's residence on south Main Street, now occupied by ERNEST PLACE.

Mrs. JOHN G. GIBBENS, of this place, has been granted a pension on the death of her husband, who died a few years ago from disease contracted while he was a Union soldier. The arrears now due her amounts to nearly $707.

Death
We are called upon to announce the loss of little SPENCER MYERS, son of ROBERT and JANE MYERS, of Burrton, KS, aged 10 years, 3 months, and 8 days, who departed this life March 28th at 11 o'clock a.m. after an illness of three weeks, during which time he bore his sufferings patiently. SPENCER was a good boy. Those who knew him best loved him most. He is sorely missed by all. He has gone home where all is bright and fair. The friends of the departed have our sincere and heartfelt sympathy in their bereavement.

Mrs. JACOB MARBLE, residing near Gessie, is lying dangerously ill. It is thought she cannot recover.

Dana News
Mr. B.F. ELLIS, of Tuscola, IL, and Miss SARAH HEDGECOCK, of Quaker Hill, were married last week, Elder JARVIS officiating.

Mrs. JOHN HASTY, who has been suffering from a gathering on her side for several weeks, is now reported better. It broke yesterday morning and ran nearly a pint of corruption. This is the third time her side has gathered.

ELI McDANIEL, of Cayuga, the newly elected Trustee of Eugene Township, was down here yesterday, gave bond, and took the oath of office.

JESSE HOUCHIN, who moved from Helt township in Montezuma about one year ago, was elected Justice of the Peace at the election, one week ago last Monday.

Marriage Bells
Last Thursday morning at 10 o'clock, at the Newport Parsonage, Mr. RICHARD HABECK and Miss HELENA RADLOFF, both of Decatur, IL, were united in matrimony by Rev. R.S. MARTIN, of the M.E. Church of this city. Mr. HABECK is a prosperous farmer with bright prospects of future success, and he has evidently selected one who will be a helpmate for coming years.

Roll of Honor for 1887-1888
The following pupils were not absent or tardy for 26 weeks: MINNIE SOUTHARD,
    25 weeks, LIZZIE HELT, EVA JAMES, BERNIE SOUTHARD
    24 weeks, ROY JAMES
    23 weeks, ELVA JAMES, CLYDE HARRINGTON
    21 weeks, SUSIE JAMES, RAY HELT, GERTIE HARRINGTON
    18 weeks, ALVIN HELT, MAX WHITE
    17 weeks, MAY HARRINGTON, GERTIE JAMES
    16 weeks, POE JAMES
    15 weeks, HARRY WHITE, MADGE HARRINGTON
    14 weeks, OLLIE JAMES, PEARL WHITE, OKIE WHITE
    12 weeks, JOHN POTTER, U. HARRINGTON
    10 weeks, EFFIE POTTER
    9 weeks, GEORGE HAMMERSLEY
    8 weeks, RAY JAMES, SANT HELT, GEORGE STRAIN, MYRTLE CRUMLEY
    7 weeks, IDA CRUMLEY
    6 weeks, NINA HARRINGTON, CLAUDE CRUMLEY
    5 weeks, MATTIE OVERPECK, BENNIE FRIST, ROSA POTTER
MINNIE SOUTHARD was not absent or tardy during the term: LIZZIE HELT was not tardy, and absent but one day.

Rev. R.S. MARTIN, pastor of the M.E. Church, accompanied by his family, left last Monday morning for Chicago to see his mother. From there, he goes to Porter County, IN, to visit relatives. He will be gone 2 or 3 weeks.

JOHN H. HENSON occupied the pulpit at the U.B. Church on last Sunday. He has been assigned to a circuit at Indianola, NE, and left for that place yesterday. He has grown from infancy to manhood in this place and will be missed.

Sheriff's Sale on Decree
    LEWIS SKINNER vs. EMELINE SANDERS, EZRA SANDERS etal
    $663.35
    Sale to be held Saturday May 5, 1888 at courthouse
        NE ¼ NE ¼ Sec 5 T 18 N R 10 W
        Part of E ½ Se ¼ Sec 32 T 19 N R 10 W
    Filed April 4, 1888
    J.B. MARTIN, Attorney for plaintiff
                        JOHN A. DARBY, Sheriff

Administrator's Sale of Real Estate
    Estate of JOHN F. STEWART, deceased
    Sale to be held Saturday, May 5, 1888
        29 acres off W side of NE ¼ Sec 20 T 16 N R 9 W
            WILLIAM B. HOOD, Administrator

Sheriff's Sale on Decree
    CHARLES W. WARD & OSCAR B. GIBSON vs. WILLIAM L. SHEWARD & CHARLES C. SHEWARD
    $35.25
    Sale to be held Saturday, May 5, 1888 at courthouse
        Undivided ½ Lot 14, town of Eugene
    Filed April 11, 1888
    WARD & GIBSON, Attorneys for plaintiff
            JOHN A. DARBY, Sheriff

Wednesday, April 18, 1888

Joint Items
KATIE LANCASTER, aged 6 years, died of measles last Saturday.

Uncle DANIEL SEARS, an old settler of this county, was buried last Monday at Carmack's graveyard. He had been feeble for a long time.

Home News
T.B. JOHNS, the great lumberman of Terre Haute, died on Tuesday of last week.

LEWIS L. BISHOP received his pension certificate and voucher on Wednesday last. His arrears amount to $572.

JACK SEARS is going to move to Terre Haute the last of this week.

TOM FOLEY, a prominent attorney of Terre Haute, is lying at the point of death. He has consumption and cannot possibly recover.

Mrs. BURSON, residing 1 ½ miles south of town, is a spry lady for one of her years. She is 80 years old, and on last Friday she made a kettle of soap by 11 o'clock, besides doing her housework, and then in the afternoon walked a half mile and quilted till night, and then came home and done her housework again.

Rev. JOHN P. HENSON, who left this place for Indianola, NE, one week ago last Tuesday, arrived safe at his destination. He ran across BEN BLANCHARD at Kansas City, MO, who is feeling fine once more.

Death
Miss KATY HELT, of Helt's Prairie, one of the early settlers of that locality, died on last Sunday evening, aged 70 years. Her funeral took place yesterday at Salem Church, after which her remains were interred in the Helt's Prairie Cemetery.

Dr. G.O. NEWTON, the newly elected Trustee of Helt Township, paid our city a visit on Saturday last.

List of Letters at Newport, IN
    HARGRAVE, Mrs. MARION   WOLF, Mrs. C.A.
    WILLIAMS, JOE   PERKINS, P.D.
    HOLLENSBY, GEORGE   FRY, T.A.

Obituary
DANIEL SEARS, who has been a resident of this township for many years, died very suddenly on last Sunday night. The deceased resided about 3 miles southwest of town, and was an Uncle of Senator R.B. SEARS and JAKE SEARS. The deceased was born in Bourbon County, KY, on June 20, 1808, and would have been 80 years of age had he lived till the 20th of June. He was married to SARAH STANFIELD in the year 1836, in Marion County, this State. He moved to this county in 1841, where he has resided ever since. His first wife died November 11, 1848. To them were born 8 children – 5 boys and 3 girls, all of whom are dead except the eldest and youngest. He was married the second time in the spring of 1855 to MARTHA CLARK, with whom he has lived ever since. For many years he had been a faithful and true Christian and member of the U.B. Church. His funeral took place on last Monday in the forenoon, and was very largely attended. The funeral discourse was preached by Rev. R.B. VAN ALLEN, pastor of the U.B. Church, after which his remains were interred in the Carmack Cemetery.

Notice to Non-Residents
    Vermillion County vs. HANNAH VALENTINE & WILLIAM H. VALENTINE
    Complaint No. 3015
    Defendants are not residents of Indiana
    Must appear before 4th Monday of May, 1888
    Filed April 17, 1888
    JUMP & DAVIS, attorneys for plaintiff
                                                    A.R. HOPKINS, Clerk

Notice to Non-Residents
    JOHN BUTLER vs. WILLIAM BUTLER etal
    Complaint No. 3031
    LEWIS BUTLER, JOHN BATES, EMILY BATES, THOMAS BATES, ELIZABETH BATES, LAURA WEILER, and JOHN WEILER are not residents of Indiana
    Must appear before 4th Monday of May, 1888
    Filed April 17, 1888
    WARD & GIBSON, attorneys for plaintiff
                                                 A.R. HOPKINS, Clerk

Wednesday, April 25, 1888

Cayuga Gaslight
HENRY HASTY moved his family to Sidell, IL, this week, where he will make his future home.

Dana News
Miss ROSA WILSON died on Friday night, April 14th, 1888, at the residence of Mr. ABE WILSON, 3 ½ miles southeast of Toronto. The interment took place Sunday under the direction of Undertaker REDMAN.

Vermillion Township
Mrs. FLORENCE TRUITT died of consumption on April 19th, 1888. The remains were buried at the Vermillion Cemetery on the 20th. She leaves a husband and three children to mourn her death.

Home News
TAYLOR PALMER has sold out at Roachdale, Putnam County, and moved to North Salem, in Hendricks County, this State.

We forgot to mention the fact in our last issue that DICK WIMSETT, of Opedee, has another coal heaver at his house. The little fellow was two weeks old last Monday.

Married
CHARLES W. SIMPSON and Miss CASSIE LEWIS, daughter of JOSHUA LEWIS, were united in wedlock on last Thursday evening by Rev. WILLIAMS. Both are residents of Cayuga, and we believe are happily mated.

Obituary
At 6 o'clock on last Friday morning, April 20, 1888, the spirit of Uncle SAMMY DAVIS took its flight to that better world. The deceased was only sick about two weeks. His ailment was lung fever. He was born on May 31, 1811, in Adams County, OH. In 1829 he moved to this township, where he had resided ever since with the exception of one year. He was married twice, his last wife surviving him. Both were also residents of this township. His first wife was ELIZABETH HASTY and the last one was CATHERINE KING. He was the father of 7 children, 6 of whom are still living. When he first moved here, this county was sparsely settled, and comparatively a wilderness country. Wild game of all kinds was plenty, and the red man was still an inhabitant of our beautiful valley. He had an extensive acquaintance with all of the early settlers, and could tell many interesting incidents of pioneer life in Vermillion County. He was a member of the M.E. Church, and had been a devoted Christian for the last 40 years or more. His funeral took place at 10 o'clock on last Sunday morning, at his late residence, in the east part of town, Rev. JOHN W. PARRETT preaching a short and appropriate discourse, after which his remains were followed to the Johnson Cemetery by the largest procession of neighbors and sympathizing friends that has passed through our city for a long time.

Obituary
CATHERINE A. HELT was born March 23, 1819. She united with the M.E. Church January 4, 1848, and died April 16, 1888, aged 69 years and 24 days, having been a devoted Christian for more than 40 years. She was an invalid all her life. Her last illness was long and her sufferings great, but she bore all with great patience. She anxiously awaited her soul's release from its clay tenement. The funeral services were conducted on Monday the 16th by Rev. W.A. SMITH, in the Salem Church. A remarkable circumstance was alluded to in the service. It was that over 40 years ago four persons united with the church at the same time. The deceased and her sister NANCY HELT, JOSEPH JAMES and DAVID MACK, and the three survivors were present at the funeral. Her body was laid to rest in Helt's Prairie Cemetery.

Obituary
Mrs. FLORENCE TRUITT, daughter of HAMILTON BETSON, of this township, died at her home, one mile west of Quaker Point, at 1 o'clock on last Thursday morning, April 19, 1888. Her funeral took place at Vermillion Chapel, on the day following her death. She leaves a husband, three little children, and a host of friends to mourn her loss. She was loved and respected by everybody, as was fully attested by the very large number who attended her funeral.

Wednesday, May 2, 1888

Home News
F.H. MUNSON has moved back to Onarga, IL.

Mrs. ELIZA DILLOW and FRED DAVIS have formed a partnership, and will furnish the people of this locality all the flowers they want this season at the lowest cash prices.

JAMES JONES, of Fountain County, after a long and tedious courtship, was united in wedlock on Wednesday last to Miss GERTRUDE WHITSON, of Hillsdale.

R.H. NIXON received a telegram on last Monday morning announcing the sudden death of his Uncle ROBERT NIXON's wife, at Oswego, KS. Mr. NIXON left on the 11:25 a.m. train for Kansas. The telegram gave no particulars. It is quite likely now that his uncle will move back here to spend the rest of his life.

A little girl of HENRY WALTHER's fell into a kettle of hot soup last Saturday afternoon and was badly burned along her back. At present writing she is resting easy and is in a fair way to recover.

Death
Mrs. SARAH RHOADS, of Waveland, mother of MARTIN G. RHOADS, of this place, died on Tuesday of last week, April 24, 1888, aged 91 years and 20 days. Her husband, GEORGE RHOADS, to whom she was married in Pennsylvania on March 30, 1824, died in June 1875. She was the mother of 6 children, all of whom survive her. All were present at the funeral, and the sons and son-in-law, acted as pallbearers. The deceased has been a member of church since early childhood, and was a true Christian lady and an affectionate mother. She has been a resident of Waveland since 1840, and but a few who were living in that locality then, are left behind. The most of them have long since gone to their long home. She was a noble and generous lady, and a person who was very highly respected by everybody.

Cayuga Gaslight
POLK HOOD has returned from Oregon. His old friends are pleased to see him.

EMERY BRILES has been offered a position at Pelmaro, IL, in a blacksmith shop.

Dana News
Miss ZOOTE JAMES, of Hillsdale, is working in the Milliner Shop with MARY TAYLOR.

SANT TAYLOR is treating his house to a new coat of paint. "RAT" CRANE is the artist.

Died
On Monday evening, in Dana, Mr. D.C. BALES died of lung fever trouble and general debility, aged 61 years and some months. The deceased had made his home with his sister, Mrs. KEYES for a number of years. The funeral was preached at Mrs. KEYES residence by Rev. J.E. WRIGHT, Tuesday evening and the interment took place at the Bales burial ground.

Application for Liquor Licenses
    WILLIAM L. HAYS – Clinton Township
    MART ADAMS – Newport Township

Wednesday, May 9, 1888

Dana News
CLINT WATSON who has been working at the carpenter trade in Terre Haute during the winter, fell from a building recently and broke his arm. He wrote home to his father for assistance and received $20 in reply.

ED H. BURNS, the sprightly little quill jerker of the Frankfort Banner, has sold out his half interest in that paper to a young man by the name of CHARLES A. JARRELL. ED does not say what he intends to do, but we suppose he will return to Montezuma and help his old dad mix mortar for fire brick.

Home News
R.E. WHITLOCK and FRED BEARD are now in Sioux City, IA, meeting with good success in their book agency business.

Miss PENE PATTERSON, of Perrysville, so it is reported, will be married sometime next month to a California gentleman, by the name of WALTHALL.

County Graduates – April Examination
    Perrysville – C.S. FLANDERS, Principal

GRACE METZGER, THOMAS HENDERSON, ROSCOE M. COMPTON, ANNA MARY JOHNSON

Newport – E.A. AIKMAN, Principal
LURA CHIPPS, EDNA BROWN, FRED DAVIS, VARA A. PATRICK, WILLIAM E. RICHARDSON, CLAUDE M. SEARS, CLARENCE ARRASMITH, SANFORD M. SWAIN, QUINCY MYERS, BERTHA FOOS, CHARLES R. GRAY, LORIE E. COIL

Quaker Hill – ELMER E. DAVIS, teacher
JOHN HAWORTH, WILLIAM WALTHALL

No. 6 – E.L. HIBERLY, teacher
ELNORA A. MILLER

Clinton – W.A. KERNS, teacher
CARRIE L. LAKE, MABEL McBETH, MARY M. HAZELET, ANNIE G. MACK, ALLIE M. ALLEN, JENNIE SHIRKIE, ALBERT GOSNELL, SILAS M. HALL, CARRIE M. HARRINGTON, CLARA S. CUNNINGHAM, MANIE E. FRIST, DEREXA WHITCOMB

List of Real Estate Transfers for Month of April
Recorded by M.B. CARTER

A.W. MALONE to I.L. ANDREWS
20 acres in Helt Township
$1000

R.A. HACKNEY etal to R. SLAUGHTER
40 acres in Vermillion Township
$580

J.A. KNOWLES to R.B. BAILEY
Lot 4 in Clinton
$110

WILLIAM GOFF to PETER COSSEY
?? acres in Highland Township
$1

H. CASEBEER to C. JAMES etal
10 acres
$210

S.H. DALLAS to E.A. THOMAS
Lot 31 & 32 in Newport
$1077

P. STEPHENS to JOHN KIGER
40 acres in Helt Township
$325

SUSAN M. COLE to PAILO STEPHENS
40 acres in Helt Township
???

L.D. THOMAS to I.M. DAVIS
120 acres in Vermillion Township
$2100

R. SLAUGHTER to WILLIAM DE HAVEN
20 acres in Vermillion Township
$300

WILLIAM EDMONSTON to L.T. EDMONSTON
81 acres in Vermillion Township
$1140

CONRAD KESPELER to GEORGE A. KESPELER
40 acres in Highland Township
$700

R. LINCH to A.D. LINCH
41 acres in ?? Township
$1

D.D. & B.C. ROBINSON to T.J. WEST
46 acres in Helt Township
$2500

T.D. McKEE etal to ELI McDANIEL
4 lots in Cayuga
$400

J.C. SAWYER to O.B. GIBSON
Lot 7 in Newport
$2600

B.J. ROLL to J.W. PARRETT
Lot 37 in Newport
$20

JAMES B. ELBERSON to C.M. ELBERSON
Part of Lot 31 in Perrysville
$200

L. AIKMAN to M.J. HUTSON
2 lots in Dana
$75

J.N. TAYLOR to A.L. WILSON
12 ½ acres in Helt Township
$200

JAMES B. ELBERSON to ART G. ELBERSON
Part of Lot 31 in Perrysville
$250

M.H. CASTLE to JOHN NORRIS
Lot 23 in Dana
$350

J.E. WHIPPLE to SARAH WHIPPLE
Out Lot in Eugene
$300

LUCY BRINDLEY to J.W. PARRETT
Lot 109 in Newport
$200

HENRY B. HAMMOND to M.J. HUTSON
3 lots in Dana
$75

D.C. WATSON to HIRAM SHEPARD
2 lots in Dana
$470

J.E. BILSLAND to CLARA McROBERTS
Lot in Dana
$1200

HENRY B. HAMMOND to JAMES CLARK
Lot in Dana
$25

S. AIKMAN to JAMES CLARK
Lot in Dana
$25

ALEX DUNLAP to L.J. PLACE
128 acres in Vermillion Township
$4242

JOSEPH SWITZER to WILLIAM SWITZER
46 acres in Eugene Township
$800

WILLIAM RUSSELL to WILLIAM RUSSELL Sr.
40 acres in Vermillion Township
$700

J.F. SORG to JAMES ASBURY
10 acres in Vermillion Township
$425

H.A. COFFEEN to J.H. BOGART
Out Lot in Clinton
$250

CLAUDE MATTHEWS to MARTHA ROBB
Lot in Clinton
$1000

HENRY B. HAMMOND to M.A. STEWART
2 lots in Dana
$37.50

A WICK to JAMES RIVERS
7 acres in Clinton
$450

HENRY THOMASMYER to C.A. ALDRIDGE
40 acres in Helt Township
$1000

MARY A. STEWART to JAMES R. FINNEL
4 lots in Jonestown
$375

CARRY ALDRIDGE to HENRY THOMASMYER
?? acres in Helt Township
$1000

C. SALTSGAVER to REBECCA SWISHER
?? acres in Highland Township
$200

J.N. DAVIS to E.C. GIBBENS
Lot 29 in Newport
$200

WILLIAM TOOPS to DAVID McBETH
2 lots in Clinton
$300

Application for Liquor License
MORGAN J. TUCKER – Clinton Township
JOHN ADAMS – Cayuga Township

Wednesday, May 16, 1888

Married Man's Predicament
D.C. JOHNSON, who has been a resident of Clinton for a number of years, and favored by the people of that township with the office of Justice of the Peace, has been distributing his affections where they brought forth the wrong kind of fruit. For a long time he has been on terms of intimacy with Miss MAY QUICK, a former resident of Clinton, but now of Terre Haute. Miss MAY is small, but rather handsome. On last Wednesday afternoon, she swore out a warrant for the arrest of D.C. JOHNSON, charging him with the paternity of her child, now three or four weeks old. CHARLEY FLAID, a detective of that city, was started out to make the arrest, but JOHNSON, getting wind of trouble brewing, lit out for tall timber, and has not been heard from since. He has probably gone west to grow up with the country. He attempted to get a divorce from his wife, who now resides in Kansas, at the last term of our circuit court, but his deserted wife filed a protest, and Judge WHITE refused to grant the decree. Miss QUICK says that JOHNSON agreed to marry her as soon as he procured the divorce, but as there is now not much chance of him securing one, she has concluded to retrieve her wrongs by resorting to the law.

Pumpkin Vine News
Mrs. AMANDA DOWDY has just received notice from the pension department that she has been granted a pension on her husband's service in the Mexican War.

MONT CASEY returned home Saturday night, having severed his position on the Oakland Ledger.

Home News
Mrs. JANE KEYES, of Dana, has been appointed Administratrix of the estate of DEWIT C. BALES, lately deceased.

MONROE PUGH, of Bethel, IL, and ALLEN J. WALTHALL of Quaker Point, were in town on last Sunday afternoon.

Z.D. JAMES of Montezuma, who recently returned from a trip to the east, is reported to be in very feeble health.

GRANT and JESSE GALLOWAY, of Monroe County, brothers of ZACH and JOHN GALLOWAY, area here on a visit

Sudden Death
On last Friday afternoon, EDWIN R. PUGH, an old and respected citizen of Quaker Point, this township, was engaged in cleaning some drift out of a little ditch near his residence, when he was stricken down with a stroke of paralysis. JOHN KERNS, the village blacksmith, happened along the road which passes in front of Mr. PUGH's house, and noticed Mr. PUGH down in the ditch, lying on his back, and moving one of his hands a little. He walked to where he was and asked him what was the matter, but the old gentleman could not speak so he could understand him. He then went to the house and told his folks, who were not yet apprised of his condition. Help was procured, and he was carried to his home, but was unable to speak more than two or three words. He was stricken down about 5 o'clock that evening, and died at 12 o'clock that night. The deceased was born in Pennsylvania in 1822, and emigrated to this county in 1856, where he had continued to live ever since. He was very highly esteemed by all who knew him. For many years he was postmaster at Quaker Point. He was a Quaker, and a member of the Friends Church near that place. His funeral took place at 11 a.m. on last Sunday, and was very largely attended. Rev. JAMES HAWORTH preached the discourse, and performed the last sad rites.

J.E. WHIPPLE has moved his Cayuga Journal office to Sidell, IL, where he will commence the publication of a paper in a few days. FRANK BLUNK, of this place, has been employed as a compositor. We wish the boys success.

On last Wednesday afternoon, just seven years after ZACH T. GALLOWAY was married, his wife gave birth to a gal baby.

Four weeks ago today, D.A. REED, of Helt Township, was thrown from a wagon by a runaway team, and so seriously injured that there is now little hope of his recovery. His skull was fractured and crushed. One day last week, Dr. SLAUGHTER, Dr. WATKINS, and Dr. NEWTON performed a surgical operation, removing a piece of the fractured skull. Dr. SLAUGHTER thinks there is no chance for the patient. He has been insensible ever since he was hurt, and has partaken of but very little nourishment.

On Thursday and Friday last, we visited the "old folks at home." Our father, Mr. DAVIS, who is past 78 years of age, is in fine health and able for his rations. Our mother, past 69, is in very poor health, and instead of weighing 160 or 170 as she did a few years ago, she now weighs but very little over 100 pounds. We hope for her speedy recovery

Died
Mrs. SARAH P. NIXON, wife of ROBERT NIXON, aged 57 years, 7 months, and 22 days, died at her home in this city on Saturday evening, April 28, 1888. The deceased was born in New Hampshire County, West Virginia, and had been sick but a few days, and while those intimately acquainted with her condition were prepared for a fatal result, her death was a complete surprise to the public. Mrs. NIXON had lived here for some 15 years, and has been not only well but favorably known by our people. The funeral services were held at the family residence last Wednesday and were conducted by Rev. JOHN ELLIOTT, assisted by Rev. JUNKINS and Rev. HAMMONS. A large concourse of neighbors and friends were present to witness the last sad rites and offer consolation to the bereaved husband.

The Oswego, Kansas, Independent

Wednesday, May 23, 1888

Home News

The widow of S.B. TATE, of Perrysville, has been granted a pension.

HARMON JONES has been appointed administrator of the estate of DAVID A. REED, late a resident of Helt Township.

DICK HANNAHS has been given a position in a telegraph office at West Wichita, KS.

Rev. JOSHUA ROGERS of Ashton, Dakota, died at 2:20 a.m. on Thursday, May 10, 1888, after a short illness. He was a brother of JOHN O. and JAMES ROGERS of Dana.

D.A. REED, of Helt Township, who was hurt in a runaway a few weeks ago, died on the 11th instant.

HURON SOUTHARD has been appointed administrator of the estate of CATHERINE A. HELT, deceased.

TOM McKNIGHT has sold his blacksmith shop to JOE HOPKINS and left here on Sunday last for Danville, IL, where he intends to locate.

Mrs. JANE McLAUGHLIN, of this place, packed her household effects and moved to Indianola, IL, on Sunday last to try living with her husband once more, who deserted her about 6 months ago.

Death

Mr. CHARLES RHOADS died yesterday at the residence of his uncle, Judge P.E. RHOADS. He was taken sick about 10 days ago with typhoid fever. He improved for a time, but pneumonia set in and death resulted from the complications of both diseases. Mr. RHOADS was employed as a traveling salesman for E.H. BINDLEY & Co. He was for several years in the firm's office, and was well known, and had many warm friends. His home was in Newport, IN. His parents, brother, and sister were at his bedside during his illness. The burial will take place at Waveland, in Montgomery County, where he was born December 17, 1866. The train will leave here at 6 o'clock Monday morning. Mr. RHOADS was a member of the Presbyterian Church of this city. The deceased was a brother of our fellow townsman, HARRY B. RHOADS, and had many warm friends, and no enemies, in this place. He was a model young man and was very highly respected by everyone.

Terre Haute Sunday Express

Commencement exercises were held at Newport High School on Saturday night. Those participants were:
QUINCY MYERS, FRED DAVIS, LEORIE COLL, MORREY SWAIN, BERTHA FOOS, CHARLES GRAY, CLARENCE ARRASMITH, VARA PATRICK, WILLIAM RICHARDSON, EDNA BROWN, LURA CHIPPS, CLAUDE SEARS, LOU E. CADY, and E.A. AIKMAN.

FRANK TURNER and wife went over to Bloomingdale, Parke County, last week, to witness the nuptials of Dr. GOLDSBERRY's daughter, who was united to a postal clerk of the C. & E.I. Railroad. The ceremony was performed by Rev. W.A. SMITH, pastor of the M.E. Church, Helt's Prairie.

Notice of Final Settlement of Estate
Estate of WILLIAM JACKSON, deceased
Must appear before May 28, 1888
Filed May 15, 1888

A.R. HOPKINS, Clerk

Birthday
Aunt BETSY JAMES, of Summit Grove, celebrated her 83rd birthday last Saturday. Sixty six friends gathered to lend sunshine and cheer to the occasion. It was thought that she would not be alive for the celebration, as she had been gradually failing for some time now. It was apparent that all the relatives and friends felt that they, in all probability, were celebrating for the last time for mother JAMES. Uncle ZACHARIAH JAMES and good wife were back from their eastern tour, and greatly added to the happiness of the gathering. Mr. W.J. HERBET, with his estimable wife, were present.
W.A. SMITH

Wednesday, May 30, 1888

Decoration Day Notes
Several celebrations were held today to honor those soldiers who have died. The following is a list of the brave boys whose remains now sleep beneath the sod:
SIMEON SHAW, THOMAS E. DIXON, PHILLIP HARRIER, JACOB REMLEY, JOHN ASBURY, JACOB YOUNT, ELI THOMAS, HENRY H. AXTON, SAMUEL BROWN, THOMPSON ARMOUR, PERRY GEBHART, WARREN THOMAS, JAMES CRAIG, WILLIAM HAMILTON, GEORGE WILFONG, ELI THOMAS, JOSEPH WALLACE, JAMES M. DIXON, CHARLEY H. DAWSON, JOHN WESLEY ARRASMITH, HENRY H. EGGLESTON

Clinton Argus
A.N. TURSHER left this week for Broadland, IL, on the Tuscola branch of the C. & E.I., where he will take charge of a night office.

The following is a list of teachers for the coming fall and winter terms:
High School and 8th Grade – W.A. KEARNS
6th and 7th Grade – R.E. WHITLOCK
4th & 5th Grade – MARY L.E. JONES
3rd Grade – ETTA EDWARDS
2nd Grade – ALICE BECKMAN
1st Grade – DAISY ROBINSON

Home News
J.T. NEWELL, of Perrysville, has been granted a pension.

Mrs. HENRY HOLLINGSWORTH, who has been confined to her bed for several weeks, don't improve any. Her stomach seems to be the seat of her trouble.

Miss PENE PATTERSON, a plump and pretty lady of Perrysville, and who is just as good as she is pretty, will be united in wedlock to a gentleman by the name of Mr. WESTAN, of Dakota, on June 7th.

Married
On last Monday afternoon, LEONARD G. GODDARD, aged 23, and Miss JANE IRWIN, aged 19, both of Putnam County, were united in wedlock, the ceremony taking place in the Clerk's office, and being performed by Rev. R.B. VAN ALLEN, pastor of the U.B. Church.

The HARRISON brothers of Bloomington, IL, are going to start a bank at Dana. They are brothers of Dr. J.C. HARRISON, of Hillsdale, and are said to be well heeled, financially.

J.B. OSMON went down to Arkansas last week, to see what was the prospect to buy cheap timber. He is talking of moving his sawmill down there. Our advice would be for him to stay here.

Wedding

A very pleasant company were gathered on last Wednesday night at the residence of Dr. GOLDSBERRY, to witness the marriage of his daughter, Miss LOLLY GOLDSBERRY to Mr. NED J. EVANS of Terre Haute, IN, by Rev. WILLIAM SMITH. The ceremony was very impressive. They will make their home in Terre Haute.

Death

Mr. WILLIAM T. FERGUSON, a resident of Highland Township, died somewhat suddenly at his residence, near Perrysville, on Saturday evening last. The funeral services were held at the house on Monday morning, commencing at 9 o'clock. Mr. FERGUSON was one of the most prominent citizens of this county. His loss will be felt by the community and district as well as by the family.

Wednesday, June 6, 1888

Dana News

R.F. GILMORE started for California Sunday morning to be gone some time. He goes for the benefit of his health.

The following is a list of the deceased comrades who were remembered with floral tokens, and the names of the respective regiments they served in, so far as known:

Thomas Cemetery
- JAMES A. BELL – 18th IN
- ED W. THOMAS – 18th IN
- WARREN THOMAS – 43rd IN
- JEROME B. DICKEN – 14th IN
- MARION McDONALD – 14th IN
- GEORGE WILFONG – 97th IN
- WESLEY CORDER – 18th IN
- SAMUEL TRUITT – 97th IN
- McCAGE HARRISON – 149th IN
- MOSE J. EMLEY – 18th IN
- ELI PALMER – 43rd IN and 123rd IN
- JOSEPH WALLACE – 55th IN
- JACOB REMLEY – 97th IN
- E.A. JONES – 22nd WI
- JOSEPH MAXWELL – 31st IN
- JACOB BROWN
- PERRY JONES
- JAMES PETTY
- DANIEL DOWNING
- I.B. LAMB
- THOMAS PIERCE
- THOMAS J. BLUNK – 123rd IN
- GEORGE HINES – 43rd IN
- VINCENT DOUGLASS

Wimsett Cemetery
- JOHN GIBBENS – 14th IN
- JOHN HALL – 43rd IN
- E.P. PHELPS
- HENRY AXTON – 14th IN
- S.V. ODEKIRK
- HENRY YOUNG

Johnson Cemetery
- JOSEPH WEBB – 14th IN

Vermillion Chapel Cemetery
- HENRY HOLLINGSWORTH – 123rd IN

    DANIEL ROBINSON
    JOHN F. STEWART – 18th IN

Miscellaneous
    JOHN FLOYD – Manley Cemetery
    HEROD FRINGER – Indianapolis
    DAVID BRUNER
    JACOB DOWDELL – Lodi, IN
    RICHARD R. UTTER – 14th IN – Highfill Cemetery
    JACK OWENS – Highfill Cemetery

Buried in the Sunny South in Unknown Graves
    J.W. ARRASMITH – 6th IN Cavalry
    WILLIAM R. DICKEN – 6th IN Cavalry
    PRESLEY JOHNSON – 6th IN Cavalry
    JASON NOYES – 18th IN Cavalry
    CHARLES DAWSON
    STEPHEN BIGNEY
    WILLIAM F. FLOYD
    HENRY H. EGGLESTON – 6th IN Cavalry

Montezuma Reporter
ED BURNS, wife and baby, of Frankfort, IN, came in Wednesday evening to attend the wedding of his sister to Mr. S.P. HANCOCK.

Died
BECKY JACKSON, wife of WILLIAM JACKSON, died at her home near Jacksonville, Monday, May 28th, 1888, at the age of 72 years. The remains were laid in their last resting place in the family burial ground May 29th. She was widely known as Widow STEELE. J. FRIST conducted the burial.

Home News
Liquor licenses were granted on Monday to the following:
    M.J. TUCKER – Clinton
    WILLIAM L. HAYS – Clinton
    MART ADAMS – Newport
    JOHN ADAMS – Cayuga
    JERRY CONLEY – Dana
    WILLIAM SLATER – Dana

Mrs. REBECCA HOLLINGSWORTH, widow of the late HENRY HOLLINGSWORTH, who served in the 123rd IN Regiment, has just been granted a pension of $12 per month for herself and $2 per month for each of her 3 children, making $18 per month. The arrears amount to $535.67. It was a God send to the worthy woman, who has been confined to her bed 6 or 7 weeks, and is in straightened circumstances.

ALLEN HALL, of Illinois, is here visiting his mother, Mrs. IRVIN LAMB.

ED KIGER, a boy raised by WALTER J. PLACE, who has been away from here 10 or 12 years, has moved back here. He is now 26 years of age.

Mrs. MALISSA EDMONSTON, mother of LEE and WILLIAM EDMONSTON of this township has just been granted a pension on her late husband, who was a soldier in the War of 1812. The arrears amount to $1088.67. The old lady will probably not live long to enjoy this bounty from the government, as she is 83 years old on the 29th of next month.

BOB GIBSON, a son of WILLIAM GIBSON, who was a former resident of this place, was married in Arkansas a few days ago to an estimable lady.

R.A. CRAIG and wife, of Eugene, will start sometime this week to Amelia, Clermont County, OH, to visit his sister whom he has not seen since 1847. They intend to be gone about 3 months.

Wednesday, June 13, 1888

Home News
Mrs. HENRY H. AXTON, of this township, has been granted a pension.

SAM MYERS, of Eugene Township, has been granted a pension of $4 per month. His first draw amounts to $118.53.

Mrs. JOHN HENSON and her children leave for Imperial, NE, on Monday to join her husband, who is traveling a circuit near that place.

Married
At Perrysville, on last Thursday, June 7th, 1888, JOHN WESTDAHL of Huron, Dakota, was united in wedlock to Miss PENE PATTERSON. Both left on the afternoon train for Cincinnati and east on a bridal tour. They will return to their home at Huron on July 15th.

Postmasters
The WILTERMOOD family don't seem to enjoy holding a government office. JOHN A. WILTERMOOD was first appointed postmaster here under the new administration, and resigned after he had held the office nearly 2 years. His brother CHARLEY WILTERMOOD was next appointed, and now is tired of it, and forwarded his resignation to the department last week. OL DAVIS has forwarded a numerously signed petition, asking for the appointment, and as he has no opposition, he will unquestionably get it.

Horseshoe Items
Miss EMMA BLACKMORE, of Judson, Parke County, IN, is visiting in our midst. If reports be true, she and CHARLEY DeHAVEN will be united in the holy bonds of wedlock before she returns home.

Mr. BUMBERGER, who has been working for Mr. JOHNSTONE, left for Brazil, Monday. We understand that he will be married soon.

Notice of Administration
  Estate of WILLIAM JACKSON, deceased
  June 2, 1888
                CHARLES W. WARD, Administrator

Wednesday, June 20, 1888

Dana News
JACOB MYERS of this place has been granted a pension on account of his son, J.H. MYERS. All his friends rejoice that Mr. MYERS has been so fortunate to secure it.

Election Inspectors
At their session last week, the Board of County Commissioners appointed the following inspectors for the November election:

Precinct	Inspector
Gessie Precinct	GEORGE SPARKS
Eugene Precinct	EMMET VAN HOUTEN
Quaker Hill	Capt. S.J. HAIL
Independence	GEORGE W. CAMPBELL
Hillsdale	WHITE JAMES
Centenary	WILLIAM WRIGHT

Clinton Argus
HARVE VAUGHN and family, of Greensburg, KS, arrived in the city last Thursday, and will make Clinton their future home. We understand HARVE has got enough of Kansas.

Rev. HOOD, recently of Blue Spring, NE, has accepted a call to preach at Dana and Clinton. He will preach here about the 4th Sunday in this month. He comes well recommended and will go to work with a vim to build up and revive the church.

Perrysville Items
NET HAVENS, the young school marm of this place, has finished her lengthly school of two months among the kids across the majestic Wabash.

Home News
GILBERT L. MACK has been appointed administrator of his wife's estate.

Mrs. JOHN P. HENSON and her four children left last Monday on the 6 o'clock train for Imperial, NE, to join her husband, who is located at that point as minister of the M.E. Church. She was accompanied as far as Chicago by W.P. HENSON, her father-in-law.

Mrs. HANNAH VALENTINE was granted a divorce yesterday from her husband, WILLIAM H. VALENTINE.

ORA DeLOSS DAVIS is reading law with CONLEY & SAWYER. He took his first lesson on last Monday.

Prof. JOHN COLLETT, of Indianapolis, left for Las Vegas, NM, on Friday last, on geological surveying expedition. He will be gone about 3 weeks.

Our old soldier friend, JOHN BARKER, is on the sick list in a pretty bad fix. He seems to be affected with lung trouble and dropsy. We hope for his speedy recovery.

WALTER PLACE Jr., who has been attending commercial college at Cincinnati, OH, since early last fall, will arrive home today, having completed his course and received his diploma.

Married
Married in Dana, Thursday, June 14th, 1888, at 4 p.m., by Rev. W.A. SMITH, Dr. W.M. JONES and Miss SALLIE L. KEYES, at the residence of the bride's mother. They will make their future home in Dana. Dr. E.E. JONES and Miss LEBO, both of Veedersburg, IN, and Miss SCOTT, of Clinton, were guests, and some other relatives and friends.

The children and grandchildren of J.M. NICHOLS, to the number of 40, gave him a happy birthday surprise party yesterday. Yesterday was Mr. NICHOLS' 69th birthday. J.R. SWAIN photographed them in one group.

Notice of Administration
    Estate of REBECCA MACK, deceased
    GILBERT L. MACK, Administrator

Wednesday, June 27, 1888

Crazy Items
SAMUEL JACKSON, who has been stricken down with consumption for a year, is rapidly sinking and there is no hope for his recovery.

Perrysville
LEN SANDERS, of this place, died last Thursday night. His funeral took place on Friday at 10 a.m. He died at his home, but his remains were taken to Mrs. AMANDA SABINS for funeral services.

Horseshoe Items
We are glad to note that LORA JOHNSON has received a pension, the amount being $175.26.

Funeral in Edgar County, IL
HARRIET RUSSELL, whose maiden name was MATER, daughter of JOHN and MARY MATER, and sister of the well known IRA MATER, was born in Parke County, IN, October 8th, 1830, and died in Edgar County, IL, May 16th, 1888, aged 57 years, 7 months, and 8 days. She was married to JOHN RUSSELL in 1849. She was the mother of 8 children, of which 7 are living – 3 sons and 4 daughters – one daughter preceded her to the world of spirits. Sister RUSSELL was converted and joined the church at the age of 19 years, and continued faithful until her death.

Home News
J.W. CROSS went to Danville, IL, last week to attend the funeral of his brother-in-law, THOMPSON ROSS.

Editor JOHNSON, of the Montezuma Reporter, is the proprietor of a new gal baby, which arrived on Friday last.

Mrs. SAMANTHA SONGER, of Cissna Park, IL, was in town over Sunday, visiting her sister, Mrs. JOHN W. CROSS.

Mrs. Dr. STADLER and her daughter CARRIE STADLER, who has been visiting her sister, Mrs. WILLIAM FRAZIER, returned last Tuesday to their home in Milwaukee, WI.

Miss ALLIE KOONSE, who taught at Premium No. 3, last winter, has been employed to teach in the city schools at Lafayette during the coming fall and winter. She is a bright teacher and a most excellent young lady.

OL DAVIS forwarded his bond, as postmaster for this place, on Monday last. He will take possession of the office about July 2nd.

Death
WILLIAM DOSS, an inmate of the county poor asylum, and who was well known to most of the citizens of this township, died from old age at 4 o'clock on last Friday morning. He was 78 years of age, and had been an inmate of the asylum since last fall. He was buried in the afternoon of the same day by Supt. JOE CONRAD.

Death
LEONARD SANDERS, who has been a resident of Perrysville for many years, and who was well known by many of our citizens here, died on Thursday last, June 21st, 1888, aged 46 years. He had been afflicted with consumption for many years, and is the third one of the family who has died from that dreadful disease in the last 12 months. He was engaged in the undertaking business, and was a useful member of society, and well respected by everybody. He was able to walk about the day before he died. He had been in very feeble health for some time. He was a brother of Mrs. JOHN L. EGGLESTON, of this place. His funeral took place on the day following his death; his remains being buried in the Hicks Cemetery, one half mile west of Perrysville.

Montezuma News
LAFE NEWELL has his new ferry boat launched and is now ready for business.

Dana News
Dr. JOHN GILMORE left last Saturday for Kansas.

Wednesday, July 4, 1888

Quaker Hill Items
Miss GRACIE ADAMS, of Illiana, was the guest of her cousin, Miss ALTA JONES, on last Sunday evening.

Miss MYRA HAWORTH, who has been visiting her sister, Mrs. FLORA COOK, returned home on last Sunday.

Big Pension
GEORGE FONCANNON received and injury during the war to his spine which affected his brain and resulted in insanity. He was sent 10 or 12 years ago to the poor house in Vermillion County. In the meantime his family has been destitute. Dr. MOORHEAD examined him, found his claim just and promptly the long delayed justice was done him. He is entitled to $72 per month for insanity until death. The arrears amount to $10,000, which will put his family in good condition.

Notice of Administration
    Estate of WILLIAM T. FERGUSON, deceased
    MARY A. FERGUSON, Administratrix

Home News
Mrs. ALICE WELHAUS, of Streator, IL, is here attending the bedside of Mrs. JOHN HASTY, who is quite seriously ill.

RAT CRANE, of Clinton, has just completed painting ELI HARLAN's residence and barn, and did a neat and tasty job.

JOE RABB, a Vermillion County boy, has been re-nominated for Circuit Judge in this district composed of Warren and Fountain counties.

JOHN G. BARKER, who is afflicted with lung trouble, heart disease, and dropsy, is no better. He is unable to lie down in bed, and what little sleep he gets is while sitting in a chair.

Capt. W.S. JEWELL, of Eugene, was in town on last Saturday and made out a voucher for the pension that has just been granted him. His first draw amounts to $1104. He gets $4 per month. He ought to get at least $16.

Mrs. C.S. DAVIS, and her two daughters, MAGGIE and NELLIE, arrived here on last Friday afternoon. They have come back to locate at some point in this county. Mr. DAVIS remained in Kansas to look after his interests there. He will probably not be here for some time yet.

The widow of the late Rev. W.Y. ALLEN, of Rockville, died on last Thursday night, aged 63 years.

Mrs. JACOB BOST, of Coal Bluff, Vigo County, arrived here on last Monday afternoon to spend a few days visiting her father, JAMES DUZAN, and others of this place.

Obituary
SAM JACKSON, a son of JOE JACKSON, of Helt Township, died on Friday last, after a long and lingering illness. His disease was consumption. He was a model young man, and very highly esteemed and respected by everyone. His funeral took place Sunday; his remains being interred in the Bales Cemetery.

JAMES H. MILLER, a brother in law of CHARLEY HACKER, is down here clerking for him in his store.

Miss MARIE LUNGER, of Chrisman, IL, was here last Monday visiting her cousin, Miss GERTIE DOWDELL.

Mrs. ELIAS PRITCHARD and Mrs. M.G. RHOADS have gone down to the French Lick Springs to recuperate their health.

Wednesday, July 11, 1888

Dear Editor,
Through the kindness of an old uncle, living in Terre Haute, I occasionally receive a copy of your paper, which gives me so many items of news from the land of my nativity, that I have concluded to become a subscriber. I was born near the old Vermillion Chapel grounds, in the year of 1837, and emigrated with my parents to the noble young commonwealth of Iowa, in 1854. What education I received was at an old log schoolhouse, one mile west of Highland. My recollection dates back to the times when SILAS BOGART, NELSON HOSS, JOHN DAVIS, MARY ANN DERR, and NAPOLEON B. MACK wielded the birch in opossum bottom district.
JOHN LYNCH
Cambria, Wayne County, IA

Clinton Argus
BRANSON HAMMOND, a member of the gallant 18th IN Regiment and a well known citizen of this township, has recently sold his farm to Dr. JOHN BOGART, and intends turning his face towards the setting sun. It is his intention to locate somewhere in Kansas.

The Clinton Bicycle Club consisting of DICK PAYTON, FRANK CAMPBELL, CHARLEY OSBORN, LAWRENCE ANDERSON, WALTER CRABB, CLAUDE ANDERSON, and JOHN STAATS wheeled to Rockville last Sunday.

Marriage
H.A. WHITE, of Augusta, KS, and his sister-in-law Mrs. FLORENCE MALONE, got married recently. Both parties are well known here, having been residents of this place. WHITE was the editor of the Western Indianian, and in the memorable campaign of 1876, was the Greenbackers' candidate for Congress in this district.

Dana News
Mr. E.E. HELT, of Helt's Prairie, was in town last Friday on his way to Paris, IL, to be examined for license to teach school. He will teach at Vermillion, IL, this year.

Perrysville Sawdust
Mrs. BILL COLE and baby son, of Kyana, IN, and Mrs. ANNA GIBSON, of Chebanse, IL, are visiting their mother, Mrs. HANNAH TATE of this place.

The 4th was celebrated at Mr. JOHN LONG's, by the appearance of a girl baby. Both mother and child are doing fine.

Home News
JACOB WOODWARD and ALICE MITCHELL, of Eugene Township, were united in wedlock on Saturday last, the ceremony taking place in the Clerk's office, and being performed by Esq. THOMPSON, of Cayuga.

SILAS HOLLINGSWORTH has returned from Lodi, where he has been working for DAVE SHIRK in the butchering business. Mr. SHIRK doesn't need his services any longer on account of numerous railroad hands having completed their work of widening the narrow gauge railroad.

The officers of the Rebekah Lodge at this place were installed on last Friday. The following is a list of them:

Mrs. ED AIKMAN	N.G.
Miss ZULA HOPKINS	V.G.
Miss GRACE CARTER	Secretary
Mrs. D.S. HOPKINS	Treasurer

WILLIAM PEARMAN has been granted a pension. The arrears amount to $1319.86. He will be getting $12 per month.

The newly elected officers for the Odd Fellows Lodge at this place were installed on Tuesday evening of last week. They are as follows:

R.A. PARRETT	N.G.
ROBERT JAGGERS	V.G.
J.R. SWAIN	Secretary
ED AIKMAN	Treasurer

Obituary
Died at her home near Eugene, IN, July 8th, 1888, Mrs. HETTIE PORTER. She was born March 20th, 1831. She married JOHN W. PORTER November 7th, 1851. To them were born 9 children, 7 of whom are still living: Mrs. MARY SMITH of Kansas, Mrs. ABBIE SMITH of Perrysville, Mrs. JENNIE ARCHIE of Ohio; MINNIE, ZOE, JOHN, and W.W. PORTER of Eugene, IN. She was a sister to Mrs. SARAH RICHARDSON of Eugene, and Mrs. ELIZABETH PERRANT of Kansas. Short funeral services were held.

Notice to Non-Residents
ALFRED M. REED vs. ELIZA A. FORD, ALBERT FORD, EMMA SKIDMORE, JASPER F. SKIDMORE, ELIZA REED, LOUISA JONES, SILAS JONES, ELIZABETH REED, CHARLES REED, CHARLES S. REED, MARY HIDDLE, CHRISTOPHER HIDDLE, PATSEY BAUM, ADAM P. BAUM, MYRTLE GREEN, OTHA GREEN, and FRANKLIN GREEN
Complaint #3016
13 of the defendants do not live in State of Indiana
Must appear before 2nd Monday of October 1888
CONLEY & SAWYER, Attorneys for plaintiff
Filed July 9, 1888
           A.R. HOPKINS, Clerk

Wednesday, July 18, 1888

Quaker Hill News
Miss LEE LINDSEY, of Eugene, is visiting her sister, Mrs. MAG SAUNDERS.

Clinton Argus
MARY CRABB and BETTIE WHITE visited their uncle, Mr. WALDEN, near Paris, IL, Tuesday of last week.

Mr. and Mrs. PETERSON HANSON lost both of their twins last week by cholera infantum. One died on Wednesday and was buried on Friday; the other died in great pain Friday night and its remains placed by the side of the one who had just gone before.

JOHN BOWEN, a well known colored man, was taken sick with cholera morbus Thursday night of last week. He died Friday evening. His funeral was held Saturday and was largely attended. JOHN was a very industrious, straight forward kind of a man and well thought of by the community. He was unmarried.

Home News

BILLY SCOTT, of Eugene Township, an old 18th boy, has been granted an increase of pension.

An infant child or LEVI CLENDENING, residing 5 miles west of town, died one day last week.

BOB LITTLE left on the 9:05 train last Friday night for Athens, TN, to visit his brother DAVE LITTLE, who moved to that delightful country last fall.

JOE CARTER, of Helt Township, has been granted an increase of pension.

Miss COE HAWKINS is visiting her grandparents and other relatives in Oakland City, IN.

Prof. ED AIKMAN, wife and mother-in-law, Mrs. MARY CHADD, are visiting relatives in Helt Township.

Miss NELLIE JONES, a clerk in the pension department at Washington, is at home on a visit. She was accompanied by her little nephew, PARK HUNTER.

A.H. CRAFT, of this township, says he has fallen heir to $173,000 in England, left him by the Will of a rich relative. He has employed RHOADS & AIKMAN to look after the matter for him.

MILTON COLLIN, of Cayuga, and Miss EMMA THORNTON, of Dana are going to splice in the near future. They have nearly all the necessary preliminaries arranged.

SAM D. COLLETT left yesterday morning for Charleston, WV, to visit his sister, Mrs. ADAM LITTLEPAGE. He took along his bicycle to coast down the Virginia mountains.

Sudden Death

Mrs. WILLIAM MORRISON, of Helt Township, aged about 30, died very suddenly last week. She was well and hearty on Wednesday morning as she ever was, and in the evening took suddenly ill and died the next day. She leaves a husband and three children. Her remains were interred in the Helt's Prairie Cemetery on Friday.

Death at the Poor Asylum

On Tuesday morning of last week, July 10th, 1888, JOHN STRAIN died at the poor asylum, at the age of 82 years. He was born in Ohio in 1806, and emigrated to Helt Township, this county in 1849, where he had resided ever since. About 4 weeks ago, he became insane, and was brought to the poor asylum where he could be cared for more properly. At one time he was in good circumstances, but in his latter days became careless, and came near squandering all his vast possessions. His sons took him in charge and saved part of his estate. On the day following his death, he was buried in the Helt's Prairie Cemetery.

Last Monday afternoon while standing in the postoffice, WILLIAM SCOTT, of Eugene Township, fainted and fell heavily on the floor. He had been bleeding at the lungs pretty freely that day, and his fainting is supposed to have resulted from the loss of blood. It was several minutes before he recovered sufficiently to get up.

Letter List

SALLY CAMER	ALLEN PLATT
SAMUEL MORRIS	HENRY BELL
T.J. BROOKS	PHILIP T. WILLIAMS

The infant child of WILLIAM F. SCHWEIZER, of Crawfordsville, died on last Monday night.

Notice to Non-Residents
> SARAH BALES vs. JAMES RUNYAN etal
> Complaint No. 3016
> Defendant CLAUDE JACKSON is not a resident of Indiana
> He lives in Illinois
> Must appear before 2nd Monday of October 1888
> CONLEY & SAWYER, attorneys for plaintiff
> Filed July 9, 1888
>
> A.R. HOPKINS, Clerk

Notice to Non-Residents
> MARY A. GEER vs. JOHN GEER
> Complaint No. 3059
> JOHN GEER is not a resident of Indiana
> Must appear before 2nd Monday in October 1888
> CONLEY & SAWYER, attorneys for plaintiff
> Filed July 11, 1888
>
> A.R. HOPKINS, Clerk

Notice to Non-Residents
> ELLA VANLEER vs. HENRY VANLEER
> Complaint No. 3060
> HENRY VANLEER is not a resident of Indiana
> Must appear before 1st Monday in October 1888
> WARD & GIBSON, attorneys for plaintiff
> Filed July 7, 1888
>
> A.R. HOPKINS, Clerk

Wednesday, July 25, 1888

1840
We want the names for publication of every man in this county who voted for WILLIAM HENRY HARRISON for President in 1840. Send them in at once. The following is a list of the names received up to date:

W.J. HERBERT	JOHN HASTY
JAMES DUZAN	THOMAS HARRISON
SAMUEL AIKMAN	JAMES F. BURNETT
ISAAC CLAWSON	THOMAS S. HOOD
RICHARD MALONE	JAMES McLAUGHLIN
HENRY RALSTON	AMOS HOOD
E.B. NOURSE	JACOB MILLER
ROBERT DAVIS	EBER HOLLINGSWORTH
ELIAS LAMB	A.V. BROWN
THOMAS A. KIBBY, Sr.	JOHN WRIGHT
WILLIAM CHUNN	OL LINDSEY
J.W. PARRETT	THOMAS CUSHMAN
WILLIAM NICHOLS	WALTER J. PLACE
JOSEPH BRENER	PETER CRIPPEN
HIRAM CHENOWETH	LEMON CHENOWETH
HUGH S. COMINGORE	JOHN DICKASON
R.J. GESSIE	HARVEY HUNT
THOMAS H. HARRISON	SAMUEL HARRIS
JAMES J. LEWIS	R.D. MOFFATT
JOHN R. McNEILL	GEORGE H. McNEILL
THOMAS J. MITCHELL, Sr.	WILLIAM NICCUM
DANIEL R. RUNYAN Sr.	DAVID SPRY

JOHN F. SMITH	WILLIAM P. SMITH
THOMAS H. SMITH	WESLEY SWISHER
ELHANAN STEVENS	WILLIAM G. TARRENCE
JOHN TATE	L.D. WOODMANSE
SAMUEL WATT	STEPHEN WEBSTER

M.L. GRIFFITH, who has been employed on the Visitor staff for several weeks past, will leave next Monday or Tuesday for Illinois, where he has purchased a half interest in the Farmer City Republican.

                                                    Winfield, Kansas, Visitor

Home News
R.M. RUCKER, of Clinton Township, has been granted an increase of pension.

An infant child or ELVIN WHEELER, of Danville, IL, died on Monday last.

W.T. CARMIN, a former citizen of Eugene, is now running a drug store at Roachdale, in Putnam County.

JOHN KERDOLFF and his daughter KATE KERDOLFF, of Cincinnati, OH, are here visiting their son, JOHN H. KERDOLFF, the jolly butcher.

GEORGE H. CARTER and wife, of Chicago, are here visiting, guests of JOE HANN and his wife. Mrs. CARTER is a cousin to Mrs. HANN. Mr. CARTER is deaf, but has a fine education and is a printer by trade. He is Supt. of a printing office in Chicago at a salary of $90 per month. His wife is both deaf and dumb, and is a daughter of T.J. STARK of Cayuga.

JAMES HEGARTY, wife and children, of Springfield, MO, are here visiting his brother, MAURICE HEGARTY.

Married
At 8 o'clock on last Saturday night, VOORHEES JONES and Miss ELLA M. FORTNER, daughter of JONAS FORTNER, was untied in wedlock by Rev. R.B. VAN ALLEN, the ceremony taking place at the residence of WILLIAM MYERS, near the Stumptown free gravel road.

Married
Miss EVA G. KERNS, a daughter of County Commissioner WILLIAM F. KERNS of Bono, was united in wedlock at the residence of her parents, to ROBERT K. PORTER, Dana, on Sunday last, Rev. W.A. SMITH performing the ceremony.

Surprise
On last Sunday, the relatives and neighbors, accompanied by the farmers' brass band, marched in procession to the residence of PHILANDER GOFF and wife, of Gessie, and informed them that they had been married 16 years. The tables were spread and about 125 persons took part.

The contract for building a schoolhouse at Stumptown, six miles west of here, was let on Thursday last to THOMAS J. NICHOLS, of Quaker Hill.

Horseshoe and Vicinity
Born to Mr. and Mrs. GEORGE W. HOWLETT, a girl. The piano thumper was born last Tuesday.

Wednesday, August 1, 1888

Home News
WILLIAM MITCHELL of Clinton has been granted a pension.

BOB CRAIG of Clinton has been granted an increase of pension.

MALINDA TUTT, of Hillsdale, mother of JOHN C. TUTT, has been granted a pension.

ED H. BURNS is now half owner of the Frankfort, IN, Daily Evening News, a spicy and newsy little sheet.

Mrs. J.A. CORBIN, of Hoopeston, has been granted a pension of $12 per month, $400 back bounty and $2500 back pay. That's a pretty comfortable sum for the widow of a soldier to receive. We congratulate Mrs. CORBIN.

Danville, IL, Commercial

1840
We have added the following names to the list of every man in this county who voted for WILLIAM HENRY HARRISON for President in 1840.

JOHN VANDUYN Sr.	JOHN STAATS
JOSEPH STAATS	JAMES CONLEY
BENJAMIN DEARDOLFF	JAMES ASBURY
JAMES KNIGHT	GEORGE RANDALL
WILLIAM B. WALTHALL	O.P. DAVIS
OTIS DERTHICH	WILLIAM R. JOHNSON

Obituary
Mrs. SUSAN A. (ROGERS) MARBLE was born in Vermillion County, IN, June 21, 1848, where she resided the greater part of her life until the summoning angel came to call her home, July 20, 1888. She was married to JACOB MARBLE, November 4, 1868. She was the mother of three children, two girls and one boy – all of whom survive her. She had been a member of the Christian Church, the last 7 years of her life. Her final illness was of long duration, being 33 weeks and 4 days. Within that time she suffered more than tongue and pen can relate, yet she bore it all with a Christian fortitude which only a true believer can. She was so reduced, having eaten very little of late and nothing from July 16th until she died. Some disease unknown to both physicians and friends by degrees stole away her vitality, all medical aid being of no value until the weakened powers finally gave way and she slept away without a struggle into a better world than this.

Bad Treatment
LAFE NEWELL, of Hillsdale, an old soldier of two wars, and now over 70 years of age, is drawing the pitiful sum of $6 per month pension. He was first placed on the rolls at $4 per month, and after a long time received an increase of $2. He cannot live many years at most, and ought to be drawing $24 per month instead of the pitiful sum of $6.

Eloped
On last Sunday night, JOE NEVINS and Miss CORA DILLOW, of this township, eloped and went to Eugene township, where they were united in wedlock by Rev. McDANIEL, a U.B. minister.

Sad Accident
VIRGIL NIXON, the little 3 year old son of Mr. and Mrs. MARSHAL NIXON, of Veedersburg, took a match last Saturday and went to the barn to burn some straw, as he said, and in attempting to do so, he set fire to his clothing and burned them nearly off. His little body was so terribly burned and his sufferings so intense as to cause his death, which came to his relief on Monday. The parents have the sympathy of our people.

Covington People's Paper

JOHN G. BARKER, who has been confined to his room for the last seven or eight weeks with heart trouble and dropsy, is gradually growing worse. His legs, up to his body, are swollen to nearly three times their natural size. He cannot lie down in bed, but has to sit in a chair day and night, and seldom sleeps over an hour in 24. Last Monday Rev. R.B. VAN ALLEN, pastor of the U.B. Church, took him into the folds of the church and baptized him. Mr. BARKER feels that his time is short, and wants to be prepared to meet his Maker.

Notice to Non-Residents
    LOUISA EDWARDS vs. WILLIAM H. EDWARDS
    Complaint No. 3062
    Residence of WILLIAM H. EDWARDS is unknown
    Must appear before 2nd Monday in October 1888
    WARD & GIBSON, attorneys for plaintiff
    Filed July 30, 1888
                                    A.R. HOPKINS, Clerk

Miss SUSAN JOHNS, of Danville, IL, is here visiting her sister, Mrs. CHARLES HACKER.

Wednesday, August 8, 1888

Summit Grove
Miss BELL MAGEE, of Newman, IL, is here visiting among her numerous friends.

Obituary
JOHN G. BARKER died at his home in Newport, IN, August 1, 1888, with dropsy. He leaves a wife and two sons – one of whom is married. The subject of this sketch was born March 1st, 1834, and was aged 54 years and 5 months. He professed religion and united with the church just before he died. He called his family around him and requested them to live Christian lives, and come to him. He told them they could come to him, he could not come back again. He died in the full triumph of a living faith and went to glory. Owing to circumstances over which we had no control, he was buried the evening of the day he died. The burial services were conducted by G.A.R. Post, of which organization he was a member. The funeral was postponed until Sabbath morning, at the U.B. Church.

Perrysville Sawdust
Little GERTRUDE BOND, daughter of Rev. BOND of this place, died on last Thursday afternoon. Her funeral took place on Friday.

Application for Liquor License
    JOSEPH HANN – Newport
    HENRY D. SPRAGUE – Eugene
    FRANK L. REEDER – Clinton
    CORNELIUS H. NORTON – Perrysville
    THOMAS J. STARK – Cayuga

Notice of Administration
    Estate of HETTIE PORTER, deceased
    BARTON S. AIKMAN, Administrator

Home News
GEORGE RITTENHOUSE, of Sidell, IL, is here taking orders for enlarging photographs.

The wife of WILLIAM PAULEY, of Helt Township, died of fever on last Monday morning. She was the daughter of ANDREW JACKSON.

T.D. SKEEN, veterinary surgeon will be in Dana on August 8, 1888.

B.S. AIKMAN has been appointed administrator of the estate of HETTIE PORTER, deceased.

Rev. JOHN W. PARRETT united in wedlock, on Sunday last, JAKE WEIR and EDITH BORRIS, both of Eugene Township.

A little son of OMER NICHOLS, of this township, died on Tuesday evening of last week, of cholera infantum, after a short illness. He was buried in the Thomas Cemetery on the day after.

Wednesday, August 15, 1888

Murder at Perrysville
Near 4 o'clock on last Wednesday afternoon, the people or Perrysville were thrown into a high state of excitement by the murder of Dr. H.H. PEYTON, a prominent citizen of that place, by SHELBY F. PARKE, a livery stable keeper. Mr. PARKE had been suspicious that the doctor was paying more attention to his young wife than the laws of etiquette permitted, and concluded that he would lay for him. The doctor keeps a large dry goods and general variety store, and in the afternoon of that day, just before the bus leaves town for the 4 o'clock train, Mr. PARKE stepped into the doctor's store and purchased the cigar, remarking at the time that he was going up to Danville on the afternoon train. He only rode a few blocks, and slipped in the back way and waited for developments.
It was not long before Mr. PARKE caught his wife in the arms of Dr. PEYTON. When words passed between them, they had a small scuffle, when the doctor broke away and started to run. Mr. PARKE followed him with revolver in hand, shooting him once in the head before he got out of the room, the ball striking in the back of the head. The next shot was fired while the doctor was getting over his garden fence. It severed the spinal cord and he was dead within 2 minutes.
The funeral of Dr. PEYTON took place at 10 o'clock a.m. on Friday last, and was very largely attended, the exercises being conducted by the Masonic order, of which he was a member.
Mr. PARKE is 26 years old, and his wife is about 20. She is the daughter of WILLIAM CAYWOOD, an honorable and respectable citizen of Perrysville. They have been married 4 or 5 years and have 2 children.
Dr. PEYTON moved from Paxton, Sullivan County, IN, to Perrysville, last September. He traded a farm in Sullivan County to J.B. McNEIL for his store building and stock of goods. He leaves a wife, a most estimable lady, and a bright and beautiful daughter, aged 14. He was in comfortable circumstances, and leaves his wife and daughter an estate worth twelve or fifteen thousand dollars.

Obituary
Little GERTRUDE BOND, daughter of Rev. GEORGE BOND and wife of this place, passed away a week ago today, after a brief and painful illness from brain disease. She was a lovable and loving child, and bore marks of no small degree of intelligence for one so young. GERTRUDE was born March 13, 1887 in the far off heathan land of Singapore, no less than 14,000 miles from the little mound beneath which her sacred ashes now lie in peace. Her parents were missionaries to that country.

Quaker Hill Gossip
Mr. DAVID WALTHALL, of Emporia, KS, who has been visiting relatives and friends for he past three weeks, will return to his western home next week.

Home News
ALVA ARRASMITH and SOLOMON DIXON, of this township, voted for General HARRISON in 1840, but reported too late to get their names in the list we have been running.

Old Mrs. CROCKETT, of Perrysville, who has been ailing for sometime, died at the residence of her son on Thursday last.

Dana News
CHARLEY LOWERMAN, of Hillsdale, a young man of 22, jumped on a freight train last Sunday, but was caught somehow between the brakes, thrown off and striking the rails at the crossing, his whole scalp was lifted from his head. It required 12 stitches to replace and hold the flesh. He is improving slowly.

JOHN W. BROOKBANK, a school teacher of Clinton township, has purchased the Clinton Free Press of L.R. BENNETT, and made his bow to the public on Saturday last. Mr. BROOKBANK is a gentleman of considerable ability, without newspaper experience, but we predict that he will get out a good paper. We suppose Deacon CASEY, the Irish wit of the west, will still be retained.

FREDDIE KESPLER, a little son of GEORGE KESPLER, of Perrysville, got a small stone in his ear four weeks ago, and none of the home doctors could extract it. He went up to Danville and Dr. POLAND removed it for him.

Sheriff DARBY went over to Indianapolis last week and brought home DUNK ANDERSON from the insane asylum as incurable. He was taken to the county asylum.

Fatal Accident
Mrs. PETER McGWIGGINS, of Nyesville, Parke County, deserted her husband 3 or 4 weeks ago, and went to Rockville, where she secured employment in the Parke Hotel as dishwasher. On last Thursday night she fell down the elevator from the third story, a distance of 60 feet, sustaining fatal injuries. Someone had carelessly left the elevator door open, and it is supposed she mistook it for her room door. She was 44 years of age.

Married
On Thursday, August 9th, 1888, Mr. DANIEL J. PEARSON and Miss ALMIRA HOBART were united in marriage by the Rev. R.S. MARTIN of the Newport M.E. Church. The ceremony took place in the parlors of the Newport Hotel at exactly 2 o'clock and was witnessed by the invited hostess and her worthy helpers. The young couple will immediately go to their farm, north of Eugene.

Notice to Non-Residents
    WORTH W. PORTER, MINNIE PORTER, & ABBIE SMITH etal vs.
    JOHN C. PORTER, ZOE M. PORTER, MARY W. SMITH, FRANK S. SMITH, FRED P. GROVES, MARY E. GROVES, & JOHN W. GROVES
    Complaint No. 3067
    MARY W. SMITH & FRANK S. SMITH are not residents of Indiana
    RHOADS & AIKMAN, attorneys for plaintiffs
    Must appear before 2nd Monday of October 1888
    Filed August 10, 1888
                        A.R. HOPKINS, Clerk

Wednesday, August 22, 1888

Clinton Spice
Mrs. NANCY FULTZ, wife of JACOB FULTZ, a worthy citizen of this township, died last Tuesday, age 61 years, 4 months. The funeral was conducted by Rev. VAN HOUTEN, at the residence, Wednesday afternoon, after which a concourse of friends followed the remains to the Hall Cemetery.

Dana Nuisance
ANDERSON HARPER, a resident of Helt Township, starts for Calloway, NE, today. Success attend him in his removal, to his western home. He sold his place here, to CHARLES WHITCOMB of Clinton.

Died
Dr. JOE WHITE, aged 26, son of ALEX WHITE, living 1 mile south of Midway, died of consumption last Tuesday. He was in Dana on Saturday, and his emaciated condition caused much comment. He practiced a few years but close application in school broke him down. J.W. REDMAN conducted the funeral Wednesday.

Died
JOHN BARRETT, living near Meator, Saline County, KS, died on August 15th, 1888, at 9 o'clock p.m. Mr. BARRETT was a former resident of Vermillion County, IN, and well known by the old settlers on Helt's Prairie. He was a member of Company D, 85th IN Volunteer Infantry, and gave three years of his life in defending the stars and stripes. He came west in the fall of 1866, and homesteaded the farm upon which he lived until death called him hence. He had been an invalid for more than four years, not being able to take care of himself since the paralytic stroke, which was the final cause of his death. Although not a member of any G.A.R. Post, yet JOHN A. LOGAN Post of this place took charge of the remains and tenderly placed them to rest in the G.A.R. Circle, in Gypsum Hill Cemetery in accordance with the burial services of the Grand Army of the Republic.
                                        Salina, KS, August 18, 1888

Married
At the Methodist Episcopal Church, August 18th, 1888, at 3:30 p.m., Mr. CHARLES SHAW and Miss RUTH M. GRIMES, both of Dana, IN, were united in marriage by Rev. R.S. MARTIN, of Newport. The young and happy couple will make their future home in Dana, in which thriving little city Mr. SHAW is building and has now nearly completed a magnificent residence, which will be one of the finest in the town.

Home News
Rev. W.N. COFFMAN, who has been out in Missouri for 2 or 3 years, is going to move back to this county and locate on his wife's farm, near Perrysville.

HARRY B. RHOADS is going to move over to Greencastle where he has accepted a position in a leading drug store at a good round salary.

Married at the residence of BRUCE BAILEY in Clinton, on Sunday evening at 7:30 p.m., by Rev. J.E. WRIGHT, Mr. R.W. WALRAVEN and Miss EMMA POTTER.

JOHN HALL, of Pine Bluff, Arkansas, is here visiting his mother, Mrs. IRVIN LAMB.

Notice
WILLIAM SAWYERS having left me, I hereby warn persons not to trust him on my accounts as I will not pay any debts of his contracting.
                                        WILLIAM H. JOHNSON

Death
Mrs. A. GISH, of Covington, mother of Mrs. THOMAS McKNIGHT, died suddenly on last Saturday night from the effects of a stroke of paralysis some time ago. She was quite an old lady, and was very highly respected by the citizens of that city.

The wife of LOUIS C. ALLEN, of Covington, a daughter of the late Major J.S. STEPHENS, and a former resident of this place, is lying at the point of death. She is afflicted with heart disease. Her many friends in this county will be sorry to here of her sad condition.

Married at the bride's home, the Rev. McDANIEL of Cayuga, IN, August 19th, 1888, Mr. JAMES DOWERS and Miss LAURA McDANIEL. The short and impressive service was performed by Rev. MATER, in the presence of select friends.

Assignee's Notice
   Appointed assignee, for the benefit of the creditors for JOSHUA LEWIS
   E.M. HEATON

Wednesday, August 29, 1888

Death
WILLIAM WOOSTER, an old and highly respected citizen, died at his residence in Montezuma, at about noon on Thursday. Mr. WOOSTER was editor of this paper for a short time, and proved himself to be a man of more than ordinary ability. He has been in the employ of the I.D.& W. Railway for several years and highly respected and esteemed by the managers of the road as well as all of the employees. He was correspondent from this place for several leading newspapers and was recognized in the political field as influential politician. The funeral services were held at the M.E. Church this afternoon, conducted by Rev. THOMAS GRIFFITH.
   Montezuma Reporter

Obituary
Miss SARAH HOLLINGSWORTH, daughter of Esq. SAMUEL C. HOLLINGSWORTH, of Terre Haute, a former resident of Opedee, died on last Sunday evening, and her remains were brought up here on Monday afternoon and interred in the Wimsett Cemetery. She was about 20 years of age, and had been an invalid for some time. She was afflicted with consumption. The funeral exercises were conducted by Rev. R.B. VAN ALLEN, pastor of the U.B. Church.

Summit Grove
Mrs. MACK, the widow of the late SPENCER MACK, and her daughters, moved to Terre Haute last week.

Home News
J.B. GRUMBLY, of Eugene township, a half brother of SHELBY PARKE, came down here on last Sunday to visit his brother.

Mrs. JOHN GIBBONS received her arrears in pension last week, amounting to $1065.73.

LOUIS G. HISE, of Clinton Township, has gone out to Colfax, IA, to spend the winter.

Died August 20th, 1888, OLLIE ANDREWS, age 20 years.

The youngest child of STEVE MILLER, of Opedee, a little girl aged about 16 months, died on Thursday last, after an illness of two months. Her remains were buried in the Wimsett Cemetery on Friday last.

SAM COLLETT, who has been at Charleston, WV, for several weeks, arrived home last Friday, accompanied by his sister, Mrs. ADAM B. LITTLEPAGE, whom he had been visiting. She will remain here until sometime in October.

GEORGE T. DOUGLAS received his pension certificate and voucher on Thursday last. He only gets about $70 back pension. He was placed on the rolls at $6 per month.

H.B. RHOADS moved over to Greencastle the first of this week to clerk for his uncle in a large drug store. He will retain his interest in the drug and dry goods store at this place.

Miss GRACE SHELATO, of Eugene, who is deaf and dumb, was down here last week visiting her brother, WILLIAM M. SHELATO. She is only 16 years of age, and will graduate in the Indianapolis deaf and dumb school in one more year.

Married by the Rev. MATER, at his residence in Hillsdale on the evening of August 25th, 1888, Mr. JASPER H. LAKE and HATTIE B. PATTERSON.

NATHAN M. TUTT, Esq., of Highland, and Mrs. EDITH ROWLAND, of Ashmore, IL, were united in wedlock on Tuesday evening of last week, the ceremony taking place at Cayuga, and being performed by Esq. THOMPSON. Mr. TUTT is 54 and his wife is 52 years of age. She weighs 196 pounds, and is an intelligent and remarkably good looking lady, and best of all she is said to be in good circumstances, owning a large farm in Sullivan County, MO.

Notice of Administration
    Estate of HARVEY H. PAXTON, deceased
    B.O. CARPENTER, Administrator

Wednesday, September 5, 1888

Quaker Hill Gossip
An infant of LORA JOHNSON, was buried at the Quaker Hill Cemetery last Friday.

Dana Nuisance
Mrs. WILLIAM CLOWSER died at her home one mile southwest of Dana last Thursday, August 24th, 1888, of a complication of diseases. She was about 26 years of age.

L.C. NORRIS had a son last Sunday night. All parties are doing well.

Home News
J.E. WHIPPLE was in town on Monday. He has sold the Sidell, IL, Journal, to a Mr. WRIGHT, and is going to start to Iowa tomorrow on a prospecting tour. FRANK BLUNK will still retain his old position of compositor.

Mrs. T.S. HOOD, and her two daughters of Dana, Mrs. J.B. FILLINGER and Mrs. GEORGE W. ALLEN, left last Monday for Iowa, on a two weeks visit to relatives.

Judge ARED F. WHITE, of Rockville, and his daughter FANNY WHITE, aged 17, were over here on Thursday last, and were guests of M.G. RHOADS and family while in the city.

GEORGE SPRAGUE, of Netawka, KS, a brother of HARRY SPRAGUE of Eugene, has been in here visiting for the last week.

School commenced in the Newport schools on Monday last. The teachers are:
    Prof. ED A. AIKMAN   Principal
    Miss BLADSEL   Grammar
    NAOMI E. EGGLESTON   Intermediate
    Miss WILLIAMSON   Primary

Mrs. CONLEY, of Helt Township, mother of attorney H.H. CONLEY, is now lying at the point of death, and it is thought she cannot possibly last more than a few days more. She is now in her 90th year, and has been an invalid for many years. She is a most excellent lady, and one among the earliest settlers of this county.

D.A. BARNHART and Miss NETTIE M. WRIGHT, of Clinton Township, will be united in bonds of wedlock at 4 o'clock this afternoon. The ceremony will take place at the residence of the bride, Mr. F.M. WRIGHT. The groom is a school teacher, and a very clever and intelligent young man. The bride is handsome, and as good as she is pretty.

Died

Mrs. SALLIE NEWELL, daughter of Mr. and Mrs. LAFE NEWELL, died of typhoid fever on Wednesday at 2 o'clock p.m., aged about 16 years. Funeral services at the residence in Alta at 7 o'clock in the morning, interment at the Morgan burial ground.

Wednesday, September 12, 1888

Death

NANCY DOWNING was born in Essex County, DE, December 23rd, 1798 and died at her home in Vermillion County, IN, September 4th, 1888. When 5 or 6 years of age, she with her parents, moved from Delaware to the State of Kentucky, then a new country. Five years afterward they moved to the State of Ohio, where they resided until the spring of 1819, when they moved to Vermillion County, IN, then a wilderness, they being among the first settlers of this county.

Soon after their arrival in this county, she was married to ELIJAH M. CONLEY, who died December 1st, 1845, leaving his widow with a family of 6 children to support – 3 girls and 3 boys. They were without property and her boys were all small, the oldest 10 and the youngest less than 3 years of age, but by her untiring industry and great energy, she kept her children together, supported them, and gave them a fair education.

At the age of 16 or 17, she gave her heart to God, joined the M.E. Church, and remained a faithful member until her death, more than 70 years. At the time of her husband's death, he was a Methodist class leader, and she lived to see all of her children who arrived at the age of accountability, members of that church.

In 1861, at the age of 63, she was thrown from a horse, both her arms broken, both wrist joints and several of her finger joints dislocated. Four long months she had to be fed, lifted, and cared for like a helpless infant, but she finally recovered and did many a hard day's work afterward.

In many things besides physical endurance Mother CONLEY was a remarkable woman. Her first and greatest concern was always for her children. For them she toiled almost day and night; for them she prayed as a mother only can pray. She had great executive ability and governed her family far better than most fathers could do, but she was never harsh or severe with her children. She ruled by love, and her master was complete.

For many years prior to her death, she had been a constant sufferer, and much of the time was helpless or almost so, and required constant watching and attention. The great burden of this care fell upon her oldest son and youngest daughter, WILLIAM CONLEY and PHEBE CONLEY. They were with her constantly, day and night, nursing and caring for her with devotion and tenderness seldom equaled and never surpassed.

For a long time, she had been waiting and longing to be at rest, though she always seemed to dread the parting hour, but the end came at last and without a struggle she passed from a life of hardship and great suffering to one of eternal joy and rest. The funeral services took place on last Wednesday, at her late residence, and were conducted by Rev. JOHN W. PARRETT, after which her remains were consigned to the tomb at the Helt's Prairie cemetery. The funeral was very largely attended by her old neighbors and many friends.

Home News

DAVE LITTLE, of this township, who moved down to Athens, TN, last fall, moved back here last week. He has weak eyes and the climate down there did not agree with him.

Miss MARY FILLINGER, of Dana, was in town on Sunday last. She came up to bring home Mrs. MARY CHADD, an aunt, who has been down there several weeks attending the bedside of her sick sister, Mrs. S.E. KAUFMAN, who is now improving slowly.

JOHN HALEY left the first of the week for Beaver, PA, to visit relatives.

WILLIAM CAYWOOD, father-in-law of SHELBY PARKE, who murdered Dr. PEYTON a few weeks ago, paid him a visit at our county jail on Monday last.

Mrs. ALLIE HANN left Monday afternoon for Kansas City, MO, to be gone several months and probably a year, visiting her mother and relatives.

On last Thursday, at the hotel in this place, Rev. R.B. VAN ALLEN, pastor of the U.B. Church, united ELI VEST and Miss JENNIE SCOTT in bonds of wedlock.

Married by the Rev. MATER at his residence in Hillsdale, on the evening of September 9th, 1888, Mr. TILMAN UNDERWOOD and Miss SAMANTHA LANGSTON.

Township Teachers

Teacher	District
Q.A. MYERS	No. 3
MARY F. RICE	No. 4
W.B. GOSNELL	No. 5
B.S. BOTHWELL	No. 6
MAGGIE HOPKINS	No. 7
L.M. CADY	No. 8
O.T. CLARK	No. 9
ELMER E. DAVIS	No. 10
BLANCHE HUPP	No. 10
SARAH WALTHALL	No. 11
EDWARD E. NEEL	No. 12
O.P. SLEETH	No. 13
EUNICE LITTLE	No. 14
LYDIA WALTHALL	No. 15

WILLIAM R. JOHNSON, of this township, is now 72 years old, and has 28 sound teeth in his head. He has never used spectacles, and can see to read and write just as well as he could when only 21 years of age.

ROBERT NIXON of Oswego, KS, and GEORGE W. ODELL and wife, Mrs. CAD HARVEY and her two children, of Hutchinson, KS, arrived here on last Sunday night to visit relatives and friends. Mrs. HARVEY and uncle ROBERT NIXON will remain sometime, but Mr. ODELL and wife will return this week.

Death
BLANCHE ARNOLD, aged 18 or 20 years, a former resident of Helt Townshop, and a granddaughter of the late JOHN BILSLAND, was brought home from Florida a corpse on last Sunday night, and her remains interred on last Monday. She was a bright and intelligent young woman, and very highly esteemed by all her young friends, and everybody else with whom she was acquainted.

Wednesday, September 19, 1888

Home News
WILLIAM K. LANCEY of Clinton, has been granted pension.

OMER LANGER, of Eugene, has been granted pension.

S.B. EGGLESTON and wife, of Jonesboro, Arkansas, are here on a visit.

MARSH HARRISON has a two year old child that is dangerously ill.

CHARLEY WILTERMOOD, of Opedee, ex-postmaster of Newport, is lying at the point of death. He was reported to be dying on Sunday last, but finally rallied. He is in the last stages of consumption and cannot possibly survive many days.

Miss ELLA TARRENCE, of Perrysville, returned last week from Austin, TX, where she had been on a visit for the last 7 months.

Killed
WILLIAM BRINDLEY, a young married man from Danville, IL, was killed on Monday last. He has been breaking for sometime on the C. & E.I. Railway, and we suppose he got caught while coupling cars. Mr. E.B. BROWN, of this place, received a telegram about 1 o'clock last Monday afternoon, stating that WILLIAM was killed and would be buried on Tuesday. He was a son of ANDY BRINDLEY of Perrysville. He leaves a young wife and one or two children.

Wedding
Mr. D.W. BELL and Miss LACIE EDMONDS were married at the home of the bride's parents, Mr. and Mrs. ED EDMONDS, in Eugene, September 12, 1888, at 8:30 p.m., in the presence of a few invited friends, the Rev. R.B. VAN ALLEN of the U.B. Church officiating. Immediately after the wedding they took the train for Cincinnati, OH, to be gone about a week. On their return they will occupy the widow LAKE property. Mr. BELL is postmaster and druggist of Eugene.

Wedding
Mr. M.W. COFFIN and Miss EMMA THORNTON, both of Cayuga, were married by Rev. R.B. VAN ALLEN at the U.B. parsonage in Newport, IN, September 13th, 1888, at 11 o'clock a.m., after which they took the train to Chicago to spend a few days. On their return they will set up housekeeping in Cayuga. Mr. COFFIN is the leading druggist in town.

Dana News
MARTIN JONES, of Quaker Hill, is the happy 'dad' of a 'gal' baby. It is more than a week old.

You can call JOHN CRANE 'Pap'. A little Cranelet of the female persuasion arrived at his house on last Thursday night.

A telegram received here on Sunday from Jacksonville, FL, informed Mrs. MAUDE LEE?, that her husband was dead.

Married
Married at the residence of PETER AIKMAN, in Helt Township, Sunday, September 16th, 1888, Mr. J. EDWIN FONCANNON and Miss IVA P. AIKMAN. The ceremony was performed by Rev. THOMAS GRIFFITH, of Montezuma, in the presence of only a few of the relatives of the bride and groom. Among those present were Mrs. MARIA JAMES, Mrs. JENNIE ALEXANDER and son HEROLD ALEXANDER, all of Hastings, NE, and Mr. and Mrs. FONCANNON, and the parents, sisters, and brothers of the bride. The groom is an honest, intelligent and energetic young man of 22 years. He is a well to do farmer and the youngest son of JACOB FONCANNON. The bride is a bright and beautiful girl of 18 summers, and the oldest daughter of PETER AIKMAN.

Wedding
A quiet little wedding took place at the residence of W.P. STANLEY's, in Annapolis, IN, Wednesday afternoon at 3:30. Miss LIZZIE was united in holy bonds of matrimony to Rev. H.L. GRIMES, of the Morton charge, M.E. Church by Rev. WILLIAM A. SMITH, of the Perrysville charge. The following are some who came from a distance: Dr. HALL and wife, of Milford, IL; Miss ANNA GRIMES; Mrs. BELL and ETHEL GRIMES; Mr. M.B. GRIMES, of Toronto, IN; Mr. FRANK STANLEY, of Sheridan, IN.

Wednesday, September 26, 1888

Dana News
Mr. MILT HAYS and Miss ALICE CRANE are attending the Cincinnati Centennial this week. They went Monday morning.

Home News

Mrs. GLANT GALLOWAY, of Hutchinson, KS, daughter of deputy County Treasurer, THOMAS CUSHMAN, is the mother of another gal baby.

J.M. HOOD, of Hanover, KS, a former resident of this place, has been nominated by the Democrats of his county for the State Legislature.

TOM McKNIGHT is working in TOM VICTOR's blacksmith shop at Clinton. Mr. McKNIGHT is one of the finest and best smiths on the Wabash.

Mrs. S.C. DUGGER and son, of Helt Township, gave us a call on Wednesday last, and was shown through our office. It was the first time she was ever in a printing office.

Miss MINA BROWN, of Kankakee, IL, is here visiting. She returns the latter part of the week.

C.M. PARKS, a former resident of this place, and mail agent of the C. & E.I. Railway, is teaching school at Parsons, KS.

BAT McCARTY, an old 18th Indiana boy, and as good a soldier as ever shouldered a musket, has been granted an increase of pension.

ELIAS LAMB was 74 years old last Monday, and is in excellent health, for one of his years.

C.S. DAVIS, of Salina, KS, is going to move back to this county. His wife and daughter arrived at Dana last week, and have rented a house and gone to housekeeping.

Agents for the Hoosier
- SMITH RABB, Postmistress — Perrysville
- JOHN CADE — Gessie
- HOSFORD & BELL — Eugene
- Dr. E.A. VANSICKLE, Postmaster — Hillsdale
- J.C. JACKSON — Hillsdale
- GEORGE W. EDWARDS, Postmaster — Clinton
- J.R. FINNELL — Jonestown
- F.N. AUSTIN — Bono
- J.E. BILSLAND — Dana
- FRANK LANGSTON — Summit Grove

Notice of Administration
Estate of NANCY FULTZ, deceased
WILLIAM HASKELL, Administrator

Notice to Non-Residents
JOSEPHINE BRACKEN vs. JOHN W. BRACKEN
Complaint No. 3068
JOHN W. BRACKEN is not a resident of Indiana
Must appear before 2nd Monday in October 1888
RHOADS & AIKMAN, attorneys for plaintiff
Filed August 17, 1888
A.R. HOPKINS, Clerk

Letter List
- ABRAHAM MILLS
- WILLIAM HOUSAND
- FRANK B. MILLER
- WILL SCHROEDER

Obituary

CHARLES W. WILTERMOOD, ex-postmaster at this place, died at the residence of his father, in Opedee, at about 10 o'clock a.m. on Wednesday last. His ailment was consumption, which disease he had only been afflicted with for a few months. The disease first developed while he was serving as postmaster, and finally growing worse and being unable to attend to the office, he resigned and went home to die. Before his death, he requested that Rev. R.B. VAN ALLEN, pastor of the U.B Church at this place, preach his funeral. The funeral was held at 10 o'clock Thursday, after which his remains were interred in the Wimsett Cemetery at Opedee. CHARLEY was a young man very highly respected by all his acquaintances and neighbors, and in his death, the community loses a good citizen, his young wife a devoted and true husband, and the parents a son whom they almost idolized.

Died

On Thursday, September 20th, 1888, GEORGIE HARRISON, the son of MARSHALL and ELLA HARRISON of Newport, died after a sickness of nearly two months, and on Friday was buried at the Thomas Cemetery. Brief and impressive services were conducted at the home and grave by Rev. R.S. MARTIN of the M.E. Church. The little one would have been 2 years old had he lived until the 4th of October.

Perrysville

Our school began here Monday last week, with Mr. FLANDERS as principal, Mr. MILLS and Miss BURT assistants.

Wednesday, October 3, 1888

Clinton Gossip

JAMES DOTY, of Marbury, IA, who in company with his wife, is visiting his brother-in-law, Mr. DECATUR DOWNING. Mr. DOTY is a prosperous farmer of that section.

Home News

PETER ZOOK, son of Rev. ZOOK, former pastor of the U.B. Church at this place, is lying dangerously ill. It is thought he cannot recover.

W.F. SCHWEIZER, of Crawfordsville, arrived here yesterday morning, and left on the midnight train for Champaign, where he intends to locate.

Mrs. PET SCHWIEZER, of Crawfordsville, is here visiting her mother and numerous friends. She has the prettiest gal baby in Montgomery County.

Married

WILLIAM G. MARTIN, of Westville, IL, and CLARINDA GOFF, of Highland Township, were married in the clerk's office on Thursday last, Rev. R.B. VAN ALLEN, pastor of the U.B. Church, officiating.

Married

Married at the residence of the bride's father, near Dana, at 2 p.m., September 25th, 1888, by Rev. J.E. WRIGHT, Mr. EDWARD A. McCOWAN and Miss ALDA McROBERTS. Quite a number of friends were present to witness the occasion.

Township Institute

The first Institute of Vermillion Township was held at the Newport Seminary, on Saturday, September 29th, 1888. The entire corps of teachers was present. They elected the following:

President	E.E. DAVIS
Vice President	B.S. BOTHWELL
Secretary	NAOMI EGGLESTON

Other teachers that attended were: SARAH WALTHALL, ELMER DAVIS, Mr. GOSNELL, ED AIKMAN, EUNICE LITTLE, LINN CADY, FRANCES RYCE.

Marriage

The residence of Mrs. SKIDMORE, wife of the late WILLIAM SKIDMORE, of Bono, IN, was brilliantly lit on Wednesday evening, September 26th, 1888, and fully 200 neighbors and friends assembled. The occasion was the marriage of Miss FIDELIA SKIDMORE and Mr. MORGAN B. GRIMES. At 8 o'clock, the bride and groom entered preceded by Rev. R.S. MARTIN, of Newport, who performed the ritual. Rev. H.S. GRIMES, a brother of the groom, and Rev. Mr. WRIGHT, of the protestant Methodist Church, were among the guests. The happy couple will live on their farm, near Bono.

Wednesday, October 10, 1888

Clinton Dumplings

Mrs. JENNIE ALEXANDER, and her mother, MARIA JAMES, after a pleasant visit with relatives and friends in this place, returned to their home in Hastings, NE, last Monday.

Miss ANNA STRAUSER, of Jonestown, died last Wednesday of typhoid fever. Two other members of the family are lying at the point of death.

CHARLEY BROOKBANK, who has been down in the wilds of Arkansas, commingling with bears, returned to this, his native heath, last week.

Home News

Mrs. Judge JUMP, of Terre Haute, is visiting her sister, Mrs. C.W. WARD.

A.G. FORTNER was elected director of the Stumptown school district on last Saturday night.

Mrs. C.M. STARK, of Madisonville, KY, arrived here last week on a visit to her sick mother, Mrs. ALVA ARRASMITH, who is dangerously ill.

Rev. ANDY WIMSETT has moved from El Dorado, KS, back to Streator, IL. He has been in poor health for sometime, being troubled with heart disease and rheumatism.

J.E. WHIPPLE, a former resident, of Eugene, has located in Vinton, IA.

Mrs. N.N. WILLEY and wife, of Clay Center, KS, are here visiting his sister, Mrs. JOHN HASTY.

Miss LAURA McCONNELL, a governess of the Knightstown Soldiers' Orphans Home, is here on a short visit.

Death

Mrs. MINERVA CONRAD, of Eugene, mother of JOE CONRAD, Superintendent of the County Poor Asylum, died on Thursday last, October 4th, 1888, aged 78 years. She was born in Kentucky, and came to Hutsonville, IL, when only 4 years of age, where she resided until after the close of the late war. About one year ago she had a stroke of paralysis, and another stroke 4 weeks ago, from which she never recovered. She leaves 7 children, 6 of whom reside in this county. Her remains were interred in the Eugene Cemetery on Friday last.

Married

On Thursday morning, at the M.E. parsonage in Newport, October 5th, 1888, Mrs. DELOSS BRACKEN, of Scotland, and Miss SARAH DUNN, of Edgar County, IL. Rev. R.S. MARTIN officiated. The happy couple will reside near Scotland, where the happy couple is favorably known.

Married
Mr. GUY WOOLEN and Miss MAGGIE LIGHT, both of Edgar County, IL, were the happy ones who on October 6th, 1888, at 2:30 p.m., were united in the holy bonds of matrimony by Rev. R.S. MARTIN of the M.E. Church.

Notice of Final Settlement of Estate
    Estate of JOHN F. STEWART, deceased
    Filed October 9, 1888
                                    A.R. HOPKINS, Clerk

Notice of Final Settlement of Estate
    Estate of CHARLES HEDGES, deceased
    Filed October 9, 1988
                                    A.R. HOPKINS, Clerk

Wednesday, October 17, 1888

Indicted for Murder
SHELBY F. PARKE, of Perrysville, who killed Dr. H.H. PEYTON, a merchant and physician of that town, a few weeks ago on account of criminal intimacy with his young wife, has been found guilty of murder in the first degree.

Home News
WILLIAM H. TATE left for Chrisman, IL, on Monday last to work there this fall and winter at his trade.

Sheriff DARBY left yesterday for Jeffersonville with JOSEPH LINDSEY, who is sent up for 2 years for burglary.

Death at Poor House
H.D. KING, a traveling stranger, who was sent to the poor asylum from Dana on June 6th, 1888, died at that institution at 2 o'clock on last Saturday afternoon, of catarrh of the stomach, aged about 65 years. He was the inventor of a patent washer which he was selling at the time he took down sick. Those who have examined the machine say it is a good one. His remains were interred by Superintendent CONRAD on Sunday.

Another Death at Poor House
DUNK ANDERSON, of Perrysville, who became insane a couple of years ago or more, and was sent to the insane asylum for treatment, and brought here two months ago as incurable, died at the poor house at 7 o'clock on last Sunday evening. He was about 40 years of age and was troubled with epilepsy. He leaves a wife and one small child in indigent circumstances. Superintendent CONRAD sent the remains up to Perrysville on the 3:35 train, last Monday afternoon for interment.

THOMAS W. DURHAM, of Topeka, KS, who served in the 11th IN during the war, has just compiled a neat Roster of all Indiana soldiers now residents of Kansas.

Dana News
Mrs. SARAH DENTON and children from Kansas are here visiting her father Mr. G.W. SHEELEY, and other friends and relatives in this township.

Notice of Final Settlement of Estate
    Estate of OWEN WRORK, deceased
    Filed October 9, 1888
                                    A.R. HOPKINS, Clerk

Mrs. A.J. YOUNT, of Fremont, NB, is at Perrysville visiting her parents and friends.

Wednesday, October 24, 1888

The Bitter End of an Old Grudge
Last Friday, a crowd gathered to hear the issues of the day from the Democratic standpoint. Among the crowd from Dana were JOHN McROBERTS, BOB NORRIS, and HARRY AIKMAN, who seemed to have held a grudge against BILLY RICHARDSON and FRANK LAMB of this place. They claim that RICHARDSON and LAMB imposed on a brother, aged 13, of McROBERTS while returning from Indianapolis some weeks ago. A fight ensued, and RICHARDSON pulled out a gun and fired 4 or 5 shots, which resulted in the death of HARRY AIKMAN.

HARRY AIKMAN was taken to M.G. RHOADS' law office, where Coroner BRINDLEY held an inquest on Saturday morning. Immediately after the tragedy, Sheriff DARBY arrested young RICHARDSON and locked him in jail. In the afternoon of the same day, the remains of AIKMAN were shipped to Clinton, where his widowed mother resides, and from there they were taken to Bono, Helt Township, on Sunday and a funeral discourse was preached by Rev. HOOK, a Presbyterian minister. It is said to be the largest funeral gathering ever witnessed in that township.

HARRY AIKMAN was the bass drummer of the Dana band that played here on Friday. He was 23 or 24 years of age. He was the son of JOHN B. AIKMAN, deceased several years ago, who was well known by many of our citizens. HARRY AIKMAN was the only son of a widowed mother, who depended upon him in part for her support. He was a pleasant young man when not under the influence of liquor. His death was a terrible blow to the mother.

Home News
IRVIN LAMB and wife have been given a position in the Reform School at Plainfield, IN, and left for that institution one day last week.

Married
GEORGE M. NEEL and MARY J. ADAM, of Highland Township, were united in wedlock, on October 14th, 1888, by Rev. W.N. COFFMAN, a minister of the U.B. Church.

Death
On last Sunday morning, in about five minutes after she arose from her bed, the wife of JOHN ADAMS, who resides near the Hannaman Chapel, in Helt Township, dropped dead. She was about 60 years of age, and was in good health, apparently. Heart disease is the supposed cause of her death.

Married
On Wednesday, October 17th, 1888, at 10:30 a.m., Mr. JEFF WIDNER, formerly of Wyoming, and Miss ORIE KNIGHT, of Dana, IN, were united in matrimony by Rev. R.S. MARTIN, of the M.E. Church.

An Afflicted Family
Mrs. JOHN HULL, of Jonestown, Helt Township, has been sorely afflicted with disease in her family during the last 9 or 10 weeks. The family consisted of the mother, two grown daughters and a 6 year old son. All were stricken down with the typhoid fever. The two daughters died, and the mother and son are still confined to their beds with that dreadful disease, but are now reported on the mend.

Quaker Hill Items
The 20th birthday party of Miss MYRA HAWORTH was celebrated by a surprise on last Tuesday evening. She received many valuable presents and was highly enjoyed by all present.

List of Letters in the Newport postoffice

JAMES CONOLY	Mr. CURTIS or CALLORNCE
Mr. L.O. CURTICE	IRVIN CURTICE
CURTIS Bros.	JOE CARTER
I. SHOE	J. SHELBY
JOHN J. PUTTMANN	LEWIS A. GREEN
Miss P.C. GROW	C. WINFRED JONES
JOHN LENOVER	J.W. DAY
HESTER OSBORN	Mrs. MAGGIE GLOVER
FLORA JOHNSTON	

Unfortunate Accident
On last Saturday afternoon, ROBERT J. HOLTZ and JOE NEWMAN, of Cayuga, 6 miles north of here, decided to take a blanket down and spend the night in a boxcar. They had taken more terrapin juice than they could carry. While walking along the tracks, they heard a train coming up from behind them, but thought they would have plenty of time to get off. In making the effort to get off the track, BOB HOLTZ fell, his right arm falling on the rail, and the big engine wheels passing over it, crushing it to a pulp from the hand to within 6 inches from the shoulder. The arm was amputated by Dr. KINDERMAN of Eugene and Dr. FLAUGHER of Eugene. At last report, he was getting along nicely.

Wednesday, October 31, 1888

Sheriff's Sale on Decree
    FRANK KINTZ, administrator of estate of GEORGE KINTZ, deceased vs.
    WILLIAM O. KINTZ, HENRY J. KINTZ, MARGARET KINTZ etal
    $3930.07
    Sale to be held Wednesday, November 21, 1888
        3 acres – SE ¼ SE ¼ Sec 27 T 15 N R 10 W
        1 acre – E side of SE ¼ SE ¼ Sec 27
        town of Jones
        also one engine and boiler, etc.
    RHOADS & AIKMAN, attorneys for plaintiffs
    Filed October 31, 1888
                              JOHN A. DARBY, Sheriff

Perrysville Pickings
Mr. GEORGE NASON, of this place, is the proud father of a fine 10 pound boy. He arrived here one week ago Saturday night.

Pension
JOE CHUNN, who has been an inmate of the poor house for the last 13 years, received the good news on Saturday last, from his attorney at Indianapolis, that his pension had been granted. He made his application in 1865, over 23 years ago. He gets $4 per month, from June 1865 to January 1st, 1888, and from that date to July 11th, $8 per month, and from that date $24 per month. The total amount is something over $1800.

Milk Sickness
WAT STEVENS, of Tangier, Parke County, well known to many of our citizens, died on Tuesday of last week, October 23, 1888, of milk sick. He was about 41 years of age, and a most excellent citizen. His wife and two children are down with the same disease, with no hope of their recovery. The attending physician thinks they caught the disease from eating fresh pork.

Clinton Gossip
A.S. BRIGHT, of Cumberland, IA, is back on a visit to his old home in this city.

Married

L.A. MORGAN and ELLA VANLEER, both of Perrysville, were united in wedlock on Sunday last. The ceremony took place in Danville, IL.

Died

Montezuma, IN, - On the 26th of October, Mrs. ELLEN BURNS, loved wife of ROBERT BURNS, and daughter of THOMAS and ANNIE CONNOR, died at her home in Terre Haute of typhus malaria fever, aged 28 years, leaving a husband and 5 children, the youngest only 5 months old. The funeral service was conducted by Rev. GRIFFITH and Rev. RIPETOE, at the M.E. Church. Interment was in Oakland Cemetery.

Died

Died at her home in Hillsdale, October 26th, 1888, of typhus malaria fever, Mrs. MARY RILEY, wife of JOHN RILEY. A devout Christian wife and mother has gone to her reward. She leaves a husband, two sons and one young daughter to mourn her loss. Funeral service here Saturday, at the Roman Catholic Church.

Wednesday, November 7, 1888

Married

On Thursday evening of this week, STANTON EGGLESTON of this place and Miss ANNA HINES, who resides two miles west of here, were united in holy wedlock. We wish them much happiness.

Birth

Mrs. CAD HARVEY, of Hutchinson, KS, who has been here visiting her mother for several weeks, gave birth to a bouncing boy on Tuesday of last week.

Sheriff's Sale on Decree
 ROBERT H. NIXON vs. GEORGE ATHERTON & SARAH J. ATHERTON
 $821.14
 Sale to be held Saturday, November 17, 1888 at courthouse
  NE ¼ NW ¼ Sec 20 T 15 N R 9 W
  SE ¼ SW ¼ Sec 17 T 15 N R 9 W
  80 acres in all
 CONLEY & SAWYER attorneys for plaintiff
 Filed October 24, 1888
         JOHN A. DARBY, Sheriff

Sheriff's Sale on Decree
 ROBERT H. NIXON vs. JOSEPH W. McCONNELL
 $222.08
 Sale to be held Saturday, November 17, 1888 at courthouse
  Part of Lot 49 in town of Newport
 CONLEY & SAWYER, attorneys for plaintiff
 Filed October 24, 1888
         JOHN A. DARBY, Sheriff

Election November 6, 1888
 County Ticket
  Sheriff   WILLIAM RHEUBY
  Auditor   WILLIAM M. HAMILTON
  Treasurer   WILLIAM B. HOOD
  Coroner   THOMAS BRINDLEY
  Surveyor   R.A. PARRETT
  Commissioner 1st Dist PHILO CURTIS

Commissioner 2nd Dist   GEORGE F. HAWORTH

Wednesday, November 14, 1888

Marriage
Mr. SANFORD TAYLOR and Miss EMMA M. MAHAN, both of Dana, IN, were united in marriage on Sunday, November 11, 1888, at 4:30 p.m. in the parlors of the M.E. parsonage. The ceremony was performed by Rev. R.S. MARTIN of Newport. Mr. TAYLOR has been a lifelong resident and prominent grain dealer of Vermillion County, and is well known as one of our most successful businessmen. The bride is the sister of Mrs. JOHN BILSLAND of Dana, and has been one of the most popular ladies in all our social circles.

Court Report for October term
State of Indiana vs. QUINTON SHEPERD
Surety of the peace – continued

State of Indiana vs. WILLIS MEADOWS
From Justice of the peace court – dismissed

State of Indiana vs. WILLIAM FOWLER
Assault & battery – continued

State of Indiana vs. JOSEPH LINDSEY
Burglary – sent to penitentiary for 2 years

State of Indiana vs. SHELBY F. PARKE
Murder – continued and bail given

State of Indiana vs. WILLIAM RICHARDSON
Continued and bail given

GEORGE A. CRABB etal vs. WINFIELD S. SCOTT etal
Partition and sale – continued

CHARLES W. WARD, Administrator of JOHN W. WEBSTER, deceased vs.
MARY H. WEBSTER etal
Partition and sale – continued

LEWIS A. MORGAN etal vs. The Perrysville Creamery Co.
Continued

JAMES M. HAYS, Administrator of CORNELIUS HISE, deceased
Partition – ordered and continued for report of Commissioner

FRANK KINTZ, Administrator vs. WILLIAM O. KINTZ etal
Foreclosure, judgment for MARGARET KINTZ
Also judgment for plaintiff

ALICE SPARKS, an infant by JOSEPH SPARKS, next friend vs. HENRY C. EATON
Seduction – judgment for plaintiff for $150

WILLIAM H. ROACH etal vs. ANDREW CURTIS
Quiet title – title quieted

ALFRED M. REED vs. ELIZA A. FORD
Partition – commissioner appointed to sell land – cause continued for report of sale

HAMILTON BETSON vs. AUGUST JENKS
Damages – continued

JERRY HAMMOND vs. MARCUS HAMMOND
Foreclosure – continued

Household Sewing Machine Co. vs. SARAH J. THOMPSON
Account $400 – judgment for plaintiff for $92.27

STEPHEN JENKS vs. SARAH J. THOMPSON
Note $60 – dismissed

DANIEL W. FINNEY vs. SARAH J. THOMPSON etal
Note $60 – dismissed

JOHN B. McNEILL vs. ROBERT B. MOUDY
Appeal from J.P. Court – judgment for plaintiff for $9.45

MAURICE HEGARTY vs. OTIS W. MILLIKIN etal
Note $50 – dismissed

HAMILTON L. STOREY etal vs. SARAH MOORE
Note $60 – judgment for plaintiff for $134.20

MARY A. GEER vs. JOHN GEER
Divorce – divorce granted

ELLEN VANLEER vs. HENRY VANLEER
Divorce – divorce granted

JONAS FORTNER vs. SILAS JONES
Complaint for breach of warranty deed – dismissed

LOUISA EDWARDS vs. WILLIAM H. EDWARDS
Divorce – divorce granted

SERENA J. DICKERSON vs. GABRIEL
Dismissed

SARAH C. BUFFEY vs. SAMUEL BUFFEY
Divorce – divorce granted

ELIJAH P. CONLEY vs. FRANK L. REEDER etal
Foreclosure $400 – judgment for plaintiff for $361.52

WORTH W. PORTER etal vs. JOHN C. PORTER
Partition – commissioner appointed to sell land – cause continued for report of sale

JOSEPHINE BRACKEN vs. JOHN W. BRACKEN
Divorce – divorce granted

JOHN F. COMPTON etal vs. HENRY E. WADE
Note $600 – judgment for plaintiff for $527.62

AUGUST L. WEBSTER vs. JOSHUA LEWIS etal
Foreclosure $400 – judgment for plaintiff $361.43

SAMUEL MOORE etal vs. JOSHUA LEWIS etal
Judgment for $221.50

JESSE KAUFMAN vs. ALBERT FORD etal
Note $125 – dismissed

REBECCA CARPENTER vs. L.D. CARPENTER
Complaint to obtain lien on land and to set aside decree – continued

SARAH M. WRIGHT vs. JACOB WRIGHT
Divorce – divorce granted

EDWARD Y. JACKSON vs. WILLIAM A. NORRIS etal
Note $175 – dismissed

MARY A. GILMORE vs. JACOB A. BROWN, administrator of MARY PAINE's estate
Claim – judgment for defendant for costs

MARION REEDER vs. WILLIAM B. REEDER
Quiet title for partition – continued

ROBERT H. NIXON vs. GEORGE ATHERTON etal
Foreclosure $1000 – judgment for plaintiff for $821.14

ANNIE R. JAMES vs. WILLIAM ANDREWS
Note $600 – judgment for plaintiff for $543.16

ROBERT WRIGHT vs. HENRY WAGGONER etal
Note $125 – judgment for plaintiff for $111.10

SEWARD LEWIS vs. CLARENCE GOSNELL etal
Note $350 – dismissed

ANGELINE VOLKILL etal vs. GEORGE W. GOFF etal
Quiet title – continued

IDORA BALES etal, by next friend, vs. SARAH A. MERCER
Quiet title and for partition – commissioner appointed to sell land
Sale reported and deed made

SOLOMON KLEIN vs. DAVID METZGER
Account $60 – judgment for plaintiff for $50.25

WILLIAM A. HAYS vs. FRANK L. REEDER
Note $125 – judgment for plaintiff for $114.65

JOHN P. SEEDS vs. ORA M. SEEDS
Partition – commissioner appointed to sell land – cause continued for report of sale

WILLIAM MAXFIELD vs. BENJAMIN F. ELLIS
Damages – continued

Clinton News
Owing to the illness of Miss ETTA EDWARDS, the room, No. 3, taught by her in the public school, is now being taught by Miss DOLLIE SCOTT.

PANZY SLATER, the 4 year old daughter of Mr. and Mrs. FRANK SLATER, died yesterday morning at 1 o'clock, of typhoid fever. Another bright and happy little soul has gone to that better world.

Mrs. JOHN CROMPTON, who sometime ago fell and crippled herself, and who has been lingering between life and death since then, quietly passed away last Wednesday morning about 3 o'clock, and was interred in Clinton Cemetery, Wednesday evening at 5 o'clock.

Death
State Senator PHIL SCHLOSS, of Terre Haute, died at 11:35 on last Monday night, of heart disease. He was about 52 years of age, and for many years has been a prominent businessman of that city, running a large merchant clothing establishment. His death will necessitate a special election. He was a Democrat but as Vigo County gave a Republican majority at the recent election, it is quite probable his successor will be a Republican.

Application for liquor license
    WILLIAM J. BROPHY – Geneva, Clinton Township
    PATRICK FLYNN – Hillsdale Township

Home News
PERRY VAN ALLEN, of the Newport Hotel, son of Rev. BOB VAN ALLEN, is on the sick list.

The wife of Dr. COOPER, of Terre Haute, committed suicide by hanging herself on Sunday last. It is supposed she lost her reason grieving over the death of two of her children.

Lafayette Courier – Mrs. GODFREY, the divorced wife of Rev. SAMUEL GODFREY, is in Chicago taking a course in a medical college with a view to prepare herself for the practice of medicine.

Miss WILLIE BROWN, of Shelbyville, IL, was here last week visiting RETA MOREHEAD. She was a former resident of this place.

Married
Married in Perrysville, IN, November 1st, 1888, by Rev. W.A. SMITH, Mr. SAMUEL G. McKEEN, of Springfield, IL, and Miss JENNIE M. DUTTON, of Perrysville. Mr. McKEEN is the son of Dr. McKEEN, formerly of Eugene, IN, but now of Danville, IL. As the telephone inspector, he commands a good salary. They will make their home in Springfield, IL.

Wednesday, November 21, 1888

Clinton News
DAVID WOLF and wife, LON WOLF and wife, CHARLEY WOLF, LEWIS REED and wife, and Dr. WATKINS, left for Ocean Springs, MS, Thursday night, where they will probably make a permanent location.

Clinton Argus
The school trustees have employed Miss DOLLIE SCOTT to teach room No. 3, made vacant by the death of Miss ETTA EDWARD.

As we go to press this Saturday morning, Mrs. JOSEPH HANSON is reported to be in a dying condition. She has been ill for some time.

Miss DORA COATES, a charming young lady, of Veedersburg, IN, is in the city visiting friends. She is a guest of the White House. She will remain in town for some time and receive instructions in painting of Mrs. DECATUR DOWNING.

Mr. CHARLEY WHITTAKER, of Sarasota, FL, and Miss SUE WHITCOMB, formerly of this city, were recently united in marriage at the home of the bride. The happy couple have a host of friends up here in Hoosierdom, who wish them a life of happiness and prosperity.

Death
Miss ETTA EDWARDS, daughter of postmaster GEORGE W. EDWARDS, of Clinton, died at 6 a.m. on last Thursday, November 15, 1888, and was interred in the Clinton Cemetery on Saturday last. She was a most estimable young lady, and at the time of her sickness, one of the teachers in the Clinton High School. Her disease was typhoid fever, which she lingered with for several weeks. Her noble and good mother died last spring. She and a brother were the only two children of the family, and in her death the father is overcome with grief. In his deep affliction he has the full sympathy of all his friends.

Home News
M.L. GRIFFITH has retired from the Farmer City, IL, Republican.

The mother of LOUIS M. HAYS, of Hillsdale, has been granted a pension.

JOHN W. DINWIDDIE, of Clinton, has had his pension increased from $8 to $18 per month.

JOHN HALEY is going to move to Camelton, PA, sometime this week, where he expects to locate and make his future home.

ROXANA HAYWARD, a 14 year old daughter of FRANK HAYWARD, the fisherman, who resides just across the river, east of here, died on the 2nd of this month.

Died
On Tuesday, November 12, 1888, Mrs. MARY L. STEVENS, wife of the late WAT STEVENS, of Tangier, Parke County, died of milk sick, after an illness of two weeks. Her husband died from the same disease on the 27th of last month. The two children were down with the disease, have nearly recovered. Mrs. STEVENS was about 34 years of age, and a niece of E.B. BROWN, of this place. They leave 3 small children to be cared for by the relatives. Mr. STEPHENS and wife were both excellent citizens, and in their death the community is deprived of two good neighbors.

Wednesday, November 28, 1888

Notice to Non-Residents
ANGELINE VOLKILL, HENRY VOLKILL, HARVEY HUNT vs.
GEORGE W. GOFF, LORETTA SANDERS, WILLIAM SANDERS, DAVID SANDERS, CHARLES SANDERS, HARRY SANDERS, EDMOND HUNT, MARY ROYES, ANNIE HUNT, CHARLES HUNT, DAVID GOFF and unknown heirs of DAVID GOFF.
Complaint No. 3087
GEORGE W. GOFF, DAVID GOFF, and unknown heirs of DAVID GOFF are not residents of Indiana
Must appear before 4th Monday of December 1888
CONLEY & SAWYER, attorneys for plaintiff
Filed November 26, 1888
A.R. HOPKINS, Clerk

Notice to Non-Residents
> MINNIE M. CURTIS vs. JOHN B. CURTIS
> Complaint No. 3099
> JOHN B. CURTIS is not a resident of Indiana
> Must appear before 4th Monday of December 1888
> RHOADS & AIKMAN, attorneys for plaintiff
> Filed November 23, 1888
>
> A.R. HOPKINS, Clerk

Romance
A dispatch from Milwaukee, WI, says Mrs. HATTIE E. PHENEGAR, of Chicago, and E. STEVENS, of Perrysville, IN, were quietly married at the Plankinton House Friday night. The bridegroom is 70 years old, and the bride is 60, and there is a spice of romance in the marriage. Years ago, in a little Hoosier town they knew and liked each other. He was a young man just starting out in life, she a young woman just leaving girlhood behind her. Somehow they drifted apart, and after awhile the young woman became Mrs. PHENEGAR and moved to Chicago. Mr. STEVENS became a prosperous merchant at Perrysville, and today is a wealthy grain buyer there. He, too, in the course of time, took unto himself a wife. Years passed and brought many changes into the lives of the old playmates. The one became a widower, the other a widow. The one accumulated riches, and the other strove to maintain herself and child in Chicago by means of her needle. One day Mrs. PHENEGAR went to Perrysville on a visit to her sister. Mr. STEVENS stood upon the depot platform, and there the old playmates renewed their acquaintance of years before. As a result of this chance meeting, a correspondence began, and the words of a Milwaukee justice ended it. Mr. STEVENS, albeit his years and the wrinkles that furrow his face, is a vigorous old gentleman with a kindly way about him, and the new Mrs. STEVENS is a buxom matron with a comely little daughter of 12 or thereabouts. Mr. STEVENS was loath to talk about the romance connected with his marriage, but was induced to tell the story, which he did in a simple unaffected way.

> Ridge Farm, IL, Times

Dana News
It is rumored that JAMES McLAUGHLIN will start for Danville this week where he intends pursuing a course in law.

Clinton News
Miss SERENA WASHBURN, one of Greencastle's fair ladies, is the guest of her cousin, Miss ANNA WASHBURN, in this city.

RATE HUPP, a Clinton boy, who has just completed his tour around the world, is now breaking on the C. & E.I. Railway.

Home News
Mrs. JOSIE HINES, of Mattoon, IL, a sister of MAURICE HEGARTY of this place, was here on a visit last week.

Married at the residence of the bride's father, in Perrysville, November 21st, 1888. Mr. EDWARD C. PATTERSON, of Champaign, IL, and Miss ELLA J. RUNYAN, by Rev. W.A. SMITH.

R.H. NIXON, wife and his daughter IDA NIXON, left one week ago this morning for the Arkansas Hot Springs. Mrs. NIXON is again seriously afflicted with rheumatism, and has gone down there to obtain relief. She and her daughter will probably stay there until spring. Mr. NIXON did not know when he left how long he would remain.

Catnip
OL GRUBB made a visit at an early hour yesterday morning, to buy some catnip that you make tea out of for babies. He told FRANK TURNER that is was a girl, arriving on the 2 o'clock a.m. train, and had pretty black hair. OL is extremely happy.

Notice to Non-Residents
    MARION REEDER vs. WILLIAM A. REEDER, & JEFFERSON FOLTZ etal
    Complaint No. 3081
    WILLIAM A. REEDER is not a resident of Indiana
    Must appear before 4th Monday of December 1888
    CONLEY & SAWYER, attorneys for plaintiff
    Filed November 26, 1888
                            A.R. HOPKINS, Clerk

MINNIE LANDERS, of Oakland, IL, a handsome young miss of 16 summers, is here visiting her uncle, JAMES W. SYKES, and family.

Dr. L.C. STADLER, of Milwaukee, WI, who is visiting relatives, returned home last Tuesday. His cousin, Miss INEZ FRAZIER, accompanied him where she will spend a couple of months visiting with relatives.

Letter List in Newport
JOHN P. SAWYER	D.G. SMITH
J.L. AUSTIN	CLINTON W. DICKINSON
GEORGE HARVEY Esq.	JAMES A. ROBERTSON
Mrs. MAGGIE SEAREY	E.W. HARTLEY

Wednesday, December 5, 1888

Died
Mr. JOHN R. HIGHFILL, a highly respected citizen of this township, died at his farm home, near Vermillion Memorial Church, November 29th, 1888, at midnight. A devoted wife and affectionate daughter, besides a large number of friends are left to mourn his death. Mr. HIGHFILL was born in Vermillion County September 4th, 1828, and has always lived in our midst, thus giving him a residence among us for 60 years, 2 months, and 26 days, during which time he has had the unbounded confidence of all who knew him. He has occupied several positions of trust and was one of the prime movers and principle workers in the erection of the new and beautiful Memorial Church near which he lived, and of which he was a member, trustee, and treasurer. For a long time he has been a silent sufferer with heart trouble and Bright's disease, which finally conquered his otherwise vigorous constitution. Funeral services were conducted at the home by Rev. R.S. MARTIN. The large number of persons present and the sympathetic words everywhere expressed are indications of the high esteem in which the deceased was held by all who knew him. In this great loss the grief stricken wife and daughter have the sympathy of the entire community.

Died
JAMES J. LEWIS, living near Gessie, died at 2 o'clock Tuesday, November 27th, 1888. He lacked only until the first of January, of being 84 years old. He had lived in this county over 50 years and was highly respected and loved by all who knew him. He was a man who always placed principle before policy, and was as unyielding as a rock where his conscience dictated either right or wrong. He had been a member of the M.E. Church for more than 60 years, and was a very prominent man in all of its affairs. He never faltered in his faith and died, as he had lived, a quiet, consistent Christian; happy in his belief and in his hope of a better life. His funeral was preached by the M.E. pastor Rev. WILEY, at Havard's Chapel at 2 o'clock Wednesday last.

Home News
Uncle ZACHARIAH D. JAMES, of Bono, Helt Township, is reported to be seriously ill.

JOE CHUNN received his first installment of pension on Saturday last. The arrears amounted to $1773.

B.S. AIKMAN has been appointed Deputy Prospecting Attorney for Vermillion County, by Prosecutor HENRY DANIELS of Rockville.

Mrs. R.J. THOMPSON, of Holton, KS, is here visiting her sister, Mrs. TAYLOR ADAMS.

W.P. HENSON, informs us that his son JOHN HENSON, a minister of Lamar, NE, is in the midst of a big revival meeting.

The wife of E.H. NEBEKER, of Covington, is dangerously ill.

R.E. NICHOLS, of Illiana, IL, was over here last week to see his father, who at the time, was dangerously ill.

The following old soldiers will be mustered into the Grand Army Post, at this place, on December 14th, 1888:

DAVE JONES	JOHN LONBARGER
CHARLES STEWART	R.T. HAWKINS
JOHN D. FRY	FROST H. HEFFLEMAN
ALBERT G. FORTNER	JOSEPH S. ANTRUM
WILLIAM P. FORTNER	THOMAS J. NICHOLS
GEORGE W. RHODENBAUGH	JOHN R. HOLLINGSWORTH

Married
At the home of the bride's parents, 8 miles northwest of Clinton, last Tuesday, Mr. LINK CHURCH and Miss GRACE ANDERSON were married.

Mrs. MARIA DOWDELL, of this place, widow of the late JACOB DOWDELL, received notice from General BLACK on Saturday last, that her pension had been granted. She gets $12 per month for each child under 16 years of age. She has 5 children under the age of 16.

FRANK TURNER has another catnip customer. GEORGE FORD, residing on South Main, made his first purchase yesterday morning. It's a girl, and arrived about 12:30 yesterday morning, December 4th, 1888. GEORGE is feeling very happy, and so is FRANK TURNER, who will furnish him all the catnip he needs at the lowest market price.

Wedding
On Thursday, November 29th, 1888, (which was Thanksgiving Day), at 11 o'clock a.m. Mr. JOSEPH M. HOPKINS of Newport and Miss ESTHER H. BALES of Helt township were united in marriage by Rev. R.S. MARTIN of the M.E. Church. The ceremony took place in the parlors of the bride's residence and was witnessed by a number of relatives and friends. Mr. QUINCY A. MYERS served as the groom's attendant and Miss ZULA HOPKINS as bridesmaid for the occasion. The groom is one of Newport's choice young men, whose sterling qualities have made him a general favorite, and the bride is one of the charming daughters of WILLIAM BALES, Esq., and is equally well known and popular in "Center Community ", where she had lived her life. Mr. and Mrs. HOPKINS will live in Newport.

Wednesday, December 12, 1888

Perrysville
WILLIAM CAYWOOD broke his arm last Friday in falling from a load of hay on the hill, north of town.

Dana News
Miss ETTA HASKELL, of Plainfield, IN, has been visiting at her aunt's Mrs. CALEB BALES, since Thanksgiving.

An infant child of OWEN T. CLARK's died last Sunday and was buried Monday by J.W. REDMAN. Mr. CLARK is a teacher in Vermillion Township.

Mrs. EMILY LEE, wife of the late JOHN LEE of West Lebanon, is visiting her numerous friends in this community. She is now at Mr. JACOB FONCANNON's.

Clinton Argus
JAMES AMMERMAN, a young man of Parke County, came over here to this county one day to visit his relatives in Helt Township. During his stay, he was taken down with a severe chill, which rapidly developed into congestion of the brain, and in two days he died. The funeral occurred last Saturday.

Sheriff's Sale on Decree
    RUSSELL & Co. vs. FRANK M. JAMES, JOHN T. DAILY, & CATHERINE DAILY
    $577.28
    Sale to be held Saturday, January 12, 1889 at courthouse
        Part of Lot 30 adjoining town of Clinton
        Also Lot 5 in Block 4 in Knowles addition to Clinton
    CONLEY & SAWYER, attorneys for plaintiff
    Filed December 11, 1888
                              WILLIAM RHEUBY, Sheriff

Home News
LAFAYETTE NEWELL, of Hillsdale, has had his pension increased.

D.T. DAVIS (deceased), of Clinton, has been granted a pension.

D.B. LENTON, of Geneva, Clinton township, has been granted a pension.

WILLIAM F. THORNTON, foreman of the Hoosier office, visited his father, who resides in Danville, IL, over Sunday. He found the old gentleman down with rheumatism in his back and legs.

Miss BESSIE OLNEY, the dressmaker, cutter, and fitter, can now be found at the residence of Mr. JOHN A. DARBY, on east Extension Street, known as the BEN BLANCHARD property.

Dr. AUSTIN MARLOW, of Terre Haute, a former physician of Clinton, and well known to many of our citizens of this county, was united in wedlock to a wealthy widow of Terre Haute, by the name of Mrs. M.M. RIDDLE, on last Monday night.

We paid our father and mother, Mr. and Mrs. DAVIS, who reside on Helt's Prairie, a short visit on Saturday last. Our father will be 79 and our mother 72 in January. Father is in fair health for one of his years, and does considerable work on the farm. Mother is feeble and in very poor health, and reduced greatly in flesh.

OLIVER H. KNIGHT, of Coolidge, KS, a former citizen of this place and typo of the Hoosier office, arrived here on last Monday night on a couple of weeks visit among his boyhood friends. He is now one of the editors and proprietors of the Coolidge, KS Citizen. He left here 7 years ago, and looks as hearty and young as he did when he left.

JOE BLACK, of Clinton, has been granted a pension.

WILLIAM H. HOOD, of Eugene, has been appointed administrator of the estate of ISAAC WAGGONER, deceased.

NORBIN RENICKS, who works for WILLIAM SHELATO, visited his parents in Waterman, Parke County, on Sunday last.

Notice of Final Settlement of Estate
    Estate of JOHN J. THORNE, deceased
    Filed December 8, 1888
                                        A.R. HOPKINS, Clerk

Wednesday, December 19, 1888

Hoosier Romance
It our last issue of November 28th, 1888, we published an article from the Ridge Farm, IL, Times, in which an old and respected citizen of Perrysville figured. It was supposed to be a happy ending of two old lovers in the bonds of wedlock. It stated that ELHANAN STEVENS, of Perrysville, and Mrs. HATTIE E. PHENEGAR, of Chicago, were married. But it is said true love never runs smooth, and it proved so in this case, for last week she packed up her traps and left for Chicago, telling her old lover and hubby that Perrysville was too lonesome for her. It is probable that they have separated for good, as it is not likely Mr. STEVENS will sell out and leave his old friends and home for a woman who prefers city life to living with him. The sad incident is to be much regretted, but Mr. STEVENS should have studied the situation thoroughly before he selected her as a partner for life.

Shiloh Post
Shiloh Post, G.A.R., was the most largely attended on last Friday of any meeting held for some time. Six new members were mustered in as follows:

    JOSEPH S. ANTRUM   ALBERT G. FORTNER
    WILLIAM P. FORTNER   THOMAS J. NICHOLS
    GEORGE W. RHODENBAUGH   DAVE JONES

New officers
    R.E. STEPHENS   Commander
    THOMAS J. NICHOLS   St. Vice Commander
    A.C. BROKAW, Jr.   St. Vice Commander
    JOHN RICHARDSON   Q.M.
    GEORGE H. RHODENBAUGH   Surgeon
    Rev. R.B. VAN ALLEN   Chaplain
    E.B. BROWN   Officer of the Day
    Z.P. THORNTON   Officer of the Guard

The new Commander appointed JOHN W. HARTMAN, Adjutant
The Adjutant appointed DAVID JONES, Sergeant Major.
The Q.M. appointed A.G. FORTNER, Q.M.S.
D.Y. FUNKHOUSER was appointed Inside Sentinel
SAM SANDERS was appointed Outside Sentinel

Died
Mr. HENRY RALSTON, aged 73, died last Sunday morning, December 9, 1883, at his home in this place. He fell from a load of hay some two weeks ago, and received an injury to the brain and spinal cord, which resulted in death. The funeral took place last Monday. An eloquent sermon was preached at the Presbyterian Church by Rev. HOOK.
                                                  Dana News

A Young Minister
A young Methodist minister arrived at Rev. R.S. MARTIN's residence on last Monday afternoon. It is a fine looking boy and weighs 8 ¾ pounds. FRANK TURNER, the catnip doctor, donated 4 pounds of catnip for the benefit of the young preacher.

Home News
LUCIAN WRIGHT, of Clinton, has been granted a pension.

MEREDITH LEWIS, of Rileysburg, has been appointed executor of the estate of JAMES J. LEWIS, deceased.

Mrs. WILLIAM KELP, an old lady of Clinton, fell down the steps leading to the kitchen door, last Sunday and broke her leg.

Mrs. BENJAMIN BLANCHARD, of South Hutchinson, KS, is in the city visiting her mother, Mrs. INSLEY.
          Terre Haute Express

Died
Mrs. SARAH B. HOWARD, an old and respected lady of Yale, Jasper County, IL, a sister of the late SAMUEL DAVIS, died here at 10 o'clock on last Sunday night, after a brief illness. She was here on a visit to relatives, and died at the residence of her nephew, JOSHUA N. DAVIS. Her remains were interred in the Thomas Cemetery, 2 miles northwest of town, on last Monday afternoon.

JIM BRAZIL and TAYLOR ADAMS have each a new catnip swigger. We did not learn whether they were of the male or female persuasion.

CHARLEY HACKER, the northside dry goods merchant, fell through a hay chute, one day last week, and hurt one of his legs so that he can hardly get around on it.

WILLIAM BALES, of Helt Township, came up here last Saturday afternoon to visit his daughter, who was recently married to JOE HOPKINS. He was accompanied by one of his younger daughters.

WILLIAM C. MYERS, who has been at Danville, IL, since some time last fall, undergoing treatment for something like a cancerous affectation of his nose, doesn't seem to be getting much relief. His nose is now nearly entirely eaten away, and the disease is seriously affecting his throat, so that he can hardly eat. BILLY is in pretty bad shape, but his doctor still has hopes of affecting a cure. In his sad affliction he has the sympathy of his many friends in this vicinity.

Married
A pleasant event occurred at the residence of SAM MALONE of Dana, at 8 o'clock last night. HORACE L. DARRAH, of Viena, IN, an operator on the J.M. & I Railway, was united in wedlock to Miss LOU THORN, a charming young lady who has made her home with Mr. MALONE for the last 3 years. Rev. R.S. MARTIN, pastor of the M.E. Church here, performed the ceremony in his usually happy way.

Married
At 4 o'clock on last Friday evening, Rev. R.B. VAN ALLEN, pastor of the U.B. Church, united in wedlock Mr. ABNER EARLES, of Danville, IL, to Miss ISABEL HUMRICKHOUSE, of Humrick, IL. As the bride's parents were opposed to the match, she had run off to escape the wrath of the old folks. The ceremony took place at the residence of HIRAM PATRICK, Eugene Township, and was a very quiet affair. Mr. EARLES is 33 years of age, and his bride is 29. It looks like they were nearly old enough to get married. As they are now married, we suppose the old folks will relent and invite them back home.

Wednesday, December 26, 1888

Clinton Argus
Capt. D.A. RANGER has been granted an increase in his pension to $6 per month.

Mr. WILLIAM PINSON, of St. Bernice, left for Arkansas last Wednesday afternoon to spend the winter hunting and trapping.

Miss SALLIE MOORE, one of Perrysville's fair young belles. Was the guest of her cousin, Prof. KERNS, a few days this week.

The SHIRKIES will shortly establish a branch grocery store at Illiana, IL, which will be under the charge of FRANK CAMPBELL.

JOHN WELLMAN, who has for 16 years, been an invalid, died at the home of his parents Tuesday night of last week. The deceased was 21 years of age.

Mr. JOHN WRIGHT, who has been growing feeble recently, was taken dangerously ill Monday morning, and for a few hours his family thought he was dying.

Accident
Thursday at 7:30 p.m., the C.& E.I. fast train coming south, when near Alvin, ran over Mr. WILLIAM P. HANNAH, a well known farmer living near that place. Mr. HANNAH was trying to board the train while it was in motion and he fell, the wheels of the car passing over one of his legs and crushing it so it required amputation. Dr. MOREHOUSE of this city, and Dr. LIVENGOOD, of Rossville, performed the operation.
                                                                                            Danville, IL, News

Vermillion Township Items
CHARLES PARRETT, who came from Tennessee last spring, started for this old home on last Wednesday. He will probably return in the spring with the birds.

Killed at Clinton
WILLIAM TRUSE, of Danville, IL, a brakeman on the C. & E.I. Railway, got caught while making a coupling of two cars, loaded with lumber, on last Thursday evening. He fell prostrate from the hurt received, and several cars ran over his legs, crushing them to jelly. He was taken to a private residence where he died in a few hours. Coroner BRINDLEY was notified, and went down to hold an inquest. His parents reside at Danville, IL, where his remains were taken on the early train Friday morning for interment.

Obituary
Miss BERTHA CARPENTER, daughter of O.C. CARPENTER, of Perrysville, died on Monday last of consumption, after a long illness. She was about 18 or 20 years of age, and a lady whom everyone respected and esteemed. Her friends were numerous, for she was kind and affectionate to everyone. In her death, the people of Perrysville lose a model young lady, and one who was held in the highest esteem by all her friends and acquaintances. Her funeral took place Monday, and was attended by a large gathering of her young friends and neighbors.

Township Institute
The Vermillion Township Teacher's Institute was held December 22nd, 1888 at Newport. Number present were FRANCES RICE, Mr. BOTHWELL, Mr. NEEL, Mr. CLARK, BLANCHE HUPP, SARAH WALTHALL, LYDIA WALTHALL, EUNICE LITTLE, LINA CADY, MAGGIE HOPKINS. Number absent were QUINCY MYERS, Mr. GOSNELL, Mr. DAVIS.

Allowances by Board of Commissioners, December Term 1888
    On account Roads
	F.M. DAVIS	$ 3.00
	S.J. HALL	3.00
	R.P. LITTLE	3.00
	S.H. DALLAS	1.50

	JOHN RICHARDSON	1.50
	R.H. NIXON	1.50
	JAMES MALONE	3.00
	HIRAM PATRICK	3.00

On account bridges

	H.S. CADY	133.33
	JOHN GALLOWAY	13.15
	JOHN MILLER	90.75
	W.M. SHELATO	6.00
	SOL WEATHERWAX	50.00
	W.K. McNEILL	295.00

On account poor

	M.L. HALL	56.25
	E.A. FLAUGHER	24.00
	JAMES T. HENDERSON	25.00
	ERASTUS MACK	25.00
	SOL WEATHERWAX	292.96
	G.O. NEWTON	223.96
	E.H. McDANIEL	142.27
	W.K. McNEILL	284.46
	S.B. DAVIS	277.54

On account books and stationery

	WILLIAM B. BURFORD	143.55
	S.B. DAVIS	75.00
	C.W. BROWN	10.00

On account gravel roads

	W.L. PORTER	7500.00

Miscellaneous

	D.S. HOPKINS, elections	4.50
	M. HEGARTY, county offices	22.64
	M.L. HALL, Board of Health	30.75
	E.E. DAVIS, criminals	8.16
	DAVID AGGRA, janitor	50.00
	S.B. DAVIS, printing	65.00
	G.W. DEALAND, Co. Supt.	238.00
	M.G. RHOADS, attorney fees	125.00
	W.L. PORTER, fees and salary	232.27
	JOSEPH CONRAD, poor asylum	610.28
	W.C. SHARP, public buildings	9.50
	WILLIAM RHEUBY, courts	8.00
	W.F. KERNS, courts	21.00
	F.M. RILEY, courts	17.50

Home News

Mrs. JAMES CRANE, of Clinton, came up here yesterday to eat Christmas turkey.

JOHN VANDEVENDER, who is working down at Terre Haute, is at home to spend the holidays.

JAMES TUTT, of Highland, who has been at Chicago for several weeks, undergoing treatment for a cancer, returned home on last Saturday night. He is in pretty bad shape, and the probabilities area that he will not live through the winter.

There will be a grand ball given at Perrysville on next Monday (New Years Eve). The Eugene orchestra will furnish the music, lead by Miss ZADAH COLLINS, of Perrysville, the best violinist in Vermillion County.

Indianapolis Journal

CHARLES B. WILEY, of Vermillion County, who was fined and sent to jail for six months for counterfeiting, by the United States district court, was discharged yesterday under the provisions of the pauper convict's act.

Matrimony

Clerk A.R. HOPKINS issued the following matrimonial permits on Monday last:
- CHARLEY SANDERS and ISA ROBBINS
- DAVE ADAMS and ANNA FOX
- WILLIAM SECRIST and MARY REFIT

Dr. FRANK JONES, who is attending medical college at Chicago, is at home to spend the holidays.

Miss CLARA MYERS, who is attending college at Champaign, IL, is at home to spend the holidays.

Mrs. BELL LINDSEY and little son, of Danville, IL, are here visiting relatives.

Miss LIZZIE BOST, of Rosedale, Parke County, is here to spend the holidays with relatives and friends.

STEVE THOMAS is going to move up near Bethel, IL, in the vicinity of Horse Shoe, this township, the latter part of the week.

Dr. C.M. WHITE, of Clinton, has been elected school trustee of that city to fill out the unexpired term of WILLIAM M. HAMILTON, who resigned.

Married

On last Thursday, December 20th, 1888, Mr. JAMES W. HUGHES and Miss NANCY E. HENDERSON, of Highland Township, were united in holy wedlock, Rev. W.A. SMITH, pastor of the Perrysville M.E. Church performing the ceremony. The ceremony took place at the residence of Mrs. COSSEY, who spread a magnificent supper.

NEWPORT HOOSIER STATE 1889

Wednesday, January 2, 1889

RANDOLPH & RANDOLPH
F.E. RANDOLPH – Salesman
Dry Goods
Cayuga, IN

J.C. JACKSON
Dry Goods
Hillsdale, In

NIXON & CATES
Lumber, Agricultural Implements
Cayuga, IN

S. BOWERS
Riverside Flouring Mills
Eugene, IN

RALPH & FOLGER
Farm Implements
Dana, IN

Dr. E.C. LOOMIS
Physician & Surgeon
Perrysville, IN

PIXLEY & Co.
Clothing
Terre Haute, IN

H.H. CONLEY
J.C. SAWYER
Attorneys at Law
Newport, IN

J.M. TAYLOR
J.L. PEER
Boys & Children's Suits
Dana, IN

CHARLES HACKER
Ladies & Men's Overcoats
Newport, IN

E.W. LEEDS
Watches, Diamonds, Jewelry
Terre Haute, IN

WILLIAM B. HOOD
Treasurer
Vermillion County

THOMAS J. NICHOLS
Furniture
Newport, IN

WILLIAM P. WRIGHT
Hay for sale
Newport, IN

ROBERT A. PARRETT
County Surveyor
Newport, IN

CHARLES W. WARD
OSCAR B. GIBSON
Attorneys at Law
Newport, IN

Notice of Administration
    Estate of JAMES J. LEWIS, deceased
    December 15, 1888

    MEREDITH LEWIS
    Administrator

Notice of Administration
    Estate of ISAAC WAGGONER, deceased
    December 1, 1888

    WILLIAM H. HOOD
    Administrator

Home News
S.E. WISHARD, of Clinton, spent last Sunday in Opedee visiting his niece, Mrs. GEORGE LINK.

T.J. NICHOLS has sold his little farm of 30 acres, near Quaker Point, this township, to Mrs. PEGGY HOLLINGSWORTH, for $1850. Mr. NICHOLS is going to move to Cayuga and engage in undertaking and furniture business.

J.B. OSMON will probably start to Arkansas this week, where he has purchased 1600 acres of fine timber which he intends to saw into lumber. He shipped his mill several days ago. Several are going from here to work for him.

WILLIAM HOOPER, of this township, has swapped his 160 acre farm for 112 acres of land in Helt township. He got less land and paid $1200 in boot money.

P.W. GRUBB, of Cherry Point, IL, was over here last week visiting his old homestead friends.

WILLIAM SKIDMORE, of Helt's Prairie, has a new baby girl at his house, which arrived on Thursday last.

Mr. FRANK SONGER, of Cissna Park, IL, spent the holidays visiting his uncle, JOHN W. CROSS and his family, of this place.

SILAS HOLLINGSWORTH has closed out his meat market and gone over to Indianapolis to work in a lard rendering factory.

Sudden death
One week ago last Friday, December 21, 1888, the wife of PERRY MORGAN, Clinton, died very suddenly from hemorrhage of the lungs. She was only sick about 8 hours. She was a most excellent and highly esteemed lady, and daughter of the late SAMUEL DAVIDSON, who resided a short distance west of that city for many years.

Reorganization
List of officers and teachers of the U.B. Sunday School for 1889:
    Superintendent – Mrs. THORNTON
    Assistant Superintendent – Mr. ED AIKMAN
    Secretary – LOU CADY
    Assistant Secretary – WALTER PLACE
    Treasurer – Miss LUCY WHITE
    Organist – Miss MARY CHIPPS
    Assistant Organist – Miss CARRIE THORNTON
    Chorister – Mr. B.S. AIKMAN
    Librarian – BOONE GIBBONS
    Assistant Librarian – WILLIE CHIPPS
    Teachers
        Class #1 – Mrs. ARRASMITH
        Class #2 – Miss MAGGIE HOPKINS
        Class #3 – Miss ANNA WILLIAMSON
        Class #4 – CHARLEY THORNTON
        Class #5 – Miss ELLA RICHARDSON
        Class #6 – Miss GRACE CARTER
        Class #7 – B.S. AIKMAN
        Class #8 – J.C. SAWYER
        Class #9 – QUINCY MYERS
        Class #10 – ED BROWN

Fodder Shock Nubbins
A six months old child of WILLIAM PEER, living 2 miles west of Dana died last Saturday of diphtheria. Rev. WRIGHT preached the funeral on Sunday.

Col. AD RANGER, of Clinton, has been granted an increase of pension.

Married
At the residence of J.E. WRIGHT on Christmas Eve, Mr. WILLIAM DOWNEY and Miss DORA WILKINS, both of Dana, were united in holy wedlock. The young couple has our best wishes.

Killed on the Rail
MARTIN KEILY, aged 28 years, an engineer on an Arkansas Railroad, was killed in an accident on Friday last, and brought to Pana, IL for burial, where he was interred on Sunday last. He was a brother of Mrs. MAURICE HEGARTY of this place, and was a most excellent and upright man. Mr. HEGARTY and his wife attended the funeral.

Broke His Leg
A little son of JAMES F. BURNETT Jr., of Dana, fell from a shed on last Saturday afternoon, and broke one of his legs in two places. It was a pretty bad accident, but the doctor thinks he can save his leg all right, and have him out again in a few months.

Pumpkin Vine News
Mr. GASSMAN, of Tuscola, IL, is in the city visiting, the guest of Miss BLANCHE HUPP.

An infant child of Mr. and Mrs. WILLIAM CLOVER was buried in Spangler Cemetery last Saturday.

Real Estate Transfers for December
OZIAS SHIPMAN etal to Indiana & Illinois Stone & Manufacturing Co.
110 acres in Eugene Township
$250,000

J.E. KNOWLES to M.S. WHITCOMB
Tract of land in Clinton Township
$100

A NOLAN to JOHN WHITCOMB
? acres in Clinton Township
$1200

S.A. BOGART to DANIEL MILLER
40 acres in Helt Township
$1600

JOHN CROMPTON to JOHN WHITCOMB
Small tract of land in Clinton Township
$500

J.W. JOHNSON to STEVE HUNT
1 acre in Highland Township
$25

WILLIAM CRABB to EMMA CRABB
? acres in Helt Township
$50

JOHN MAST etal to W.F. HARVEY
39 acres in Helt Township
$?

JOHN S. HOUCHIN to M. & H. AIKMAN
Lots 21 & 22, Dana
$216

J.W. PARRETT to ELLA PARRETT
Lots 99 & 100, Newport
$100

M. AIKMAN to J.S. HOUCHIN
34 acres in Helt Township
$700

ELLA PARRETT to J.C. SAWYER
Lot 100 in Newport
$160

U.E. THORNE to F.P. THORNE
65 acres in Helt Township
$859

L.W. THORNE to F.P. THORNE
65 acres in Helt Township
$850

JOHN W. JARVIS to WILLIAM B. PAULEY
Lots 26 & 27, Dana
$80

HENRY NEBEKER to WILSON & CRANE
Part of Lot 4, Clinton
$350

N.C. ANDERSON to WILSON & CRANE
Part of Lot 4, Clinton
$350

WILSON & CRANE to HENRY NEBEKER
Lot 4, Clinton
$350

H.G. WASHBURN to A. NEBEKER
Out lot 15, Clinton
$1000

A NEBEKER to SERENA J. WASHBURN
Out lot 15, Clinton
$1000

NELSON HANSON to SYLVESTER DOUGLASS
Lot 4, Block 16, Clinton
$100

MATTHEW A. GRAY to A.W. TRUITT
Lot 10, Block 5, Clinton
$550

F.M. HELT to ERASTUS K. CRANE
10 acres in Helt Township
$300

W.B. PAULEY to HARRIET BARRON
Lots 26 & 27, Block 7, Dana
$184

ELI H. McDANIEL to PORTER MILLIKIN
Lots 67 & 68, Cayuga
$310

J.D. McKEE etal to CHRISTIA A. TODD
Lot 162, 3rd addition
$150

EDMOND HUNT to HARVEY HUNT
6 acres in Highland Township
$215

JOSEPH HANN and uxor to J.F. WILTERMOOD & E.E. DAVIS
Lot 2, Collett's subdivision of 55 & 56, Newport
$2100

WILLIAM MORRISON to MARY E. PORTER
Tract of land in Helt Township
$850

JAMES LUCAS to E.D. STEEN
30 acres, Eugene Township
$1000

J.H. BOGART to MARY S. DAVIS
Out lot in Clinton
$350

S. AIKMAN to O.B. LOWRY
Lot 6 & 7, Dana
$40

R.M. KILGORE to H.M. KILGORE
45.15 acres, Eugene township
$1000

Notice of Final Settlement of Estate
    Estate of LEVI M. WESTBROOK, deceased
    Court to be held January 18, 1889
    Filed December 29, 1888
                                      A.R. HOPKINS, Clerk

Wednesday, January 9, 1889

Mrs. MAURICE HEGARTY and her daughter NELLIE HEGARTY returned home from Mattoon, IL, yesterday where she went 10 days ago to attend her brother's funeral.

JAMES SHORTER, a Clinton coal miner, who was seriously injured the first part of last week by a premature blast, still lingers in a critical condition, without much hope of his recovery. He was badly pulverized.

JIM OSBORN and his partner have already invested $10,000 in their fire brick factory at Hillsdale, and it will take fully that much more money to place them on a good footing to do business.

Home News
Montezuma has a case of scarlet fever, the daughter of PHILLIP BIPUS.

Mrs. W.P. HENSON went out to Sodorus, IL, on Saturday last, to visit relatives.

W.P. WHITE, of Helt's Prairie, is lying at the point of death. His physicians have given up all hope of his recovery.

J.M. HARPER, of Helt's Prairie, who has been seriously ill for two or three weeks, is still lying very low, with chances against his recovery.

Mr. and Mrs. JAMES BARNES, of Montezuma, are happy over a New Year's gift in the shape of a nine pound boy, that arrived New Year's Eve.

WILLIAM GALLOWAY and wife, of Hutchinson, KS, were here last week visiting relatives. Mrs. GALLOWAY is the daughter of Deputy Treasurer THOMAS CUSHMAN.

Mrs. AGNES STEAVERS, of Parke County, is over here visiting her mother, Mrs. JACOB DOWDELL.

Rev. J.E. WRIGHT, of Dana, was a caller at the Hoosier State office on Friday last. He was accompanied by his son, JOHN WRIGHT, a bright young man, who was on his way to Perdue University, where he is attending school.

There was a report in town yesterday that JOHN WADE, of this township, and Miss MAGGIE EDMONDS, of Eugene, were married. When JOHN left home a few days ago, he told his folks that he intended to marry before he came back.

At Montezuma, on the 3rd instant, S.P. WELSHAN and wife celebrated their golden wedding anniversary. Fifty years is a long time for two persons to trot together in double harness. The children and grandchildren, and several noted guests were present and had a good time.

Left for Arkansas
J.B. OSMON, who intended to leave for the timber regions of Arkansas last week, did not get off till last Monday morning. He took quite a little colony of people with him. Among them were EMERY BRILES, FRANK DICKEN, FRANK HASTY and family, and one of the gravel pit boys.

Our Club Agents
The following are authorized to receive subscriptions to the Hoosier State
    Miss E. DICKASON & SMITH RABB – Perrysville
    JOHN CADE – Gessie
    HOSFORD & BELL – Eugene
    Dr. E.A. FLAUGHER – Cayuga
    J.C. JACKSON – Hillsdale
    J.E. BILSLAND – Dana
    F.N. AUSTIN – Bono
    E.F. McCOWN – Jonestown

FRANK LANGSTON – Summit Grove
S.R. FINNELL – Clinton

Fodder Shock Nubbins
Dana News
Mrs. J.P. YORK went to Waveland, IN, last Tuesday to visit her parents and friends for several days.

ALBERT FONCANNON has traded his town property here for 40 acres of land near him, belonging to a man who lives in Illinois. The land that Mr. FONCANNON got is known as the MASSA SMITH Farm.

Prof. FRED RUSH and EMMET LANG left last Friday night for a trip to southern Georgia. Mr. RUSH went to Thomasville, GA to visit his father who is in very poor health. EMMET goes for a rest and recreation. They expect to get back in a week.

Handsome Gift
Mrs. Rev. R.S. MARTIN was recently the recipient of a complete wardrobe outfit, for the special use of the unnamed son, who arrived three weeks ago. The wardrobe is beautiful and was valued at $30, and was the gift of the ladies who are members and friends of the Newport M.E. charge.

Wednesday, January 16, 1889

OZRO CRANER, a former resident of this place, is a member of the lower house of the present legislature from Delaware County. Since he left here, he has been studying law, and is now a full fledged attorney. He is married and has 2 or 3 children.

Obituary
Death of W.P. WHITE
On last Sunday afternoon, we attended the funeral of WARREN P. WHITE, better known as "PICK" WHITE, the interment taking place at the Clinton Cemetery. The deceased was a son of JAMES A. WHITE Sr., who resides three miles north of Clinton, and just in the edge of Helt's Prairie. Mr. WHITE had been confined to his room 6 or 8 weeks, and was kindly cared for by his parents, where he had made his home since the death of his wife in 1879. His brother CHARLEY WHITE, of Clinton, was his attending physician, and did all in his power to alleviate his sufferings and restore him to health once more, but his disease was beyond the reach of medicines, and he lingered until 10 o'clock Saturday morning, January 12, 1889, when the death angel claimed him for its own. Those who were present when the last sparks of life left his body, say he passed away without a struggle. His funeral occurred at 2 o'clock on Sunday afternoon at the residence of his parents, and was very largely attended by his neighbors and friends, who came to pay their last tribute of respect before his remains were consigned to the silent tomb. The officiating minister was the pastor of the Presbyterian Church at Clinton. The pastor in his remarks said:

WARREN P. WHITE was born in July 1848, and died January 12, 1889, aged 40 years and 6 months. He was married to SARAH M. FILLINGER April 9, 1873 who died November 1, 1879. Two children survive him – PEARL WHITE, aged 14 years, and OKIE WHITE, aged 12."

Pumpkin Vine News
Clinton Argus
The infant child born to Mr. and Mrs. LINK McWETHY a few weeks ago, died Tuesday night.

MORT WICKS will leave for Washington Territory in a few days, where he will make his future home.

FRANK J. BORGMAN and son JOHN BORGMAN start for Mississippi Sunday night, where they have a contract for manufacturing staves for a London firm.

W.H. CALE left Tuesday morning on a trip to Virginia, where he will visit his father and mother. He has not seen his parents for 15 years.

Clinton Echoes
SILAS TAYLOR, an old and respected citizen of Parke County, pulled up stakes and moved to Clinton last week.

JOHN AMMERMAN and family, formerly of this township, but now of Effingham, IL, returned to their home last Saturday after a two week's visit with Mr. AMMERMAN's father, JAMES AMMERMAN.

FRED AMMERMAN, eldest son of THEOPOLIS AMMERMAN, and who was killed by the explosion of a boiler in a sawmill in Jasper County near his home, was brought here for burial last Thursday. Six weeks ago, JAMES AMMERMAN, a second son of Mr. AMMERMAN, came here on a visit, took sick while at his uncle's and died before his father and mother could reach his bedside.

Vermillion Township Items
Mrs. MARGARET ROGERS, widow of Rev. JOSHUA ROGERS, a former citizen of Newport, now of Ashton, Dakota, is here visiting her numerous relatives and friends. She arrived here the last of October and intends returning to Dakota in the spring.

Fodder Shock Nubbins
Dana News
The little infant child of Mr. and Mrs. A.M. FOLGER, is quite sick with congestion of the lungs.

Mashed His Hand
Prof. BARNABAS C. HOBBS met with an accident last Friday, which resulted in the loss of two fingers of his right hand. He was engaged with a workman repairing the dam at his fish pond. The man was driving a stake, which Prof. HOBBS wanted to straighten, and asked him to stop for a moment. He did not understand the command, and brought the heavy maul down with full force. The two fingers were crushed terribly and were at once amputated.

Stricken With Paralysis
P.S. WESTFALL, editor and proprietor of the Terre Haute Mail, was stricken down with paralysis on last Thursday night, and is now in a very critical condition. His whole left side is paralyzed. It is doubtful if he recovers.

Robbery
AMOS HOLYCROSS, an unsavory citizen of Highland Township, stole a load of corn from MARK STEELY, north of Covington, Fountain County, one day last week, and hauled it down to Perrysville where he had disposed of it for cash. Officers came in on him at Perrysville before he got it unloaded, but he got wind of their coming in time to make his escape. He is about 30 years of age, is married and has two children.

Home News
A small child of NATHAN KIGER, who resides northwest of here, died of congestion on Monday last, aged one year. Its remains were interred in the Thomas Cemetery on Tuesday. Rev. R.B. VAN ALLEN preached the funeral.

BOB HOLTZ, of Lodi, Parke County, was in town on Wednesday last. He has affected a compromise with the heirs of the late Mrs. NORBIN THOMAS, who willed him 120 acres, by which they release all claims against him for $625.

Miss EFFIE HALL did not leave for Jonesboro, Arkansas, last week, but left for that point on the 6 o'clock train this morning. She was accompanied by her brother JOHN HALL.

CHARLEY STEWART, JOHN LONBARGER, and JONATHAN ELLIS were mustered in as members of the Shiloh Post of this place, on last Friday night.

JOHN HASTY has again had his pension increased. He now gets $30 per month. Awhile back he got an increase and re-rating, getting over $1000 back pension. This time he gets $168 in arrears.

Married
On January 9th, 1889, by Rev. W.A. SMITH of Perrysville, at the residence of Mr. JOHN WANN's, Mr. EDWARD J. JONES and Miss ALICE THOMPSON, all of Vermillion County. The young couple will live at the old Jones home, now owned by the happy bridegroom.

Married
On December 25th, 1888, in Perrysville, Mr. THOMAS B. DUKES and Miss ALICE M. BOYD. They will live at Rosedale, IN.

Death
PETER CRIPPEN, who resided 4 or 5 miles west of Perrysville, and who was one of the oldest residents of Highland Township, died on Friday last, and was buried at the Hughes Cemetery on the day following.

Fractured His Skull
News was received here yesterday that ALFRED CHIPPS, of Maysville, MO, a former resident of this place, was kicked by a wild horse a few days ago, and that his skull was seriously fractured. The physician does not think it a dangerous hurt.

Death
Mrs. CATHERINE DAILY, of Parke County, residing east of Clinton, died on Saturday last, aged 82 years. One of her sons is one of the Honorable Board of Commissioners of Parke County. Mrs. DAILY was a noble woman, and loved by everyone. She was a member of the Campbellite Church, and a true Christian lady in every respect. In her death society loses a valuable member, and her children a kind and affectionate mother.

Delinquent Tax List for Vermillion County for the year 1887

Highland Township

NAME	SECTION	TWP	RANGE	ACRES	TAX
GOODNER, JOSEPH P.	20	18	10	25	10.48
GOODNER, JOSEPH P.	21	18	10	83	91.85
GOODNER, JOSEPH P.	21	18	10	11	21.70
TROSPER, MAHALA	29	19	9	8.50	8.88

Eugene Township

NAME	SECTION	TWP	RANGE	ACRES	TAX
FULTZ, HENRY	19	18	9	70	89.99
FULTZ, CLARA B.	17	18	9	40	
FULTZ, CLARA B.	28	18	10	30.32	55.22
FULTZ, CLARA B.	18	18	9	120	
FULTZ, CLARA B.	18	18	9	120	327.99
FULTZ, CLARA B.	18	18	9	19	29.02
PETTY, MALINDA	9	17	9	69	
PETTY, MALINDA	9	17	9	20	11.51

Vermillion Township

NAME	SECTION	TWP	RANGE	ACRES	TAX
ALDRIDGE, JOHN E.	30	17	10	30	17.43
BROWN, DAVID	34	17	9	2	7.61
COLLETT, JOSEPHUS	13	16	9	30	
COLLETT, JOSEPHUS	14	16	9	61.30	50.70
FOLGER, URIAH	30	16	19	9.87	2.36
GILLESPIE heirs	5	16	10	26.50	50.92
JOHNSON, WILLIAM H.	2	16	9	26	11.68
MANNING, JOHN	14	17	9	78.50	60.38
MORGAN, CHARLES	9	16	10	1	6.76
RYAN, JESSE	32	17	10	15	
RYAN, JESSE	5	16	10	20	31.32
SIDEBOTTOM, AARON S.	33	17	10	20	40.10
WILTERMOOD, MARTHA	3	16	9	40	
WILTERMOOD, MARTHA	2	16	9	12	8.80
YOUNG, SQUIRE	2	16	9	3	18.40

Helt Township

NAME	SECTION	TWP	RANGE	ACRES	TAX
ATHERTON, GEORGE	20	15	9	40	
ATHERTON, GEORGE	17	15	9	40	32.70
COLLETT, JOSEPHUS	23	16	9	60.80	
COLLETT, JOSEPHUS	22	16	9	40	
COLLETT, JOSEPHUS	22	16	9	40	46.51
COMPTON, L.H.	34	16	9	11.25	13.77
COMPTON, CATHERINE	34	16	9	8	
COMPTON, CATHERINE	34	16	9	10	12.95
COLE, PHILA	10	15	9	5	3.09
DOUGLAS, DAVID	34	16	9	.54	16.51
HAYS, JOHN F.	20	15	9	.75	
HAYS, JOHN F.	20	15	9	45.25	
HAYS, JOHN F.	20	15	9	17.50	32.71
JOHNSON, ALBERT W.	27	16	9	40	
JOHNSON, ALBERT W.	27	16	9	25	10.29
PERRIN, SUSAN	31	15	9	20	35.98
STRAUGHN, JOHN W.	7	15	9	2	8.00
SLATER, WILEY G.	28	16	9	40	
SLATER, WILEY G.	28	16	9	30	
SLATER, WILEY G.	28	16	9	22.50	47.66
SLATER, WILEY G.	34	15	9	80	78.97

Clinton Township

NAME	SECTION	TWP	RANGE	ACRES	TAX
BROPHY, WILLIAM J.	5	14	9	.20	11.08
CARPENTER, MARTIN heirs	24	14	19	5	3.79
DOWDY, AMON	12	14	10	10	16.64
DOWDY, AMON	31	14	9	13	
DOWDY, AMON	31	14	9	26	41.78
JOHNSON, ELIZABETH	13	14	10	7.50	29.90
MORRIS, SARAH	33	14	9	23.72	30.60
SHEPERD, JAMES N.	17	14	9	30	18.42

Town Lots in Perrysville

NAME	LOTS	TAX

BISHOP, GEORGE R.	Out lot 7	7.51
CROCKET, ALLEN S.	Out lot 53	2.07
FOX, ELISA J.	G. & C's addition In lot 13	15.35
GIBSON, MINAS T.	McNeill's addition In lot 1	3.49
PATTERSON, SARAH E.	G. & C's addition In lot 18	22.88
SCOTT, MINERVA	Steven's addition In lot 5	9.28
SHEWMAKER, JOHN	Lacey's addition In lot 11 & 12	7.84

Town Lots in Eugene

NAME	LOTS	TAX
HOLTZ, JOSEPH	In lot 19	13.51
HOLTZ, JOSEPH	Out lot 6	6.36
SHEWARD, JAMES heirs	In lot 14	5.48

Town Lots in Cayuga

NAME	LOTS	TAX
PENN, GEORGE	G. & McK's addition In lot 55	16.15

Town Lots in Newport

NAME	LOTS	TAX
KILDOW, ADAM H.	Blanchard's addition In lots 1, 2, 3	
KILDOW, ADAM H.	Blanchard's addition In lots 4, 5, 6, 7, 8	
KILDOW, ADAM H.	Parrett's addition In lots 7 & 8	54.88
VANDUYN, ELLA	East one half In lots 37 & 38	25.65

Town Lots in Alta

NAME	LOTS	TAX
McCUNE, HENRY C.	In lots 41 & 42	4.36
THOMPSON, WALLACE	In lots 81, 82, 83	3.15

Town lots in Dana

NAME	LOTS	TAX
AIKMAN, ADALINE	In lot 18, Block 6	9.64
WATSON, D.C.	In lot 11 & 12, Block 3	
WATSON, D.C.	In lot 13 & 14, Block 2	22.13

Town lots in Clinton

NAME	LOTS	TAX
CANADAY, WILLIAM A.	19 feet Northside In lot 1, Block 18	
CANADAY, WILLIAM A.	South one half In lot 2, Block 18	
CANADAY, WILLIAM A.	In lot 3, Block 18	33.91
COOPER, JOHN	North one half In lot 1, Block 18	
COOPER, JOHN	Knowles addition In lot 1, Block 4	15.31
HAYS, J.M. & W.A.	North one third In lot 1, Block 3	37.96
PERRIN, HYDE heirs	In lot 5, Block 16	22.61
ROGERS, LEONARD	Knowles addition In lot 1, Block 3	15.96
ROGERS, LEONARD	In lot 7 & 10, Block 3	3.19
WELLS, GEORGE heirs	In lot 7, block 30	26.92

Wednesday, January 23, 1889

Pumpkin Vine News
A rumor has reached this place that JOHN DINWIDDIE, who went to Arkansas shortly after the election, died upon his arrival there. We do not vouch for the authenticity of the story, however.

According to the Vinton, IA, Eagle, two of our former Vermillion County boys, J.E. and W.P. WHIPPLE, of Eugene, have located at that place to engage in the law and real estate business. J.E. WHIPPLE is the real estate man and W.P. is the lawyer in the firm GILCHRIST & WHIPPLE. Luck to you boys.

Fodder Shock Nubbins
Dana News
At the residence of Mr. JAMES OSBORN, a birthday party was given in honor of Miss MAGGIE DAVIS, on her 15th anniversary, last Friday night. Quite a number of young folks participated in the splendid supper and social enjoyment.

Summit Grove Items
CREWS JAMES and CY DOWNS are talking of planting 40 acres of sorghum in the spring to be manufactured into vinegar, which they will ship to Siberia.

Mr. JAMES CONLEY got off of the southbound train last Wednesday morning and started to walk home. He had gone about one mile from Summit when he became very sick, somewhat delirious, lost his way and started back again. Mr. FRIST happened to meet him, and seeing his condition, helped him to the house of JOE JAMES. After resting a short time, JOE took him in his buggy and started home with him, but about two miles out he became so sick that he had to stop again. His family was notified, and in the evening he was taken home where he has since been in a dangerous condition. Fears are entertained that he will not recover.

Sheriff's Sale on Decree
    State of Indiana vs. WILEY G. SLATER & MARTHA J. SLATER
    $695.64
    Sale to be held Saturday, February 16, 1889
    Sale at courthouse between 10 and 4
        SE ¼ NW ¼ Sec 28 T 16 N R 9 W – 40 acres
        N end of W ½ SE ¼ Sec 28 – 30 acres
        N end of E ½ SW ¼ Sec 28 – 22 ½ acres
    Filed January 25, 1889
    RHOADS & AIKMAN, Attorneys for plaintiff
                      WILLIAM RHEUBY, Sheriff

Home News
GEORGE H. McNEILL, of Perrysville, has been appointed administrator of the estate of PETER CRIPPEN, deceased.

JOHN GALLOWAY, who is working in the blacksmith shops of the street railway company of Terre Haute, will move his family down there this week.

SILAS HOLLINGSWORTH, who is working in a fertilizing establishment at Indianapolis, came home last Saturday night and returned to his work yesterday morning. He is getting $1.75 per day and board.

Dr. FRANK TURNER, wholesale and retail dealer of catnip for this locality, has a young swigger at his house of the female gender, which arrived promptly at 5 o'clock on last Thursday evening, and gave three unearthly war whoops for a bowl of catnip before it was 15 minutes old.

W.C. MYERS, an ex-sheriff of this county, who has been undergoing treatment at Danville, IL, since last fall for catarrh or cancer of the head, does not seem to be improving any. His nose is all eaten away, and the roof of his mouth, and his throat do not seem to heal. He had a gathering in one of his ears a few days ago, which is supposed to have originated from the disease of his throat and nostrils.

Dr. FRANK TURNER sold REESE MITCHELL 10 pounds of catnip one day last week, at the usual 3 % discount for cash. It is a boy and arrived one week ago last Thursday.

Surprise
Friday, January 18th, 1889 was the 69th birthday of ABEL SEXTON, Esq., who is one of the many successful and prominent men of our county seat, and is universally esteemed for his manifest interest in town, county and state, but in nothing has his interest been deeper than in the home Sunday School work. His record is a remarkable one, he having served for 21 years as S.S. Supt. of the M.E. Church in Newport, and with such efficiency and general favor, that he has recently been re-elected to serve another term. The pastors, teachers, officers, and choir of the Sunday School learned of his birthday and gave him a surprise party.

Lingering
FRANK ARRASMITH, the victim of the billiard ball matinee in the north side saloon of this place, five weeks ago last Saturday night, is gradually growing worse, and his chances for recovery are now very slim. He has not taken any nourishment to amount to anything for a week, and for the last day or two refuses to take medicine. He lies in a comatose condition, and does not pay any attention to anyone. He is unable to rise up in bed, and complains of his head and neck hurting him. He has fallen away very much in flesh in the last two weeks, and we doubt if he survives.

Death
Mr. PERRY S. WESTFALL, editor of the Terre Haute Saturday Evening Mail, who was stricken down with paralysis one week ago last Friday evening, died at 6:15 o'clock on last Thursday morning, January 17, 1889. Mr. WESTFALL had been identified with the newspaper interests of Terre Haute for many years, and was a man whom everybody respected. He learned the printing trade in the Express office, and in 1860 became manager of that paper. In 1872 he embarked in the newspaper business in his own hook, purchasing the Saturday Evening Mail of Major O.J. SMITH. The Evening Mail under his good management gained a strong foothold in Indiana, and today is one of the best literary papers published in the state. In his sad and unexpected death, the city of Terre Haute loses one of its best and most highly respected citizens. The deceased leaves a wife, four sons, and two daughters, and a host of friends to deeply sympathize with them in their sad affliction. The remains were consigned to their last resting place on Sunday last.

Death
MAHALA NICHOLAS, living four miles north of Gessie, died on January 12, 1889, aged nearly 74 years. She had been quite an invalid for a number of years past, and for the last seven months was confined entirely to her bed. She was a daughter of RICHARD SHUTE, of this county, long since deceased, and sister to EPHRAIM, DANIEL and JOHN SHUTE, all prominent men in this county. She was born in Gallia County, OH, and came with her father's family to this county in 1820. In 1835 she was married to WILLIAM NICHOLAS, who, at the age of 80 years, still survives her. She was the mother of 6 children, three of whom are living to mourn for a mother who will never come back to them. She had been a member of the Methodist Church for more than 30 years, and bore her long and tedious illness with fortitude and Christian resignation. Her funeral was preached in Howard's Chapel by her pastor, the Rev. Mr. WILEY, and was largely attended – many being her friends and neighbors who had known her for more than 30 years.

Death
Mrs. NANCY HAYES, of St. Bernice, Helt Township, was stricken down with paralysis on last Friday night and died the next day. Her remains were interred in the Sugar Grove Cemetery, west of that village, in the edge of Illinois. She was 71 years of age, and only recently received a pension, getting nearly $1000 in arrears.

Death

Col. R.H. WASHBURN, of Clinton, informed us a few days ago that his brother, WILLIAM O. WASHBURN, was dead. He died at Wichita, KS, where he was teaching in the public schools at the time he took sick. He died sometime last November, but Col. WASHBURN was only recently informed of the sad event. He had written him two or three letters, and getting no answer from him, finally wrote the postmaster of that place, who answered his letter and told him that his brother had died.

Sudden Death

Mrs. LUCINDA BROWN, landlady of the Brown Hotel of Eugene, died very suddenly of heart disease on last Thursday night, after an illness of only about one week, aged 68 years. Mrs. BROWN owned the hotel, and had been running it since the death of her husband several years ago. She was a very estimable lady, and we believe a member of the M.E. Church. Her funeral took place on Saturday last, her remains being interred in the Eugene Cemetery. She leaves two children, both daughters, who have made their home with her for many years.

Married

FROST HEFFLEMAN and Mrs. MATILDA MAXWELL, both of this township, were united in wedlock yesterday morning by Esq. ALBERT HENDERSON.

Wednesday, January 30, 1889

Official Directory
County Officers

A.R. HOPKINS	Clerk
WILLIAM B. HOOD	Treasurer
WILLIAM M. HAMILTON	Auditor
MELVILLE B. CARTER	Recorder
WILLIAM RHEUBY	Sheriff
GEORGE W. DEALAND	County Superintendent
ROBERT V. PARRETT	Surveyor
THOMAS BRINDLEY	Coroner
FRANK RILEY	Commissioner
GEORGE HAWORTH	Commissioner
WILLIAM F. KERNS	Commissioner

Eloped

On last Tuesday, JOHN JONES, son of JOSEPH JONES, living two miles north of Highland, Helt Township, eloped with a woman by the name of SOPHIA GARDNER. This Mrs. GARDNER is a grass widow, and a sister to HENRY BABCOCK's wife, and an own aunt of JOHN JONES' wife, the man she ran off with. HENRY BABCOCK resides one mile west of Hillsdale, where Mrs. GARDNER has been stopping for some time, making it her home. JOHN JONES resides about one half mile west of BABCOCK's, on JOHN OSBORN's farm. It has been known for some time that JONES and Mrs. GARDNER were too intimate, but the news never got into circulation until JONES told his wife, a few days before he left for Indianapolis. JOHN JONES leaves a good wife in very poor circumstances.

Fodder Shock Nubbins
Dana News

On last Sunday, while toying with a blank cartridge at home, TOM ALLEN, son of Mr. GEORGE ALLEN, was quite seriously injured in the hand by the explosion of the cartridge.

We learn that our old friend and former businessman ALF McDONALD, late of Montezuma, has rented the Boyles building on Front Street and will put in a mammoth stock of dry goods, etc.

A little melee occurred last Thursday night at the residence of S.E. KAUFMAN about two miles east of town, which resulted in a painful fracture to Mr. KAUFMAN and the flight of the assailant. JOE FRENCH, who had worked at the KAUFMAN Brickyard for some time, got into an altercation with Mr. KAUFMAN, and struck him with a long club, the blow crushing Mr. KAUFMAN's shoulder. The wounded man sent out here for an officer to arrest FRENCH, but he could not find his game. At this writing, Mr. KAUFMAN is improving.

Married
On last Monday night at the residence of ALEX HARRISON at this place, Mr. WILLIAM MORRISON and Miss IDA HOWARD, Rev. J.E. WRIGHT officiating. Mr. MORRISON is about 40 years of age, and his bride yet under 19. They will locate in Dana.

Died
JESSE RUNYAN, commonly known as Uncle JESSE, died at his home January 24th, 1889, after a short illness of four days. Mr. RUNYAN was an old and respected citizen. He was born in Ohio in 1810, moved to Vermillion County in 1841, and was 79 years old at the time of his death. He was universally respected by all who knew him. Ten children, 46 grandchildren, and 6 great grandchildren survive him.

Home News
GRANT DAVIS, of Dana, is jubilating over his first baby. It is a fine boy, and arrived on last Saturday night.

Mrs. H.O. PETERS, of Brimfield, IL, has donated a beautiful lot in Eugene for the erection of the new Presbyterian Church.

Miss EFFIE HALL writes back from Jonesboro, Arkansas, that she is well pleased with her home among the dusky natives of the south.

We are glad to learn that J.M. HARPER, of Helt's Prairie, who has been near death's door for several weeks, is now beyond the danger line, and is rapidly convalescing.

The wife of NEWTON COCKRUM, of Benton, IL, last week gave birth to twin girl babies weighing 26 pounds. They are regarded as monstrosities in the baby line.
                                          Sullivan Union

JAMES HENRY of Clinton, and HENRY SHAFFER of Helt Township, have received the pleasing information that their pensions have been increased. Both were old soldiers of Company C, 18th IN Regiment.

Notice
The partnership of GALLOWAY & BRILES is dissolved. All persons knowing themselves indebted to said firm, will please not settle until books have been straightened and a collector appointed.
                                          J.W. GALLOWAY
                                          Terre Haute, IN

Died
The infant child of GEORGE and MATTIE FORD, died of whooping cough at 2 o'clock this morning. It was eight weeks old yesterday.

Letter List
    A.M. KIMBER   ORSEN WHITE
    Miss ELIJA FRIST   Miss EVA MYERS
    Miss NANCY J. ISINBUGER

Notice of Administration
> Estate of LUCINDA E. BROWN, deceased
> Filed January 23, 1889
>> HUGH H. CONLEY, Admininstrator

Notice of Administration
> Estate of PETER CRIPPEN, deceased
> Filed January 21, 1889
>> GEORGE H. McNEILL, Administrator

Married
ALBERT HENDERSON, of this township, united in wedlock on Sunday last, Mr. MICHAEL RUSK, of Parkerville, Parke County, and Miss SARAH R. REMLEY, of this township. The marriage was brought about by an advertisement inserted in the Hoosier a few months ago by Mr. RUSK, who stated that he wanted a wife.

Died
Mrs. SARAH GREGG, of Frankfort, wife of ROBERT GREGG, while engaged in a giddy dance at her residence on Tuesday night of last week, suddenly took sick and started for the door. Her husband noticed there was something the matter with her as she passed out the door, and followed her. He found her lying on the steps, and at once carried her in the house where she expired in a minute or two. She was afflicted with heart disease. She was 46 years of age, and had children grown. Her son was dancing with her at the time she became sick.

Married
On the 25th of January, 1889, at 1:30 p.m., Mr. HENDERSON RIDGELY, Esq. and Miss EMILY S. PARKER were united in the holy bonds of matrimony at Newport, IN, Rev. R.S. MARTIN of the M.E. Church officiating. There were present to witness the event, Judge C.W. WARD, County Clerk HOPKINS, and others who joined the congratulating the handsome and happy pair. The groom is a man of fine physical appearance, and in business circles is both prominent and successful. He is at present City Controller of Springfield, IL, and for many years has been one of the Government's trusted officials. The bride is a tall, handsome, and intelligent blonde, and will be a worthy companion and helpmate. They will make their future home in Springfield, IL.

Sheriff's Sale on Decree
> State of Indiana vs. DAVID S. HOPKINS, JOHN MANNING, etc.
> $878.17
> Sale to be held Saturday, February 16, 1889
> Sale at courthouse between 10 and 4
>> W ½ NE ¼ Sec 34, T 17 N R 9 W – 80 acres
> Filed January 23, 1889
> RHOADS & AIKMAN, attorneys for plaintiff
>> WILLIAM RHEUBY, Sheriff

Notice of Assignment for creditors
> All property of JOHN W. JARVIS & JOHN NORRIS, partners in business in Dana
> Business known as JARVIS & NORRIS
> All individual property of JOHN NORRIS
>> JAMES C. SAWYER, Assignee

Home News
SAM D. COLLETT, who is attending the polytechnic institute at Terre Haute, spent last Sunday with his parents and young friends of this place.

ED SMITH, the colored barber of Danville, IL, is whiling away his precious time in the jail of that city on the charge of running a house of ill fame. He was a former resident of this place.

Married
At the residence of the Rev. MATER, in Hillsdale, on January 24th, 1889, Mr. ALBERT SHORT and Mrs. MAGGIE LADD, both of the Prairie State.

Married
SEVREE BROWN, of Cayuga, and Miss LYDIA HOGUE, of Vermillion County, IL, were joined in wedlock on Sunday last, at the residence of the U.B. parsonage, by Rev. R.B. VAN ALLEN.

Wednesday, February 6, 1889

Real Estate Transfers for January 1889
MARY E. HINES etal to ALONZO JOHNS
80 acres in Helt Township
$3,600

SMITH McCORMACK, guardian, to E.G. McCORMACK
Part of Lot 13 in Perrysville
$78

W.W. PORTER to JOHN C. PORTER
3 acres in Eugene Township
$1,500

JAMES PEYTON to JOHN C. PEYTON
40 acres in Helt Township
$800

EMMET ANSTEAD and husband to A.V. BROWN etal
2 lots in Clinton
$600

F.A. DUDLEY to DAVID McBETH
Lot in Clinton
$700

B.F. ELLIS to REBECCA R. ELLIS
50 acres in Vermillion Township
$800

PEGGY HOLLINGSWORTH to JESSE GIBSON
40 acres in Vermillion Township
$800

JOHN WHITCOMB to R.J. CRAIG
Lot in Clinton
$300

J. RANDALL to J.E. HANN
20 acres in Clinton Township
$200

J. PICKES to J. RANDALL
20 acres in Clinton Township
$200

H.B. HAMMOND to HARRY J. SPRAGUE
2 lots in Dana
$50

D. CRAIG to H.B. DUDLEY
Lot in Dana
$300

WILLIAM WOOD to F.M. SHORES
40 acres in Clinton Township
$900

H. HAMMOND to HARRY J. SPRAGUE
2 lots in Dana
$50

J.O. LUCE to ISAAC STRAIN
Lot in Clinton
$200

J.R. BERTOLETT to E.H. McDANIEL
Lot in Cayuga
$499

H. JORDAN to F.P. THORNE
25 acres in Helt Township
$1

F.P. THORNE to H. JORDAN
15 acres in Helt Township
$1

F.D. McKEE to W.T. MORGAN
Lot in Cayuga
$125

J.F. WILTERMOOD to E.E. DAVIS
Lot in Newport
$1,500

E. HOLLINGSWORTH to O.P. DAVIS
Land in Vermillion Township
$410

JOHN NORRIS to GEORGE P. NORRIS
2 lots in Dana
$500

JOHN W. NEEL to MARTHA J. NEEL
80 acres in Highland Township
$500

JOHN A. STRAIN to J.N. FRIST
Lot in Clinton
$150

E. ASBURY to T. St. L. & K.C. Railway
A strip of ground in Eugene Township
$52

R. HOLLINGSWORTH to OMER LUNGER
Lot in Newport
$1

SILAS HOLLINGSWORTH to OMER LUNGER
Lot in Newport
$100

L. SNYDER to GEORGE W. SNYDER
Out lot near Highland
$30

F.D. McKEE to MARY SIMPSON
Lot in Cayuga
$400

PRISCILLA POTTER to M.H. RANDALL
26 acres in Helt Township
$1,000

M.G. RHOADS to J.F. COMPTON
Lot in Perrysville
$950

EPHRAIM SHUTE to MARY McLAUGHLIN
10 acres in Highland Township
$462.10

A NICHOLS to PEGGY HOLLINGSWORTH
40 acres in Vermillion Township
$1,850

PEGGY HOLLINGSWORTH to J. HOLLINGSWORTH
? acres in Vermillion Township
$250

PEGGY HOLLINGSWORTH to C.H. CARTER
11 acres in Vermillion Township
$1

PEGGY HOLLINGSWORTH to PATIENCE HOLLINGSWORTH
15 acres in Vermillion Township
$1

S.D. GALLAHER to W.H. SKIDMORE
Lot in Dana
$100

JAMES A. ARRASMITH to MARY A. KUNKLE
? acres in Vermillion Township
$250

WASHINGTON POTTER to EMMA F. SHANNON
? acres in Clinton Township
$69

THOMAS J. WEST to JOHN A. FONCANNON
46 acres in Helt Township
$600

Z.P. THORNTON will vacate the Newport Hotel on the first of next month. He will move into his residence on South Main Street, and still continue to run the "bus line", carry the mail, freight and express goods. A man by the name of TOM ELLIS, of Marshall, IL, formerly a resident of Eugene Township, will take charge of the hotel.

Home News
EL FORTNER, of Heckland, Vigo County, was in town yesterday.

ROY VAN ALLEN, the little son of Rev. R.B. VAN ALLEN, is dangerously ill.

Squire N.M. TUTT, of Highland, on Saturday last, bought out WILLIAM SWINDELL of that village, paying him $1,000 cash for his drug store and stock, and his residence.

FRANK WILTERMOOD, of Opedee, has purchased the Hollywood Saloon at Waterman, Parke County, and will move over there this week.

Married
JOHN C. PORTER, of Portertown, and Miss ALICE WOODARD, of Cayuga, Eugene Township, were married at 11 o'clock a.m. on Sunday last, Rev. R.B. VAN ALLEN, pastor of the U.B. Church performing the ceremony.

Obituary
On Wednesday last, PAUL DAVIS, son of HOWARD and LUELLA DAVIS of Helt Township, died after an illness of only a few days, aged nearly 7 months. The funeral occurred on the day following his death at Salem M.E. Church, Rev. MEREDITH preaching a short discourse, after which the remains were interred in the Helt's Prairie Cemetery. He was a bright and beautiful little child, and the idol of his parents, who will sadly mourn the loss of their dear little one.

Matrimony
Mr. JOSEPH T. COONCE, of Humrick, IL, was united in wedlock to Miss MARIA NICHOLS, daughter of T.J. NICHOLS, of this place, on last Saturday evening, the ceremony taking place at the residence of the bride's parents. Rev. JOHN W. PARRETT, of the M.E. Church, was the officiating minister.

Married
By Rev. W.A. SMITH, on the evening of January 31st, 1889, in Perrysville, at the residence of Mrs. LANGLEY, Mr. WILLIAM H. TATE, of Chrisman, IL, and Miss NELLIE LUSADDER, of Perrysville. Their home is to be in Chrisman. The young couple are favorably known here.

The Eugene fair society have elected the following officers for the ensuing year:
    JAMES MALONE, President
    H.D. SPRAGUE, Vice President
    J.S. GRONDYKE, Secretary
    M.G. HOSFORD, Assistant Secretary
    GEORGE L. WATSON, Treasurer

Pumpkin Vine News
Clinton Argus
Mrs. MICHAEL CASEY received a telegram from Minnesota Thursday, that her brother, CHARLES CUNNINGHAM, was about to die. She leaves Saturday.

Mrs. FRANK SHEPHERDSON, wife of editor SHEPHERDSON of the Granville Ohio Times, and son, are visiting her parents, Mr. and Mrs. JOHN WHITCOMB of this city.

Fodder Shock Nubbins
Dana News
JOHN MALONE has sold out to OMER NICHOLS his poultry establishment. He could not attend to it and the gravel road also.

Following are some of the names of those who have united with the M.E. Church at Bono:
> MYRTLE & OSA BARNHART, ROSE BOREN, Col. HIGHFILL and wife, GEORGE PUETT, ROY AIKMAN, BIRD MALONE, WILLIAM PEER and wife, ANNIE CHEESEWRIGHT, ERVAN SANDERFORD and wife.

Public Sale
> Auction at residence 4 miles SW of Perrysville, IN, on the Eugene & Danville Road
> Saturday, February 23, 1889
> All household goods, farm implements, cows, pigs, etc.
>> J. MART SMITH
>> W.J. MOORE, Auctioneer

Notice to Non-Residents
> MEREDITH LEWIS & MEREDITH LEWIS, Executor
> Vs.
> MARY LEWIS, ISAAC LEWIS, ELLEN HOWARD, SARAH NICHOLS, NANCY FLEMING, JOSHUA LEWIS, JOHN LEWIS, FRANK LEWIS, CHARLES H. LEWIS, EMMA LEWIS, CHARLES J. STUTLER, JOHN F. LEWIS, AMERICUS LEWIS, EMMA L. RAINBOLE
> RHOADS & AIKMAN, Attorneys for plaintiff
> ISAAC LEWIS, ELLEN HOWARD, NANCY FLEMING, JOHN W. LEWIS, FRANK LEWIS, & AMERICUS LEWIS are not residents of Indiana
> Must appear before 2nd Monday in March
> Filed January 23, 1889
>> A.R. HOPKINS, Clerk

Death
We are called upon this week to chronicle the death of Uncle ALVA ARRASMITH, which occurred at 9 a.m. on Thursday last at the residence of his son-in-law, MARTIN HARRIS, who resides 2 miles south of Camargo, IL. Uncle ALVA had made his home with Mr. HARRIS since the latter part of last October. His wife died on the 13th of that month and after her death he concluded he would rather spend the rest of his days with his daughter. He had been a resident of this township since 1851, moving here from Putnam County, near Greencastle, where he has a sister still living. The deceased united with the M.E. Church when only 14 years of age, and was a consistent member up to the day of his death. He was 80 years old on the 26th of last October, but for several years had been in feeble health. The remains were interred in the Thomas Cemetery.

Clinton Echoes
The prospect of opening a new coal works near is good. A vein 5 ½ feet thick and of extra quality has been found on the J.J. HIGGINS' farm.

It is an evident fact that many of our boys are happy again to be endowed with the power of matrimonial proposition. During the past week the following persons appeared before CADI McDOUGALL and joined their fates for the remainder of their natural lives:
- LEVI TAYLOR and ANNA CHUNN
- BRUCE HARRISON and BELLE SHEW
- OTIS SHANON and MATTIE FREEMAN

Justice McDOUGALL performed the ceremony and Justice WISHARD offered congratulations.

Wednesday, February 13, 1889

County Clerk A.R. HOPKINS issued the following marriage licenses during the month of January:
- WILLIAM F. KELTZ to LAURA A. VESTAL
- EDWARD J. JONES to ALICE THOMPSON
- FRED CLOUSER to ELIZABETH WILKINS
- BENJAMIN S. HOWE to LORA CROSS
- JOSEPH V. SIMS to ELIZABETH DAVIS
- WILLIAM F. MORRISON to IDA HOWARD
- F.H. HEFFLEMAN to MATILDA MAXWELL
- ALBERT SHORT to MAGGIE LADD
- HENDERSON RIDGELY to EMILY S. PARKER
- SEVREE BROWN to LYDIA A. HOGUE
- MICHAEL RUSK to SARAH REMLEY
- WILLIAM H. TATE to NELLIE LUSADDER
- JOHN C. PORTER to ALICE WOODARD
- BRUCE HARRISON to AURILLA B. SHEW
- LEVI TAYLOR to ANNA CHUNN

Made an Assignment
ANDY JACKSON, a farmer and stock dealer of Helt Township, has made an assignment for the benefit of his creditors. He selected M.G. RHOADS as assignee to settle up his business. He had recently negotiated for a loan to bridge him over, and pay off his indebtedness, but his new wife refused to sign the mortgage, and now he has to sacrifice the earnings of a lifetime to pay his debts. He owns 320 acres of land, all of which is under mortgage.

The following is a list of divorces and the names of the parties to whom granted, during 1888:
- MATTHEW A. GRAY vs. NETTIE G. GRAY, granted to plaintiff
- HANNAH VALENTINE vs. WILLIAM A. VALENTINE, granted to plaintiff
- MARCELLUS TRAPHAGAN vs. SUSAN TRAPHAGAN, granted to defendant
- DAVID BARKER vs. KITTY A. BARKER, granted to plaintiff
- CATHERINE WATSON vs. DEWIT WATSON, granted to plaintiff
- MARY A. GEER vs. JOHN GEER, granted to plaintiff
- ELLA VANLEER vs. HENRY VANLEER, granted to plaintiff
- LOUISA EDWARDS vs. WILLIAM H. EDWARDS, granted to plaintiff
- SARAH BUFFEY vs. SAMUEL BUFFEY, granted to plaintiff
- JOSEPHINE BRACKEN vs. JOHN W. BRACKEN, granted to plaintiff
- SARAH M. WRIGHT vs. JACOB WRIGHT, granted to plaintiff
- MINNIE M. CURTIS vs. JOHN B. CURTIS, granted to plaintiff
- JOHN W. NEEL vs. MARY J. NEEL, granted to defendant

Clinton Echoes
Miss VIOLA BRUCE is very low with lung and pneumonia fever, and is not expected to recover.

Uncle TOM KIBBY, an old and respected citizen of Clinton Township, died last Saturday evening after a brief illness of one week. Uncle TOM was 78 years old, but as hale as most men at 50.

Died
Little DAN HARRISON, son of BENNY HARRISON, after a lingering illness of many weeks with that dread disease, typhoid fever, died last Friday night at 11 o'clock. Another of Mr. HARRISON's boys is very low with dropsy.

Death
Uncle TOM KIBBY, who resided a short distance west of Clinton, died at 6 o'clock last Saturday evening of lung fever, after an illness of only a few days. He was born in Ohio in 1810 and settled in Clinton Township in 1830, being one of the old settlers of our county. He was 79 years of age, and was stout and active, before his last sickness, for one of his age. Everyone liked Uncle TOM. Col. R.H. WASHBURN, of Clinton, furnishes us the following brief biographical sketch of Uncle TOM KIBBY, who died on last Saturday night: He was born February 8, 1810, at Jeffersonville, Clark County, IN. He died February 9, 1889, aged 79 years and one day. He moved to Clinton in 1830, and was married to JANE VANNEST who died some years ago. He made 63 trips to New Orleans on flat boats, making his first trip in 1833. He leaves two sons, THOMAS A. and ISAAC. He was sick 9 days, his ailment being lung fever. He leaves his two sons 300 acres of land.

Obituary
Being requested, I send the notice of the death of Mrs. CARRIE JAMES, wife of MAURICE JAMES and daughter of WILLIAM KEARNS, who died at her residence, 3 miles west of Hillsdale, on Wednesday, February 6th, 1889. The remains were interred at the Helt's Prairie Cemetery the next day. She left a husband and two sons, with many friends to mourn her loss. She said a short time before she died that she was going to be with her two small children, parents, mother JACKSON, and other friends who had passed on before.

Death
At 10 minutes before 1 o'clock on last Thursday afternoon, the spirit of FRANK ARRASMITH took its flight to that unknown world. His death makes the fourth person who has been murdered in this county since the 18th of last March. In this case there does not seem to be much division of opinion. Nearly everyone thinks that CHARLEY VANVLEIT, the murderer, was justified. But this matter will be for the jury to decide. ARRASMITH was hit in the head by a billiard ball on Saturday, December 15th, 1888. The ball, when it struck him, was thrown with such force, it felled him. When an autopsy was held, it was found that the concussion had injured the brain and formed a sack of puss. How he managed to live as long as he did, is a mystery. On last Saturday at 10 a.m., the funeral occurred at the residence of his mother, there being a large attendance of neighbors and citizens present. The services were conducted by Rev. R.B. VAN ALLEN, pastor of the U.B. Church, after which his remains were conveyed to the Johnson Cemetery, 2 miles north of town.

Home News
The applicants for the Newport Postoffice are LEN WHEELER, Z.P. THORNTON, D.R. GRAY, and WILLIAM F. THORNTON.

It is now thought that it will not be long until OMER LUNGER and MARIA DUZAN will commence trotting in double harness.

JAMES CHIPPS, a doorkeeper of the Indiana Senate, came over here last week to attend the funeral of his nephew, FRANK ARRASMITH.

JOHN D. BROWN, an old soldier of the 11th IN, who resides in this place, has had his pension increased from $14 to $17 per month.

Esq. THOMPSON and MILT COFFIN, of Cayuga, are the aspirants for the postoffice at that place. We doubt if the squire is eligible, on account of being a Justice of the Peace.

SILAS HOLLINGSWORTH and family, including WILLIAM RITTENHOUSE, moved to Indianapolis yesterday morning, where they will make their future home.

R.H. MYERS, of Hutchinson, KS, arrived here on Wednesday last to spend a few days visiting relatives and old friends. He talks as though he might move back here, if he can find a good opening.

W.P. HENSON is crippling around on a crutch and cane, caused by his wound received in the foot, at Perrysville, KY, while fighting for Uncle Sam. PERRY gets the pitiful sum of $4 per month pension. He ought to have $30 per month.

Obituary
Died at Evanston, IL, Saturday, February 2, at 8:30 p.m., W.C. TOWLE of Eugene. The deceased was born at Exeter, Maine, July 29th, 1829. In 1859 he came to Eugene and went into business with his brother-in-law W.L. NAYLOR, and has since made that place his home. Mr. TOWLE was a man of strictest honesty, upright in his dealings and respected by all. He gave liberally to churches, Sabbath Schools, and all charitable objects. The remains were interred at Rose Hill on Tuesday of last week at 2 p.m.

Paralyzed
One evening last week, MADISON NICHOLS, of this place, who has been confined to his bed for a long time, was stricken down with paralysis, and for two or three days was unable to speak so that his family could understand him. But we are glad to note that he is now slowly improving, and that his attending physician has hopes of his speedy recovery.

Notice of Petition to Sell Real Estate
    WILLIAM H. HOOD, Admr. of Estate of ISAAC WAGGONER, deceased
    Vs.
    DANIEL WAGGONER, HENRY WAGGONER, REBECCA N. KROUT, MARY E. FARR, LYDIA M. DAVIESS, SARAH J. BOWERMAN, ELLEN F. HYBARGER, MARY J. WAGGONER
    Permission to sell real estate to pay debts
                                      A.R. HOPKINS, Clerk

Death
TOM McKNIGHT, of Clinton, informs us that his good old mother died at Dayton, OH, on the 1st of January, 1889, aged 85 years. She was a member of the Quaker Church, and died as she had lived, a true Christian woman. Mr. McKNIGHT informs us that his father, now 95 years of age, is still living. He has not seen his father for 25 years.

Notice to Non-Residents
    The Interstate Investment Co.
    Vs.
    JULIA B. HOSFORD
    WILLIAM EGGLESTON
    EDWARD REED
    Must appear before 2nd Monday in March 1889
                                      A.R. HOPKINS, Clerk

Notice of Application for Liquor License
    MONROE STARK – Newport
    EDMOND EDMONDS Jr. – Eugene
    CHARLES W. SIMPSON – Cayuga

Wednesday, February 20, 1889

Pumpkin Vine News
Clinton Argus
BRUCE BAILEY has withdrawn his name from the list of postoffice applicants.

A special telegram from Terre Haute brings the news of the sad death of Miss MAY QUICK at home in that city Friday morning of this week.

President CLEVELAND's overcoat wouldn't make a vest for attorney ISAAC H. STRAIN now-a-days. It's a fine healthy boy and arrived last week.

Death
Mr. VANHUSS, who has been for some time a helpless and penniless invalid, died last Wednesday at the residence of his son, near Jonestown, and was interred in the Spangler Cemetery on Thursday. Mr. VANHUSS is one of those persons to whom death was a pleasure. Being possessed of a meager amount of the world's goods, and his physical health destroyed, he became a pensioner on the county. His son made the best home for him that he could, but owing to the fact that he is a poor man and has a large family to support, he could not soothe the declining years of his aged parent, as he should like to have done.

Fodder Shock Nubbins
Dana News
Mrs. WILLIAM SLATER went, last week, to Iowa, to visit her mother who has been seriously ill.

JOHN WOODGATE and his wife were called to Waveland last week to attend the funeral of Mr. WOODGATE's father.

Mrs. HUNM, of Memphis, TN, and Mrs. G.W. TERRY, of Humboldt, IL, visited her brother, HORACE WELLS, of this place last week.

We hear that ALF McDONALD, who had intended to come to this place soon, has failed in business, and is completely broke and now of course will not come here.

BILLY MORRISON has bought SOLOMON CARPENTER's farm in the Tennessee Valley neighborhood, and he and his young wife have gone to housekeeping this week.

Home News
Miss ELMA VAN ALLEN, daughter of pastor VAN ALLEN of the U.B. Church, who has been ill for a couple of weeks, is now said to have the typhoid pneumonia fever. She is a sick girl, but the attending physician has hopes for her recovery.

Wednesday, February 27, 1889

Pumpkin Vine News
Clinton Argus
The 12 year old daughter of Mr. and Mrs. ISAAC ROGERS died on the 18th instant.

RILEY HOPKINS will establish a broom factory in town in a short time. Success to you RILEY.

Perrysville Items
Dr. J.T. HENDERSON has moved his office to Covington. His family will go as soon as school is out. We have not heard who will take his place.

Quaker Hill Siftings
ALLEN WALTHALL went to Wilmington, OH, last week to visit his brother and sister that are attending school there.

Clinton Echoes
JOHN WRIGHT and Dr. BOGART have purchased the Central House and livery stable of JOHN McMILLEN. Mr. McMILLEN and family are talking of going to Washington Territory. Wherever he strays, he will ever have the best wishes of his many friends at this place.
FLORENCE WHITE talks of leasing the hotel.

Stricken Down
At an early hour in the morning, on Wednesday last, the wife of WILLIAM DARNALL, who resides near Bono, Helt Township, was stricken down with paralysis, and at last account was in pretty bad condition. On that morning, she was sitting on a chair in front of the fire, when one of the little children came in with his hands nearly frozen. Mrs. DARNALL attempted to take off his gloves, her fingers seemed to be numb and she could not remove them. Her little daughter noticed that her face was drawn to one side. At this time, Mrs. DARNALL attempted to get up and go and look in the glass to see what was the matter with her face. On arising from the chair, she fell over on the floor as limp as a rag and as helpless as a child. Assistance soon arrived, when she was placed in bed and a physician called for. She is in a very dangerous condition, and fears are entertained that she might not recover.

Death
News was received here last week that JOHN GIBSON, son of WILLIAM GIBSON, ex-Clerk of this county, was shot in a row in Missouri recently, and died in three days after receiving the wound. The ball passed through his eye and into his brains. It is said that his brains oozed out of the wound, and that he was insensible from the time he was shot until death occurred. We did not obtain full particulars of the tragedy, but is supposed that he was engaged in gambling at the time the row occurred. In the spring of 1885, JOHN was arrested at Vincennes with some more gamblers for burglarizing a saloon in that place, and sentenced to the penitentiary for 4 or 5 years. Through the influence of his father and some influential political friends in this state, they persuaded Gov. GRAY to let him out on parole after he had served 2 years. He only remained in this state a short time after being released, and took his leave for Hutchinson, KS, where his father was then living. His father still resides in Kansas, but has moved out on to a large farm near that city. The deceased was about 30 years of age, and had an ungovernable temper.

From Helt
Miss TOTTIE CRANE came in from Augusta, KS, Monday. She said she had a lovely winter there.

Home News
Miss INEZ FRAZIER, who has been visiting relatives in Milwaukee, WI, for the past 3 months, returned home last Tuesday.

Mr. WILLIAM BISH, of Wayne County, this state, a brother of Mrs. ELIAS LAMB of this place, died on the 16th instant, aged 77 years.

JOSHUA DAVIS, of Newport, IN, came in Sunday to attend the funeral of his niece, Miss FLORA DAVIS.
						Altamont, KS, Sentinel

Uncle SAM HOOD and wife, of Dana, who have been trotting together in double harness for 50 years, will celebrate their golden wedding tomorrow. They were married in Helt Township, this county, and have always lived near where they now reside. We hope they live to celebrate many more wedding anniversaries.

Uncle MADISON NICHOLS, who has been on the sick list for a long time, and who was stricken down with a stroke of paralysis a few weeks ago, continues to about hold his own. He does not seem to improve or get worse. Some days he feels a little better, and then again not quite so well.

Mrs. JACOB DOWDELL received her pension certificate on Monday last. She gets $22 per month for herself and five little children. She gets arrears from April 9th.

Rev. JOHN P. HENSON, of Lamar, NB, arrived back here last week, on a short visit to the old folks. He looks as natural as ever. He is well pleased with his new home in the west.

W.P. HENSON is still confined to his room from the effects of the wound he received in his foot while serving Uncle SAM in the US Army. He was shot clear through the foot, near the instep, and his foot is now so swollen and sore that he cannot put on his shoe. The doctor thinks there is a gathering and that his foot will have to be lanced.

Sudden Death
The infant child of REESE D. MITCHELL, a bright little boy aged about 10 weeks, died very suddenly at an early hour on last Sunday morning. The little fellow seemed to be in his usual health at bedtime, but near 12 o'clock at night showed symptoms of not feeling well. He was given medicine which seemed to relieve him at the time, but at 3 o'clock in the morning he grew worse, and died before a physician could get there. The doctor pronounced his ailment paralysis of the stomach. The remains of the dear little one were interred in the Thomas Cemetery in the forenoon on last Monday. Brief funeral services were conducted at the home and cemetery by Rev. R.S. MARTIN of the M.E. Church, on Monday, February 25, 1889.

Died
Saturday, at 10 o'clock p.m., February 16th, 1889, at the home of her parents, Mr. and Mrs. R.A. DAVIS, one mile northwest of town of consumption, Miss FLORA DAVIS, aged 20 years, 11 months, and 10 days. Miss FLORA was born in Fairmount, Vermillion County, IN, March 6th, 1868.
                                                                       Altamont, KS, Sentinel
The father of the deceased was a son of the late Uncle SAMMY DAVIS, of this place, and at one time was a resident of Newport.

Marriage
In the parlors of the M.E. parsonage at Newport on February 23rd, 1889, Mr. SOLOMON DeVOSS and Miss ROSETTA GRAVES, both of Perrysville, IN, were united in matrimony by Rev. R.S. MARTIN. The young couple will make their future home 20 miles north of Perrysville, where a farm has already been secured by them.

Birthday Surprise
Yesterday, Mr. ROBERT D. MOFFATT, of Perrysville, was 77 years old, and was very pleasantly surprised by his friends calling at noon with full baskets of good things, and setting up a spread that would be good enough for a king. Among those present were his daughters, Mrs. M.G. RHOADS of Newport, Mrs. Judge B.E. RHOADS of Terre Haute, Mrs. JOHN F. COMPTON of Perrysville and their husbands; his son WALTER E. MOFFATT of Terre Haute, and all the grandchildren, and Mr. R.J. GESSIE and THOMAS CUSHMAN.

Marriage
On last Sunday night, at 8 o'clock, Rev. R.B. VAN ALLEN, pastor of the U.B. Church, united in wedlock Mr. OMER LUNGER of Eugene, and Miss MARIA DUZAN of this place, the ceremony taking place in the parlor of the Newport Hotel. They will occupy their residence in this place, and make Newport their future home.

Public Sale
Sale to be held Thursday, March 7, 1889 at farm 1 ½ miles north of Eugene
Horses, colts, ponies, cows, farming equipment, etc.
H.O. PETERS

Wednesday, March 6, 1889

Made His Escape
On last Saturday night, SYLVESTER GRUBB, who is under the sentence of death for killing his sweetheart, because she would not marry him, escaped from the Vincennes Jail by drilling his way through the top of his cage. The time fixed for his execution was April 19th.

Perrysville Items
The Misses IMO and ZADAH COLLINS will go to Ridgefarm Monday evening to furnish music for a dance at that place. Miss IMO COLLINS has been teaching music this winter at Logansport.

Fodder Shock Nubbins
Dana News
JESSE KAUFMAN, living near Staats School house has traded his farm of 80 acres to J.F. COOK for his livery stable and stock at Cayuga. Mr. KAUFMAN has moved to that place.

Mr. WILLIAM HENDRIX, of Highland, has bought SOLON JOHNSON's farm, of about 140 acres, on old Clinton Road near "No. 17". Mr. HENDRIX was out here last Wednesday fixing up the deeds. He will not move on the place until after harvest.

Married
On Wednesday night, February 27th, 1889, Mr. LON CLEARWATERS and Miss EMMA HOLLINGSWORTH were united in wedlock or were to be. Both live in Vermillion Chapel neighborhood.

Clinton Echoes
Mr. and Mrs. T.B. MYERS celebrated their 12th wedding anniversary February 22nd, 1889. Quite a large crowd of invited guests were present and enjoyed the occasion.

WILLIAM SOLIDAY, who has been at work some time on the paper in St. Louis, is visiting his parents at this place.

Home News
WILLIAM P. BELL and his brother-in-law, J.T. HARVEY, returned home from Kansas City, MO, on last Friday night. They talk of remaining here.

Dr. FRANK TURNER received a telegram from C.S. DAVIS, of Dana, at an early hour on last Monday morning, requesting the immediate shipment of 28 pounds of catnip. It is a girl, weighs 9 ½ pounds, and arrived at 11 o'clock on last Sunday night.

Dr. E.C. LOOMIS, of Millbrook, KS, has located at Perrysville to practice medicine. He comes very highly recommended by eminent physicians, and has opened out at the old stand lately occupied by Dr. HENDERSON. He is an old soldier, having served 3 years and 8 months in the Union Army.

DORA STEWART, of this township, was united in wedlock one day last week to a Miss FRAZIER, who is said to be a very estimable lady. The ceremony was performed by Rev. R.B. VAN ALLEN, pastor of the U.B. Church.

CASPER LAKE, son of JOHN LAKE of Hillsdale, aged about 23 years, died of consumption on last Saturday night, and was interred on Monday.

List of letters

WILLIAM PARRETT   H.G. DENNIS
DOCK BRUSH   JASPER SINGLETON
C.W. HAMILTON

Marriage
Wednesday evening, February 27th, 1889, at 7 o'clock, the cozy farm home of Mr. JOHN BRINDLEY, near Vermillion Memorial Church, was taken possession of by a number of invited guests, who witnessed the marriage ceremony of Mr. WILLIAM ALONZO CLEARWATERS and Miss EMMA HOLLINGSWORTH, both of Vermillion County. Rev. R.S. MARTIN, of the Newport M.E. Church officiated at the ceremony. The happy couple will continue to reside in the home community where they have been so long and favorably known.

Marriage Licenses issued by Clerk A.R. HOPKINS for February
   JOSEPH T. COONCE to MARIA NICHOLS
   SOLOMON DeVOSS to ROSETTA A. GRAVES
   JAMES E. SPENCER to SARAH M. LANGLEY
   OMER LUNGER to MARIA DUZAN
   WILLIAM A. CLEARWATERS to: EMMA HOLLINGSWORTH
   HARRY C. MALONE to MARY BARNHART
   DORA STEWART to FLORELLA D. FRAZIER

Marriage
At the town residence of Mr. LEVI ARRASMITH, on the evening of March 1, 1889, Mr. WILLIAM HOUT, of Danville, IL, and Miss MOLLIE MYERS, of Indianola, IL, were united in matrimony by Rev. R.S. MARTIN. The groom is a successful millwright of Illinois and the bride is a niece of Miss LEVI ARRASMITH of this city.

Obituary
GRACE RUHL was born December 21st, 1874, in Perrysville, IN, and died in the same place February 14th, 1889, 15 minutes past 10 o'clock of consumption. She was a bright, beautiful, little girl, and had many friends among the young people. About 14 months ago she took a severe cold that never left her; she had a strong determination not to give up, but the serious effects of which she at length yielded, and though loving her school and books, her school days on earth are ended, and she was taken to the school above. She received the ordinance of baptism and was taken into church fellowship February 5th. She died as one in sweet sleep. A large audience followed her remains to the cemetery, where a funeral discourse by Rev. J.M. MILLS, was held. A father, mother, and one little sister here, and one grown sister in New York are left to mourn her.

Real Estate Transfers for February 1889
   W.W. PORTER to JOE COLLETT
   58 acres in Eugene Township
   $3,600

   T.D. McKEE etal to S.W. COFFIN
   Lot in Cayuga
   $150

   SAM AIKMAN to JOHN MALONE
   Lot in Dana
   $25

   WILLIAM JAMES to SILAS DAVIS
   2 lots in Clinton
   $30

H.D. SPRAGUE to JAMES SHEWARD
Lot in Eugene
$75

S.P. HEDGES to MATTHEW W. SCOTT
Lot in Clinton
$950

MARTIN PATRICK to GEORGE L. PRIEST
2 acres in Eugene Township
$?

T.D. McKEE etal to W.T. COFFIN
Lot in Cayuga
$125

HIRAM DROLLINGER to ELIZABETH CAROLINE DeVOSS
2 lots in Perrysville
$200

HAM BETSON to ARTHUR BETSON
? acres in Vermillion County
$3,000

JNO. CLARK to J.H. BOGART
40 acres in Clinton Township
$1,600

R.H. NIXON to KERDOLFF & DILLOW
Lot in Newport
$454

MARGARET HOLTZ to C.W. SIMPSON
Lot in Cayuga
$550

W.H. SKIDMORE to HOMER D. DAVIS
Lot in Dana
$500

MARTIN PETTY to LUCINDA LLOYD
2 lots in Clinton
$400

J.L. EGGLESTON etal to SAM J. HALL & J.C. SAWYER
Tract of land in Vermillion Township
$600

WILLIAM COLLETT to C.B. HOOTEN
165 acres in Eugene Township
$7,500

ADAM ZENER to W.C. ARRASMITH
2 lots in Newport
$150

CORA A. McMILLEN to J.H. BOGART & JOHN WRIGHT
3 lots in Clinton
$3,000

W.H. SKIDMORE to WILLIAM HOOPER
115 acres in Helt Township
$5,500

JOHN McKEE etal to E.L. HIBERLY
Lot in Cayuga
$490

S.E. KAUFMAN to W.B. PAULEY
3 lots in Dana
$75

WILLIAM COOK to MONROE NOLAN
12 acres in Helt Township
$400

WILLIAM SWINDELL to EDAH TUTT
3 lots in Highland
$1,099

Auditor to H.C. & A.S. DIES
2 lots in Clinton
$53.41

Auditor to H.O. PETERS
70 acres in Eugene Township
$59.72

J. WILTERMOOD to R.H. NIXON
Lot in Newport
$400

ROBERT ADAMS to JOHN QUINCY ADAMS
Lot in Dana
$1,200

T.D. McKEE to MARY E. CARR
Lot in Cayuga
$75

SAM MALONE to D. PEER
80 acres in Helt Township
$3,600

SOLON JOHNSON to W.J. HENDRICKS
120 acres in Helt Township
$2,600

NANCY HAWKINS and husband to J.A. BENNETT
2 lots in Newport
$600

Wednesday, March 13, 1889

Helt Hollerings
AL STOKESBERRY and daughter are on the sick list. So is Uncle CHARLEY HELT.

Fodder Shock Nubbins
Dana News
On Thursday of last week, Mr. and Mrs. T.S. HOOD celebrated their golden wedding. Fifty years is a long period of time for a couple to dwell together in this time of life. We offer congratulations. Only their children and their families participated. Mrs. DUNCAN of Oskaloosa, IA came and will visit awhile among other relatives.

Clinton Echoes
Mrs. SUE WISHARD, of Crawfordsville, returned to her home last Friday, after a pleasant visit of a week with her sister, Mrs. MOREY, of this place.

A family by the name of POWERS, who moved from Paris, IL, to this place last fall has fallen heir to a large fortune from relatives in Ohio. Mr. POWERS left last week in company with Mrs. HIGGINS, of this place, to look after this new interest. It is supposed to amount to nearly $100,000.

Summit Grove Items
Rev. THOMAS DAVIS will now have the pleasure of being called Papa. A pot slinger arrived at his house Sunday night. Boys, don't bother THOMAS about his girl for a few years.

Mistress HARRINGTON, with her daughters of this place, was called to mourn the loss of her daughter, Mrs. SMITH, of Toronto. Mrs. HARRINGTON has children about 50 years old, and this is the first time death has bereft her of a child.

An infant child of Captain WILLIAMS, in the west part of this township, died one week ago last Sunday night.

Sudden Death
The little son of EDWARD E. & LAURA DAVIS, of this place, took down with spasms on last Monday morning. Physicians were with him from the time he took ill until his death, but could do nothing to alleviate the sufferings of the dear little one. He was about 4 years of age, the only child, and was a bright and intelligent boy for one of his years. He was idolized by the parents, and his sudden and unexpected death is a sad blow to them. The funeral will take place from the family residence at 10 o'clock this morning. The remains will be interred in the Wimsett Cemetery at Opedee.

Death
SAMUEL C. JOHNSON, who resided two miles north of Gessie, this county, died one week ago last Monday, March 4, 1889, aged 73 years. He was the father of ex-Superintendent A.J. JOHNSON, and had been on the sick bed of affliction for the last 13 months. He was a man whom everybody respected, and had been an elder in the Baptist Church for 40 years. In his death the community loses a good citizen, the church an exemplary Christian and the children a kind and affectionate father.

Obituary
MATTIE JONES, an old and respected citizen of Jonestown, Helt Township, died on Tuesday night of last week. We did not learn any particulars connected with his illness or history.

Obituary
DANIEL LASHLEY, father of JOHN H. LASHLEY, of Eugene, and who resided 4 miles west of that town, in the edge of Illinois, died on March 4th, 1889, aged nearly 82 years. He had been a true and consistent member of the Cumberland Presbyterian Church since he was 14 years of age, and died in hope of being rewarded a happy home beyond the grave. His wife preceded him to that better world about 6 years ago. He leaves 6 children – 3 boys and 3 daughters, all grown to man and womanhood. His remains were interred at the McKindree Chapel Cemetery.

Sudden Death
Mrs. LAURA SMITH, wife of NAT SMITH of Helt Township, died suddenly on last Thursday morning. She had visited a sick neighbor the day before, and was in apparently good health. She took down ill about 8 o'clock on Wednesday evening and died at 1 o'clock the next morning. She was the daughter of STEPHEN HARRINGTON, now deceased, who was well known to the older residents of this county. The writer was acquainted with Mrs. SMITH in her younger days and knows that she was a most excellent lady. She was kind and affectionate, and had the good will of everyone. In her death the husband loses a true and devoted wife, and the children a kind and noble mother.

Death
Last Monday morning, Rev. S.C. ZOOK, of West Newell, IL, 4 miles north of Danville, IL died. The deceased had been on the sick list for sometime, but was not considered dangerously ill. His daughter, Mrs. ELMER HENSON, of this place, on receiving the sad news, left on the next train. She had received news on Friday stating that her father was better, and when she received the telegram on Monday, it was a very great surprise to her. Her brother, PETER ZOOK, is also lying at the point of death. The Rev. ZOOK was once pastor in charge of the Newport circuit, and had a host of warm friends in this county who will regret to hear of his sudden and unexpected death. He was 67 years of age, and had been in the ministry for 47 years. He was a good and true Christian, and his death will be a great loss to the U.B. Church.

Obituary
WILLIAM McCAULIFF, who resided one half mile northeast of Dana, died on last Thursday morning, aged 100 years. He had been a resident of this county for nearly 40 years, and had been totally blind for the last 10 or 12 years. The first work he did when he came to this country from the Emerald Isle, was for STEPHEN GERARD, of Philadelphia. He worked on the old Indiana and Illinois Central, now the I.D. & W Railway, in 1854, 1855, when it was being constructed through this county. His wife and 4 children are still living. The deceased was a member of the Catholic Church, and died a true and consistent Christian.

Home News
JOHNNY PAYTON, of Clinton, was up here visiting his uncle, ELIAS PRITCHARD.

J.B. OSMON, who came home from the timber regions of Arkansas 3 or 4 weeks ago, has been on the sick list ever since his return.

CHARLEY BROKAW moved to Terre Haute on Friday of last week.

FRANK BLUNK, foreman of the Sidell, IL, Journal, spent last Sunday here with his mother.

J.M. NICHOLS is very poorly. He gets no better, but is gradually growing worse, if anything. He suffers a great deal, and is nearly as helpless as a child.

Rev. FIN D. NEWHOUSE, of Williamsport, who was sent as a Missionary to India a few years ago, is on his way home. He returns on account of his wife's health.

The latest reports from Mrs. WILLIAM DARNALL, of Helt Township, who was stricken down with paralysis a couple of weeks ago, are favorable for her recovery. Her numerous friends in this place will be glad to hear this cheerful news.

Notice of Administration
    Estate of ALVA ARRASMITH, deceased
    Filed March 6th, 1889
                                            THOMAS T. ARRASMITH, Administrator

Public Sale of Personal Property and Real Estate
    Notice to Creditors of WILLIAM GROVES, JULIUS GROVES, & JOHN GROVES
    Auction to be held Friday, April 12th, 1889 at residence near Lebanon Church
        Horses, colts, cows, farming implements, etc.
                                            SPENCER H. DALLAS, Assignee

Wednesday, March 20, 1889

Suicide at Clinton
A big sensation was created yesterday morning, at an early hour, by the startling news that Mrs. BELL CRANE, wife of JAMES CRANE, the druggist of that place, had committed suicide. The full particulars, which we learned from Attorney WILTERMOOD, who came up here yesterday on the noon train, are about as follows: Mr. CRANE got up to build a fire about 6:15 o'clock yesterday morning as near as he can remember, and had gone out to split up some kindling. On his return to the house, his little 4 year old child was screaming with all its might. He laid down his kindling and went to the bedroom to see what was the matter, but did not find his wife in bed. He asked the child what was the matter, which continued to scream. The child pointed down to the floor, back of the bed, where he found his wife weltering in her own blood. He immediately gave the alarm, and Mrs. WALLS, a near neighbor came over in haste, and when she arrived, she found her in the throes of death. She had shot herself through the left temple with her husband's revolver, which was in a bureau drawer in the same room. She was left handed which accounts for her shooting herself on the left side. The ball did not pass through her head, but lodged in her brain. As soon as her husband had stepped out after the kindling, she got up and procured the revolver from the press and committed the fatal deed. Her husband did not hear the report of the weapon. She had never dressed herself, but was in her nightgown when she took her life. She was awake at the time her husband got up, and the last thing her husband remembers of she was rubbing her forehead with her hand. It is said she has been down hearted for sometime over loss sustained by her husband's store catching fire some time ago, but had never shown any signs of insanity, or in any way threatened to take her life. On last Sunday she told her husband that she was afraid she was going to lose her mind. On Monday night she attended church and seemed to be in good spirits. She was 28 years of age, and the daughter of GEORGE W. ODELL, of Arlington, KS, a former citizen of this place. She was a bright and intelligent young woman, always very lively, and was very highly esteemed by everyone. She was born and raised at this place, and moved with her father to Kansas several years ago, where she was united in marriage to JAMES CRANE. Both lived very happily together, and there could have been no cause from any source for her to take her own life except mental derangement. She left no note stating why she had concluded to end her life. Coroner BRINDLEY was telegraphed and went down there on the 9 o'clock train yesterday morning to hold an inquest. It is probable that her remains will be brought to this place for interment. She leaves a husband, and a bright and sweet little daughter, aged 4 years.

Clinton Echoes
Ohio seems to be a lucky state for wealthy uncles to die and leave fortunes to Indianans. This week the news comes to us that ELIAS BIDWELL and his sister EMMA BIDWELL have suddenly fallen heir to a fortune of $5,000 by the death of an uncle at Ozark, OH.

Estray Notice
Taken up by ELIPHAZ LOWRY, Helt Township, February 15, 1889, 3 estray heifers
W.J. ANDREWS, J.P.

Home News
WILLIAM H. YOUNT, of Highland Township, is reported to be down with the consumption. He has been on the sick list for quite awhile.

Rev. JOHN S. BROWN, pastor of the U.B. Church at Sheldon, IL, is down here visiting his father-in-law, Uncle SAMMY DeHAVEN, and will probably remain over Sunday.

We understand that BILLY HOSFORD has been appointed postmaster at Eugene.

Miss BELL CAMPBELL, of Clinton, who has been visiting her brother at Dixon, IL, for several months, and recuperating her health, was up here last week, visiting friends at Opedee and this place.

R.H. NIXON and wife left yesterday morning for Arkansas Hot Springs for the benefit of his wife's health, who is troubled with rheumatism. Mr. NIXON will visit his Uncle at Oswego, KS before his return.

JONES and OL LINDSEY, of Eugene Township, were in town on Friday last. They are brothers, the first mentioned being 71 and the latter 82 years of age. Both are in splendid health, and were among the first settlers of the county now living. They took dinner with Esq. JOHN L. EGGLESTON.

Fodder Shock Nubbins
The town Board of Trustees have elected Mr. MILT HAYS to the vacancy on the school board occasioned by the removal of WILL COOK. Mr. HAYS is no doubt a good selection as he has had several years experience at Clinton.

Obituary
OLIVER P. DAVIS, the only and dearly beloved son of E.E. and LAURA DAVIS, of Newport, died March 12th, 1889, of congestion of the brain, lingering but a short time after he was stricken with the fever. Little OLLIE, as he was familiarly called by the fond parents and loving friends was taken sick on Sunday night and on Tuesday morning at 2 o'clock fell asleep in Jesus. He was an unusually bright, intelligent, and lovable child, and was the pet of all who knew him. Funeral services were conducted at the residence Wednesday March 13th, by Rev. R.S. MARTIN. A large number attended the remains to the Wimsett Cemetery near Opedee.

Obituary
Col. E.M. BENSON, of Montezuma, who was well and favorably known to many of our older citizens, died of pneumonia, on Monday night, March 11th, 1889, after an illness of only a few days. He was a Virginian by birth and had been a resident of Parke County since he was 14 years of age. At the time of his death he was past 75 years of age. For 40 years or more, he was one of the leading and prominent businessmen of Montezuma. Everybody esteemed and respected Col. BENSON, and had implicit confidence in his integrity. During his business career he accumulated a large fortune, which, by bad management of some kind, disappeared like a morning dew later on and left him in straightened circumstances in his old days. There never was a more generous hearted man lived in Parke County than the subject of this notice. At one time JOHN G. DAVIS, who represented this district in Congress, was a partner of his in business. Two children survive him; Miss GERTIE BENSON, the present postmistress of Montezuma, and HENRY BENSON, a crippled son. The remains of the deceased were interred in the cemetery at that place at 2 o'clock on last Wednesday afternoon.

Pumpkin Vine News
GEORGE PATTERSON, formerly of this city, and son of Mr. and Mrs. T.A. PATTERSON, is now doorkeeper of the Colorado Senate, and expects a prominent government appointment soon.

Allowance by Board of Commissioners, March Term 1889

Roads
JOHN RICHARDSON	1.50
JAMES CHIPPS	1.50
J.N. DAVIS	3.00

Public Buildings
D.W. WATSON & Sons	9.25
NIXON & CATES	30.00
WILLIAM RHEUBY	8.00
W.C. ARRASMITH	22.00
FRANK McNULTY	12.79
W.C. SHARP	4.00

Books & Stationery
M. POST	5.00
C.W. BROWN	13.00
O.H. HARSHORN	24.40
WILLIAM B. BURFORD	146.28

Inquests
WALLACE & HALL	30.00
E.A. FLAUGHER	10.00
LEWIS SHEPARD	10.00
M.L. HALL, Board of Health	53.50

Poor
M.L. HALL	56.25
HENRY NEBEKER	97.25
ERASTUS MACK	25.00
J.T. HENDERSON	25.00
G.O. NEWTON	263.37
SOL WEATHERWAX	130.83
E.H. McDANIEL	262.36
W.K. McNEILL	320.24
S.B. DAVIS	295.54
E.A. FLAUGHER	25.00

County Offices
M. HEGARTY	6.70
W.B. HOOD	.35

Fees & Salary
W.B. HOOD	200.00
W.M. HAMILTON	491.46

Gravel Roads
W.L. PORTER	126.25
WILLIAM B. HOOD	1838.20
H.S. CADY, Bridges	3.00
JOHN MILLER, Bridges	110.50
FRED RUSH, Bridges	10.00

E.F. DAVIS, Criminals	1.00
CHARLES HACKER, Criminals	3.00
WILLIAM RHEUBY, Criminals	42.70
WILLIAM RHEUBY, Courts	54.20
W.F. KERNS, Courts	17.50
F.M. RILEY, Courts	14.00
GEORGE F. HAWORTH, Courts	28.00
DAVID AGGRA, Janitor	50.00
S.B. DAVIS, Printing	129.85
M.G. RHOADS, Attorney fees	125.00
GEORGE W. DEALAND, County Superintendent	257.00
JOSEPH CONRAD, Poor Asylum	592.58

Marriage

The event of last week was the marriage of WILLIAM BROWN to Miss MARY E. WISE, both of this place. The knot tying took place at the U.B. parsonage, at Portertown, Eugene Township, on last Thursday afternoon, Rev. R.B. VAN ALLEN performing the pleasant duty.

Big Meeting

One of the most stirring, spiritual and successful revival meetings ever held in this place, was brought to a close last Sunday evening at the M.E. Church. Following is a list of those who united with the church on probation and letter: WILLIAM RHEUBY, ELIZABETH RHEUBY, ESTER C. HOPKINS, ANNA MASON, MAGGIE HACKER, ELMER HENSON, IDA HENSON, PAUL CONLEY, ADA MAY PLACE, URA ASTON, FLORA RICHARDS, JOSIE M. CROSS, JOHN GRUBB, JOHN HARRISON, MARY DOWDELL, LUCY WHITE, EARL HOLLINGS-WORTH, OLIVER GRUBB, JENNIE H. AGGRA, AGNES YOUNG, HATTIE DAVIS, MINTON HARRIS, NELLIE HARRISON, W.C. ARRASMITH, MARY HARRIS, JOHN MILLER, ANNA WILTERMOOD, GRACE RHEUBY, MARY HILLER, WILLIAM M. SHELATO, HATTIE PORTER, SARAH YOUNG, WILLIAM PORTER, GOULD G. RHEUBY, HANNAH FORTNER, and FRED CAIN.

Wednesday, March 27, 1889

Clinton Echoes

ED McFADDEN and his brother-in-law, CHARLES CURTIS, spent Sunday with friends and relatives here.

If some of those persons who are saying so much about Sexton JONES refusing to dig the grave for JOSEPH LONG's child, unless he was paid for it, would have taken the amount they spend on beer every week, and contributed that amount toward the digging of the grave, they would have shown sympathy for Mr. LONG and his family. Mr. JONES is a poor man and his earns his bread by the sweat of his brow, and it is nothing more than right, for him to be paid for his work at the cemetery.

Obituary

Aunt AMASSA MALONE, who has for several years made her home with HUGH MALONE, JOHN RICHARDS, and ISAAC AMBROSE, died very suddenly last Monday morning, aged 82 years, at HUGH MALONE's house. She had been complaining some, but was not sick to speak of for a week. About 3 o'clock Monday morning she aroused the family and complaining of feeling a suffocation and a blindness. Mr. MALONE ran over to a neighbor for aid, but before he returned she breathed her last. Deceased was the stepmother of RICHARD and SAMUEL G. MALONE. Her husband, Col. WILLIAM MALONE, died during the Civil War. Her remains were taken to West Union in Parke County for interment.

Died – on Wednesday of last week, the 4 months old child of GEORGE MYERS and wife, died after a short illness. He was one of God's flowers which "budded on earth to bloom in Heaven."

Fodder Shock Nubbins
Dana News
Mrs. SIB DUNCAN, of Oskaloosa, IA, returned to her home last Tuesday, accompanied by her niece, Miss GRACE ALLEN.

CHARLEY HOOKER returned last Saturday night from Toronto, Canada, where he and FRANK BALES attended the Veterinary College during the past winter. He left FRANK at Toledo, OH, who intended to visit his sister Mrs. JULIA TOWLE at Defiance. FRANK arrived home Tuesday.

The Clinton Suicide
The suicide of Mrs. BELL CRANE, wife of JAMES CRANE, of Clinton, on Tuesday morning of last week, was a very sad affair. The news of her death when conveyed to her father, GEORGE W. ODELL, of Arlington, KS, completely prostrated him so that he was unable to come here to attend the funeral, which occurred on last Thursday afternoon, the remains being brought here on the 3:30 afternoon train, and then followed to the Thomas Cemetery by a procession of her many friends at this place and Clinton. It was the largest funeral procession that has been seen in this locality for a long time.

Her two brothers, EDWARD and OTIS ODELL, of Hutchinson, KS, arrived on the same train that brought her remains from Clinton to this place. The casket was opened at the cemetery in order to give her friends here and her two brothers a chance to take a last look at her earthly form. The scene was a very sad one, and will be long remembered by all those who witnessed it. Her death was so unexpected and sudden to her brothers, that they could hardly bear up under the severe shock. Only a few days before one of them had received a letter from her, and then flashed upon the wires the sad news that their dear and only sister was dead.

Her husband met several small losses by fire last fall, and from that time on she worried about his losses, but no one noticed that her mind was failing until quite recently. On the Sunday before she committed the act, she approached her husband and told him that she believed she was going crazy. She complained of her head hurting her. On the day she shot herself, her husband was going to take her up to Dana to visit her relatives and friends a few days, and then if she made no improvement, he intended to take her on a trip to Kansas, where her father and two brothers reside.

Her little daughter, who is only 3 years old instead of 4 as stated by us last week, slept in a small bed near her mother's, and on the morning of the sad event, the little girl had woken up and crawled over and got in bed with her mother before Mr. CRANE got up to build the fire. When Mr. CRANE passed out of the room, the sweet and innocent little daughter was caressing and kissing her mother. As soon as Mr. CRANE had gone out to the wood house to get some kindling to start the fire, the little daughter says her mama kissed her, and then got up in her nightgown, walked to the press, and after procuring her husband's revolver, walked back to the bed and gave her little child a farewell kiss, and then placing the revolver to her left temple, pulled the trigger and fell to the floor a bleeding corpse.

She had been married about 5 years, and had only one child, little EDNA. She and her husband had always lived together pleasantly, and had everything that heart could wish for. The report that she is the fourth one of the family that has committed suicide is false. She is the first and only one of the name that ever committed suicide.

Death
BENJAMIN DEARDORFF, of Eugene Township, died at 12 o'clock on last Thursday night, aged 69 years, 6 months, and 20 days. He had congestion of the lungs, was ill only a few days, and was confined to his bed a few hours. He had been a member of the Cumberland Presbyterian Church for 10 years. The funeral took place at 11 o'clock Friday morning at his residence, Rev. R.B. VAN ALLEN, pastor of the U.B. Church conducting the service. Burial at Eugene Cemetery.

Home News
JACK SEARS, who moved from here to Terre Haute last fall, has recently moved to Clinton, where he has been placed in charge of a section on the C & E.I. Railway.

BOB HOLTZ, owner of the Lodi Ferry, across the Wabash at that point, has just completed a new boat, that he says is hard to beat. His brother JIM HOLTZ is in charge of the new ferry.

Matrimony
On Sunday last, at 3 o'clock in the afternoon, at the residence of the bride's father, ARTHUR PAYTON, of Helt Township, Mr. MORRIS H. RANDALL and Miss ELLA E. PAYTON were untied in wedlock, Rev. R.B. VAN ALLEN, pastor of the U.B. Church performing the ceremony.

School No. 16
The highest average made by the following pupils during the term beginning September 17, 1888 and closing March 15, 1889:

BETSEY HELT	99	Grade 5
MADGE HARRINGTON	98	
RAY JAMES	98	
SUSIE JAMES	96	
GERTIE HARRINGTON	96	
MARTIN RHOADS	96	
MAX WHITE	95	
SANT HELT	95	
PEARL WHITE	92	
ABBIE FRIST	80	
MINNIE SOUTHARD	100	Grade 4
EVA JAMES	99	
GERTIE JAMES	98	
ALVIN HELT	74	
RAY HELT	56	
RAY JAMES	97	Grade 3
IDA CRUMLEY	94	
HARRY WHITE	87	
OKIE WHITE	82	

MINNIE SOUTHARD was not absent a day.

Teacher – CARRIE McDOWELL

Wednesday, April 3, 1889

Death
HENRY WILTERMOOD, who resided about two miles southeast of town, died on last Wednesday afternoon, after a short illness of kidney troubles. The deceased was born May 19, 1825 in Harrison County, this state.

Real Estate Transfers for the month of March, M.B. CARTER, Recorder

JOE L. MACK to LEWIS SHEW
15 acres in Vermillion Township
$115

WILLIAM C. GROVES to J.D. HUNTER
10 acres in Vermillion Township
$800

GEORGE ATHERTON to A.B. WILLIS
80 acres in Helt Township
$1,000

JAMES VANGILDER to WILLIAM PEER
156 acres in Helt Township
$5,600

WILLIAM F. HAYS to J.F. HAYS
Lot in Dana
$200

JOHN W. JARVIS to W.A. HAYS
Lot in Dana
$600

SARAH A. WHITE to ANN NICHOLS
Lot in Newport
$650

J.W. BEARD to SOLOMON CARPENTER
10 acres in Helt Township
$1,000

EPHRAIM SHUTE to ISAAC PRATER
40 acres in Highland Township
$1,000

J. McLAUGHLIN to JOHN MILLER
Lot in Newport
$140

WILLIAM HAYS to WILLIAM L. HAYS
Lot in Clinton
$200

J.H. BOGART to SARAH SPARKS
Lot in Clinton
$125

R.D. MOFFATT to THOMAS CUSHMAN
2 lots in Perrysville
$600

W.A. HAYS to H.C. & SOPHIA DICE
Out lot near Clinton
$200

W.M. TAYLOR to FRED STAATS
Lot in Clinton
$3,100

MARGARET J. THOMAS to WILLIAM JONES
40 acres in Vermillion Township
$580

MARY J. NEEL to SUSANA NEEL
17 acres in Highland Township
$400

CHARLES S. NEEL to MARY J. NEEL
17 acres in Highland Township
$400

REBECCA REYNOLDS to D. MOSBARGER
6 acres in Highland Township
$220

THOMAS D. McKEE to LUCINDA DOWERS
Lot in Cayuga
$75

W.L. TINCHER to SARAH A. MORGAN
40 acres in Helt Township
$1,800

JOSEPH F. COOK to JESSE KAUFMAN
Lot in Cayuga
$1,000

JESSE KAUFMAN to J.F. COOK
79 acres in Helt Township
$2,000

W. GIBSON to SARAH WHITE
Lot 5 in Newport
$450

JNO. LLOYD to J.W. JONES
Lot in Clinton
$75

LUCINDA LLOYD to JNO. LLOYD
Lot in Clinton
$80

CARRIE M. TAYLOR to W.J. SWINDELL
Lot in Dana
$350

REBECCA SWIFT to JAMES WICKENS
Out lot in Hillsdale
$25

M. KING to W. VIRGIN
5 acres in Highland Township
$140

S.B. KIGER to M. KING
2 lots in Gessie
$200

EMMA HOPKINS to W.H. GUILLIAMS and wife
60 acres in Helt Township
$200

W.H. GUILLIAMS to EMMA HOPKINS
30 acres in Helt Township
$900

W.J. HENDRIX to HENRY SMITH
Tract of land in Helt Township
$250

D.W. FINNEY to OMER DAVIS
Lot in Dana
$35

JESSE RUNYAN to D.C. RUNYAN
Undivided ½ of 40 acres
$300

ALENA EVANS to ABRAHAM GEBHART
Lot in Eugene
$100

Marriage Licenses
WILLIAM F. HAYS to MOLLIE M. MYERS
CHARLES A. STULTZ to GLENDORA EATON
WILLIAM S. BROWN to MARY E. WISE
HARRY D. WHETSEL to SUSAN A. PAULEY
ASA HINTON to LUCINDA A. RAMSEY
JOSEPH DOULEY to CLARA B. DEPUY
WILLIAM E. PORTER to HARRIET E. HANNUM
MORRIS H. RANDALL to ELLA E. PAYTON
GILBERT L. MACK to MARY J. EARLES

Summit Grove Items
Last Thursday evening, Mr. GILBERT MACK and Mrs. JENNIE EARLES were united in wedlock at the home of the bride. Rev. THOMAS DAVIS performed the ceremony.

Wednesday, April 10, 1889 (unreadable)

Wednesday, April 17, 1889 (unreadable)

Wednesday, April 24, 1889

Fodder Shock Nobbins
Dana News
Rev. S.S. AIKMAN and family of Lebanon, IN, visited in this township this week.

Rev. H.C. LISTON, of Rockville, immersed the following persons last Sunday afternoon in Little Vermillion, near the iron bridge: Miss ALLIE THOMPSON, Miss MINNIE McCOWEN, BERT THOMPSON, and JOSEPH BELL.

Mr. CHARLES M. GILMORE, of Terre Haute, mustered in the Sons of Veterans Camp at Hillsdale last Friday night. The following is a list of members: JAMES B. SMITH, CHARLES JAMES, CHARLES BARNS, ED OXFORD, JOSEPH LAKE, FRED LANE, HUBERT LANE, JAMES GARLINGHOUSE, VES GARLINGHOUSE, LAURA JOHNSON, LEVI POTTER, and FRANK STRAIGHT.

Summit Grove Items
BURT SOUTHARD was in Summit last Friday. BURT is clerking in a store at Terre Haute. He used to be a clerk in a store at this town, and was a straight forward young man.

Postmaster DAVIS
When we published our last issue of our paper, we did not think it possible for Postmaster DAVIS to survive another week, but he still lingers on the brink of eternity, with no hope of his recovery. He is getting very weak, and is delirious the most of the time. It was four weeks ago last Sunday since the last time he was up town. It don't seem possible that he can last many days. He is kept under the influence of chloral most of the time.

Hydrophobia
A young man named SOLOMON SHOAF, a farmer of Sugar Creek Township, Parke County, is reported to be dying of hydrophobia. He has to be handcuffed and tied down in bed to keep him from biting anyone. He tried to bite everyone who comes near him.

P.S. Since the above was put in type, we learn through the Terre Haute Express that Mr. SHOAF has died. It is now stated that the same day, he also bit a boy by the name of MYERS in the same neighborhood, and he is now sick, and his hand totally swollen, and that he shows almost the same symptoms that SHOAF did.

Real Estate Transfers since our last issue:

HENRY C. DUTTON etal to PETER S. MOUDY
2 lots in Perrysville
$20

SARAH CASTLE to D. McDONALD
Part of lot in Dana
$372

B.S. AIKMAN to SARAH NOWLING
5 acres in Clinton Township
$125

J.W. JONES to W.F. BUTLER
Lot in Clinton
$112

D.W. FINNEY to M.A. COMBS
Lots in Dana
$105

C.M. TAYLOR to E. THOMPSON
2 lots in Dana
$200

WILLIAM SANDERS to C.M. SANDERS
? acres in Highland Township
$1,100

SARAH R. HAINS to J.M. SULLIVAN
169 acres in Highland Township
$5,400

S.J. HALL to J.C. SAWYER
? acres in Vermillion Township
$300

Home News

W.P. SWAIM, a prominent stock raiser of Bellmore, Parke County, died on the 14th of this month of paralysis. He was 52 years of age.

We understand that WILLIAM L. PORTER and MATTHEW LYTLE will leave for Arkansas this week, but will retain Newport as their voting place.

Mrs. O.J. INNIS, of Rockville, is dead. She died one week ago last Thursday.

ALFRED DePUY, residing southwest of Bono, Helt Township, is quite seriously ill with the quinsy. He was thought to be a little better yesterday morning.

Obituary

On Friday last, a little son of FRANK WHIPPLE, aged 18 months, of Cayuga, died after an illness of several days. His remains were buried on Saturday. The parents have the sympathy of their neighbors and friends in the loss of their dear little boy.

Notice of Administration
    Estate of BENJAMIN F. DEARDORFF, Sr., deceased
    Filed April 8, 1889
                        BENJAMIN F. DEARDORFF, Jr., Admr.

Sheriff's Sale on Decree
    HIRAM SHEPARD
    Vs.
    JULIUS C. GROVES, LAURA GROVES, SPENCER H. DALLAS
    $1,867
    Sale on Saturday, May 4, 1889 between 8 and 4 at courthouse
        W ½ NW ¼ Sec 16 T 16 N R 10 W
            North of Harrison boundary
            Except 10 acres belonging to WILLIAM GROVES
        Also except 20 acres off S end
        Therefore containing 50 acres
    5 acres off S end of E ½ of NW ¼ of SW ¼ Sec 9 T 16 N R 10 W
    CONLEY & SAWYER, attorneys for plaintiff
    Filed April 1, 1889
                        WILLIAM RHEUBY, Sheriff

Sheriff's Sale on Decree
    MELVIN L. HALL
    Vs.
    JOHN W. GALLOWAY & FLORA GALLOWAY
    $211.70
    Sale on Saturday, April 27, 1889 between 8 and 4 at courthouse
        30 feet off W end of W ½ Lot 49 in original plot of Newport
    CONLEY & SAWYER, attorneys for plaintiff
    Filed March 28, 1889
                        WILLIAM RHEUBY, Sheriff

Notice of Petition to Sell Real Estate
    ROBERT J. HOLTZ, Admr. of Estate of JOSEPH HOLTZ, deceased
    Vs.
    MARY E. HENSON, JOHN HENSON and JAMES T. HOLTZ
    Must appear in court June 17, 1889
    Filed April 23, 1889
                        A.R. HOPKINS, Clerk

Nuptials
On last Thursday evening, MORTON HOLLINGSWORTH and Miss GERTIE DOWDELL, both of this place, were united in wedlock at the residence of the bride's mother. The ceremony took place at 8:30 o'clock, Rev. R.B. VAN ALLEN, pastor of the U.B. Church, tying the knot. About 30 or 40 friends were present to witness the happy event.

Obituary
Death of the Oldest Lady in the County
Mrs. SARAH E. MOORE, who resided about 3 miles north of Eugene, died on Saturday, aged 84 years. She had been ailing for three or four months, and her end was not unexpected. She had been a resident of the county since 1833, and was probably the oldest woman in the county. She was the widow of JOSEPH MOORE, who died in 1863, or 1864. She was the sister of Uncle ALEX DUNLAP, of this township, who is now the only survivor of the family. The deceased was not a member of any church, but was a true Christian lady in every sense of the term. No one had a more generous heart than she. She was kind and affectionate to all, and every one who knew her was her friend. She was one of the noble women in this country, and in her death society loses a most estimable lady. Her funeral occurred on Monday last, and was very largely attended by her relatives, neighbors, and friends.

Arrived
C.S. DAVIS arrived here from Salina, KS, at 6 o'clock on last Wednesday evening, making the run on a freight train in 4 days. This is pretty quick time. He had a car chartered, which he had filled with his household goods, horse, and buggy.

We omitted to state in our last issue, that HARRY B. RHOADS of Greencastle, a former resident of this place, is the proud father of a fine looking girl baby. HARRY is feeling extremely happy.

Wednesday, April 1, 1889

Clinton Echoes
WILLARD GOSNELL, of Vermillion Township, was in town Saturday. He informs us that he will soon start to travel for the Centennial Manufacturing Company of Cincinnati.

Blue Mountain Joe's show attracted quite a crows Saturday night. There was a $5 prize to be given to the best looking girl and the ugliest man was to be pointed out but no reward was offered for him. The consequence was that most of the crowd consisted of women, every one of them was looking her prettiest, all smiles and full of expectation. Miss CARRIE WEBER, who has never made any pretensions to be pretty was pronounced to be the prettiest girl, and now you can't find another girl in town that will admit that she was there. CONEY SHEW was the ugliest man.

Death
W.H. YOUNT, who had been confined to his bed for several weeks, died on Monday night of last week, from a complication of diseases. His burial took place on the Wednesday following his death, the funeral discourse being preached by Rev. TAYLOR, pastor of the U.B. Church, after which his remains were interred in the Hicks Cemetery, one half mile west of Perrysville. The deceased was never married, and was 46 years and 5 months of age. He was one of the ablest writers in the county, and for many years was the Perrysville correspondent to the Hoosier. As a sarcastic writer, he was equal to the late GEORGE D. PRENTISS. He wrote several beautiful poems which were published in the Hoosier, among them one on Decoration Day that cannot be beaten by any one. It paid a high tribute to the fallen heroes who had given up their lives in their country's defense, and was very pathetic and touching. If the poor fellow had let liquor alone, and properly used his talents, he might have been one of the most brilliant writers of the country today. He was his own worst enemy, and is now dead.

Aunt SALLIE MOREY is very bad sick with congestion of the stomach, and at present writing is not expected to live.

Summit Grove Items
FRANK WILES is obligated to suspend work on account of cutting off two of his toes while chopping wood the other day.

CORA HARPER is attending the county normal school at Perrysville.

Fodder Shock Items
Dana News
At the residence of Rev. J.E. WRIGHT, at 11 o'clock a.m. Sunday last, Mr. JOHN PAYTON and Miss MOLLIE DOWDY were united in wedlock. They were both residents of Center Church neighborhood. After the ceremony the couple went to Mr. J.H. HEARN's, cousin of the bride, and took dinner.

At the residence of her son-in-law, Mr. WILLIAM REED, three and one half miles northeast of Dana, Mrs. MELISSA SLATER, widow of JAMES SLATER, died of Bright's disease on Tuesday April 23, 1889, aged 68 years. The funeral took place at Vermillion Chapel at 1 o'clock p.m. Wednesday. The deceased was one of the pioneer women of Vermillion County and was respected by all.

Home News
BILLY HOLLINGSWORTH left for Indianapolis yesterday morning, where he has secured work.

ELIJAH P. CONLEY, of Gosport, a former resident of Helt Townshi and Clinton, has been granted a pension.

SAM D. COLLETT, who is attending the Rose Polytechnic School at Terre Haute, and one of his classmates, spent Sunday here with his parents.

HARRY B. RHOADS, who is clerking in a drug store at Greencastle, was over here Monday and Tuesday visiting his uncle, M.G. RHOADS, and numerous friends. He is in splendid health and looking better than we ever saw him.

The wife of JOHN FOX, of Perrysville, died on Wednesday after a short illness, aged about 30 years. She leaves a husband and 5 little children, the youngest being only a few weeks old. It is said that she was a most estimable and highly respected by every one.

ETHEL MADALINE WILTERMOOD, the little two year old daughter of ALBERT B. and ALWILDA WILTERMOOD, of Terre Haute, died on Friday last, April 26, 1889, and was interred in the Wimsett Cemetery at Opedee on Saturday last. She was born August 28, 1886, and was a bright and interesting child, and idolized by her parents.

Real Estate Transfers since our last issue:
    JAMES C. TUTT to JOE CONRAD
    100 acres in Helt Township
    $2,500

    L.M. TERRY to JOS. JACKSON
    40 acres in Helt Township
    $1,600

    LEWIS NORRIS and wife to L.M. TERRY
    40 acres in Helt Township
    $1,600

LAURA WISHARD and husband to CARRIE McDOWELL
120 acres in Helt Township
$500

HARRY E. SANDERS to WILLIAM SANDERS
? acres in Highland Township
$1,600

WILLIAM GIBSON to JONES LINDSEY
40 acres in Eugene Township
$150

DAVID SPRY to HENRY TATE
Lot in Perrysville
$200

Notice of Petition to Sell Real Estate
BENJAMIN O. CARPENTER, Admr. of Estate of HARVEY H. PEYTON, deceased
Vs.
ELLA PEYTON and LOLA PEYTON
Heirs of HENRY H. PEYTON, deceased
Filed April 28, 1889

A.R. HOPKINS, Clerk

Wednesday, May 8, 1889

Death
Postmaster OLIVER L. DAVIS, who took down with Bright's disease of the kidneys the latter part of March, died at 11:30 o'clock on last Wednesday night, May 1st, 1889. He passed away quietly with a pleasant smile on his face. The deceased was born September 30, 1862, at Homer, IL, and was united in wedlock to Miss ELLA JAMIESON, of Ellettsville, this state, June 6, 1882. He leaves a wife and two sweet little children, BLANCHE and FARMER. Both are bright and interesting children and were the idol of their father. The deceased was a young man, full of energy and good business qualifications, and made an exceptional good postmaster. He was kind and obliging, and had the good will and esteem of everyone. He always gave everybody a pleasant answer, and was generous to a fault. In his death our little city loses an active businessman, the wife a kind and affectionate father. He was a friend to everyone, and no person in Newport had a larger host of warm personal friends than postmaster OL DAVIS. The fact of his great popularity was fully attested at his funeral, which took place on last Friday morning. It was the largest procession that has passed through the town for many years, the procession of carriages and buggies being over a half mile long. The funeral services were conducted at his late residence one block east of the Hoosier office, Rev. JOHN W. PARRETT, a retired minister of the M.E. Church, performing the last sad rites, after which his remains were laid to rest at the Thomas Cemetery, 2 miles northwest of town.

Clinton Echoes
The Hon. Doctor JOHN Q. METCALF and Mrs. CATHERINE BOREN were united in wedlock on Tuesday of last week, Esq. WISHARD officiating. Mrs. BOREN is an experienced wife and no doubt will look well after the doctor's suspenders, buttons, and laundry department, as this is her fifth matrimonial vow. The doctor informs us that he is ever ready to obey her with fear and trembling.

Mr. WILLIAM J. SEWELL, of Casey, IL, and who worked last fall on the Free Press, is now in Tacoma, Washington Territory.

Pumpkin Vine News
Clinton Argus
Mrs. JANE DAVIDSON and children left for Marshall, Michigan, where they will make their future home with Mrs. DAVIDSON's brother, ED PERRIN.

Mrs. SALLY MOREY has been dangerously ill this week with inflammatory neuralgia. At this writing she is slightly improved. Her brother JAMES WISHARD and sister SUE WISHARD came Wednesday.

Died
Mrs. CHASE, an aged lady, died at the home of her son-in-law JOHN ROBERTS last Wednesday night. She had been ill for a long time with consumption. She leaves three children: Mrs. JOHN ROBERTS, ALICE CHASE, and HENRY CHASE. Her remains were carried to their last resting place Friday, followed by a number of mourners and sympathizing friends. Rev. HANDLEY officiated in the last sad rites.

Obituary
SARAH MOORE, nee DUNLAP, was born August 30, 1803, in Maryland, near Baltimore. When 11 years of age, she removed with her parents to Ohio, where she was married to JOSEPH MOORE in 1823. In 1833 she came with her husband and 5 children to Indiana, entering land near Eugene, where she had since resided to her death, April 30, 1889, being nearly 80 years of age. Mrs. MOORE has survived her husband since 1861, having reared to manhood and womanhood 11 children, 9 of whom survive their mother – 4 sons and 5 daughters.
      Friendly Recollection
Mrs. MOORE was in every respect a true woman, wife, mother, and member of society; ever kind in sickness, visiting the sick and distressed to do them good; very charitable and ready to aid everyone about her need; none were turned hungry from her door. In addition to rearing a large family of her own, she gave the last years of her life to the earnest care of a family of grandchildren. He work is finished, and well done; she has gone over for the reward in store for the faithful. Although severely afflicted for some months prior to her death, Mrs. MOORE bore her afflictions with the Christian fortitude so characteristic of her life.

Death
Nearly all the prominent citizens of this county, and especially the old soldiers, are acquainted with Capt. JOHN LINDSEY, who resided west of Clinton, and near the old Indiana furnace, of which he was superintendent for many years. This old soldier's warfare is over. His spirit took flight for that better world on Monday last. We did not learn any particulars connected with the illness. A simple telegram was received by Senator SEARS' stating that he would be buried at the Clinton Cemetery yesterday afternoon. The deceased was born in Ohio in 1815, and had been a resident of this county since 1840. When the war broke out in 1861, he was one among the first to enlist to defend his country's flag. He was elected Capt. of Company I, 14th IN Regiment, and fought gallantly for the old flag until he was severely wounded in the leg, making a cripple of him for life. But he did not resign on account of his wound. He took quarters at Terre Haute, where he enlisted hundreds of men for the Union Army. No braver or better regiment went from Indiana that the bloody old 14th. This regiment saw more hard service than any regiment that went from the state. It was made up of brave and true soldiers, the most of whom were killed in battle or died in camp. No man was more highly respected and honored.

Post Office
Mr. E.F. DAVIS, father of the late postmaster of this place, who was on his bond, received a letter from Postmaster General WANNAMAKER, on Monday last, instructing him to appoint a postmaster temporarily for this place, until a permanent one could be selected by the department. Mr. DAVIS selected Mr. S.H. DALLAS, who has been in charge of the office for several weeks.

Mr. MICHAEL SNYDER, third great uncle of Mrs. LEE J. PLACE, and HATTIE STEARNS, a relative, both of Muncie, IL, are here on a visit. Mr. SNYDER is 81 years of age, and in good health for one of his years.

Home News
JESSE KAUFMAN has sold out his livery outfit at Cayuga to ROBERT J. HOLTZ.

JOHN D. COLLETT, cashier of Collett & Co. Bank, and his wife, left for Charleston, WV, to visit his brother-in-law, ADAM B. LITTLEPAGE.

Rev. GALLAHER, of Veedersburg, father of STEVE GALLAHER, of this place, was in town on Friday last. He was on his way to Chrisman, IL, where he preached on Sunday last. He is a minister of the Christian Church. He is a very dignified looking gentleman.

Mrs. HULDAH E. BARKER, of this place, was made happy on last Monday, by receipt of the news that her pension had been granted at the rate of $12 per month from the second of August, the date of the death of her husband, JOHN G. BARKER.

Death
Mrs. JOHN KEILY, of Pana, IL, mother of Mrs. MAURICE HEGARTY, of this place, died on last Sunday afternoon, aged 65 years. Her husband survives her. She was only sick a short time. Her daughter, Mrs. HEGARTY, received a telegram on Saturday, announcing her serious illness, and immediately left for Pana, arriving there a short time before her mother passed beyond the shores of time. The deceased was a member of the Catholic Church, and a consistent Christian lady. Her remains were interred on Monday last.

Funeral
Mrs. ADALINE V. JONES; maiden name was BEAUMONT. She was born in Charleston, WV, July 16, 1812. She was married to Mr. J.N. JONES, January 20th, 1832, in Terre Haute, IN. They settled in Perrysville about the year 1832, and her husband was one of the most active and successful businessmen of that place, accumulating a handsome property and with it they were liberal in aiding all charitable and religious objects. He died some 14 years since, and his widow has lived in this place, loved and respected by all. She was a kind mother, a good neighbor, liberal in distributing to the necessities of the poor and needy. She was a good friend and helper in sickness and sure to be found at the bedside of suffering, and a true Christian, ever adorning her profession of Christianity and often praying at the bedside of the sufferer, and successfully pointing them to the friend of sinners. The last place she was ever at on earth from her home was church. She had been going down with something like an abscess in her stomach for some two months. All was done that could be done to prolong her life. The summons came on Friday afternoon. She passed away without a struggle. Her daughter, Mrs. LIDA BENTON, was unceasing in her ministrations of kindness to her mother until the last. She was dearly beloved by them and her grandchildren. The funeral was conducted on Sunday in the old home, conducted by Rev. W.A. SMITH. There were present a nephew, Mr. JONES, from Chicago, and grandson, Mr. DUNLAP and wife, from Indianapolis, and a granddaughter, Miss DUNLAP, from South Bend.

Dead Letter List
- Miss NONA BURGESS
- Miss HARRIET E. HANUM
- Miss LULA ROBANON
- Mrs. MARY WILLIAMS
- WILLIAM GIBBONS
- Miss CALEY HOLLINGSWORTH
- Mrs. W.C. WALKER

Real Estate Transfers
WILLIAM P. HUNTER and wife to I. SAGERS
2 lots in Eugene
$500

MARTHA J. THOMPSON and husband to JAMES F. JOHNSON
20 acres in Vermillion Township
$$165

THOMAS HINES and wife to R.J. GESSIE
128.72 acres in Highland Township
$3,711.98

CHARLES W. SIMPSON to MARY F. NIXON
Part of one lot in Eugene Junction
$$65

ELIZABETH LEATHERMAN to MARCUS HARDING
6 lots in town of Highland
$365

LESLIE D. THOMAS to WILLIAM HENRY & AMELIA OWENS
Tract of land in Eugene Township
$200

Target Gun
On last Saturday, while GOTLIEB HEIBREDER, of Eugene, was sitting in POLLARD's blacksmith shop at that place, he was struck in the eye by a spent ball, supposed to have been fired from a target gun, and his eye completely destroyed. Mr. HEIBREDER is an old and respected citizen of that place, and is engaged in the furniture and undertaking business. Who fired the shot is more than anyone is able to find out.

Wedding
A very quiet but decidedly handsome affair was the wedding ceremony of last Wednesday evening, which linked the lives of two of our prominent and most highly respected citizens. The groom was none other than Hon. J.C. SAWYER, the lawyer partner of H.H. CONLEY, and the bride was Miss MINTA HARVEY, one of Vermillion County's favorite young ladies. The wedding service was performed by Rev. R.S. MARTIN of the M.E. Church, in the parlors of the bride's home, 1 mile north of town, none but the immediate relatives of the bride being present.

Death
DAVID J. WOLFE, who resided 12 miles southwest of Jonestown, Helt Township, died on Tuesday of last week, aged 76 years. He was born in Virginia in 1812, and had been a resident of this county since 1844. He died from blood poisoning caused by a splinter he ran under his fingernail 3 years ago. He went down to Ocean Springs, MI, last fall, to see if that climate would not benefit his failing health, but he received no relief, and about 4 weeks ago came home to die. He was a member of the U.B. Church, and was buried at Sugar Grove Cemetery, IL on the day following his death.

Obituary
Mrs. HARRIET UTTER HOLMES, of Williamsport, Warren County, a former resident of this place, and who was well known to many of our citizens, died on April 22, 1889. She had been an invalid for 2 or 3 years, and suffered intensely at times. The deceased was born in this town in 1847, and was united in wedlock to A.V. HOLMES on January 17, 1870. She leaves a husband and 6 children, 3 boys and 3 girls. She had been a member of the M.E. Church since 1881.

On last Wednesday, Esq. JOHN L. EGGLESTON received a letter from his son SELDON B. EGGLESTON who is in business at Jonesboro, AR, stating that a destructive fire had prevailed there the Saturday night before, destroying 42 buildings and entailing a loss of over half a million dollars. He also stated that EMERY BRILES and JERRY DICKEN were there.

Notice to Non-Residents
> MARY LEWIS
> Vs.
> WILLIAM W. CREVISTON & ADELIA CREVISTON
> Defendants are not residents of Indiana
> Must appear before 4th Monday in May 1889
> RHOADS & AIKMAN, attorneys for plaintiff
> Filed April 15, 1889
>> A.R. HOPKINS, Clerk

Administrator's Sale
> Estate of BENJAMIN DEARDORFF, Sr., deceased
> Auction to be held Saturday, May 25, 1889
> Held at late residence in Eugene Township
> Personal property
>> Horse, buggy, harness, tools, etc.
>> BENJAMIN DEARDORFF, Jr., Admr.

Wednesday, May 15, 1889

Pumpkin Vine News
Clinton Argus
WILLIAM VAUGHN, of this city, had a finger cut off in a sawmill at Cayuga Tuesday. On Monday another man lost 3 fingers in the same mill. We did not learn whose fingers.

Clinton Echoes
The following pupils of the Clinton High School received county diplomas this spring: INDIA BULLINGTON, CLARA AIKMAN, EVA CLARK, LUCRETIA STONE, CORA TWEEDY, NELLIE MALONE, NEMA WHITCOMB, GRACE SOLIDAY, MYRTLE WRIGHT, ARTHUR ROBERTS, BERNARD STOKESBERRY, and ED THOMPSON.

Montezuma News
FRANK FONCANNON, M.D. of Kansas, is visiting his father and mother, Mr. and Mrs. J.C. FONCANNON of Helt Township, Vermillion County.

Born
A girl baby to J.W. JARVIS and wife, Thursday, May 2, 1889.

Farm for Sale
I have a farm of 140 acres, situated 3 miles southwest of Clinton, which I wish to sell. 100 acres is under cultivation, and the rest is timber. A good one story frame house, with 5 rooms and good cellar, a splendid barn, 40 feet square, with 16 foot siding, a good orchard, well, spring, and splendid stock water. The soil is clay and rich, 5 ½ foot vein of good coal underlies the farm. Price $40 per acre.
>> FRANK L. REEDER

Filed March 6, 1889

Death
The wife of Uncle JOE STAATS, of Helt Township, who has been an invalid for a long time, died on last Friday. She was about 85 years of age, and had been a resident of this county since 1830. Her husband, to whom she was married about 60 years ago, survives her. She was a true Christian lady, and had been a member of the M.E. Church for many years.

Death
JOE JACKSON, of this township, died yesterday morning. We did not learn the cause of his death. He was a bright young man, and was the son of WHIT JACKSON.

Home news

Mrs. M.B. CARTER bought property of Miss ELLA PARRETT yesterday, on the east side of George Street, now occupied by D.Y. FUNKHOUSER, consideration $750.

JERRY DICKEN and EMERY BRILES, returned from the alligator swamps of Arkansas on Wednesday last. They were not very highly impressed with that malarial climate.

CHARLEY THOMAS, of Eugene, who went to the Arkansas Hot Springs a short time since, for the benefit of his health, died here on the 3rd of May, 1889, of Bright's disease of the kidneys. He was the son-in-law BENJAMIN DEARDORFF Sr., lately deceased.

ROBERT DICKASON, of Highland Township, aged about 65 years, died on Friday last.

Real Estate Transfers since our last issue:

WILLIAM A. HAYS to MORGAN J. TUCKER
Lot in Clinton
$1,750

N.C. ANDERSON to LAURA J. JEFFRIES
2 lots in Clinton
$250

E.J. HAGER to C. HAGER
Lot in Clinton
$100

CHARLES WHITCOMB to J.F. BOWEN
Lot in Clinton
$110

S.E. ANDREWS to W.P. ANDREWS
Tract of land in Helt Township
$25

JOHN RUNYAN to CHARLES D. RUNYAN
Undivided 1/20 of 80 acres in Clinton Township
$85

EMMA F.A. FONCANNON to THOMAS CARLIN
8 acres in Clinton Township
$200

MARY J. HUMPHRIES to THOMAS CARLIN
8 acres in Clinton Township
$200

PHOEBE RUNYAN etal to M.J. HUMPHRIES
8 acres in Clinton Township
$1

PHOEBE RUNYAN etal to J.P. RUNYAN
8 acres in Clinton Township
$1

J.S. HOUCHIN to E. VANSICKLE
113 acres, more or less, in Helt Township
$4,520

Rileysburgh Notes
Mrs. DAVID SHUTE, of Missouri, is visiting her sister, Mrs. JOSEPH SHUTE, of this place.

Executor's Sale
    Estate of SARAH MOORE, deceased
    Personal property
    Auction to be held Saturday, June 1, 1889
    Held at residence in Eugene Township
        Hogs, cows, wheat, etc.
    Also 210 acres of farming land S ¾ of S ½ Sec 18, T 18 N R 9 W
            MILO J. RUDY, executor of Will

Wednesday, May 22, 1889

Committed Suicide
CHARLES MORRIS, aged only 13 years, a resident of Terre Haute, committed suicide by hanging himself with a leather strap from a beam in a barn on last Monday afternoon. No cause is assigned.

Clinton Echoes
Mrs. OTIS PERRIN started last week to Michigan to join her husband. Mr. PERRIN has purchased a farm there, and they will make that their future home.

Mrs. HANEY, wife of Capt. JOHN HANEY, formerly of this place, died at her home in Galena, OH, last week, and her remains were brought to Terre Haute for burial.

Clinton is to have a postmistress. JAMES WILSON received a telegram last Thursday that Mrs. BLYTHE had been given the post office at Clinton. Mrs. BLYTHE is the widow of a Union soldier, who lost his health in the army, and now she receives no pension.

New Postmasters
The following new postmasters were appointed for this county:
    Perrysville – Mrs. ELLEN HANSICKER
    Gessie – J.J. CARUTHERS
    Cayuga – M.W. COFFIN
    Newport – WILLIAM F. THORNTON
    Quaker Hill – JOHN A. KERN
    Hillsdale – Major J.A. SANDERS
    Dana – HENRY H. AYE
    St. Bernice – B.F. SPICER
    Clinton – Mrs. M. BLYTHE

Home News
JEROME DICKEN and Miss MINNIE BURKE were married on last Saturday night, Rev. R.B. VAN ALLEN, pastor of the U.B. Church performing the ceremony.

Wedding Bells
On May 20, 1889, in the parlors of the Newport M.E. parsonage, Mr. JAMES REID and Miss SARAH E. BROOKS, both of Illinois, were united in marriage by Rev. R.S. MARTIN. Mr. REID is a mill man of considerable success, and the bride is a lady of excellent qualities.

Killed at This Place
ED TAYLOR of Danville, IL, who was temporarily braking on the A.E.I. Railway, met with an accident at the gravel pit, just north of town on Tuesday of last week, which proved fatal. He was braking for a friend who was attending a funeral.

Birthday
Aunt BETSY JAMES, of Summit Grove, Helt Township, celebrated her 84th birthday on Monday last. There were about 80 relatives and friends present to enjoy the day with the good old lady. Aunt BETSY is in exceedingly good health for one of her years.

Obituary
Mrs. SARAH STAATS, wife of Uncle JOE STAATS of Helt Township, this county, died on Saturday, May 11, 1889, aged 84 years the 10th of last March. She was a Virginian by birth, but had been a resident of this county since 1830. She had been a member of the M.E. Church for over 65 years, and was a Christian lady who was respected and esteemed by everybody. She was a kind and devoted mother, and raised to man and womanhood a large and interesting family, being the mother of 11 children, 9 of whom survive her. She and her husband shared in the pleasures and hardships of this world together for over 63 years, and had always been true and devoted to each other. Theirs has truly been a long and happy life, and now the good wife has passed to her home of rest, while the husband is permitted to remain on earth a short time longer. Her funeral took place on the Sunday following her death, Rev. MEREDITH and Rev. J.E. WRIGHT, ministers of the M.E. Church performing the last sad rites, after which she was laid to rest in Helt's Prairie Cemetery.

Real Estate Transfers since last issue:
> G.D. McKEE etal to C.& E.I. Railway
> Right of way through Cayuga
> $1
>
> WILLIAM RHEUBY to LEWIS S. SKINNER
> 55 acres in Highland Township
> $750
>
> JOHN S. GRONDYKE to C.&E.I. Railway
> Right of way through Cayuga
> $1
>
> JOHN ADAMS to JACOB MYERS
> 30 acres in Vermillion Township
> $900
>
> DANIEL LASHLEY to ELIZ. GEBHART
> 20 acres in Eugene Township
> $500
>
> JOHN HENDERSON and wife to AARON H. CRAFT
> 30 acres in Vermillion Township
> $875
>
> URIAH FOLGER and E.C. FOLGER to MARY P. HAMILTON
> 5.87 acres in Eugene Township
> $150

Wednesday, May 29, 1889

Birthday

Last Monday was Coroner THOMAS BRINDLEY's 64th birthday. He did not suspect anything unusual was going to happen at his house that day, and loafed around town until near noon, when he went home for dinner, and was greeted by a house full of relatives and friends. It was a happy surprise for him. Among those from a distance were: Mrs. MARY REED and Mrs. B.F. PATTON, of Danville, IL; and Mrs. ANNIE EADS, Miss LAURA REEDER, Miss IDA COX, Mr. and Mrs. FRANK REEDER and CHARLES COTTRELL, of Clinton.

Fodder Shock Nubbins
Dana News

HENRY SKIDMORE, of Robinson, IL, was here last week attending to business affairs. He reports his family well pleased, and his wife's health much improved since moving there.

Home News

WILLIAM F. THORNTON, the new postmaster for this place, filled out his bond on Thursday last, and expects to receive his commission sometime this week. His bondsmen are R.H. NIXON and CHARLEY POTTS. The two are worth over $100,000.

WILLIAM JOHNS and wife, of Danville, IL, were down here two or three days last week visiting their brother-in-law, CHARLEY HACKER.

LEVI COVINGTON, of Eugene Township, an honest and worthy old soldier, who wore the blue during the late war, has just been granted a pension.

CHARLES S. JACKSON has been appointed administrator of JOSEPH A. JACKSON, deceased.

J.J. KNIGHT, of Carbon, Clay Co., a former resident of Helt Township, was in town yesterday.

JAMES WOODWARD, of Eugene Township, has been granted a pension, and is a happy man.

Sentenced

DAVID WATSON, aged 56 years, who killed JOHN HUDSON at Judson, Parke County, last September by stabbing him to death with a butcher's knife, was tried in the Parke Circuit Court last week, and sentenced to the penitentiary for life. HUDSON accused WATSON of poisoning his dog when WATSON, who has an uncontrollable temper, flew into a rage, and grabbing a knife, plunged it into his victim's heart.

Pumpkin Vine News
Clinton Argus

The following teachers have been selected for the Clinton schools for the next year:

    J.H. TOMLIN, Superintendent
    W.A. KEARNS, Principal High School
    R.E. WHITLOCK, 6th & 7th Grades
    J.W. BROOKBANK, 4th & 5th Grades
    DOLLIE SCOTT, 3rd Grade
    BLANCHE HUPP, 2nd Grade
    DAISY ROBISON, 1st Grade

Wednesday, June 5, 1889

Clinton Echoes

BEN DAVIDSON, a former Clinton Township boy, but now of Tuscola, IN, visited his sister, Mrs. WILLIAM HILL, last week. BEN is now numbered among the prosperous young farmers of his county.

Sudden Death
Our people were startled on last Thursday morning by the announcement that Mrs. RUTH PORTER, an old and respected citizen of this place, was dead. She had gotten up to prepare the morning meal and had barely dressed herself when her brother-in-law, WILLIAM I. PORTER, who happened in the room at the time, noticed that there was something the matter with her. He immediately called to his assistance Dr. LEWIS SHEPARD, her nephew by marriage. They picked her up and started to the bed with her, when she gave one gasp for breath and was dead. She was 78 years of age, and was one of the oldest residents of Newport. Her husband, RICHARD PORTER, who died during the late war, was at one time among one of the wealthiest farmers of this township, but broke up by speculation in cattle, and died a poor man. No inquest was held, and it is generally supposed that she died of paralysis of the heart. She was a good citizen, and very highly respected by everyone. She had been a member of the M.E. Church for many years, and the last sad rites were performed by Rev. R.S. MARTIN, pastor of the church at this place. Her interment took place on Saturday, her remains being taken to Montezuma and buried beside her husband.

Obituary
ROBERT WRIGHT, of West Upland, Parke County, formerly a resident of this place and the father of WILLIAM P. WRIGHT, died on Friday last. He would have been 82 years of age. He was afflicted with Bright's disease of the kidneys, and had been ailing for some time. His wife died here one year ago last winter. The deceased leaves an estate worth $30,000, most of which is in cash, to be divided between his children. The funeral took place on last Saturday afternoon. His remains were interred at the Linebarger Cemetery,

Death
Mrs. ELIZABETH HOLLINGSWORTH, of this township, who was making her home with JOHN F. HUNT, 7 miles southwest of town, died quite suddenly on last Thursday night. She retired to bed at about 9 o'clock at night in her usual health, and took a coughing spell and choked to death before 10 o'clock. The deceased was born at Breckenridge, KY, in 1813, and emigrated with her parents to Corydon, this state, when it was the capitol of Indiana. She had been a resident of this state 65 years, and the county 60 years, and was the last survivor of a family of 10 children. She was a sister-in-law of Hon. O.P. DAVIS, of Opedee, and was a very estimable and highly respected lady. She was a good Christian, and had been a member of the U.B. Church for 27 years. Her funeral took place at Opedee on Saturday last and was very largely attended. The discourse was preached by Rev. R.B. VAN ALLEN, pastor of her church.

Clinton
The commencement exercises here, of both Professor TOMLIN and KEARNS' classes, far surpassed anything of the kind that has ever been in town. On Thursday evening, Prof. KEARNS' class, which had completed the common school course, gave their entertainment. These were 10 of them: GRACE SOLIDAY, EDDIE THOMPSON, CORA TWEEDY, NELLIE MALONE, ARTHUR ROBERTS, CLARE AIKMAN, MYRTLE WRIGHT, INDIA BULLINGTON, EVA CLARK, and NETTIE WHITCOMB. On Friday evening, Prof. TOMLIN's class, which had completed the High School course, gave an entertainment. The members of this class were: MARY WELLS, MAGGIE HALL, and WILLIAM WEBER. The following graduates received a gold watch as a graduating present: ARTHUR ROBERTS, NELLIE MALONE, CORA TWEEDY, MARY WELLS, and MAGGIE HALL.

Death
Uncle ISRAEL WOOD, one of our old and respected citizens of this township, died very suddenly last Sunday. Mr. WOOD was a loving father, a kind neighbor, and all who knew him, loved and respected him. He was ever ready and willing to lend a helping hand to all in need.

Home News
Mrs. OL DAVIS, wife of our late postmaster, has gone down to Ellettsville to live with her people.

ALBERT ANDERSON, a 17 year old son of DANIEL ANDERSON of Clay County, committed suicide on Thursday last by hanging himself in his father's barn.

J.W. NEEL, of Highland Township, was down here yesterday and made a Will. He wills all his property, real and personal, at his death, to his 4 grandchildren – FRANK HOLDER, FLORA HOLDER, BERTIE MAY HOLDER, and AMOS HOLDER – children by his first wife's daughter. He cut out all his own children because he says they refuse to speak to him when they meet him.

List of Letters
    Miss FLORA STEWART   Mrs. N. SHIELDS
    J.N. GRISWOLD   CURT HOLLAND
    W.H. LAEFF   F.F. PETERS
    H. HOUCHIN   OLIVER L. READ

Death
ISRAEL WOOD of Clinton, died very suddenly at 1 o'clock on last Sunday. He was about 61 years of age and had been a resident for many years. He was a loving father, a kind neighbor, and all who knew him loved and respected him. He was only sick 4 days. He was a member of the Masonic fraternity, and was buried by that order yesterday afternoon.

Wednesday, June 12, 1889

Death
JOSEPH CHUNN, who had been making his home with MILTON HARRIS, one mile south of town, since early last winter, died very suddenly at 8 o'clock on last Saturday night. On the Tuesday before, he was in town and executed his voucher for his quarterly payment of pension, and was in his usual health. On Friday night when he retired for rest, he did not complain of any ailment, but during the night he took sick, and the next morning a physician was called to attend him. In the afternoon of that day he had a stroke of paralysis, and laid perfectly helpless until death, not being able to utter a single word after being stricken down. His daughter, ALICE CHUNN, who lives at the Soldiers' Orphans' Home, at Knightstown, was immediately notified, and Senator SEARS left on the early morning train Sunday, to meet her and bring her back here, arriving here on the 6:22 train Monday morning. The other daughter, who is married, resides in Illinois. He only had two children. The deceased had been an inmate of the poor house for many years, and last year after the government granted his pension, which had been pending for 16 or 17 years, he went to live with Mr. MILTON HARRIS. He was afflicted with rheumatism, and had been walking on crutches for many years. During the late war, he was a member of the 6th IN Cavalry, and had recently joined the Grand Army Post at this place. His remains were taken down to Clinton for interment, where they were laid to rest on last Monday afternoon, the Grand Army Posts of Clinton and this place conducting the exercises. The officiating minister was Rev. HANDLEY, pastor of the M.E. Church at that place.

Fodder Shock Nubbins
Mr. JAMES RUSH and wife, father, and mother of Prof. RUSH of this place arrived here last Monday night from Thomasville, GA, accompanied by their son MARK RUSH. The elder gentleman is in very feeble health and desired to see his friends in Vermillion while he could.

Clinton Echoes
MILT HAYS, administrator of the HISE estate, was in the city last week making his final settlement with the creditors. The estate paid 65 cents on the dollar.

Col. R.H. WASHBURN left last Friday for Michigan where he will make his future home. While we are loth to lose HARLOW from our midst, he has the best wishes of a host of friends. FRANK WELLS will take care for his widow while he is away.

Mr. WHITLOCK, one of the corps of teachers here, returned to his home in Dana last week, and has accepted a position as deputy postmaster at that place.

Home News
ED HEGARTY, aged about 15, of Mattoon, IL, is over here visiting his uncle, MAURICE HEGARTY.

County Surveyor BOB PARRETT called around at Dr. FRANK TURNER's catnip foundry last Monday, and laid in a supply of that staple article. BOB says it is a fine looking boy.

Attorney M.G. RHOADS has been appointed administrator of the estate of RUTH PORTER, deceased, with the Will annexed, which was made a long time ago, and is said to be no good now.

ED E. AIKMAN yesterday gave bond as deputy treasurer of this county. His bond is for $10,000. Mr. CUSHMAN, who has so long been the watch dog of the county treasury, retires, and Mr. AIKMAN takes his place today.

J.M. NICHOLS, who has been on the sick list for over 6 months, is still confined to his room. He had to have another surgical operation performed on Saturday last. He has had a long and tough siege of it. We do hope he will now take a change for the better.

Mrs. S.C. ZOOK, widow of the late Rev. ZOOK, of Vermilion County, IL, was down here last week visiting her daughter, Mrs. IDA HENSON.

WILLIAM C. BENNETT, of this place, received notice on Friday last that his application for pension had been granted. He gets $4 per month, and gets over four years arrears. BILL was a good soldier, and we are glad to hear that he has been placed on the pension rolls, but are sorry the rate is so small. He is justly entitled to a more liberal rate.

Married
In the parlor of the Newport Parsonage, at 10 o'clock a.m., June 8th, 1889, by Rev. R.S. MARTIN of the M.E. Church, Mr. GEORGE A. HARPER and Miss MATTIE GREENHILL, both of Danville, IL, were united in marriage in the presence of a few friends. Mr. and Mrs. HARPER will make their future home in the city of their former residence.

Matrimony
On Tuesday of last week, June 4th, 1889, Miss MATTIE McDONALD, of Hoopeston, IL, daughter of the late MARION McDONALD, of this place, was united in wedlock to Mr. LAWRENCE SCOOLER, a traveling salesman of New York. The ceremony took place at the residence of the bride's mother, Mrs. KATE CORBIN. On the Wednesday afternoon following the couple took a trip to Springfield, IL, and St. Louis, MO. They will make their home in New York City. The bride is 18 and the groom is 32 years of age.

Real Estate Transfers
>JAMES OSBORN and wife to JOSEPH BURNS
9 acres in Helt Township
$270

>DAVID McBETH and wife to M.J. STOKESBERRY
Part of lots 5, 8, & 9, Block 1, in Clinton
$500

>JAMES J. KNIGHT and wife to EDWARD L. WATSON
80 acres in Helt Township
$3,600

JOSEPH F. COOK and wife to CLAY E. THOMAS
80 acres in Vermillion Township
$2,700

Death
OSCAR AYERS, of Dana, a young man aged about 21 or 22 years, died on last Monday evening, of consumption. He had been an invalid for a year or more. He recently returned from Florida, where he went to see if the climate would not benefit his failing health, but the trip did him no good.

Helt Hollerings
HENRY SHAFFER has a nice little girl baby, 4 weeks old.

Wednesday, June 19, 1889

Killed
A sad accident happened at Gessie, this county, on Thursday last. JOHN HAWORTH, agent on the C.&E.I. Railway at that place, attempted to board a passing freight train and missed his footing and fell under the train, 13 cars passing over his body. Mr. HAWORTH was a general favorite among the people in his vicinity. He leaves a wife and 3 little children.

Home News
The Fairmont Veto, published by Miss IDA ROBISON, has pulled up stakes and moved to Homer, IL, where a newspaper will be started by the fair IDA on a much larger scale.

WILLIAM WOOD has been appointed administrator of the estate of ISRAEL WOOD, deceased.

RICHARD HAWORTH, of Quaker Hill, this township, who has been attending college at Richmond, this state, is at home.

Rev. JOHN P. HENSON, of Lamar, NE, arrived back here last Saturday afternoon on a visit and maybe to stay.

FRANK BLINK, foreman of the Sidell, IL, Journal, came over here on Saturday last and spent Sunday with his mother.

Miss CLARA MYERS, who has been attending school at Champaign, IL, returned home last week. She will go back again in September to complete her course.

Real Estate Transfers
FRANK M. RILEY et ux to WILLIAM E. ISRIG
½ acre in Highland Township
$109

JAMES OSBORN et ux to SARAH J. SMITH
Lots 10 & 11, in Osborn's addition to Dana
$100

JAMES QUINLAN et ux to CHARLES G. THOMAS
Lot 2, Block 5, in Dana
$350

JAMES T. BARNES Sr. to AMANDA BUSH
Lot 8, in Barnett's addition to Dana
$500

H.B. DUDLEY et ux to JOHN WHITCOMB
Part of Lot 2, Block 4, in Clinton
$100

Obituary
The infant child of OSCAR NICHOLS, residing 8 miles southwest of here, aged 5 or 6 months, died on Wednesday of spinal trouble. Its remains were interred at the Thomas Cemetery on Thursday, the day following its death.

Wednesday, June 26, 1889

Another Murder
Little PARLEY SNIDER, aged 13 years, of Highland, this county, was brutally murdered on Tuesday evening of last week. Near noon of that day his mother sent him on an errand to Hillsdale, located about ¾ of a mile from Highland. While he was down there, two sons of DAVE DOUGLASS - KERSEY DOUGLASS and HOSEA DOUGLASS, aged 10 and 12 years, and a son of ADAM PEARMAN, named OSCAR PEARMAN, aged 13 years, ran across PARLEY SNIDER, and persuaded him to go the swimming hold, ¼ mile west of Hillsdale. This was the last time that PARLEY SNIDER was seen alive……… Later OSCAR PEARMAN told his mother that SNIDER had drowned that afternoon at the swimming hole. A search was made, and his body was recovered. It showed that he had indeed not drowned, but had evidence of several blows to the head. An investigation is being made. The victim was interred at 4 o'clock on last Monday afternoon, his remains being followed to the cemetery by his grief stricken parents and a large concourse of sympathizing friends.

Fodder Shock Nubbins
Dana News
Mrs. ABIGAIL THOMPSON is quite low with erysipelas at this writing.

Death
Mrs. J.B. DURHAM, who died in this city Thursday, June 13th, 1889, was born in Paris, KY, November 10th, 1807, and was therefore 82 years of age at the time of her death. She was the daughter of HARRISON and RUTH RUBY WALKER, and at an early age developed those traits which throughout her life marked her as one of the noblest Christian women and made her a model wife and mother. She united with the Methodist Episcopal Church at 9 years of age, remaining a devoted and exemplary member until death. She was educated at the nunnery at Bardstown, KY, and was married to J.B. DURHAM, January 22, 1833, removing to Montgomery County, IN, in March following. To them were born 9 children, 6 of whom are living and 3 of them residents of this city, viz: T.W. DURHAM, Mrs. J.J. HANNA, and Mrs. C.W. WELCH. One son is living in Seattle, Washington Territory, and 2 daughters in Indiana. Mrs. DURHAM removed with her husband and family to Topeka in 1868, where her husband died in 1882, and a daughter, Mrs. W.H. WHITE, in 1885. She was well known to all who came here in the earlier years of the city's history and universally beloved. Dr. LIPPINGOOD, assisted by Dr. McCABE will conduct the funeral services this morning at 8 o'clock.
                                                Topeka, KS, Capitol, June 15, 1889

Real Estate Transfers
    JOSHUA JUMP, Commissioner to SMITH McCORMACK
    Part of 5 lots in Perrysville
    $?

    JOHN L. FOX et ux to JAMES W. HUGHES
    133.72 acres in Highland Township
    $5,150

ELIZA A. DOWNING and husband to ALBERT F. HARMESON
Lot 113 in Grondyke & McKee's addition to the town of Cayuga
$755

MATTHEW W. SCOTT et ux to JOHN H. BOGART
Lot 4 in Block 10, in Clinton
$20

MORTON WICK to LUCY ANN WICK
Lot 6, Block 3, in Knowles addition to town of Clinton
$60

Notice of Administration
Estate of JOSEPH CHUNN, deceased
Filed June 19, 1889

JAMES CHIPPS, Administrator

Tin Wedding
Rev. R.S. MARTIN, pastor of the M.E. Church here, had been trotting in double harness 10 years yesterday, and his many friends here concluded they would celebrate his tin wedding last night by giving him a surprise. There was quite a large crowd to greet him when he returned home from the country.

Married
At the residence of Rev. MATER, in Hillsdale, on June 19th, 1889, Mr. CHARLES D. SELCH and Miss JESSIE E. GARLINGHOUSE were married.

Home News
JAMES TUTT, of Highland, who has been afflicted with cancer of the head for many years, is now lying at the point of death, and it is thought he cannot survive many days.

Mrs. IRVIN LAMB, of the Reform School at Plainfield, was over here all of last week visiting her relatives and host of friends. On Monday she went out to Urbana, IL, to visit her daughter, Mrs. PET SCHWEIZER.

Pumpkin Vine News
Clinton Argus
Miss ORA JOHNSON, who has recently graduated from the State Normal School of Kansas, has been employed in the city school of Emporia, KS, for the ensuing year at a good salary.

Died
Mrs. HEDGES, an aged and well known citizen of Clinton, died at her home west of here Wednesday. The funeral was conducted Thursday. Mrs. HEDGES leaves quite a family of grown children. She was a member of the Baptist Church and was a true Christian lady. She was nearly 80 years old.

Divorced
ELHANAN STEVENS and HATTIE A. STEVENS, his wife, after 6 months of married life, found that was impossible for them to harmonize and were on Friday of last week duly divorced in the Circuit Court. Mrs. HATTIE A. STEVENS changed her name to her former name, HATTIE A. PHENEGAR. No charges were made upon either party.

Pension
W.P. HENSON was made happy with the notice that his pension was being increased. In 1862 he was granted a pension of $2 per month. It was then increased to $5 14 years later. It has been increased to $8 effective in 1862, which will give him $1,428, and increase to $30 per month.

Administrator's Sale
    Estate of ADALINE V. JONES, deceased
    Auction of personal property at late residence in Perrysville
    Auction to be held Saturday, June 22nd, 1889
                              B.O. CARPENTER, Administrator

Wednesday, July 3, 1889

    Dana Notes
Miss GRACE ALLEN returned Thursday from a visit to the family of her uncle, W.A. DUNCAN, at Oskaloosa, IA.

SIMEON HOLLINGSWORTH, an old and respected citizen residing one mile north of Dana, died on Tuesday night of last week of congestion of the stomach. He was buried on Thursday under the auspices of the Dana Masonic Lodge, Rev. R.B. VAN ALLEN conducting the service.

Miss GRACE WHITLOCK closed her school at the Mandlay school house last Saturday.

    Summit Grove Items
Miss ELVA, OLLIE and FRED JAMES returned home from the Normal School at Terre Haute last week.

    Other News
JOHN LEECHMAN, aged 70 years, residing at Center Point, Clay County, died on Sunday last from the effects of a snake bite, received several days ago.

Mrs. CHARLES FISCHER, of Brazil, was fatally burned on Monday last while trying to start a fire in the kitchen stove with coal oil. The contents of the can ignited and exploded, setting her clothing on fire.

D.C. GREINER has been appointed postmaster at Terre Haute. We are glad of it. He is an old soldier and a very clever gentleman, and we predict will make a good postmaster. He is poor and is deserving of a good office for the active work performed during the last campaign.

Our old friend, E.Y. JACKSON, is able to be out on the streets again. He has had a three months siege with a lame hand which has confined him to the house most of the time. We are glad to see him out again.
                                              Altamont, KS, Sentinel
Mr. JACKSON was a former resident of this place, and is well known to many of our citizens.

    Circuit Court Proceedings
        State of Indiana vs. CLARK CONKLIN
        Malicious trespass – Nollied

        State of Indiana vs. WILLIAM RICHARDSON
        Murder in the 2nd degree – Continued

        State of Indiana vs. STEVE BROWN
        Murder in the 1st degree – Sent to penitentiary for 10 years

        State of Indiana vs. JOSEPH CONRAD
        Giving false list of tax values – Dismissed

        State of Indiana vs. ABRAHAM SIMS
        Carrying concealed weapons – Fined $1 and costs

State of Indiana vs. JOHN C. PORTER
Carrying concealed weapons – Fined $1 and costs

State of Indiana vs. JOSEPH HANN
Selling liquor to minor – Continued

State of Indiana vs. JOHN R. PORTER
Allowing minor to play pool – Fined $5 and costs

State of Indiana vs. JULIUS ALDRIDGE
Allowing minor to play pool – Fined $5 and costs

State of Indiana vs. JOSEPH DAVIS
Appeal from J.P. Court – Discharged – Not guilty

State of Indiana vs. CORNELIUS H. NORTON
Selling whiskey to minor – Discharged – Not guilty

State of Indiana vs. CORNELIUS H. NORTON
Selling whiskey on election day – Fined $10 and costs

State of Indiana vs. JOHN H. SMITH
Selling beer to minor – Not guilty – Discharged

State of Indiana vs. DANIEL MACK
From J.P. Court – Continued

State of Indiana vs. HENRY KUNKLE etal
From J.P. Court – Dismissed

GEORGE A. CRABB etal vs. WINFIELD S. CRABB etal
Partition and sale – Continued

CHARLES W. WARD, Admr JOHN W. WEBSTER, dec. vs. MARY H. WEBSTER etal
Sale – Continued

SARAH BALES vs. JAMES RUNYAN etal
Partition made

WORTH W. PORTER etal vs. JOHN C. PORTER etal
Partition – Continued

SAMUEL B. DAVIS, Trustee vs. WILLIAM POOR
Sent to Reform School

SAMUEL B. DAVIS, Trustee vs. FRANK MASON
Sent to Reform School

SAMUEL B. DAVIS, Trustee vs. WILLIAM MASON
Dismissed

SAMUEL B. DAVIS, Trustee vs. WILLIAM TATINAN
Dismissed

HESTER A.B. EMERSON vs. WILLIAM H. EMERSON
Complaint to set aside decree of divorce – Continued

The Interstate Investment Co. of the State of Kansas vs. JULIA B. HOSFORD etal
Quiet title – Continued

TRAVIS P. YORK vs. JAMES QUINLAN
Change of venue from Parke County – Judgment for defendant

CHARLES COOPER etal, SAMPSON REED etal, vs. MARTIN L. WRIGHT
Foreclosure $150 – Continued

BELL WRIGHTMIER vs. RICHARD WRIGHTMIER
Divorce – Granted to plaintiff

SUSAN NEFF vs. JOSEPH BARRIS
Note - $170 – Continued

SAMUEL WAGGONER etal vs. MARY J. WAGGONER etal
Quiet title – change of venue to Parke County

RANDOLPH SMOCK vs. JAMES PEGG etal
Change from Parke County – Continued

JOHN H. BOGART vs. SARAH J. ENGLISH etal
Quiet title – Judgment for plaintiff

MARY LEWIS vs. WILLIAM W. CREVISTON etal
Quiet title – Judgment for plaintiff

HIRAM CHENOWETH vs. AMANDA FERGUSON, Admr
Claim $1118.47 – Continued

MOSES SWAIM etal vs. LAFAYETTE SWAIM etal
Quiet title – change of venue from Montgomery County – finding for plaintiff
Continued on verdict

MARY A. FERGUSON, Admr vs. HARRY W. ROBINSON etal
Petition for a Commissioner to make deed – Commissioner appointed – deed made

DAVID B. DINSMORE vs. JOHN S. HOUCHIN
Complaint for release from Guardian bond – released – defendant filed new bond

MARTHA FOUTS etal vs. SAMUEL & MALONE
Partition – Continued

WILLIAM W. BAILEY vs. BENJAMIN O. CARPENTER
Claim $12.80 – Dismissed

ELLEN HAWKINS vs. JOHN W. JARVIS etal
Note $725 – Judgment for plaintiff

HENRY NEBEKER vs. JAMES E. KNOWLES etal
Account $100 - Continued

JOHN J. BRAKE vs. WILLIAM ORTH
Partition – Dismissed

JOHN WHITCOMB vs. AMON DOWDY etal
Note $550 – Default judgment $125.25 – foreclosure

JAMES C. FORTNER vs. SILAS JONES
Quiet title – Reform deed continued

CHARLES WHITCOMB, REA WHITE vs. DAVID L. WRIGHT
Notes $115 – Default – Judgment $102.84

ELLEN DICKSON vs. MARY A. FERGUSON, Admr.
Claim $232.58 – Judgment for plaintiff $238.32

S.P. LINK etal vs. ISAAC KIBBY
Note $75 – Default judgment $70.09

WILLIAM PETTINGER vs. JOHN KONKLE
Note $250 – default judgment $242

ELHANAN STEVENS vs. HATTIE STEVENS
Divorce – granted

Real Estate Transfers
SMITH McCORMACK et ux to EDWIN G. McCORMACK & CHARLES McCORMACK
Part of Lot 50, in Perrysville - $500

ELIZABETH MOORE and husband to MARTIN B. RUDY
20 acres in Highland Township - $1100

ANN P. KESPLER to ELNORA B. HAHNA
Undivided 1/3 of out lot No. 10, in Perrysville - $58.93

Pumpkin Vine News
Clinton Argus
Mrs. EMELINE WHITCOMB is visiting her father, JAMES GREEN, at Buffalo, NY.

WILLIAM HAMILTON has purchased PERRY MORGAN's residence for Mrs. RUTH FONCANNON. The amount paid was $1200.

Miss CLARA WHITCOMB returned home last week from the south, where she has been engaged in teaching during the last year.

JOHN C. CHANEY, of Sullivan County, has been appointed Assistant Attorney in the Department of Justice, at Washington.

Home News
Miss MYRT BALES, of Jonestown, who has been up here visiting her sister, Mrs. J.M. HOPKINS, returned home last Sunday evening, after a pleasant stay of two months.

CLIFFORD K. STOUT and wife, of Cincinnati, OH, are here on a visit, the guests of JOHN H. KERDOLFF and wife. Mr. STOUT was a former resident of this place, and is well known by many of our citizens. He is now accountant and bookkeeper for the P.C. & St. L. Railway at Cincinnati, and is receiving a big salary.

Mrs. MARY J. HUMPHRIES, of Clinton Township, has just received notice that her husband's pension has been granted. The arrears amounts to $5,000. Mr. HUMPHRIES has been dead sometime, and the money will now go to his wife and children.

Uncle MADISON NICHOLS is again in very poor health. He is troubled a great deal with shortness of breath, and much of the time has to do his sleeping while sitting in a chair. It begins to look like his time here is getting short, unless there is a sudden change for the better. Nearly all his children were here on Sunday last to see him.

Mrs. FRED HACKER and son, WILLIAM HACKER, of Danville, were thrown down an embankment Friday afternoon by a runaway team. Mrs. HACKER was severely cut above and below the eye and her head was severely bruised. The son, WILLIAM, suffered a compound fracture of the left leg below the knee, both bones being broken.
Terre Haute Express

The little 3 year old daughter of County Surveyor R.A. PARRETT, of this place, fell while tripping over the floor on Wednesday last, and broke her left arm near the elbow joint. As it is broken so near the elbow, it will very likely make a very stiff joint for her.

WILLIAM H. DARNALL, of Bono, was up here on Sunday last. He says his wife, who was stricken down with paralysis several months ago, is still improving, and he thinks she will entirely recover in the course of time. She is now able to do considerable work, and can lift six pounds with her hand on the side she was paralyzed.

Miss MAY WISEMAN, of Winchester, IN, will be the guest of Misses ELLA and LOU WIMSETT during a part of the summer.

CHARLEY WRIGHT, of Sidell, IL, formerly editor of the Journal at that place, was over here several days last week, the guest of JOE HANN and family.

Sudden Death
SIMEON HOLLINGSWORTH, of this township, who resided about 2 miles north of Dana, on the Dana and Stumptown free gravel road, took suddenly ill with congestion of the stomach at 10 o'clock on Tuesday morning of last week, and by 10 o'clock that night he was a corpse. He was up here all the week before as a petit juror, and was in his usual good health, and his sudden death was a great surprise to his old friends in this locality. The deceased was 57 years and 29 days of age, and a most excellent citizen. He was honored and respected by everyone. He leaves a wife and one son, grown to manhood. He had been a Master Mason since 1881, and was buried by that order on Thursday last. The services were conducted by Rev. R.B. VAN ALLEN, pastor of the U.B. Church, of which church he had been a true and faithful member since he was a young man. He was born in Helt Township, in a short distance of where he had resided all his life. His remains were interred at the Wesley Chapel Cemetery, five miles west of Dana. It was the largest funeral procession that has been seen in that location for several months.

Marriage Licenses
The following is a list of marriage licenses issued by County Clerk A.R. HOPKINS, for June:
GEORGE HARPER and MATTIE GREENHILL
CORA M. BUMGARDNER and MAY HARRISON
CHARLES E. SELCH and JESSIE E. GARLINGHOUSE

Wednesday, July 10, 1889

Home News
JOHN GRUBB and ALMETTA FOOS were married on Saturday last.

JOEL HOLLINGSWORTH has been appointed administrator of his father's estate.

Miss EVA PARRETT, daughter of Judge WILLIAM F. PARRETT, of Evansville, is here on a visit, the guest of her cousin, Miss ELLA PARRETT.

LYMAN B. WILLIAMS, for nearly 30 years school superintendent of Steuben County, committed suicide on Sunday last. Grief over the death of one of his family is the supposed cause.

Rev. WILLIAM F. HENDERSON, of Quaker Hill, left for Ashville, TN, on Monday last, for the benefit of his failing health. He has consumption, and has been in very poor health for a long time. We hope the trip will benefit him.

Pumpkin Vine News
Clinton Argus
Mr. GUS D. FRENCH, of Dodge, WI, and Miss EMMA KNIGHT, of this city, were united in marriage last Tuesday evening at the residence of EVAN DAVIS, Rev. HANDLEY officiating. They will make their home in Wisconsin.

Mrs. BLYTH and her deputy Miss EUNICE NOURSE, were duly sworn into Uncle SAM's service Monday. After they have learned the ropes, they will no doubt be able to serve more promptly in the way of distributing and delivering the mail.

Real Estate Transfers
> WILLIAM R. HOLLINGSWORTH to JAMES WARD
> 15 acres in Vermillion Township - $125
>
> M.G. RHOADS, exec. of RUTH S. PORTER to LEWIS SHEPARD
> Lot 46 in Newport - $550
>
> HENRY NEBEKER et ux to JAMES C. CRANE
> Lot in Clinton - $300

Obituary
On last Thanksgiving Day, JAMES MADISON NICHOLS, of this place, took down sick, and lingered until about 8 o'clock last Saturday evening, when his spirit took its flight to that better world. During his long illness, he would take changes for the better, and his relatives and friends were encouraged with the belief that he would get well. But these periods were not of long duration. During these long months, he suffered intense pain at times, and death was really a relief to the veteran Christian, who had been a member of the U.B. Church since August, 1840, and who had always lived an exemplary Christian life. He was born in Mercer County, KY, on June 19, 1819, and consequently at the date of his death was 70 years and 17 days of age. When only 13 years of age in 1832, he emigrated to this county with his parents and had always been a resident of this township. When a young man he taught school in this locality for many years, and was one among the first school teachers in this township. For over 20 years he was assessor of this township, and was acquainted with nearly every person in this township, who always respected and honored him as a respectable and upright citizen. His death is a great loss to the community, and especially to the church, of which he was an active and zealous worker. He always tried to do by others as he would wish to be done by, and we believe if there ever was a true and conscientious Christian, MADISON NICHOLS was that man. He was kind and courteous to all, and raised a family of children who are highly respected by everyone. His good wife, whose heart is broken with grief over the loss of her dear companion, is one of the noblest women of this land, and in her hours of sorrow, she has the sympathy of everyone. The funeral occurred at 3 o'clock on last Sunday afternoon at the U.B. Church, Rev. IRA MATER, of Hillsdale, preaching the discourse. His remains were followed to the Thomas Cemetery by the largest funeral procession that ever passed through the town – nearly 500 people. The last sad rites at the grave were performed by pastor R.B. VAN ALLEN.

Deserted

Young DeHART, aged about 25, who was working for HAM BETSON and supporting his widowed mother, has deserted the old lady, who is between 60 and 70 years of age, and unable to support herself. On Monday last, the trustee ordered her taken to the poor house, where she will have a comfortable home and be kindly cared for.

Celebrating the Fourth

AARON H. CRAFT, who resides two miles west of town, celebrated the 4th by getting married the day before so he could have some one to help him enjoy the National holiday. The name of the lady is Mrs. PHOEBE PHILLIPS, a resident of this place. She is 48 and Mr. CRAFT is 55. Both are good citizens, and we wish them a pleasant and happy future.

Killed

On last Wednesday afternoon a small boy by the name of VAN DUNLAP, the son of a widow lady of Clinton, was run over and instantly killed, about one mile north of that town, by a C. & E.I. Train. He was horribly mangled, his head being severed from the body. Coroner BRINDLEY was notified and went down on the night train and held an inquest over the remains, and rendered a verdict of accidental killing. The boy was engaged in herding cattle in the vicinity of the accident, and it is supposed he attempted to board a passing train and was pulled under the train.

Matrimony

FRANK FORTNER, of Terre Haute, formerly of this place, was united in wedlock on last Sunday evening to Miss LAURA B. HOWELL, residing six miles southwest of here. Rev. WILLIAM E. HENDERSON performing the ceremony.

Wednesday, July 17, 1889

Dana Notes

IRA PEER went to Paxton, IL, last Thursday to which place his father's stock of dry goods has been shipped. He will there engage in the dry goods business with a Mr. RAMEY, a former traveling salesman.

Pumpkin Vine News
Clinton Argus

Died – FREDERICK STAATS, infant son of Mr. and Mrs. HARRY STAATS, died at the residence of Mrs. PHOEBE STAATS on Sunday evening. The funeral occurred from the house Tuesday afternoon. The little boy was about six months of age. The grief stricken family has the sympathy of their many friends in their hour of affliction.

While our young drayman, ED CUNNINGHAM was working at a pile of beer kegs in Walker's beer house Wednesday morning, he got his right hand caught between the chimes of two kegs which were falling together. They cut off the two forefingers of his right hand. He was taken at once to Dr. NEBEKER's office where his wounds were dressed. It was a very painful accident, and will no doubt lay ED up for some time to come, and maybe change all his plans for life.

Died – CHARLIE REED, son of Mr. and Mrs. D.A. REED, died at the home of his parents at the Edwards residence on Monday morning at the age of five years and 3 months. The funeral was conducted Tuesday afternoon and was well attended by friends of the family. CHARLIE was a very bright little fellow, and although he had been a terribly afflicted invalid for 3 years, was a very sweet dispositioned child and was perfectly willing and even anxious to die.

Fodder Shock Nubbins
Dana News

Mr. J.F. PEELER has sold his drug and grocery store to Mr. CHARLES WOLFE, of St. Bernice.

Uncle DICK MALONE is 73 years old today, Wednesday.

Mrs. JAMES KAUFMAN, her friends will be glad to learn, was able to be out for a buggy ride last Saturday.

J.L. PEER is moving his large stock of dry goods this week to Paxton, IL. He will retire from business himself, and his son IRA PEER and another partner will conduct the business.

Obituary
ELIZABETH SWANK was born May 20, 1805, in Ohio; was married to EDMUND JAMES June 9, 1822; joined the M.E. Church in 1823, of which she was a most exemplary member till her death, which occurred in Summit Grove, Vermillion County, IN, Friday about 12 p.m, July 12, 1889. Her age was 84 years, 1 month, and 23 days. She was sick but 2 days, and was able to spend the day Wednesday visiting at Rev. THOMAS DAVIS'. She died without a struggle, full of years and full of honors – loved by God and her neighbors and children and grandchildren. Her home was always a welcome one to itinerant ministers in early Methodism in Indiana. JOHN STRANGE, J.F. THOMPSON, R. HARGRAVE and A. WOOD have rested under her hospitable roof, and shared of her Christian hospitality, and while we today miss her from our circle she doubtless is with her dear companion. Her children and grandchildren have for years been in the habit of celebrating her birthday. I was permitted to be at her 82nd and 83rd. These were occasions of great pleasure to her and all her numerous friends. The funeral services were conducted by Rev. T.C. DAVIS, at 2 p.m. Saturday, July 13, 1889, at the Summit Grove Church. Her remains were laid to rest in the beautiful cemetery of Summit Grove.

Died
NANCY ELLIS, wife of JAMES ELLIS, who lives on JAMES HAWORTH's farm, died last Monday morning at 4 o'clock, and was buried at the Thomas Cemetery at 10:30 a.m. yesterday. There was a large crowd of friends at the funeral. JOHN HENDERSON conducted the exercises at the cemetery. She leaves a husband and a daughter, aged 6 or 7 years. She had been an invalid for 5 years, and had suffered much and no doubt death was welcomed by her.

Birthday
The children and relatives of Mrs. SAM SANDERS, of this place, took the old lady by surprise on Friday last. On that day she was 54 years of age, and the children and relatives thought it would be nice to give her a happy surprise, and all come in and spend the day with her.

Married
At Danville, on Saturday, July 13, 1889, by the Rev. W.W. SWERINGEN, Mr. C.L. HOON, of Denver, CO, and Miss M.M. CHENOWETH, of Perrysville, IN.

Wednesday, July 24, 1889

Saturday afternoon, THOMAS HESTER, aged 72, filed suit at Brazil for a divorce from his wife, MARTHA HESTER, aged 69 years. They had been married for 26 years.
Terre Haute Express

Death
Mrs. BOTHWELL, wife of B.S. BOTHWELL, who taught the Opedee School last winter, died very suddenly on last Friday morning. She took down with a congestive chill at about 10 o'clock on Thursday night, and was a corpse by 7 o'clock in the morning. She was a daughter of LEVI and EMILY MYERS of Parke County. She was born April 14, 1866 and died July 19, 1889, aged 23 years, 3 months, and 5 days. Her funeral was preached by Rev. R.B. VAN ALLEN, pastor of the U.B. Church, after which her remains were interred in the cemetery at that place. She leaves a husband and 3 little children to mourn her death.

Marriage

The people of Dana were somewhat surprised last week, by the announcement that Dr. HIRAM SHEPARD, of that brisk little city, had been spliced to the young widow of 'TRAP' HIGGINS. He was an old bachelor, over 50, and she a blushing widow of 22. The wedding took place at Galesburg, IL, on the 11th of the month, and was kept a profound secret for several days. H.W. BULLOCK acted as right hand bower for the groom. Mrs. HIGGINS was a dressmaker of Dana, and did a big business. We wish them success.

Montezuma News

Mrs. JAMES RAIRDON, who has been very sick for the past two weeks at the home of her father northeast of town, with intermittent fever, is slowly improving, though not yet able to come home.

Real Estate Transfers

    DANIEL LASHLEY to MARTHA J. SOLLARS
    20 acres in Eugene Township for $5

    E.D. JAMES et ux to F.M. JAMES
    190 acres in Helt Township for $2,000

    JESSE RUNYAN et ux to THOMAS CARLIN
    8 acres in Clinton Township for $225

    THOMAS CARLIN et al to JESSE RUNYAN
    8 acres in Clinton Township for $1

    O.P. MORGAN to GEORGE W. FONCANNON
    Lots 8 & 9, Block 30, in Clinton for $1500

    THOMAS McKEE et al to Mrs. LUCY CLIFTON
    Lots 120 and 121 in Cayuga for $200

    FRED A. STAATS to EMMET B. LANG
    Lots 11 & 12, Block 4, in Dana for $350

Home News

The infant child of ELMER E. DAVIS, of Quaker Hill, this township, was buried on Thursday last. It was only sick a few days.

Uncle JIMMY TUTT, of Highland, who is suffering with cancer of the head, still lingers, notwithstanding. It was the opinion of his neighbors many months ago, that he could not possibly last many days. The old gentleman has suffered untold misery, and death would be a great relief to him.

Wednesday, July 31, 1889

Obituary

Montezuma, IN – July 29, 1889 – Mrs. CHARLOTTE L. JONES, wife of R.O. JONES, died July 24th, 1889, aged 57 years. Mr. and Mrs. JONES had been married 39 years. The deceased was a homely woman, seldom ever going away from home on account of ill health. But she loved to have her friends visit her. And to know her as did the writer, was to love her. She leaves a husband and one daughter. Mrs. GRACE GENTRY, and a host of other friends. Funeral services were conducted by Rev. J.C. KEMP at the family residence on Tuesday evening.

Pumpkin Vine News
Clinton Argus
O.B. SIMS has resigned his position as night operator at this place, and returned to Urbana, IL.

Miss CARRIE WILSON, of Crawfordsville, is the guest of her sister, Mrs. Dr. NEBEKER.

Missing
On Saturday last, the landlord of the Newport Hotel at this place, TOM ELLIS, mysteriously disappeared, and up to date no information of his whereabouts has been received. He had only $5 when he left, which he received for a hog which did not belong to him. His wife, who is a most excellent lady, is running the hotel now, and is giving general satisfaction. Mr. ELLIS was a very clever and good hearted fellow, but strong drink has the upper hand of him, and he cannot resist the temptation.

Marriage
AUSTIN MILLER and Miss ANNA DICKEN, of Terre Haute, both former residents of this place, were united in wedlock, one day last week. Mrs. DICKEN, the mother of the bride, who recently separated from her husband, is living with the newly married couple.

Clinton Echoes
FRANK THRIFT has secured a position at Indianapolis and will dispose of his property here and remove his family to that place. Mr. THRIFT is an industrious and honest man and we wish him success in his new home.

Miss MAGGIE PINSON has an offer of $50 per month to go to Illinois to teach this winter. Miss PINSON taught at the same place last spring, and her work was much appreciated.

FRANK FUNKHOUSER is soon to quit the sawmill business. He has accepted a position as agent for the Sanford Fork and Tool works of Terre Haute.

Fodder Shock Nubbins
Dana News
The infant child of Mr. and Mrs. CHARLES SHAW died of spinal ailment last Thursday. It was a bright little child, and its loss is a great bereavement to the parents.

Rev, C.C. PALMER, a Baptist preacher, who formerly preached at this place, but lately stationed at Brookston has been cutting some serious antics. He has left his wife and child, and jumped the country with a Miss MARY McGOON of Pawpaw, MI, a dressmaker. During the past season, he has been visiting her claiming that she was his cousin.

Unrequited Love
CHARLEY PARRETT, a young man who is working for WILLIAM Y. RICE, three miles southwest of here, was dead gone on a young lady who did not reciprocate his love. He wanted to marry the young lady, but she rejected his offer, preferring to earn her living by teaching school a little while longer. Without her this world was no pleasure to him, and so on last Sunday evening he concluded to end his earthly career here. He took enough laudanum to accomplish his object, but his scheme was discovered in time by someone of Mr. RICE's family who gave the alarm, when Dr. J.C. HARRISON, of Hillsdale, was dispatched for and arrived in time to prevent a funeral. Mr. PARRETT is a native of Tennessee, and had been a resident of this township about 2 years, working for different farmers. He was strictly temperate and industrious and bore a good reputation.

Home News
A.J. BECK, of Highland Township, an old Co. I, 43rd IN boy, has been granted a pension. His arrears amounts to between six and seven hundred dollars.

EMERY BRILES left here on the early south bound train on Saturday morning for Plainfield, where he has been given employment by the Superintendent of the Reform School. The Superintendent will find him a clever gentleman, and the most ingenious fellow.

C.S. DAVIS will leave for Salina, KS, on Tuesday next, to look after his business at that place.

Real Estate Transfers
JOHN ELLIS to JOHN HENDERSON
18 acres in Vermillion Township for $210

JAMES R. FINNELL to SQUIRE McCOWAN
80 acres in Helt Township for $3,000

SQUIRE McCOWAN to JAMES R. FINNELL
80 acres in Helt Township for $3,000

HENRY B. HAMMOND & SAMUEL KAUFMAN to SARAH C. SMITH
Lot 3 in Dana for $50

Wednesday, August 7, 1889

Fodder Shock Nubbins
Dana News
An eight pound boy arrived at the residence of Mr. WILL RHOADS last Friday night.

On Friday night last, Mr. and Mrs. DAN THOMAS, of Bono, were the happy recipients of a fine nine pound boy.

Sheriff's Sale on Decree
FRANK R. BYERS, Admr. of Estate of MICHAEL BYERS, deceased
Vs.
RUFUS DARLING & SUSAN DARLING
$1199.95
Sale on Saturday, September 7, 1889
Sale at courthouse between 10 and 4
NW ¼ SW ¼ Sec 33 T 19 N R 9 W
NE ¼ SW ¼ Sec 33 T 19 N R 9 W
RHOADS & AIKMAN, Attorneys for plaintiff
Filed August 3, 1889
WILLIAM RHEUBY, Sheriff

Sheriff's Sale on Decree
JOHN WHITCOMB
Vs.
AMON DOWDY & MARIAH C. DOWDY
$427.35
Sale on Saturday, August 31, 1889
Sale at courthouse between 10 and 4
SE ¼ SE ¼ SE ¼ Sec 12 T 14 N R 9 W – 10 acres
CONLEY & SAWYER, Attorneys for plaintiff
Filed July 26, 1889
WILLIAM RHEUBY, Sheriff

Home News
A child of WILLIAM ALLY, of Cayuga, aged 4 years, died on Wednesday of whooping cough and brain fever. The funeral was preached by Rev. R.B. VAN ALLEN, pastor of the U.B. Church.

Mrs. PAT FLYNN of Hillsdale, accompanied by her aunt, Mrs. WATSON of Illinois, gave the editor a pleasant call on last Saturday afternoon.

Mrs. J.M. NICHOLS has gone out to Illiana, IL, to reside with her son ROBERT E. NICHOLS.

TOM BASINGER, who resides on TIP DALLAS' farm, lost an infant child by death on Sunday last.

Miss HATTIE STEARNS, of Muncie, IL, was here the latter part of last week visiting her cousin, W.M. PLACE.

Death
Mrs. SALLIE NICHOLS, wife of HENRY C. NICHOLS of Perrysville, died on Thursday last and was interred in the Hicks Cemetery, west of that town, on the day following her death. She was 60 years of age, and had been an invalid for the last six or seven months. In her death the community loses a most excellent and highly esteemed lady.

Unclaimed Letters
    Miss JULY ANDBOW   J.D. WHITE
    R.F. BROWNBAUGH   JOHN MOSEWELL
    LULU FOLSOM

Marriage Licenses
    AARON H. CRAFT and PHOEBE PHILIPS
    FRED G. FRENCH and EMMA E. KNIGHT
    FRANK FORTNER and LAURA B. HOWELL
    JOHN GRUBB and ALMETTA FOOS
    ROBERT SKIDMORE and NANCY J. STUTSMAN
    LEONIDAS DRAKE and SARAH E. CRAIG
    JESSE T.S. WILSON and ARMINDA E. CRAFT

Application for Liquor License
    FRANK L. REEDER – Clinton
    HENRY D. SPRAGUE – Eugene
    EDWARD E. DAVIS – Newport
    THOMAS J. STARK – Cayuga
    WILLIAM J. BROPHY – Clinton

Pumpkin Vine News
Clinton Argus
WILLIE JAMES is lying dangerously ill at the residence of JOHN HORNEY, with fever.

HENRY BLAIR, a C & E.I. Railway employee, lost his forefinger on his right hand Monday, while working among some rails at Atherton. One of the rails fell on his hand, completely severing the finger.

Wednesday, August 14, 1889

Real Estate Transfers
    JOHN WHITCOMB to JOSEPH HANSON
    Lot in Clinton for $100

    JOSEPH HANSON to DAVID M. LARR
    2 lots in Clinton for $700

    EMMA F. SHANNON and husband to ANTON DOMIS
    3 acres in Clinton Township for $100

SILAS HUGHES to JOHN L. FOX
5 acres in Gessie for $750

JOHN W. PARRETT et ux to L.F. PURKY & J.M. ORR, as partners
3 lots in Newport
$100

WILLIAM WOOD et al to WILLIAM WRIGHT
243 acres in Clinton Township for $1

L.J. PLACE et ux to PURKY & ORR
Lot in Newport for $1

Obituary
Mr. JAMES C. TUTT, of Highland, who has been near death's door for many weeks, died at about 12 o'clock noon, on Saturday last, August 10th, 1889. He had been afflicted with cancer of the head for 30 years, but it did not trouble him much until a few years ago. During the last months of his illness, he suffered intensely, and for nearly two weeks before his death, he became totally blind and was neither able to eat or drink. His wife has also been an invalid for the last year and was unable to assist in caring for him, which wholly devolved upon their daughter SARAH, who has watched over them with the greatest care, and attended to their every need. It is thought the mother cannot last long. Mr. TUTT was born in Virginia on November 6th, 1816, and moved to this county in 1837, where he had lived ever since. The greater part of his life was spent in Eugene Township, where he had numerous friends and no enemies. Everybody respected and honored him. He was temperate in his habits, and one among the most industrious men in the county. Rev. IRA MATER, of Hillsdale, a U.B. minister, who frequently visited him during his illness, conducted the funeral services at his late residence on Sunday afternoon, after which his remains were followed to the cemetery, one fourth of a mile north of Highland, by relatives and sympathizing friends, and his body lowered into the grave to await the morning of the resurrection.

Miss MATTIE CUMMINGS, of Bloomingdale, Parke County, daughter of JAMES and RACHEL CUMMINGS, and a niece of Mrs. J.L. EGGLESTON, of this place, died on Tuesday of last week, August 6th, 1889, of consumption. She makes the third one of the family who has died of the same disease in the last 2 years.

Miss MATTIE DAVIS, a former resident of this place, who was born and raised here, but moved to Altamont, KS, a few years ago, has been appointed assistant postmistress of that place. The office pays $700 a year.

Fodder Shock Nubbins
Dana News
PORTER THOMPSON, who has been in this office for about 10 months, has retired and JOHN JORDAN has taken his place.

Notice to Non-Residents
    IDA HARVEY vs. HOMER H. HARVEY
    No. 3173
    Divorce
    Defendant is not a resident of Indiana
    Must appear before first Monday in October 1889
    CONLEY & SAWYER, Attorneys for plaintiff
    Filed August 12th, 1889
                                A.R. HOPKINS, Clerk

Home News
ED VANSICKLE, the station agent at Hillsdale, has gone to Buffalo, NY, for treatment at the World's Dispensary. He has been in poor health for some time.

R.A. PARRETT has established a ferry across the Wabash, at the old Reed Ferry, one and one half miles east of here, and is now prepared to ferry all those who will favor him with their patronage. It is a new boat, and no one need have any fears of accidents, as he has a good ferryman.

Mr. and Mrs. L.R. MITCHELL, of Ft. Scott, KS, who are visiting her parents, Sheriff RHEUBY and wife, had the pleasure of entertaining Mr. H.W. JAMES and family of Summit Grove, and Mr. and Mrs. R.C. NESBITT, of Georgetown, IL, on Saturday last.

Postmaster COFFIN, of Cayuga, is the proud father of a nine pound gal baby, which arrived on August 3rd, 1889.

D.R. GRAY has moved to Terre Haute, where he has been given a position as telegraph operator by the C. & E.I. Railway.

Misses MARY and EVA PARRETT, daughters of Judge WILLIAM PARRETT, of Evansville, are here visiting their uncle, Esq. J.W. PARRETT, and family.

ELIAS LAMB, is quite seriously sick, and is out of his right mind part of the time. He thinks an abscess is coming on his side, and fears it will break on the inside.

Summit Grove Items
Mr. HENRY WATSON, a young man of this place, has gone to Dana to run a barber shop.

Last Monday afternoon, while Rev. JOHN P. HENSON's kids were playing with the lawn mower, ROSWELL HENSON, aged between 2 and 3 years, undertook to pull out some grass that was lodged on the sickle bar, while the machine was in motion, and had his two middle fingers, on the left hand, clipped off smooth at the first joint.

Wednesday, August 21, 1889

Death of an Inhuman Monster
SILE JONES, who lived just across the line from Quaker Point, in the edge of Illinois, died on Tuesday of last week, and was buried on the day following in the Friends' Cemetery. Very few friends or relatives wept over his death. During his lifetime he was cruel and inhuman to his family. He drove one of his sons from home, who was in the last stages of consumption, and when he died a neighbor called to notify him of the fact, and ask for advice in regard to the burial. He told his neighbor he did not want to see his son and to go ahead with the funeral. The coffin and burial robe were purchased at Dana, and when the bill was presented to SILE JONES, he refused to liquidate. He was then sued in the Edgar County, IL, court, and beat the case on the ground that his son was 21, and he was not accountable for his debts. He drove his wife from home several times, and once when she was sick and not able to wait upon herself, he agreed to give his little 12 year old daughter, who was the only help about the house, a nice horse and buggy if she would starve his wife to death. The little girl who was not old enough, hardly, to know the crime she was committing, was obeying her father's instructions, and at the end of 2 days, without anything to eat or drink, the wife made an effort to get out of bed, when she fainted and fell out on the floor. The children became alarmed and notified the neighbors who came in and placed the sick woman back on the bed, and when she recovered she told them that she was nearly starved and had not had anything to eat for 2 days. Upon his death, the neighborhood is better off without him. At the time of his death, he was worth nearly $20,000, and could well afford to be generous to his family. When he realized that he was close to death, he wanted to get all his property into money, so he could burn it so that none of his family could have it.

Afflicted Family

FELIX FRAZIER, who was born in this township, and resided near here until a few years ago when he moved to Illiana, IL, situated 3 miles west of Dana, is favorably known to many of our people, all of whom will regret to hear of his sad affliction. On last Thursday, his bright and pretty little daughter, aged nearly 2 years, died and was buried at the Thomas Cemetery, two miles northwest of here, on Friday last. On the same night of the day they buried their daughter, their son WILLIAM FRAZIER, aged 20 years, 11 months and 12 days died of consumption, after an illness of four months. His disease was due to exposure last winter. The little girl died of fever and whooping cough. The son's funeral took place in the U.B. Church, in this place, shortly after noon on Sunday last, the sermon being preached by Rev. THORNE, U.B. Pastor of the Brouillette Creek circuit. It was a very large funeral procession. After the services the remains were followed to the cemetery by 57 vehicles, and there laid beside his dear little sister. On the day she was buried, before they started with her, he had her brought to his bed and planted on her cold cheeks an affectionate kiss, and before the rise of the morning sun, he was cold in death. Mr. FAZIER seems to be unfortunate with his children. A few years ago, he lost a couple within a few days of each other.

Home News

The wife of OTIS M. ODELL, of Hutchinson, KS, is reported to be in very delicate health. Her many friends here will be sorry to bear this sad news.

Rev. JOHN P. HENSON was made the proud father of a girl baby, at about 4 o'clock, on last Wednesday morning. It weighs 9 pounds and is spry as a kitten.

F.M. BISHOP, a former resident of this place, has been elected Marshall of Syracuse, KS. For many years he was Marshall of this town, and made an excellent officer.

HARRY B. RHOADS, of Greencastle, is here on a visit. He has been in poor health for sometime, and is going out west to see if he cannot gain some relief. His wife is at Terre Haute with her parents.

We understand that JOHNNY GROVES' wife is suffering from cancer of the breast.

Mrs. CHARITY DAWSON, of Cameron, Warren County, IL, is here visiting her mother, Mrs. REBECCA HOLLINGSWORTH.

We are sorry to learn that Uncle JOE STAATS, of Helt Township, is confined to his bed, and cannot possibly last many more days.

The widow of the late WILLIAM WOOSTER, at one time editor of the Montezuma Reporter, was united one day last week in wedlock to a Rockville gentleman by the name of MILLER. We wish them a pleasant and happy journey down the road of time together.

JOSEPH W. McCONNELL, the old photographer of this place, received the welcome news from Commissioner TANNER last week, that his pension had been granted at the rate of $12 per month for double hernia. He only gets pay back to September 1st, 1888, the date of his application.

Mrs. HENRY THOMASMYER, who resides a short distance north of Dana, and who has been undergoing treatment for a long time for cancer of the breast, by a physician of Danville, IL, and is now said to be in a very critical condition. The doctor now says he cannot do anything for her.

Mrs. SARAH E. DICKEN, of Terre Haute, was granted a divorce from her husband, ANDY DICKEN, in the Vigo County court on Friday last. Both were former residents of this place.

ED TARRENCE, of Austin, TX, arrived here last Monday to spend a few hours shaking hands with his many young friends. His mother is at Terre Haute, and his father is in poor health.

On last Monday the following Newporters left for various parts in Kansas to visit relatives and friends: Esq. JOHN L. EGGLESTON and wife to Topeka, to visit TOM MOFFATT and family; BELL THORNTON to Hutchinson, KS, to visit her sister, Mrs. FLORA ODELL, who is in very poor health; BELL KERDOLFF to Garden City, to visit Mrs. SALLIE LOWRY; LIZA DILLOW to Coolidge to visit OLIVER KNIGHT and wife; PERRY VAN ALLEN to Hutchinson, KS, for the benefit of his health and to visit relatives and friends.

Desertion
MARTHA FOOS filed a complaint in the circuit court yesterday, for a divorce from VALENTINE FOOS. They were married in 1871, in Vermillion County, and for several years they lived together. On February 18, 1878, the wife claims, her husband abandoned her, and up the present time has refused to provide for her support.
Indianapolis Journal of Friday last

Eloped
Catlin, August 19th – BETTIE CULP, aged 16 years, disappeared from this place last Friday, and was not heard from until today, when word was received that she had eloped with HENRY GEORGE, a farmer of this township. They were married at Newport, IN.
Indianapolis Journal

Surprise Dinner
The friends of DAVID PEARMAN thought they would give him and his estimable wife a happy surprise before leaving a neighborhood. On last Monday, August 14th, while DAVID was up to Cayuga, (his wife also being away from home), a host of friends and relatives congregated at the residence and prepared a bountiful dinner. JESSE KAUFMAN, who understood the trick, accompanied DAVID home.

Geneva Items
WILLIAM STOKESBERRY, who resides on the old homestead, near Center, is blessed with an 8 pound boy of his own.

Real Estate Transfers
    JAMES E. KNOWLES etal to OLIVER P. MORGAN
    Lots 1 & 4 in Clinton
    $300

    W.H. SALTSGAVER et ux to JOHN CADE
    Lot in Gessie
    $30

    DANIEL E. STRAIN et ux. to JAMES E. KNOWLES & CHARLES B. KNOWLES
    Lot 1 in Clinton
    $125

    MARY MILLER to ANDREW J. INGRAM
    4 acres in Vermillion Township
    $40

    EMMA KIBLEY and husband to MARY S. DAVIS
    4 acres in Clinton Township
    $150

Wednesday, August 28, 1889

Col. R.N. HUDSON, of Terre Haute, is lying dangerously ill.

L.A. McKNIGHT, a former merchant of Gessie, this county, is now holding forth at Boswell, IN.

Dana Scribblings
CARL TEMPLE and wife, with some friends from Chrisman, visited Dana Sunday.

Pumpkin Vine News
The miners ceased work Tuesday and Wednesday of this week, and showed their respect for the dead, by attending the funerals of the infants of CHARLES GARDNER and JOE HARDING.

Fodder Shock Nubbins
Dana News
SETH JONES, who has been at Brookston for more than a year past, came home last week on a visit.

Hon. D.W. FINNEY, ex-Lieutenant Governor of Kansas, visited his brother DAVID FINNEY, at this place this week.

Miss HATTIE THORNE leaves today for Vienna, IN, to spend the coming winter with her sister, Mrs. LOU DARRAH.

Montezuma Items
Mrs. Dr. ANNA B. CAMPBELL, of Rockville, will leave next week for New York City to be with her daughters, Misses EVA and LILLIE, who are studying painting and music respectively. She will be absent about 6 months.

Perrysville Items
Miss BERTIE SMITH will leave for Westfield, IL, the 31st. She intends to graduate in the United Brethren College of that place.

Death
At about 8 o'clock on Tuesday morning of last week, a good old Quaker lady of this township passed from earth to that better world. She was the estimable wife of WILLIAM B. WALTHALL, who resides 7 miles west of here, and near Quaker Point. She was born in Belmont County, OH, and had she lived until the 16th of next month, she would have been 63 years of age. She was united to Mr. WALTHALL in the fall of 1855, being his second wife, and had been a resident of this county since her marriage. She was a Christian in the true sense of the term, having been a member of the Friends Church since early childhood. She always lived a consistent life, and adhered strictly to the golden rule. She was charitable and kind to everyone, and everybody loved and respected Mrs. WALTHALL. She was a grand and noble woman, and in her death the people of that neighborhood lose a valuable citizen, and one whose death is universally mourned. The funeral occurred at the Friends Church, near her late home, on Wednesday last. There was no regular funeral discourse.

Home News
OTHO SHARP, of Waveland, is here visiting his brother BILL SHARP.

ELIAS LAMB, who has been seriously afflicted with an abscess on his side for several weeks, is now on the mend and able to ride out in a buggy.

Newport is to have a new millinery store. Mrs. J.L. NELSON is going to open our in the Hegarty building.

D.B. WALTHALL, of Emporia, KS, who came home to attend the funeral of his mother, was in town on Saturday last with his father and brother ALLEN WALTHALL.

Trustee WEATHERWAX and Uncle BEN HARRISON, of Clinton Township, were in town on Monday last. The old squire is in very feeble health, and cannot get around without assistance.

Death
Montezuma, IN, August 25, 1889 – Died at the family residence, August 25th, after a short illness, Mrs. INDIANA QUINLAN, wife of JAMES QUINLAN. Mrs. QUINLAN was the daughter of WAKE and SUSAN INGRAM. She was born in Vermillion County, January 18, 1851, and married 15 years. She leaves a husband and 3 children. She was a devout Catholic. Funeral services from St. Joseph Catholic Church at 9 o'clock Tuesday morning by Rev. Father BOWERS of Terre Haute, then the remains were taken to Armiesburg and laid to rest.

Surprise
Last Saturday forenoon, Mrs. SOPHIA ROBISON, living at Cedar Corner, 3 miles south of here, on returning from town and opening the door of the house, was completely astonished and bewildered. There she found her room and back porch filled with relatives and friends who had gathered during her absence and spread a generous table of tempting food from well filled baskets. She was a loss for words or actions until someone informed her it was her 64th birthday.

New Shoe Shop
I have opened a shoe shop in the building occupied by Henson's Harness Shop in Newport.
　　　　　　　　　　　　　　　　WILLIAM H. TATE

A.L. MACK, of Helt's Prairie, and EURA SOUTHARD, of Clinton Township gave us a call on Monday last.

Mrs. JANE McLAUGHLIN, son and daughter, of Indianola, IL, are here visiting relatives and friends.

STANT EGGLESTON returned from Jonesboro, AR, last week, where she has been for several days visiting her brother SELDON EGGLESTON.

AL C. WHEELER will leave for Jonesboro, AR, next week to take a position in S.B. EGGLESTON's big railroad restaurant at that place.

Mrs. CHARITY DAWSON and her children, who have been here for the last 10 days visiting her mother, left for home yesterday morning. She was accustomed as far as Danville by her sister, Miss MARY HOLLINGSWORTH.

Newport is getting to be a religious center. On the 15th of next month, 2 of our young men will go to Evanston, IL, to take a thorough theological course. It will take them 3 years to prepare themselves for the ministry. Both are intelligent and smart, and we predict they will make their mark in the Christian field of labor. Their names are JOHN P. HENSON and QUINCY A. MYERS. Both are educating themselves for the M.E. Church.

Accident
On last Monday morning, RICHARD T. MITCHELL, of this place, met with a serious accident, by which he lost three fingers on his left hand. He and two or three others were taking his traction engine from WATSON PARRETT's to TAYLOR ADAMS' to thresh wheat, and while on their way, the pump got out of fix and would not work. Mr. MITCHELL hopped off the engine and attempted to fix it while it was running. He stumbled and fell, his left hand striking the cogs in the big drive wheel. Three of his fingers were so badly mashed, they had to be amputated.

Real Estate Transfers
JOHN WADE to THOMAS V. WADE
37 acres in Vermillion Township
$500

JOHN BLAKESLEY to ALONZO L. MACK
40 acres in Helt Township
$1600

ISAAC KIBBY et ux to THOMAS A. KIBBY
110 acres in Clinton Township
$3000

JAMES HARRIS, of Idaho, a former resident of this township and an old soldier of the 43rd Indiana, accompanied by his sister, MARY JANE JACKSON of Colorado, arrived back here last week on a visit. Mrs. JACKSON is a sister to ELIZABETH SOUTHARD, five miles south of here, whose guest she now is. Mr. HARRIS left yesterday for Milwaukee to take in the soldiers' reunion. He is now engaged in the mining business and is quite wealthy. It has been 20 years since he left this township.

Wednesday, September 4, 1889

Marriage
BAYLESS RUTHERFORD and Mrs. A. SMITH, both of Cayuga, were joined in wedlock by Rev. R.B. VAN ALLEN, pastor of the U.B. Church, at 8 o'clock on last Thursday evening, the ceremony taking place at the residence of bride's son-in-law, JESSE KAUFMAN. Mr. RUTHERFORD is 65 and Mrs. SMITH is 62. We wish them a pleasant and happy life.

Pumpkin Vine News
Clinton Argus
The infant child of Mr. and Mrs. LIGE ALLEN died Sunday morning, and the funeral services were conducted at the residence on north Main Street by Rev. HANDLEY, Monday afternoon, and the remains interred in the Clinton Cemetery.

Mrs. JAMES WHITE (nee ELIZABETH J. CRABB) died at her home, 3 miles north of this city, on the 27th of this month, after a lingering illness with consumption. The funeral service was conducted at the house by Rev. HANDLEY, whose remarks were appropriate and comforting. Mrs. WHITE was born April 3, 1851, and was married to JAMES WHITE in 1871. Her death is mourned by a kind and affectionate husband and 3 children, the oldest being a bright and winsome girl, EVA WHITE. She united in the M.E. Church some 17 or 18 years ago, and has always lived the life of a quiet, uncomplaining patient Christian.

Marriage
The Georgetown, IL, correspondent of the Danville of the Danville Daily News, gives that paper the following particulars of nuptials of ARCHIE McCONNELL and Miss ALLIE NORMAN, who were united in matrimony a few days ago. Mr. ARCHIE McCONNELL, of Indianapolis, IN, a lumberman who has been in our neighborhood for some weeks, was met by Miss ALLIE and ANNA NORMAN, of Eugene, IN, at Danville on Saturday last. Mr. McCONNELL selected Miss ALLIE and called upon Judge EVANS, who pronounced them man and wife.

Fodder Shock Nubbins
Dana News
FRANK WALTHALL has been appointed administrator of the estate of the late SILAS JONES.

Dr. NEBEKER and Col. WASHBURN, of Clinton, were in town Tuesday. The doctor performed a surgical operation upon the person of LEWIS NORRIS. The patient is improving.

Death
Col. ROBERT N. HUDSON, one of the old and prominent citizens of Terre Haute, and for many years connected with the newspapers of that city, died on Friday last, after a four week's illness. He had been a resident of Terre Haute since 1840, and was a graduate of Asbury University. He was editor of the Express from 1856 to 1864. He served two years as a member of the Indiana legislature, and was Col. of the 133rd Indiana during the late rebellion. The Col. was generous and warm-hearted citizen, and was very highly esteemed by his neighbors and acquaintances. His funeral took place on Sunday last and was very largely attended.

Last week, we mentioned the marriage of HATTIE M. WOOSTER to PETER J. MULLER. The bride of the 13th of August had answered the great English question on the 22nd by filing, through PUETT & HADLEY, her attorneys, an application for divorce. The complaint alleges that her husband immediately quit work after they were married and laid around beastly drunk. Although she importuned him to quit drinking, he only got the drunker. He became such a nuisance that the railroad company, for which Mrs. MULLER ran the I.D. & S. water tank, gave notice that she must fire her husband or leave. She prefers to do the former.
                                    Rockville Tribune

Summit Grove Items
Brother MEREDITH preached his farewell sermon at Salem last Sunday.

Brother THOMAS DAVIS will soon leave us and try ministry.

DULIN JAMES and family, of Newman, IL, visited here last week.

LEWIS STUTSMAN and JOSEPH STRAIN, the promising young ornithologists, visited east of Terre Haute, last Sunday.

Home News
LEVI McINTYRE and wife, of Eugene Township, returned home on Saturday last from Missouri, where they spent a week pleasantly visiting his wife's relatives. Mr. McINTYRE is not favorably impressed with that country, and prefers Indiana to Missouri.

JERRY CONLEY is tending bar for JULIUS ALDRIDGE of Cayuga.

AL WHEELER will leave for Jonesboro, AR on Saturday next, to accept a clerkship with S.B. EGGLESTON. He gets $25 per month and board.

Married
On September 1st, 1889, a the residence of the bride's parents near Gessie, IN, by W.N. COFFMAN, Mr. CHARLES HUGHES and Miss LAURA DYE. The bride was elegantly attired for the occasion, making a handsome couple. There were present, 20 invited guests to witness the solemn and impressive ceremony. The bride and groom both are from highly esteemed families.

Death
The little 2 year old daughter of HAL WHEELER, of Dana, died at an early hour on last Friday morning, of whooping cough and intermittent fever. She was a bright and pretty little child, and the idol of the household, and in her death the parents are deeply grieved. The remains of the dear little one were interred at the Thomas Cemetery on Saturday last.

Mrs. NICHOLS, an aged sister, died at her residence in Perrysville, IN, August 1st, 1889. Resolved by Rebekah Lodge, No. 118, of Perrysville, IN.
                                    CORA CHISLER
                                    KITTY CHISLER
                                    IMOGENE COLLINS

Home News

Miss FLORENCE ASHBY leaves the 10th of this month for Nebraska, where she will make her future home. Her many young friends here regret to see her leave.

Mrs. MATT WHITLOCK and her daughter, GRACE WHITLOCK, of Dana, were up here on Saturday last visiting Rev. R.B. VAN ALLEN and family. Mrs. WHITLOCK is a sister of pastor VAN ALLEN.

Liquor licenses were granted on Monday last, by the Board of Commissioners on Monday last, to the following parties: WILLIAM J. BROPHY, FRANK L. REEDER, HENRY D. SPRAGUE, and THOMAS J. STARK.

Marriage Licenses
    CHARLEY NEVINS to MARIETTA MOORE
    RICHARD PARKER to ANNIE M. EDWARDS
    MARION WICK to MARY BUTTS
    SCOTT HOLD to ELLEN HOGUE
    JOHN T. CARSON to ROWENA DAVIS
    GEORGE RIGHTSELL to OLLIE PAYTON
    BAYLESS RUTHERFORD to AMASSA SMITH
    CHARLES G. HUGHES to LAURA E. DYE

Notice of Final Settlement of Estate
    Estate of MARY COX, deceased
    Filed August 25, 1889

                                      A.R. HUGHES, Clerk

Notice of Final Settlement of Estate
    Estate of HETTIE PORTER, deceased
    Filed August 25, 1889

                                      A.R. HUGHES, Clerk

Death

Uncle JOE STAATS was born in Virginia on May 13, 1801, and died at his residence in Helt Township, on Saturday last, at 10 a.m. He was one of the old residents of this county, having moved to Helt Township in 1830, where he resided up to the day of his death. His wife died early last spring. Uncle JOE STAATS, as he was familiarly called, had been in feeble health for sometime, and death was not unexpected by his children. He had been a member of the M.E. Church since boyhood, and for many years had been a minister of that church. He lived a consistent Christian life, and always tried to do by his neighbors, as he would wish to be done by. His death is very deeply regretted by those who knew him. His death is very deeply regretted by those who knew him best, and his loss will be sadly felt by the church, of which he was one of the beacon lights. The funeral occurred from his late residence on Sunday last, Rev. MEREDITH performed the last sad rites, assisted by Rev. HOOK, Pastor of the Clinton Presbyterian Church after which his remains were followed to the Helt's Prairie Cemetery.

Real Estate Transfers
    JOHN KIGER et ux to PHILA A. STEVENSON
    4 ½ acres in Helt Township
    $325

    BEN HARRISON to C.P. HARRISON
    66 acres in Clinton Township
    $500

WILLIAM WRIGHT et ux to THOMAS MYERS
Lot 7 in Newport
$50

ANN HOPKINS and husband to MARY ENNIS
Lot 79 in Perrysville
$160

R.B. STOKES to Z.T. GALLOWAY
Part of Lot 72 in Newport
$600

LUCINDA KONKLE to JOHN KONKLE
40 acres in Clinton Township
$1800

Unclaimed Letters
- Mrs. ELIZA DOWNING
- Mr. L. MILLER
- GEORGE TEMPLE
- Miss REBECCA J. WOOD
- CHARLES W. CUMMINGS
- T.P. HAUGHNEY
- Mrs. KATY LOHRMANN
- Miss LIZZIE STERLING
- CHARLES H. HARTER
- Mrs. MARY CONOVER
- J.B. CUMMINGS

Wednesday, September 11, 1889

Township Teachers

Teacher	District
ANNA RICHARDSON	No. 3
EDNA BROWN	No. 4
W.B. GOSNELL	No. 5
OLIN M. CADY	No. 6
ELSIE ANDREWS	No. 7
E.E. NEEL	No. 8
OWEN T. CLARK	No. 9
B.S. BOTHWELL	No. 10
MAGGIE HOPKINS	No. 10
CHARLEY HUNT	No. 11
SARAH WALTHALL	No. 12
FRACIE M. RICE	No. 13
LOU CADY	No. 14
ELMER E. DAVIS	No. 15

Fodder Shock Nubbins
Dana News
WILLIE FINNEY and JOHNNY WRIGHT left Tuesday for Purdue University at Lafayette.

WILLIAM H. DARNALL received the sorrowful news last week that his youngest sister, Mrs. CHARLES HALLER, living at Frederick City, MD, is dead. She leaves a husband and 5 children.

IRA PEER came from Paxton, IL, last Saturday night to spend a few days with parents. He reports that they are doing big business there, 6 clerks being constantly engaged.

On last Friday, Miss EVA MALONE received a telegram from Decatur, IL, informing her that she had been selected to take charge of one of the city schools. We heartily congratulate Miss MALONE over her deserved position. She left last Saturday.

Montezuma News

Mrs. WILL DOWNEY and daughter GERTIE MAGERS, have been visiting relatives in Vermillion County.

O.P. BROWN has purchased from ANDREW LINEBARGER, a farm a little over 145 acres in this township, northeast of town, for which he paid $9,330.

At the table of ANDREW LINEBARGER on last Sunday sat 5 men whose aggregate age was 383 years. They were Judge DONALDSON aged 87; Rev. CUMMINGS age 76; A. LINEBARGER age 74; Rev. MUSSER age 73 ½; and Rev. PARRETT age 72 ½.

Cayuga Clatter

Mrs. S.W. SIGLER and Miss MINNIE SWITZER, of Portland, OR, are visiting friends in this vicinity.

Home News

Mrs. MARY STILLAR, of Remington, this state, accompanied by her two little children, arrived here yesterday on a visit to her sister, Mrs. HENRY DILLOW.

JOHN P. HENSON and Q.A. MYERS, of this place, leave for the theological college at Evanston, IL, near Chicago to prepare themselves for the ministry in the M.E. Church.

Mrs. Dr. WILLIAM M. JONES and her sister, Mrs. TOM CLARK, wife of the operator and station agent of the I.D. & W. Railway at that place, were in town on Monday last and gave us a short call.

Attorney SCOTT AIKMAN and Miss MARY CHIPPS have about made all the necessary preparations for their marriage, which will take place in the near future.

H.O. PETERS and wife, of Brimfield, IL, were at Eugene, last week, attending the county fair and visiting their relatives and numerous friends. Both are in good health.

ADAM B. LITTLEPAGE and wife, of Charleston, WV, are here visiting his father-in-law, STEPHEN S. COLLETT and family, and their numerous friends.

SELDON B. EGGLESTON and wife, of Jonesboro, AR, are here on a visit. Mr. EGGLESTON came here sick and is still confined to his bed.

DICK MITCHELL has purchased the north side saloon, owned by E.E. DAVIS. The sale took place yesterday. The consideration was $2150.

Notice of Final Settlement of Estate
    Estate of JOHN BILSLAND, deceased
    Filed September 9, 1889
                                A.R. HOPKINS, Clerk

Our Town Schools

Our town schools commenced on Monday. The schools are classified as follows: Prof. W.E. CLAPHAN, Principal of the high school with 32 pupils in attendance; Miss JENNIE BLASDALE, grammar department with 34 pupils; Miss MATTIE DOWELL, intermediate, with 26 pupils; and Miss LYDIA PIKE, primary, with 33 pupils.

Real Estate Transfers
    LAFAYETTE NEWLIN et ux to CLARA SULLIVAN & CORA L. NEWELL
    Lots 1, 2, 3, 4, 5, & 6, in Alta
    $1

WILLIAM SWINDELL to FRED LINDSEY etal
1 ½ acres in Helt Township
$80

WILLIAM C. COOK et ux to CATHERINE AXTON
10 acres in Vermillion Township
$400

FRANKLIN AIKMAN et ux to ALFRED NOLAN
60 acres in Helt Township
$2700

M.J. TUCKER et ux to WILLIAM L. WRIGHT
Lot 5, in Block 27, in Clinton
$1000

Wednesday, September 18, 1889

Fodder Shock Nubbins
Dana News
Mr. T.S. HOOD and his granddaughter, Miss IDA DOWDY, left last Tuesday to visit relatives and friends in Kansas, Iowa, and Nebraska.

Mrs. CALEB BALES took a relapse last week and is now seriously afflicted with rheumatism.

Mr. JOHN CASTLE of Ridge Farm, and his sister, Mrs. A.M. FOLGER, of this place, left Tuesday for Hutchinson, KS, to visit relatives for a few weeks.

Rev. R.S. MARTIN, for 3 years pastor of the M.E. Church here, received a well deserved promotion at the late Brazil Conference. Valparaiso is a city of nearly 6,000 population, and the seat of a fine college.

Rev. DEMETRUS TILLOTSON received a first class appointment at the M.E. Conference. He goes to Crown Point, county seat of Lake County, which is a town of 2,000 population or more. It borders on Lake Michigan.

Clinton Echoes
Miss ALICE BECKMAN went to Terre Haute last Monday to attend the Normal. She resigned her position in the school here for the purpose of graduating at the State Normal.

LARZ and ARTHUR WHITCOMB and WILLIS HANDLEY left last Monday for Greencastle where they will attend school for the coming year.

Death
JOHN ROBBINS, a young man of Tangier, Parke County, accidentally shot himself through the palm of the hand two weeks ago last Monday. The wound was dressed and seemed to be getting along all right until one week ago last Monday, when, late in the afternoon, he suddenly took the lock-jaw and died in a few hours. He was able to go about every day after he shot himself, and did not suffer any pain from the wound until lock-jaw set in. He was a respectable and very highly esteemed young man, and his sudden death was a terrible shock to his relatives and many young friends.

Married on last Thursday evening at 7 o'clock, at the residence of JOHN PORTER, TICE WILLIAMS, of Pana, IL, and Miss MINNIE BAILEY, of Clinton Township, were married by Rev. HANDLEY. They will locate at Pana, IL.

Death

ANNA JAMES, wife of Z.D. JAMES, of Newman, IL, died last Wednesday night, September 11, 1889, aged about 31 years. She was the daughter of JOHN S. ANDERSON, of Helt Township, and was a most estimable lady. She and her husband were both former residents of Helt Township this county. The deceased had been an invalid for 2 or 3 years, but was able to be up and about. Not over two weeks ago, she was over to visit her parents and relatives. On the day she died she did not seem to be ailing more than common, until a few hours before her spirit took its flight to that better world. Her remains were brought back to this county for burial, the funeral discourse being preached at the residence of her brother-in-law, WRIGHT JAMES, by Rev. THOMAS C. DAVIS, on Friday last, after which her remains were interred in the Helt's Prairie Cemetery.

Home News

GEORGE CLOUSER and wife, of Monticello, IL, celebrated their 65th wedding anniversary on Monday last.

Mrs. LILY LANGTRY, the actress, has secured a divorce from her husband, and now little FREDDIE GEBHART will have an open field and can marry the LILY if he wants her.

BOB YOUNGER, the noted bandit, died in the Minnesota penitentiary of consumption, on last Monday night. He belonged to the Younger gang and was a desperate character.

PHILO CURTIS, the newly elected county Commissioner of Clinton Township, who takes his seat on the first Monday in next December, was in town yesterday, accompanied by WILLIAM WRIGHT, an ex-county Commissioner.

Married by Rev. IRA MATER, at his residence in Hillsdale, on the evening of the 15th instant, Mr. EDMUND R. OXFORD and Miss HULDAH A. PRICE, all of Vermillion County, IN.

JOE and Miss RETA MOREHEAD, residing just north of town, left for Chattanooga, TN, on last Sunday night. Mr. MOREHEAD has been in poor health for 3 years, and thought a trip down south might benefit him. His sister RETA went along to take care of him.

This evening at 7:30 o'clock, attorney BARTON SCOTT AIKMAN will lead Miss MARY CHIPPS to the hymeneal altar, and make solemn pledges that he will maintain and support her in the future. SCOTT is a model young man and MARY is equally as good. We believe they will make a happy match.

Miss CLARA MYERS leaves today for Champaign, IL, to attend college.

A.W. JOHNSON, of Ashmore, Coles County, IL, is over visiting relatives.

Mrs. MARY GOFF, a wealthy widow of Brown Township, Montgomery County, committed suicide on Monday last. No cause is assigned.

B.F. DOSS, of Dillard, OR, who is back here on a visit, gave us a call on Wednesday last. He will not return to Oregon until some time next spring.

JAMES T. HOOD of Eugene, better known as POLK HOOD, has been granted a pension after so long a time. It has been 8 or 9 years since he first made his application. He will probably get a good round sum.

The many friends of Prof. J.W. PERRIN will be pleased to learn that he has been appointed assistant county superintendent of Cook County at a salary of $150 per month.

Danville, IL, News

Death
PEIRSON FENNIMORE, who was brought to the poor asylum from Clinton Township on the 26th of February, died at 4 o'clock on last Saturday morning of rheumatism and heart disease. He was 78 years of age. He was known to many of the citizens of this county as Dr. FENNIMORE, which name he derived from having manufactured a liniment bearing his name several years ago, and which was pronounced a good medicine for many ailments.

Marriage
On last Sunday, after morning services at the new Presbyterian Church at Eugene, Rev. FYFFE, the pastor, united in bonds of holy wedlock, Dr. ALEX KINDERMAN and Miss LUCY GADD.

Wednesday, September 25, 1889

Cayuga Clatter
AUGUST JOHNSON, a young man who has been working in the rock quarry west of town, had his middle finger mashed off last Thursday.

Miss CORA THOMPSON has resigned her position as deputy postmaster. We will miss her smiling face at the general delivery window.

We are glad to hear that JOSEPH DILLOW is going to become a citizen of Cayuga, next week. He is going to build a first class blacksmith shop north of KAUFMAN's livery stable.

WILL MILLIKIN, who has accepted a position in the Arcade Clothing store of Danville, was home visiting last Wednesday.

Montezuma Items
Mrs. JAMES HOLTZ left on Wednesday for Kansas, to join her husband, who has been out there several weeks and where they will live in the future.

H.H. and GERTRUDE BENSON left on the 11 o'clock train on Tuesday for the West, where they will in the future reside.

Pumpkin Vine News
Clinton Argus
Miss ALICE BECKMAN left Sunday morning to attend the State Normal at Terre Haute. She intends taking a two years course.

An infant child of Mr. and Mrs. JAMES LEWIS, of Geneva, died Monday. The funeral took place Tuesday.

We regret to learn that our friend ED VANSICKLE, of Hillsdale, is in poor health. He had returned from Buffalo feeling considerable better, but is not so well now.

Allowances by Board of Commissioners September term 1889

M.L. HALL, poor	56.25
J.A. BARNES, poor	25.00
HENRY NEBEKER, poor	37.25
E.E. SMITH, poor	25.00
E. MACK, poor	25.00
E.H. McDANIEL, poor	177.64
W.K. McNEILL, poor	194.53
S.B. DAVIS, poor	182.08
G.O. NEWTON, poor	176.00
SOL WEATHERWAX, poor	226.96
G.F. HAWORTH, courts	21.00

W.F. KERNS, courts	31.50
F.M. RILEY, courts	28.00
WILLIAM RHEUBY, courts	6.00
C.W. BROWN, books and stationary	78.75
BAKER & THORNTON, books and stationary	9.83
WILLIAM B. BURFORD, books and stationary	120.00
M. HEGARTY, county offices	3.20
R.H. NIXON, county offices	73.40
M.L. HALL, board of health	53.50
J.C. HARRISON, inquest	10.00
T.C. HOOD, inquest	10.00
JOSEPH CONRAD, poor asylum	543.33
WILLIAM MORRIS, board of equalization	2.00
JOHN R. STAHL, board of equalization	2.00
J.H. NICHOLAS, board of equalization	2.00
THOMAS CUSHMAN, public buildings	1.60
WILLIAM RHEUBY, public buildings	9.00
L.J. PLACE, public buildings	22.75
JOHN MILLER, public buildings	3.57
DAVID AGGRA, janitor	50.00
GEORGE W. DEALAND, county superintendent	210.00
SOL WEATHERWAX, funeral expense of soldier	45.00
J.L. SMITH, printing	153.00
S.B. DAVIS, printing	246.60
W.K. McNEILL, enumeration	50.00
E.H. McDANIEL, enumeration	40.00
G.O. NEWTON, enumeration	50.00
SOL WEATHERWAX, enumeration	60.00
J.C. JACKSON, bridges	5.00
JOSEPH CATES, bridges	31.31
OSCAR KERNS, bridges	11.00
W.M. HAMILTON, fees and salary	606.50
WILLIAM RHEUBY, roads	5.10
ED TIFFANY, roads	3.00
HENRY JENKS, roads	1.50
G.B. TILLOTSON, roads	1.50
W.P. HASKELL, roads	.50
WILLIAM RHEUBY, elections	30.00
WILLIAM RHEUBY, criminals	79.65
M.G. RHOADS, attorney fees	125.00
MART FLEENER, examining Treasurer books	483.75
R.E. STEPHENS, examining Treasurer books	196.56
ANNA ROSS, examining Treasurer books	210.00

Real Estate Transactions

MANFORD E. STEWART et ux to FRANKLIN AIKMAN
2 ½ acres in Helt Township
$700

WILLIAM SWINDELL to A.B. CASEBEER etal in trust
Part of lot 23 in Hillsdale
$35

CHARLES R. TATE et ux to AMANDA E. ALDRICH
¼ acre in Perrysville
$90

JOHN F. WALTER to DAISY E. ROBISON
Lot 3 in Clinton
$125

ROBERT J. GESSIE et ux to CHARLES L. CARITHERS
Lot 35 in Gessie
$400

JOHN F. WALTER to JESSIE A. ROBISON
Lot 2 in Clinton
$150

WILLIAM C. COOK to CATHERINE AXTON
10 acres in Vermillion Township
$400

MARY GIBSON to E.E. JOHNSON
Kits 10, 11, 12, & 13 in Hillsdale
$100

Home News
Mrs. SELDON EGGLESTON was up at Urbana, IL, last week, visiting her sister, Mrs. PET SCHWIEZER.

Mrs. ANNA TARRENCE, of Austin, TX, a former resident of Newport, is here visiting her relatives and numerous friends.

Miss LILLIE SPROULS, of Eugene, and Miss ELLA BAILEY, of Grant Park, IL, who have been visiting their cousin, Miss GRACE RHEUBY, returned home yesterday morning.

Mrs. PENE WESTDAHL, of Huron, Dakota, a former resident of Perrysville, took in the U.B. conference basket picnic here on Sunday last. She is in remarkably fine health.

Miss LISTA LAMB, of Economy, Wayne County, this state, is here on a visit to relatives and intends to remain several weeks. She is the guest of her grandfather, ELIAS LAMB.

Rev. F.M. GEE, the new M.E. pastor, arrived here last week, and is a fine and bright looking gentleman. He is 26 years old and is very sociable. He has a wife and one child, and has been in the ministry for 5 years. He is a son of Elder GEE. He will hold his first quarterly meeting on the 19th and 20th of next month at the Lebanon Church.

While in Danville, IL, on Thursday last, we met M.G. COLEMAN, formerly principal of the Newport Schools. He has quit the school business and entered the ministry of the M.E. Church. He is now located on the Atwood, IL, circuit.

A.J. ADAMS and wife, of Danville, IL, will leave this week for Cincinnati, to spend the winter with their daughter EVA. Mr. ADAMS is in poor health and is slowly recovering from an attack of apoplexy.

Obituary
Died at 6 o'clock a.m. Saturday, September 21st, 1889, an infant son of Mr. and Mrs. WILLIAM SHELATO. The little darling suffered three days and then its spirit took its flight to that upper and better world. WILLIAM and INEZ SHELATO want to express their thanks for the kindness expressed by the citizens of Newport for their support during their bereavement.

Marriage
While attending conference here last week, Rev. DAVID BREWER, of Pilot Grove circuit, IL, was united in wedlock to Mrs. ELIZABETH WETHERSPOON of Fairmount, IL. The ceremony took place on Thursday night, at the residence of JAMES W. SYKES, one mile west of town, Elder A.M. SNYDER tying the double bow knot. This is the third wife for Brother BREWER.

Marriage
Attorney BARTON SCOTT AIKMAN and MARY CHIPPS, of this place, were united in holy wedlock at 7:30 o'clock on last Wednesday evening, September 18, 1889. The ceremony took place at the residence of the bride's parents, Rev. THOMAS GRIFFITH, of Montezuma performing the pleasant duty in his usual happy way. The young couple went to Dana after the ceremony.

Missing
Two weeks ago this morning, GEORGE FORD, an insurance agent who has been a resident of this place about 2 years, left for Chicago to get $200 due him from the company he represented. He told his wife before leaving to come up to Momence on the G.A.R. excursion on the following Saturday (which was one week ago last Saturday) and he would meet her there. She went as directed, but failed to find her young husband there. She wrote to her brother-in-law, SAM RITTENHOUSE, of Sidell, IL. He came down last Monday, but was unable to give her any information. Mr. FORD and his wife, to whom he was wedded less than two years ago, had always gotten along pleasantly and happily, and his absence is a mystery.

Wednesday, October 2, 1889

Cayuga Clatter
JAMES B. ILES will remove from the farm to Eugene in the very near future. He will occupy the former residence of his sister, Mrs. NAYLOR.

Fodder Shock Nubbins
Dana News
Mrs. J.E. BILSLAND and Mrs. Dr. SMITH went to Terre Haute Tuesday to arrange to put their daughters in school at St. Mary's College. The girls will go week after next.

Married
Mr. MATTHEW HAWS and Miss ALICE MOORE were united in holy wedlock at 4 o'clock p.m. on the 24th instant at the residence of the officiating minister, J.E. WRIGHT. Both parties live in St. Bernice.

Pumpkin Vine News
Clinton Argus
Little MARY GOSNELL, the 4 year old daughter of Mr. and Mrs. CLARENCE GOSNELL, died on the 17th of this month. She was a bright and winsome little creature, and her departure has cast a gloom over the hearts of her loving parents.

Mrs. HUTCHINSON, wife of WILLIAM HUTCHINSON, of Geneva, died at her home, 3 miles northwest of here, last Saturday. The interment gook place at Mt. Pleasant Cemetery, in Parke County, Sunday morning. She leaves a devoted husband, one son aged about 6 years, and an infant one week old.

A harsh fate seems to hang over the family of Mr. and Mrs. HENRY BLAIR. Wednesday, of this week, their daughter, LILLY BLAIR, died at her home, after a lingering illness with consumption. This is the third daughter they have lost in 3 years. The funeral was conducted at the house of Elder JACOBS, of Stanford, and was well attended by her young friends. The afflicted family has the heart felt sympathy of the community in their dire affliction.

Mrs. JAMES HENRY died at her home in this city Sunday morning, rather unexpectedly to most of her neighbors, as it was not generally known that she was dangerously ill. She had been ailing for some time, and suffered a great deal of pain. The funeral was postponed until Wednesday in order to enable her son JOHN HENRY to arrive from Chicago. He happened to be up in Wisconsin and was greatly delayed. Mrs. HENRY was a native of this place, and has resided here all her life. She leaves a small family consisting of the husband and one son. She was about 45 years of age, and was a member of the M.E. Church. The funeral was well attended.

JAMES H. VAUGHN, born near Dayton, OH, December 16th, 1823, and died at Clinton, IN, September 24th, 1889, aged 65 years, 9 months, and 8 days. He was married to Miss ANNA HACKETT in Ohio in 1848. He came to this state about 34 years ago and has made this part of the state his permanent residence ever since. He was a carpenter by trade, and altogether a good, quiet, industrious citizen and a gentle husband and father. Mr. VAUGHN was one of the most learned men in the country, a Shakespearian and historian of great ability. He leaves a wife and 5 grown children to mourn his loss. Rev. HANDLEY conducted the funeral services at the house Wednesday afternoon, and the remains were followed to their last resting place by a large number of sympathizing friends.

Clinton Echoes
MATTHEW SCOTT and his daughter, Mrs. MANN, are visiting Mr. SCOTT's daughters in Missouri.

Esq. WISHARD surprised his many friends, last Friday, by bringing home from Illinois a brand new bride. The old couple have the best wishes of a host of friends.

Death
During the latter part of last February, the wife of WILLIAM DARNALL, of Helt Township, was stricken down with a stroke of paralysis. It was several months before she recovered sufficiently to get around. Recently her husband and friends were elated over the prospect of her full recovery. But their hopes were of short duration. On Thursday morning of last week she was again stricken down, and at 11 o'clock a.m. on the day following her spirit took its flight to that better world on high. In her death the husband loses a good wife, and the children a noble and kind hearted mother. Mrs. DARNALL was a good Christian lady, and always noted for her charity. When the present editor of the Dana News, a ragged urchin of 11 years of age, came from New York with many other orphan boys, seeking a home in the west, he went to Mr. DARNALL, who was poor and felt unable to care for him but by the sympathetic persuasion of his good wife, he took Mr. SMITH and gave him a home, and he was treated as one of their own children. He was clothed and given a good education, and much credit is due the noble woman who now rests from work and has gone to reap the reward laid up for her in a better world than this. Her funeral, which took place on Saturday last, was very largely attended, fully attesting the high esteem in which she was held by her neighbors and friends.

Home News
JOHN W. GALLOWAY, of Terre Haute came up here on Saturday night to visit his sick brother-in-law, S.B. EGGLESTON.

ED A. AIKMAN leaves on Monday next to attend the Rush Medical College of Chicago, to prepare himself to physic people.

E.B. BROWN has been appointed Deputy County Treasurer.

JASPER ANDREWS, of St. Bernice, Helt Township, came up here on Sunday last to visit his daughter, Miss ELSIE ANDREWS, who is teaching at the Thomas Schoolhouse.

MOSES THOMPSON and his two sons left Tuesday on the 11 o'clock train for St. Paul, NB, to look at their farm recently purchased.

PERRY VAN ALLEN has resigned his position at the Plainfield Reform School, and accepted a clerkship in a grocery store at Brazil.

Obituary
WILLIAM RUSSELL Jr. of Helt Township, a son of WILLIAM RUSSELL Sr., a nonagenarian, died at his residence on Thursday last, aged 43 years. He died of typhoid fever, and was only sick about two weeks. His funeral took place on Friday and was very largely attended by his neighbors. He leaves a wife and several small children.

Marriage
A few days ago, EDWARD McDOWELL, of Helt Township, took out license to wed Miss LYDIA WALTHALL, of this township, but it seems there was a flash in the pan, and the event did not take place. What was the cause, we have not been able to learn, but understand that she wanted to wait until next spring.

Married
On Friday last, LEWIS SHOE and MARY E. QUICK, of this township, were united in wedlock. This is Mr. SHOE's third matrimonial venture. He got a young girl this last time.

Death
WILLIAM P. DOLE, who was commissioner of Indian affairs under President LINCOLN, died at Washington City on Monday last, aged 78 years. For many years he was a resident of Paris, IL, where his remains will be taken for burial. He was a resident at one time, of Clinton, this county.

Marriage
SAMUEL E. WISHARD, of Clinton, this county, aged 72, and Mrs. LEVINA BARNHARDT, of Maroa, IL, aged 66, were united in marriage on Thursday last, the ceremony taking place at Maroa. This is the fourth time Mr. WISHARD has been spliced, and the second time for his lovely young bride. We wish them lots of amusement and a long and happy life.

Dying
Mrs. HENRY THOMASMYER, of Dana, who has been suffering from cancer of the breast for a long time, was reported to be dying on last Monday evening.

Marriage Licenses issued by Clerk A.R. HOPKINS during the month of September:
    MELVIN H. WELLS and RILLA S.D. NATION
    DANIEL A. REMLEY and PATIENCE HOLLINGSWORTH
    ULYSSES G. KEARNS and ROSE RICHARD
    TICE W. WILLIAMS and MINNIE B. BAILEY
    ALEXANDER KINDERMAN and LUCY M. GADD
    EDMUND R. OXFORD and HULDAH A. PRICE
    DANIEL V. MACK and ROSE A. ROSS
    BARTON S. AIKMAN and MARY B. CHIPPS
    EDWARD McDOWELL and LYDIA WALTHALL
    DAVID BREWER and ELIZABETH WETHERSPOON
    MATTHEW HAWS and ALLIE MOORE
    JOSEPH M. HOLLINGSWORTH and ROSA LACEY
    ALBERT J. DOUGHTY and ADDIE MOORE
    ERNEST TRUMAN and GRACE G. WHITE
    LEWIS SHOE and MARY E. QUICK

Real Estate Transfers
    JOHN L. KNIGHT et ux to MARY E. KENOVER
    75 acres in Helt Township
    $800

GEORGE DAVIS et ux to BELL CLEM
4 acres in Highland Township
$200

STEPHEN MILLER et ux to EDWARD H. YOUNG
½ acre in Vermillion Township
$200

MORGAN J. TUCKER et ux to JOHN WHITCOMB
20 acres in Clinton Township
$300

PETER COSSEY et ux to CHRISTIAN GLINDMEIER
20 acres in Highland Township
$500

JOHN T. NEWELL to NATHAN COLLINS
20 acres in Highland Township
$500

Notice of Final Settlement of Estate
    Estate of HARVEY H. PAYTON, deceased
    Filed September 26th, 1889
                        A.R. HOPKINS, Clerk

Wednesday, October 9, 1889

Home News
Mrs. HENRY THOMASMYER, residing just north of Dana, who is afflicted with cancer of the breast, is lying at the point of death, and liable to die any hour.

Mrs. MAURICE HEGARTY, left for Mattoon, IL, on last Monday afternoon, accompanied by her son WILLIE HEGARTY, who is going to enter the Catholic School at that place.

Mrs. LIZZIE BOST, of Rosedale, Parke County, and Mrs. ALMA DUZAN of Terre Haute, came up here to attend the funeral of their brother and brother-in-law, FRED DUZAN, on Monday last.

The following are the grand jurymen for this term of court: CHARLES P. POTTS, foreman; PETER COSSEY, ANDREW J. BECK, WILLIAM H. DARNALL, NATHAN A. CORDREY and FRANCIS M. DAVIS.

A thirteen year old son of ROBERT FOSTER, of Quaker Hill, died on Sunday last.

STANT EGGLESTON, residing two miles west of town, is the happy father of a girl baby, which arrived yesterday morning.

JOHN BLAKESLEY, of Helt Township, has purchased Mrs. ALEX WHITE's farm, consisting of 100 acres or more. He paid $2400, cash down.

Mr. ED AIKMAN left on the fast train last Monday morning for Chicago to attend the Rush Medical College, and prepare himself for the practice of medicine.

SELDON EGGLESTON, who is afflicted with the Arkansas swamp fever, is still lying at the point of death, with very little hope of his recovery.

Married
On the 2nd of this month, at the residence of the bride's parents in Highland Township, this county, ERNEST TRUMAN and GRACE G. WHITE were united in wedlock, Rev. W.N. COFFIN, pastor of the U.B. Church performing the ceremony.

Married
By the Rev. MATER, at his residence in Hillsdale, on the evening of the 9th instant, FRANK MALONE and ANNIE BROCK, all of Vermillion County, IN.

Death
We are sorry to learn that Mrs. MATTHEW LYTLE, who left here early last spring with her husband for Fordyce, AR, died on the 30th of September.

Dying
Uncle JOHN WRIGHT, of Clinton, who has been a resident of that township since 1820, having moved to this county with his parents when only 2 years old, was reported to be dying yesterday morning.

Dangerously Ill
Esq. GEORGE W. VANDEVENDER, residing near the depot, who has been ailing with what the doctors pronounce a cankered sore mouth for several weeks, is now thought to be in precarious condition, and his recovery considered doubtful. Large chunks of flesh rotted and fell out of his mouth, and the soreness is now extending down his throat. He is delirious most of the time.

Insurance Agent
On September 25th, 1889, we published an item stating that GEORGE FORD, an insurance agent of this place, was mysteriously missing. About 10 days ago, his wife sold off her household goods at a great sacrifice, and went up to Alvin, IL, to live with her husband's brother-in-law. She returned here on Saturday last and says her husband has gone to Canada for protection of the law, he having forged notes to secure commissions from the insurance company he represented.

Fodder Shock Nubbins
Mrs. JULIA TOWLE, of Defiance, OH, is here visiting her father, WILLIAM F. BALES, and other relatives.

FRANK BALES is home from Brazil to remain until school opens at Toronto, Canada, when he will go back this winter and graduate.

Died, at the country residence of SAM MALONE, of consumption, Mrs. WILLIAM AIKMAN, on Wednesday of last week. Deceased leaves a husband and three little children. Rev. RUSMISEL, of Bono, preached a funeral discourse. The remains were interred in the Bono Cemetery.

Accident
On the second of last month, FRED DUZAN, of this place, while hewing timber for E.D. WHEELER with a foot adz, met with an accident which proved fatal at 3 o'clock on last Sunday morning. The adz glanced and struck him about two inches above the knee on the right leg, cutting a large gash to the bone. The next day after the accident he was around on crutches, and the next day he dispensed of them, although he was warned not to stir around any. On the 18th of September his wounded leg became so painful that he had to call in a physician. Blood poisoning set in and there was no relief for him. He was born in this town on the 15th of December, 1858, and had he lived until the 15th of next December he would have been 31 years of age. His funeral took place at 2 o'clock last Monday afternoon from the M.E. Church, Rev. JOHN W. PARRETT preaching a short and appropriate sermon. The remains were taken to the Thomas Cemetery and interred. The G.A.R. band of which he was formerly a member, turned out and furnished music for the occasion. The deceased leaves a wife and one child, a little girl between 2 and 3 years old.

Pretty Democrat
We have always had sincerity in the Democracy of JOHN L. SMITH, editor of the Dana News. He has been married about 2 years, and on Sunday last his good wife, who is a thoroughbred Republican, took advantage of the political situation, and gave birth to a girl baby, weighing 10 ½ pounds.

Seriously Hurt
Mrs. LOUISA HAIN, wife of WILLIAM HAIN of Highland Township, and sister to Mrs. JOHN RICHARDSON of this place, met with quite a serious accident on Sunday last. She was thrown out of a two seated rig while her daughter was in front driving. They were going to JAMES BLUNT's to spend the day. Mrs. HAIN is a very large lady, and struck the ground hard, breaking two ribs and her shoulder blade.

Accident
On Thursday, while an old lady of Perrysville, the widow of the late Dr. SMALL of that place, was boiling down some cider in a large kettle, under a fire in the back yard, her clothing caught fire and burned off her before assistance could come to her relief. The hired girl heard her screams, and started with an old quilt or blanket to smother the flames, but Mrs. SMALL ran so fast away from her that when she reached her it was too late. Her body was charred from head to foot. She suffered great misery until Saturday, when death came to her relief. She was a very highly respected lady, and if we mistake not, was the sister of J.F. SMITH, with whom she had been making her home for a number of years. Her husband, when living, was the leading physician of Perrysville.

Our County Fair Awards
Class 1
    SAMUEL MOORE, E.N. BOWMAN & PETER AIKMAN – awarding committee
    Jack of any age – H.C. NELSON, 1st
    Span of mules in harness – JOHN HENDERSON, 1st
    Mule colt sucking – RAYMOND FONCANNON, 1st
    Mule 2 year old – JOHN HENDERSON, 1st
Class 2 – Light harness
    H.C. HANNA – Judge
    Stallion, 4 year old and over – DAVID SWAIM, 1st, SI MERRIWETHER, 2nd
    Stallion, 3 year old – WILLIAM McMURTRY, 1st, JOE COOK, 2nd
    Stallion, 2 year old – A. FONCANNON, 1st, J.M. WELCH, 2nd
    Stallion, 1 year old – ALF NIER, 1st, ALBERT McMULLEN, 2nd
    Stallion colt sucking – Mr. DIXON, 1st, SI MERIWETHER, 2nd
    Mare, 4 year old or over – C.C. HOOKER, 1st, CALEB BALES, 2nd
    Mare, 3 year old – J.M. WELCH, 1st, J.M. SHIRK, 2nd
    Mare, 2 year old – A.G. HARDING, 1st, STARRY brothers, 2nd
    Mare, 1 year old – ISAAC JORDAN, 1st, SI MERRIWETHER, 2nd
    Mare colt sucking – Mr. DIXON, 1st, Chrisman Horse Co., 2nd
    Gelding in harness – C.C. HOOKER, 1st, STANTON EGGLESTON, 2nd
    Span horses or mares in harness – DAVID SWAIM, 1st, S. MERRIWETHER, 2nd
    Saddle nag – JOHN D. COLLETT, 1st
Class 3 – Heavy Draft
    H.C. HANNA, Judge
    Stallion, 4 year old and over – Scotland Horse Co., 1st, LEVI HADLEY, 2nd
    Stallion, 3 year old – H.C. NELSON, 1st, Dana Shire Horse Co., 2nd
    Stallion, 2 year old – JOHN BELL, 1st
    Stallion, 1 year old – CHARLES JACKSON, 1st
    Mare, 4 year old and over – I.D. SAYRE, 1st, J.B. THOMAS, 2nd
    Mare, 3 year old – J.B. THOMAS, 1st
    Mare, 2 year old – J.B. THOMAS, 1st, TOM WATSON, 2nd

Mare, 1 year old – I.D. SAYRE, 1st, H.C. NELSON, 2nd
Mare colt sucking – J.B. THOMAS, 1st, I.D. SAYRE, 2nd
Gelding any age – PERRY DeHAVEN, 1st, B.E. WHITLOCK, 2nd

Class 4 – Fine Wools
WILLIAM F. BALES, JACOB WIMSETT, JAMES HARLAN – Awarding Committee
Buck, 1 year old or over – B.W. HARVEY, 1st
Ewe, 1 year old or over – B.W. HARVEY, 1st
Ewe, under 1 year – B.W. HARVEY, 1st and 2nd

Class 5
Buck, 1 year old or over – B.W. HARVEY, 1st, ALBERT FONCANNON, 2nd
Buck, under 1 year – Mr. DIXON, 1st, A. FONCANNON, 2nd
Ewe, 1 year old or over – B.W. HARVEY, 1st, A. FONCANNON, 2nd
Ewe under one year – Mr. DIXON, 1st, B.W. HARVEY, 2nd

Class 7 – Sweepstakes
Buck of any age – B.W. HARVEY, 1st
Ewe of any age or class – A. FONCANNON, 1st
Buck with 5 lambs on ground with sire – ALBERT FONCANNON, 1st

Class 8 – Berkshires
Boar, 1 year old or over – JOE MOREHEAD, 1st

Class 9 – Chester Whites
I.D. SAYRE, A.M. WATSON, ISAAC RICE – Awarding Committee
Boar, 1 year old or over – WILLIAM MYERS, 1st, ELIZABETH HINES, 2nd
Boar, under 1 year – WILLIAM MYERS, 1st, B.W. HARVEY, 2nd
Sow, 1 year old or over – B.W. HARVEY, 1st, WILLIAM MYERS, 2nd
Sow, under 1 year – B.W. HARVEY, 1st, WILLIAM MYERS, 2nd
Brood sow with 5 sucking pigs – WILLIAM MYERS, 1st, B.W. HARVEY, 2nd

Class 10 – Other Breeds
Boar, 1 year old or over – Mr. McMENDENHALL, 1st, WILLIAM WRIGHT, 2nd
Boar, under 1 year – CHARLES DUNLAP, 1st, WILLIAM WRIGHT, 2nd
Sow, 1 year of over – WILLIAM WRIGHT, 1st and 2nd
Sow under 1 year – WILLIAM WRIGHT, 1st, ALBERT McMULLEN, 2nd

Class 11 – Sweepstakes
Boar, any age or grade – WILLIAM WRIGHT, 1st
Sow, any age or grade – B.W. HARVEY, 1st

Class 12 – Horses for general purposes
H.C. HANNA, Judge
Stallion, 4 year old or over – Chrisman Horse Co., 1st, CHIPPS, DARBY & Co., 2nd
Stallion, 3 year old – J.D. VARNER, 1st, L.H. BELL, 2nd
Stallion, 2 year old – A. FONCANNON, 1st, JAMES ALDRIDGE, 2nd
Stallion, 1 year old – DAVID SWAIM, 1st, CHARLES JACKSON, 2nd
Stallion, colt sucking – Mr. DIXON, 1st, ERNEST HIBERLY, 2nd
Mare, 4 year old or over – DAVID SWAIM, 1st, BRUCE MERRIMAN, 2nd
Mare, 3 year old – J.M. SHIRK, 1st, ALEX DUNLAP, 2nd
Mare, 2 year old – Mr. DIXON, 1st, DAVID SWAIM, 2nd
Mare, 1 year old – CHIPPS, DARBY & Co., 1st, ALF NIER, 2nd
Mare sucking colt – ISAAC RICE, 1st, Chrisman Horse Co., 2nd
Gelding any age in harness – C.C. HOOKER, 1st, JOHN T. WILSON, 2nd
Span horses or mares – DAVID SWAIM, 1st, A.M. WATSON, 2nd
Carriage team – DAVID SWAIM, 1st, MONROE PUGH, 2nd

Class 13 – Short horn
ZERA CASTLE, H.C. NELSON – Awarding Committee
Bull, 2 year old or over – J.D. VARNER, 1st, L.H. AIKMAN, 2nd
Bull, 2 year old – J.D. VARNER, 1st
Bull, 1 year old – J.D. VARNER, 1st, L.H. AIKMAN, 2nd
Bull calf under 8 months – J.D. VARNER, 1st, L.H. AIKMAN, 2nd
Cow, 3 year or older – J.D. VARNER, 1st and 2nd

Cow, 2 year old – J.D. VARNER, 1st, L.H. AIKMAN, 2nd
Heifer calf under 8 months – L.H. AIKMAN, 1st

Class 14 – Dairy cattle
Cow, 1 year old or over – H.H. CONLEY, 1st

Class 15 – Breeding cattle
Bull producing 3 best calves all on groud with sire – L.H. AIKMAN, 1st
Cow with at least 2 of her produce – L.H. AIKMAN, 1st

Class 16 – Sweepstakes
Bull any age or grade – J.D. VARNER, 1st
Cow any age or grade – J.D. VARNER, 1st
Herd of Shorthorns, Herfords, or Polled – J.D. VARNER, 1st, L.H. AIKMAN, 2nd

Class 17 – Poultry
N.M. TUTT, E.B. BROWN – Awarding Committee
Pair Langshans – J.M. COX, 1st and 2nd
Pair white cochins – LEWIS SHEPARD, 1st and 2nd
Pair buff cochins – TOM HARLAN, 1st, J.M. COX, 2nd
Pair Plymouth rocks – ELIZABETH HINES, 1st, E.G. McCORMACK, 2nd
Pair white Plymouth rocks – LEWIS SHEPARD, 1st and 2nd
Pair black javas – LEWIS SHEPARD, 1st
Wyandottes, white – E.G. McCORMACK, 1st, J.M. COX, 2nd
Pair golden sebright bantams – J.M. COX, 1st
Pair silver sebright bantams – J.M. COX, 1st
White leghorn, rose comb – E.G. McCORMACK, 1st, J.M. COX, 2nd
Brown leghorn – E.G. McCORMACK, 1st
Brown leghorn, rose comb – J.M. COX, 1st
Common turkeys – VINA HART, 1st
White guineas – IKE JORDAN, 1st and 2nd
Toulouse geese – J.M. COX, 1st
Best and largest collection of poultry – J.M. COX, 1st, E.G. McCORMACK, 2nd

Class 18 – Light Harness Sweepstakes
H.C. HANNA – Judge
Stallion, any age – DAVID SWAIM, 1st
Brood mare showing not less than two of her produce – DIXON, 1st
Mare of any age – A.G. HARDING, 1st

Class 18 – Heavy Draft Sweepstakes
Stallion, any age – Scotland Horse Co., 1st
Horse producing 3 best colts on the ground – CHIPPS, DARBY & Co., 1st
Brood mare – I.D. SAYRE, 1st
Mare of any age – J.B. THOMAS, 1st

Class 19 – General Purpose Sweepstakes
Stallion of any age – Chrisman Horse Co., 1st
Horse producing 3 best colts – Chrisman Horse Co., 1st
Brood mare – ALF NIER, 1st
Mare of any age – DIXON, 1st

Class 20 – Agricultural
R. STOKES, F.M. DAVIS, A. BETSON – Awarding Committee
White wheat – GEORGE W. BRINDLEY, 1st
Red wheat – FRANK HARVEY, 1st
White corn – J.N. SPARKS, 1st
Yellow corn – EL HARLAN, 1st
Any variety corn – EL HARLAN, 1st
Barley – J.W. MENDENHALL, 1st
Oats – J.W. MENDENHALL, 1st
Pop corn – GEORGE W. BRINDLEY, 1st
Sweet corn – S.W. COFFIN, 1st
Clover seed – CHARLES VANVLEIT, 1st

Timothy seed – CHARLES DUNLAP, 1st

Class 21

Watermelons – W.S. THOMPSON, 1st
Pumpkins – EL HARLAN, 1st
Hubbard squashes – JACOB WIMSETT, 1st
Parsnips – ELIZABETH ARRASMITH, 1st
Turnip beets – G.W. BRINDLEY, 1st
Sugar beets – G.W. BRINDLEY, 1st
Red peppers – EL HARLAN, 1st
Pie plant – G.W. BRINDLEY, 1st
Red tomatoes – MARY A. ROWLAND, 1st
Lima beans – W.H. DALLAS, 1st
Snap beans – CHARLES VANVLEIT, 1st
Red onion sets – MARY A. ROWLAND, 1st
Potato onions – W.S. THOMPSON, 1st
Squash – W.S. THOMPSON, 1st
Carrots – ELIZABETH ARRASMITH, 1st
Early Ohio potatoes – GEORGE W. BRINDLEY, 1st
Early Rose potatoes – GEORGE W. BRINDLEY, 1st
Early Vermont potatoes – GEORGE BRINDLEY, 1st
Beauty of Hebron – CLIFTON WHITE, 1st
Any variety potatoes – GEORGE BRINDLEY, 1st
Turnips – W.S. THOMPSON, 1st
Red sweet potato – J.W. MENDENHALL, 1st
Yellow sweet potato – GEORGE BRINDLEY, 1st
Collection of potatoes – GEORGE BRINDLEY, 1st
Soft soap – LINK SANDERS, 1st
Hard soap – MARY A. ROWLAND, 1st
Mango pepper – Mrs. D.W. FINNEY, 1st

Class 22

Best collection and greatest variety of apples – S.W. COFFIN
Best 12 varieties, 4 fall and 8 winter apples – EMMA HESS
6 varieties for commercial purposes – S.W. COFFIN
Dozen quinces – MARY A. ROWLAND
3 bunches Concords – Mrs. D.W. FINNEY
3 bunches Delaware – J.W. MENDENHALL
3 bunches Hartford – J.W. MENDENHALL
3 bunches not enumerated – J.W. MENDENHALL

Class 23

DANIEL WISE, WILLIAM REED, EL HARLAN – Awarding Committee
Two seated top carriage – L.J. PLACE
One seated top carriage – L.J. PLACE
Wooden pump – D.W. FINNEY
Pump any description – D.W. FINNEY
Sewing machine – HORACE WELLS
Aquarium – Mr. HAYS
Stoves – H.S. COMINGORE

Class 24

Two horse plow – D.W. FINNEY
One horse plow – D.W. FINNEY
Sulky plow – D.W. FINNEY
Double shovel plow – D.W. FINNEY
Single shovel plow – D.W. FINNEY
2 horse harrow – D.W. FINNEY
Cultivator – D.W. FINNEY
Reaper – RALPH & FOLGER

Mower – RALPH & FOLGER
2 horse wagon – D.W. FINNEY
Display farm implements – L.J. PLACE
Sweep feed mill – T.J. HAWORTH & Son
Steam feed mill – T.J. HAWORTH & Son
Force and lift pump – T.J. HAWORTH & Son

Class 26

H. MARKLE, Mrs. W. ALLEN – Awarding Committee
Display and variety of plants in bloom – ADA PLACE
Collection of geraniums in pots – Mrs. S.S. COLLETT
Hanging basket – MARGARET EGGLESTON, 1st, ADA PLACE, 2nd
Display of cut flowers – Mrs. L.M. WHEELER
Display of dahlias – Mrs. L.M. WHEELER
Display of roses – Mrs. L.M. WHEELER
Display of tube roses in pots – Mrs. M.G. RHOADS
Display of floral designs – Mrs. M.G. RHOADS
Basket of flowers – Mrs. M.G. RHOADS
Collection of verbena – Mrs. M.G. RHOADS
Collection of pansies in bloom – ADA PLACE
Oleander in bloom – ADA PLACE
Basket bouquet – SARAH C. DAVIS

Class 27

ETTA AIKMAN, AMANDA FRAZER, G.F. TRUITT – Awarding Committee
Cheese – JANE MENDENHALL
Butter – ELIZABETH HINES, 1st, MARY MOREHEAD, 2nd
Wheat bread, salt rising – VINA HART
Wheat bread, yeast rising – Mrs. E. DUNLAP, 1st, ELLA KELLEY, 2nd
Corn bread – TIP DALLAS, 1st, SARAH C. DAVIS, 2nd
White cake – LIZA DILLOW
Jelly cake – Mrs. J.D. COLLETT, 1st, LIZA DILLOW, 2nd
Fruit cake – MARY A. ROWLAND, 1st, ELIZABETH ARRASMITH, 2nd
Pound cake – LIZA DILLOW
Sponge cake – LIZA DILLOW, 1st, SALLIE MARKLE, 2nd
Orange cake – Mrs. J.D. COLLETT, 1st, LIZA DILLOW, 2nd
Marble cake – SALLIE MARKLE, 1st, LIZA DILLOW, 2nd
Chocolate cake – OLLIE COLLETT, 1st, LIZA DILLOW, 2nd
Cocoanut cake – OLLIE COLLETT, 1st, SALLIE MARKLE, 2nd
Angel food cake – Mrs. E. DUNLAP, 1st, MARY A. ROWLAND, 2nd
Collection of cakes – LIZA DILLOW, 1st, SALLIE MARKLE, 2nd
Yeast biscuit – TIP DALLAS, 1st, SALLIE MARKLE, 2nd
Lemon pie – JANE HOPKINS
Mince pie – JANE HOPKINS
Pumpkin pie – RETA MOREHEAD
Peach pie – RETA MOREHEAD
Green apple pie – JANE HOPKINS
Cherry pie – RETA MOREHEAD
Gooseberry pie – JANE HOPKINS
Brown bread – Mrs. E.N. BOWMAN
Boston baked beans – SARAH C. DAVIS

Class 28

BELL F. STAATS, Mrs. JAMES HARLAN, Mrs. AMOS BETSON, Award Committee
Tomato pickle – ELLA KELLEY
Cucumber pickle – Mrs. JOHN DARBY
Sweet pickle – CARRIE MITCHELL
Preserve – Mrs. E.N. BOWMAN
Apple jelly – JANE HOPKINS

Currant jelly – MARY A. ROWLAND
Raspberry jelly – MARY A. ROWLAND
Pear jelly – Mrs. E.N. BOWMAN
Grape jelly – MARY A. ROWLAND
Gooseberry jelly – Mrs. E.N. BOWMAN
Blackberry jelly – Mrs. E.N. BOWMAN
Plum jelly – MARY A. ROWLAND
Strawberry jelly – JANE MENDENHALL
Collection of jellies – MARY A. ROWLAND
Canned strawberries – JANE MENDENHALL
Collection of fruit jellies – ELLA KELLEY
Canned peaches – BESSIE OLNEY
Canned cherries – VINA HART
Canned blackberries – VINA HART
Canned currants – MARY VANDEVENDER
Canned gooseberries – MARY VANDEVENDER
Canned pears – VINA HART
Canned plums – ELLA KELLEY
Canned grapes – JANE MENDENHALL
Canned tomatoes – JANE HOPKINS
Currant wine – MARY A. ROWLAND
Blackberry wine – MARY A. ROWLAND
Strawberry wine – JANE MENDENHALL
Grape wine – MARY A. ROWLAND
Blackberry cordial – JANE MENDENHALL
Collection canned fruit – HATTIE WHEELER
Maple sugar – JOE MOREHEAD
Molasses – Mrs. CHARLES STEWART

Class 29
SUSAN P. ELDER, H. MARKLE – Awarding committee
Scrap work silk – Mrs. J.T.H. MILLER, 1st, Mrs. E.N. BOWMAN, 2nd
Scrap work worsted – Mrs. C.W. VANCE, 1st, Mrs. J.N. SPENCE, 2nd
Scrap work cotton – Mrs. C.W. VANCE, 1st, ELLA KELLEY, 2nd
Patch work quilt – Mrs. J.T.H. MILLER, 1st, Mrs. E.N. BOWMAN, 2nd
Worked quilt by hand – Mrs. J.T.H. MILLER, 1st, Mrs. J.N. SPENCE, 2nd
Bed comfort – Mrs. J.T.H. MILLER, 1st, ELLA KELLEY, 2nd
Beautifully wrought undergarment set – Mrs. J.N. SPENCE

Class 30
BELL F. STAATS, SIBBELL J. FISHER, MATTIE ELDER – Awarding committee
Kensington embroidery – EMMA DUNLAP, 1st, PET JACOBS, 2nd
Macrame lace – Mrs. C.W. VANCE, 1st, Mrs. J.N. SPENCE, 2nd
Baby afghan – Mrs. J.T.H. MILLER, 1st, Mrs. E.N. BOWMAN, 2nd
Crochet worsted lace – ZULA HOPKINS
Crochet silk lace – Mrs. C.W. VANCE
Fancy apron – Mrs. C.W. VANCE
Pillows and bolster shams – Mrs. J.N. SPENCE
Table cover – BERTHA WRIGHT
Tucked shirt by hand – Mrs. E.N. BOWMAN
Mantel lambrequin – Mrs. J.N. SPENCE
Lamp mat – Mrs. E.N. BOWMAN
Lincoln embroidery – Mrs. E.N. BOWMAN
Cotton embroidery – Mrs. J.N. SPENCE
Child's embroidery dress by hand – Mrs. C.W. VANCE
Tattin – EMMA DUNLAP
Chair tidy – Mrs. J.N. SPENCE
Silk embroidery by hand – Mrs. C.W. VANCE

Toilet set of mats – ELLA KELLEY
Piece of tapestry – Mrs. J.N. SPENCE
Sofa cushion – Mrs. J.T.H. MILLER
Fancy worsted work not tapestry – Mrs. C.W. VANCE
Yoke ank sleeves by hand – Mrs. J.N. SPENCE
Fancy work basket – Mrs. J.T.H. MILLER
Crochet shawl – Mrs. E.N. BOWMAN
Crochet opera hood – ADA PLACE
Hearth rug – ELLA KELLEY
Sun bonnet – JANE MENDENHALL
Calico dress – MARY A. ROWLAND
Child's sacque – MARY A. ROWLAND
Child's apron – SARAH C. DAVIS
Lady's cap – Mrs. C.W. VANCE
Lady's night dress – CLARA MARSHALL
Shirt made by hand – ELLA KELLEY
Crochet tidy – EMMA DUNLAP
Slipper case – Mrs. J.T.H. MILLER
Pin cushion – Mrs. E.E. FREEMAN
Infants robe – Mrs. C.W. VANCE
Display lace work – Mrs. E.N. BOWMAN

Class 31

SUSAN R. ELDER, H. MARKLE, Mrs. M.R. STURM – Awarding committee
Pair woolen blankets – JANE MENDENHALL
Rag carpet – L. PARRETT, 1st, D.W. FINNEY, 2nd
Woolen knit stockings – Mrs. E.N. BOWMAN. 1st, MARY A. ROWLAND, 2nd
Pair socks – MARY A. ROWLAND
Pair cotton stockings – Mrs. J.N. SPENCE
Pair woolen knit gloves – ELLA KELLEY
Pair mittens – Mrs. E.N. BOWMAN

Class 32

CALDIE McMECHEN, R.E. STEPHENS, J.E. WRIGHT – Awarding committee
Water color painting – ELLA KELLEY
Landscape painting – SUE STANLEY
Animal painting – E.E. FREEMAN
Fruit painting – SUE STANLEY
Flower painting – E.E. FREEMAN
Portrait painting – Mrs. D.E. PRINGLE
Grecian painting – MARY A. ROWLAND
Pencil drawing – N. BOWMAN
Pastel painting – SUE STANLEY
Collection of photographs – J.R. SWAIN
Plain penmanship – M.L. DOVE
Ornamental penmanship – M.L. DOVE
Collection of oil paintings – D.E. PRINGLE
Painted plate – N. BOWMAN
Painted fan – E. FREEMAN
Crayon drawing – ELLA KELLEY
Painted plaque – SUE STANLEY
China painting – SUE STANLEY
Painting on silk – SUE STANLEY
Point lace handkerchief – N. BOWMAN
Hammered brass – N. BOWMAN
Lace linen, drawn work – Mrs. J.N. SPENCE
Lace rick rack – Mrs. J.N. SPENCE
Feather edge lace – Mrs. J.N. SPENCE

Button holes by hand – ELLA RICHARDSON
Painting on satin – Mrs. D.E. PRINGLE
Painting on plush – Mrs. E.E. FREEMAN
Show of living birds – Mrs. LIZA DILLOW
Painting on panels – Mrs. C.W. VANCE
Still life study from nature – Mrs. D.E. PRINGLE

Wednesday, October 16, 1889

Death
Our citizens were startled on last Friday morning by the announcement that WILLIAM P. WRIGHT, a farmer and fine stock breeder of Poland China hogs, residing at the west end of town, was dead. On that morning he was in his usual health, and ate a hearty breakfast, after which he went out to the barn lot to feed his stock, intending to go to Terre Haute on the 9 o'clock train to attend the races. While feeding his stock, he had an attack of apoplexy, and was unable to move without help. He hallowed for help, but his family was unable to hear him. Coroner BRINDLEY, who was returning from taking his cow to the pasture, heard him and went to his relief as soon as possible. As he passed his residence, his wife was coming out, and the two managed to get him to the house. He died within a few minutes after the physician reached the house. He was about 40 years of age and leaves a wife and one child. The funeral took place on Sunday afternoon, and was very largely attended. Rev. F.M. GEE, pastor of the M.E. Church, held short services at the residence, after which his remains were taken charge of by the Knights of Pythias, of Rockville, of which order he was a member, and interred in the Johnson Cemetery, two miles north of town.

Death
A few weeks ago, SELDON B. EGGLESTON returned here from Jonesboro, AR, where he has been running a big railroad restaurant for the last 2 years, to visit his father and recuperate his health. After he had been here a few days, he improved sufficiently to come downtown, and took a relapse and had to take to his bed again. He continued to grow worse until 3 o'clock last Friday morning when death claimed him for its own. He was about 29 years of age, and married. The funeral occurred on last Saturday afternoon, Rev. F.M. GEE and Rev. J.W. PARRETT officiating a the residence, after which the Knights of Pythias of Clinton took charge of the remains and buried him in the Thomas Cemetery according to the rites of that order, of which deceased was a member, having joined during his residence at Jonesboro, AR. The procession was very large, which was headed by the Newport cornet band, which furnished music for the occasion.

Death
Mrs. ELIZABETH THOMASMYER, wife of HENRY THOMASMYER, who resided a short distance north of Dana, this county, died at 10 o'clock last Wednesday night, and was buried at the Thomas Cemetery, two miles northwest of here on last Friday afternoon. The deceased had been troubled with cancer of the breast for many years, which resulted in death. She was born in England in December 1835, and came to this county when a small child. Her parents first settled in Ohio, afterwards in Wisconsin, and moved to this county in 1866. Her husband and four children survive her – two boys and two girls, who have grown to man and womanhood. Her funeral discourse was preached by Rev. LISTON, a Baptist minister of Rockville, of which church she has been a member since she was 13 years of age. A large and respectable procession of her neighbors and friends followed her to the last resting place.

Death
The wife of JOHN MANGES, residing about 6 miles west of here, died on Thursday last, and was interred in the Thomas Cemetery on Friday afternoon. Mrs. MANGERS took sick while attending our county fair. She was about 40 years of age, and a lady that never went out very much. She leaves a husband, but no children.

Death
A son of JOHN W. REMLEY, residing about 6 miles west of here, died on last Wednesday night at 10 minutes of 11 o'clock, aged about 7 years, and was interred in the Thomas Cemetery on Friday afternoon.

Death
BELLE W. COFFIN, daughter of S.W. and R.A. COFFIN, was born January 18th, 1863 and died October 7th, 1889, at 8 ½ p.m. She united with the Cumberland Presbyterian Church during the winter of 1886, and has lived a devoted earnest Christian. She was possessed of wonderful patience and trust and through her long illness, was always cheerful and loving. Five years ago watchful friends noticed that her health was failing and she and her father spent that winter in the south, but only temporary good was effected, and soon after her return, she was again afflicted, and has been a constant sufferer from consumption until relieved by death. Perhaps no young lady in this community had a larger circle of friends; in fact she was not known to have a single enemy, her lovable and sunny disposition remaining with her. The funeral was conducted Wednesday, October 9th, 1889, at 10 o'clock a.m. from the family residence, one mile and a half south of Cayuga, Rev. GEE, of Newport, officiating in the presence of a large concourse of friends after which she was laid to rest in the Thomas Cemetery.

Injury
JAMES HARNEY, residing 6 miles west of here, is said to have been quite seriously hurt by a gravel bank caving in on him, near Lodi, Parke County, on Thursday last. He is a young man, about 20 years of age.

Montezuma News
Mr. WOODY has engaged Miss NETTIE STEPHENSON as organist while instructing the class in vocal music at Hillsdale.

Died – Mrs. CORA SWAIM, wife of JOSEPH SWAIM, two miles east of Bloomingdale, October 9th, 1889, of consumption. Mrs. SWAIM was the daughter of Mr. and Mrs. J.P. HUNT. The interment took place at Bloomingdale Cemetery at 2 p.m. October 10th. The funeral sermon was preached by Rev. CUMMINGS of Rockville.

Cayuga Clatter
J.M. SHIRK has moved his family from Covington to this place.

Fodder Shock Nubbins
Dana News
Mrs. LOU DARRAH, nee THORNE, became the mother of a big 9 pound boy, one week ago last Sunday.

Died – at her home near Sugar Grove, IL, on Wednesday, Mrs. FRANK REED, at an advanced age. She was the mother of the late SILAS JONES' wife. Undertaker REDMAN says that she was the largest corpse he has ever handled, her weight being 350 pounds.

Real Estate Transfers
    GEORGE FISHER to EMMA CLARK
    10 lots in Dana
    $350

    DAVID McBETH to E.R. MURRY
    Part of lot in Clinton
    $250

M. RANDALL to S. & A. PYLE
20 acres in Helt Township
$600

W.B. WALTHALL to THOMAS B. WALTHALL
? acres in Vermillion Township
$500

J.S. HOUCHIN to F. MALONE
Lot in Alta
$150

J.C. GREGORY to JAMES QUINLAN
Lot in Dana
$300

JAMES M. ORR etal to HENRY V. NIXON etal
4 lots in Newport
$4,500

HAMMOND & AIKMAN to W.E. FULWIDER
2 lots in Dana
$100

SARAH WHITE to JOHN BLAKESLEY
100 acres in Helt Township
$2,400

MARY GIBSON to JOHN S. HOUCHIN
3 lots in Hillsdale
$125

GEORGE M. LOUGH to W.E. EDMONSTON
3 lots in Dana
$1,100

Home News
Our brother TOM DAVIS, of Summit Grove, left last Friday morning for Illinois City, IL, where he has been given a circuit by the Central Illinois M.E. Conference.

Col. WILLIAM E. McLEAN's wife, who died in Washington DC, last week, was brought back to Terre Haute yesterday afternoon and interred in the cemetery at that place. She had been an invalid for several years.

JOHN WRIGHT, an old and respected citizen of Clinton, who has been a resident of that township since 1820, died near 11 o'clock a.m. on Wednesday last, aged 71 years. His funeral was very largely attended.

JONATHAN MERRIMAN, who was a member of the 6th Indiana cavalry, received notice on Saturday last, that his pension had been granted, allowing him $6 per month from the 5th of April, 1886. His arrears will amount to about $260.

WILLIAM F. SCHWEIZER and wife, of Urbana, IL, came down here on Saturday last to attend the funeral of S.B. EGGLESTON, and remained with the editor and family over Sunday. Mrs. SCHWEIZER is a sister of Mr. EGGLESTON's wife.

LINK CHURCH, of Helt Township has a new girl baby at his house. It arrived last Monday.

A small child of PETE RHODENBAUGH, of Cayuga, died on Friday last, and was interred in the Eugene Cemetery on Saturday.

Judge WILLIAM EGGLESTON and wife, of Terre Haute, came up here to attend the funeral of his nephew, S.B. EGGLESTON, which occurred on Saturday last.

"BUD" SAGERS, a cousin of S.B. EGGLESTON, who was clerking for him at Jonesboro, AR, came home last Saturday to attend the funeral of his employer, reaching here on the afternoon train, just as they were ready to leave the house for the cemetery.

Mrs. IRVIN LAMB of the Plainfield Reform School, who came over here last week to attend the funeral of her son-in-law, S.B. EGGLESTON, left for home on the early morning train last Monday.

Mrs. CAROLINE DALLAS, of Colorado, a former citizen of this place, is back on a visit after an absence of 6 or 7 years. She will probably remain all winter.

ZAN MOREHEAD, residing a short distance northeast of here, is now the proud father of two fine boys, the second one having arrived one day last week.

Married
Mr. ISAAC T. CLINES and Miss ROSA CARTER, all of Vermillion County, were married by the Rev. MATER at his residence in Hillsdale on the 10th instant.

Married
At 12 o'clock on Thursday last, at the U.B. parsonage in this place, Rev. R.B. VAN ALLEN united WILLIAM MATTHEWS and AGNES L. KERN in holy wedlock.

Operation
JOHN BROWN, of Parke County, a brother of E.B. BROWN of this county, went up to Danville on Saturday last, and had Dr. MOREHOUSE remove a cancer from his under lip. He cut it in a V shape, taking out about one inch of his lip. The cancer had been coming for about 3 years, and was rapidly growing larger. The doctor thinks he will never by bothered with it anymore. The wound made in the lip was stitched together so that when it heals up it will leave a very small scar.

Married
On last Sunday afternoon at 2 o'clock, ALLEN HOLLINGSWORTH and Miss NORA CHAPMAN, both of this township, were united in bonds of wedlock, the ceremony taking place at the residence of the bride, and being performed by Rev. R.B. VAN ALLEN, pastor of the U.B. Church.

Wednesday, October 23, 1889

Clinton Echoes
Last Wednesday was the 8th wedding anniversary of Mr. and Mrs. G.A. CRABB. Quite a number of invited guests did honor to the occasion.

Mr. and Mrs. FRANK MANN were called to Bloomfield last week to attend the bedside of their son WIN MANN, who is quite sick with lung fever, and whose recovery is considered doubtful.

Mrs. Dr. HENRY SHEPHERD, of Hartford, KS, is visiting her parents, Mr. and Mrs. MORGAN. The doctor is about to lose his eyesight.

Montezuma News
Miss ERIN JOHNSTON, of Beatrice, NE, is visiting relatives in Montezuma.

O.P. FULTON and wife, of Beatrice, NE, are visiting relatives in Montezuma this week. Mrs. FULTON is a sister of J.E. JOHNSTON.

Fodder Shock Nubbins
Dana News
Mr. FRANK HICKS and a wife, of Indianapolis, visited the BILSLAND and MALONE families at this place over Sunday. Mr. HICKS is a cousin of Mr. BILSLAND and Mrs. MALONE.

Pumpkin Vine News
Clinton Argus
After an illness of several months, ABNER THOMPSON died at his home in the north part of town, Thursday morning. The deceased was about 45 years of age. He leaves a wife and 3 children, Miss DELLA THOMPSON and two boys. AB was a genial hearted soul but too much liquor shortened his life.

Home News
Mrs. ELIZABETH SCONCE of Danville, IL, and her mother, Mrs. CATHERINE BELL of Eugene Township, came down here on a visit on Friday last. Mrs. SCONCE left for home on Monday afternoon, but her mother, who is nearly 84 years of age and as spry as a kitten, expects to remain several weeks. She is now the guest of the editor's family.

Death
JACOB WHITE, who was a resident of Helt Township, this county, for many years, and moved to Saline County, KS, in 1867, died of fever on the 20th of last month.

Death
Miss JESSIE VAUGHN, who resided one mile north of Helt's Prairie, died yesterday morning, of intermittent fever, after a two weeks' illness. She was 16 years of age, and an amiable young lady.

Marriage
On Friday last, at the residence of the U.B. pastor, Rev. R.B. VAN ALLEN united in wedlock LEE J. BENNETT, aged 22, to Miss CORA DAVIS, aged 13, both of this township. The mother claimed that her daughter would be 15 on her next birthday, but the daughter was very positive that she was only 13.

Notice of Assigment
Notice is hereby given that ALFRED McDONALD, of Dana, has made an assignment of all his property, real and personal, to the undersigned in trust, for the benefit of his creditors.
BARTON S. AIKMAN, assignee

Real Estate Transfers
WILLIAM S. PONTON to OLIVER PONTON
86 acres in Helt Township
$400

MINERVA C. SCOTT to JOHN L. WEBSTER
Lot in Perrysville
$50

SYLVESTOR INGRAM et ux to JOHN W. BEARD
40 acres in Helt Township
$1,200

HEZEKIAH CASEBEER et ux to ROBERT A. PARRETT
40 acres in Helt Township
$688

Wednesday, October 30, 1889

Halos From the Hill
Mr. and Mrs. JOHN HENDERSON, who returned last week from their pleasant western trip, were visited Thursday and Friday by their sister and family, Mrs. CHARLES LINDLEY, of Parke County.

Montezuma News
Cards are out for the marriage of FRANK M. CONNER, our obliging and popular agent of the I.D. & W. Railway, to Miss LULU HORN, at the residence of the bride's parents in Cloverdale, IN, next Wednesday evening, October 30th.

Pumpkin Vine News
Clinton Argus
Little LOTTIE SEDGEWICK, a bright girl of 7 years died at the residence of SAMUEL NEWLIN near Libertyville, last Tuesday. She was a member of the Coal Creek Sabbath School, and was a great favorite among her numerous young friends and associates.

Clinton Echoes
Sunday morning at 4 o'clock, Mrs. WILLIAM POWERS died at her residence just south of town in the edge of Parke County. Mr. POWERS, it is reported, had a large fortune left to him last spring by the death of an uncle in Ohio. He went to see about it and came back much elated over his prospects, expecting to get the money at the close of the year. At the time of his wife's sickness, he was working to get money to go to Ohio to sign certain papers and take possession of his newly acquired property. Mr. POWERS has been a poor man and his wife, who has been an honest, hardworking woman all her life, is called away just as an era of prosperity begins to dawn.

Home News
R.H. MYERS and family, who moved to Hutchinson, KS, about 7 years ago, arrived back here last week, and they have come to stay. Says he has gotten all he wants of Kansas.

LEM and ELISHA DAVIS, of Pittsburg, IN, are here visiting their brother, E.F. DAVIS.

Mr. SAM McKEE of Ogden, IL, was in town yesterday afternoon.

WILLIAM F. HENDERSON, of Quaker Hill, this township, who has been at Maryville, TN, for some time to recuperate his failing health, is now at Courtland, AL.

Mrs. EMMA BARR and son, of Waveland, IN, are here visiting, the guests of her brother, WILLIAM SHARP.

Marriage
SAMUEL R. COFFMAN and Miss ELLA SYKES were united in marriage in the forenoon of the 16th instant by Rev. J.E. WRIGHT.

Married
Our old friend, JOE BURNS, of Montezuma, startled our people by a happy surprise in getting married to Mrs. ANNA E. CANNON, of Genoa, NE on the 16th of this month. His new wife is an estimable lady, and the widow of the late Dr. CANNON, who, for sometime, has been matron of the Indian School at Genoa, NE. She is the daughter of Esq. W.C. DONALDSON, who is now 87 years of age, and in good health.

Death
GEORGE W. VANDEVENDER, who resided near the depot, died at 9 o'clock on last Friday morning, aged about 50 years. His ailment was what the physicians pronounced canker sore mouth, from which he suffered 10 weeks and one day before death came to his relief. Great chunks of rotten flesh was taken from his mouth, many of which he swallowed, being unable to spit them out. It was with great difficulty and severe pain that he swallowed food of any kind, his principal diet being soup. He was delirious most of the time the last 3 weeks. He had been Justice of the Peace of this township for nearly 4 years, and made a most excellent officer. He funeral took place on last Sunday afternoon.

Marriage
On the evening of the 16th instant, Mr. CHARLES FARRIS, of St. Bernice, and Miss LIZZIE McROBERTS, of Dana, were united in holy matrimony at the home of the bride, Rev. J.E. WRIGHT officiating.

Notice of Administration
    Estate of JOHN PAYTON, deceased
    Filed October 8, 1889
                          F.E. JAQUES, Administrator

Notice of Administration
    Estate of WILLIAM RUSSELL, deceased
    Filed October 8, 1889
                          AUGUSTUS O. MILLER, Administrator

Notice of Administration
    Estate of JOHN WRIGHT, deceased
    Filed October 24, 1889
                          ULYSSES G. WRIGHT, Administrator

Notice of Application for Liquor License
    JACOB I. MARTIN – Gessie
    PATRICK FLYNN – Hillsdale
    RICHARD T. MITCHELL – Newport
    WILLAM R. BOWEN – Newport
    SAMUEL HAIN – Clinton

Real Estate Transfers
    JOHN PAULEY et ux to MARY E. BROCK
    10 acres in Vermillion Township
    $200

    WILLIAM S. BOREN etal to REUBEN PUFFER
    40 acres in Helt Township
    $240

    JOHN A. WILTERMOOD et ux to ALBERT H. NICHOLS
    Lots 22 and 23 in Dana
    $550

    WILLIAM J. SWINDELL to CARRIE M. TAYLOR
    Part of lot 9 in Dana
    $350

SILAS DAVIS to JOHN H. BOGART
Lot in Clinton
$500

CHARLES F. BRILES et ux to LYDIA BALLAH
20 acres in Highland Township
$700

DANIEL W. FINNEY et ux to CHARLES SMITH
Lot 7 in Dana
$35

Wednesday, November 6, 1889

Fodder Shock Nubbins
WILL FINNEY returned to school at Purdue University on Monday.

Miss ALICE CRANE and little niece, EDNA CRANE, of Clinton, are in Dana on a two weeks visit.

LEE BELLUS has sold his property in the west part of town to Mrs. EMILY JONES, of Edgar County, IL.

W.B. PAULEY, of our town, went away to Kentucky last week and brought a wife back with him. He has resumed housekeeping at his own home.

Cayuga Clatter
The two Misses ILES went to Danville Monday, to witness the marriage of "FOXY" STURM and Miss NETTIE LUKE.

Notice to Heirs and Creditors of Petition to Sell Real Estate
    Estate of EHUD HUGHES, deceased
    Filed November 5, 1889
                WILLIAM HUGHES, Administrator

Notice to Non-Residents
    JEMIMA SWAIM vs. WILLIAM SWAIM
    Complaint #3203
    WILLIAM SWAIM not a resident of Indiana
    Must appear before 4th Monday in December 1889
    Filed November 1, 1889
                A.R. HOPKINS, Clerk

Notice to Non-Residents
    JONAS C. FORTNER
    Vs.
    SAMANTHA MILLER, JAMES JONES, DELILAH JONES, ROSA JONES, ELMER JONES, LACIE JONES, ORA JONES, SILAS JONES, & LAURA A. JONES
    Complaint #3154
    All defendants are not residents of Indiana
    Must appear before 4th Monday in December 1889
    Filed November 4, 1889
                A.R. HOPKINS, Clerk

Notice to Non-Residents
- REBECCA J. HATTREY vs. HARVEY HATTREY
- Complaint #3204
- HARVEY HATTREY not a resident of Indiana
- Must appear before 4th Monday in December 1889
- Filed November 4, 1889

                        A.R. HOPKINS, Clerk

Sheriff's Sale
- HIRAM CHENOWETH vs. DAVID B. JOHNSON & HELEN B. JOHNSON
- $632.87
- Sale to be held Saturday, November 30, 1889
- Sale at courthouse between 10 and 4
  - Lot #26 and 20 feet off S side of Lot 47 in Perrysville
- CONLEY & SAWYER, attorneys for plaintiff
- Filed November 2, 1889

                        WILLIAM RHEUBY, Sheriff

Sheriff's Sale
- FERDINAND BREIDENBACK
- Vs.
- JOHN NORRIS, SARAH E. NORRIS, JAMES C. SAWYER, trustee, HIRAM SHEPARD, SUSAN F. WARREN & ELLEN HAWKINS
- $2458.28
- Sale to be held Saturday, November 30, 1889
- Sale at courthouse between 10 and 4
  - Sec 22, T 16 N R 10 – 12 acres
  - Sec 22, T 16 N R 10 – 33 acres
  - Sec 22, T 16 N R 10 – 40 acres
- MAXWELL & MAXWELL, attorneys for plaintiff
- Filed November 2, 1889

                        WILLIAM RHEUBY, Sheriff

Sheriff's Sale
- JOHN WHITCOMB vs. FRANK REEDER & LUCINDA REEDER
- $2863.53
- Sale to be held Saturday, November 30, 1889
- Sale at courthouse between 10 and 4
  - N ½ SW ¼ Sec 28
  - W ½ W ½ NE ¼ SE ¼ Sec 28
  - SE ¼ SW ¼ Sec 28
  - All in T 14 R 9 W – 140 acres
- CONLEY & SAWYER, attorneys for plaintiff
- Filed November 2, 1889

                        WILLIAM RHEUBY, Sheriff

Pumpkin Vine News

Mrs. ELIZA PAYTON, widow of the late JOHN PAYTON, this week received a very pleasant surprise in the way of a remittance of $251.04 from Uncle SAM for which was due her husband for services as postmaster at this place during the war. It seems as though Mr. PAYTON did not receive all his pay, and it has lain there all these 28 years, until now.

Ridge Farm News

ISAAC SIDERS was indicted by the grand jury Thursday for the murder of his uncle, THOMAS SIDERS, of Camargo, in July.

ABLE W. PAYNE, aged 49, obtained a divorce at Danville, a few days since, from his wife HARRIET PAYNE, to whom he had been married over 20 years. He immediately took out a license to marry ELIZABETH PAYNE, his brother's widow.

Rileysburg Notes
Mr. MACK ROUSE and Miss KATE CONNER were married on Thursday last.

Obituary
MARY E. CARR, of Cayuga, died on Thursday last, aged 29 years, 3 months, and 23 days. She had been a member of the Christian church for 5 years. She was the daughter of LEVI and MARY GEBHART, and was married to JOHN F. CARR on December 9, 1886. The funeral was preached by Rev. R.B. VAN ALLEN, pastor of the U.B. Church.

Married
On Thursday last, at high noon, WILLIAM P. BELL and Miss NAOMI C. EGGLESTON, both of this place, were united in wedlock, Rev. F.M. GEE, pastor of the M.E. Church performing the ceremony.

The following marriage licenses were issued by Clerk A.R. HOPKINS during October:
- JOHN W. BRACKEN and LUCY GOOD
- WILLIAM R. HENSLEY and CELESTA HILON
- FRANK MALONE and ANNIE BROCK
- JASPER N. STARK and JULIA A. HANE
- HARVEY TOSSER and FLORENCE DOUGLASS
- ISAAC T. GLINES and ROSA CARTER
- WILLIAM MATTHEWS and AGNES L. KERN
- ALLEN HOLLINGSWORTH and NORA CHAPMAN
- CHARLES FARRIS and LIZZIE McROBERTS
- SAMUEL R. KAUFMAN and ELLA SYKES
- LEE J. BENNETT and CORA DAVIS
- ISRAEL WILSON and ISRAEL STONEBRAKER
- LEONARD H. SWITZER and ADALINE MORRISON
- ISAAC McKOUSE and CLARA B. CONNER
- WILLIAM P. BELL and NAOMI C. EGGLESTON
- JASPER A. SINGLETON and HATTIE M. PAYTON
- ABRAM SIMS and VINA GRIFFIS

Notice of Administration
Estate of NORMAN C. SKINNER, deceased
Filed October 30, 1889
W.K. McKNEILL, Administrator

Home News
JOE GARRETT is the proprietor of a new girl baby which arrived on Thursday last.

Grandma HIBERLY, mother of FRED and ERNEST HIBERLY, was 88 years of age on Monday, October 28th, 1889. She is still active and spry for one of her years.

Mrs. JANE NICHOLS and her daughter-in-law, Mrs. OSCAR NICHOLS, of this township, went up to Henning, IL, on Friday last to visit BRENTON NICHOLS and family.

Mrs. L.J. PLACE was happily surprised on Tuesday of last week by the arrival of her aged mother, Mrs. EMILY McBROOM, who is now past 73 years of age and gets around quite lively for one of her age. She was accompanied by her youngest daughter, Mrs. SHEPHERD and little son, all of Fairmount, IL.

Real Estate Transfers
> ELIAS PRITCHARD et ux to REBECCA TILLOTSON
> 1/3 of an acre in Helt Township
> $200
>
> ELIZABETH HITE to WILLIAM S. BROWN
> Lot 8 in Zener's addition to Newport
> $175
>
> S. AIKMAN etal to Z.R. CONNER
> Lots 17 & 18 in Dana
> $100
>
> L.D. THOMAS to JOSEPH COLLETT
> ? acres in Eugene Township
> $9,294.75
>
> A.C. HENDERSON to S.J. MOREY
> Lot in Clinton
> $500
>
> WILLIAM ROACH etal to ASA DOWERS
> 35 acres in Eugene Township
> $500

Wednesday, November 13, 1889

Reunion
ORPHA WIGLEY's two sisters came to see her last Monday the 4th instant; her oldest sister, JERUSHA TEEGARDEN, is 86 years old, and her youngest sister, MARY ANN LEWIS, is 71 years old. ORPHA is 84 years old. They all went out to WILLIAM WIGLEY's Thursday and had a picnic. There they found the old dinner pot that their mother bought 97 years ago. They were raised on grub cooked in the same old dinner pot, so they brought the old pot in, and ORPHA and MARY ANN cooked dinner in it by the old fashioned fireplace. JERUSHA baked a regular old fashion Johnny cake on a board before the fire. JERUSHA and ORPHA's wedding dinners were cooked in this same old pot. JERUSHA had not seen her sister MARY for 60 years. Of course she would not have known her if she had met her any place else. JERUSHA TEEGARDEN lives in Vincennes, IN. MARY ANN LEWIS lives in Osgood, IN. MARY's husband and daughter, MAGGIE LEWIS came with her. They are all Christian ladies, and expect soon to be called home. The 3 sisters went over to Cates' Station Monday to visit Aunt JERUSHA's son and grandchildren.

Halos From the Hill
Miss MYRA HAWORTH, her brother WILL HAWORTH, and FRANK PETERS, who are Bloomingdale students, spent Sunday here.

Miss GRACE SHEPARD is studying German and Algebra preparatory to entering Coates College next year.

Rileysburg Notes
Mrs. SARAH JOHNSON and Miss MELVINA KING, of Gessie, were up to visit Mrs. ELIZABETH RODGERS, their sister, last Sunday.

Fodder Shock Nubbins
Dana News
Born, October 31, 1889, to Mr. and Mrs. ALBERT AYE, a big boy.

Pumpkin Vine News
FRANK L. REEDER and family started for Washington Territory this week where they will make their future home. FRANK leased his saloon to OTE PERRIN.

Home News
Dr. JOHN H. BOGART, of Clinotn, has been appointed administrator of the estate of ELIZA SWEM, deceased.

Postmaster THORNTON's father of Danville, IL, and his grandfather of Sodorus, aged 88, came down here yesterday for a visit.

Mrs. ANGELINE ALEXANDER, residing near Vincennes, will arrive here today to pay her daughter, Mrs. WILLIAM C. MYERS, a short visit.

Mrs. MARY CHADD and her daughter, Mrs. LAURA AIKMAN, have gone down to Dana, to spend a month visiting relatives and friends.

JAMES M. WRIGHT, of Hillsdale, a former resident of Opedee, has advertised for retail liquor license, to sell by the small at Tangier, Parke County.

Mrs. Z.T. GALLOWAY returned home from Ellettsville, Monroe County, on Thursday last, where she had been for the last two weeks visiting her parents, relatives, and friends.

JOHN VANDEVENDER, of this place, will be united in marriage tomorrow to a young widow of Terre Haute by the name of ORPHA BROWN, who is the mother of 3 children.

E.Y. JACKSON Jr., of Altamont, KS, a former resident of this place, was elected a Justice of the Peace at the election held in that state, on Tuesday of last week.

PHILO CURTIS, the newly elected county commissioner of Clinton Township, will take his seat as one of the Board on the first Monday in next month. He is intelligent, with considerable business experience, and we believe will make a good guardian of the county's interests.

JAMES BEARD, of Helt Township, gave us a pleasant call yesterday. He is 66 years old, and has been a resident of this county since he was 11 years old.

In a Bad Fix
The wife of Uncle JOHN HASTY is afflicted with a large gathering in her side which has been coming for the last three weeks. It is now as large as a man's fist. About one year ago, she had a gathering on her side which laid her up for quite a while. This one is forming about six inches below the other one. She is confined to her bed and unable to help herself.

Death
JOE GARRETT's infant child, born October 31st, died at 3 o'clock on last Monday afternoon, aged 11 days. The funeral took place at 2 o'clock yesterday afternoon, Rev. R.B. VAN ALLEN, conducting the services at the residence, after which the remains were taken to the Thomas Cemetery and interred.

Real Estate Transfers
    T.D. McKEE etal to FRANK C. RICHARDSON
    Lot 149 in Cayuga
    $150

DAVID HINES to SILAS HUGHES
Lots 13 & 14 in Gessie
$200

ELIAS WALRAVEN et ux to HENRY H. ANDERSON
35 acres in Clinton Township
$1200

SARAH A. BURGESS and husband to IDA DAVIS etal
24.46 acres in Helt Township
$300

L.D. THOMAS, assignee of WILLIAM COLLETT, to THOMAS PATRICK
Out lot in Eugene
$300

JAMES L. HACKLETHORNE et ux to ETTIE B. PERRIN
Lot 10 in Knowles' addition to Clinton
$400

L.T. DICKASON et ux to J.G. ENGLISH
110 acres in Highland Township
$4000

Notice to Non-Residents
    WILLIAM WRIGHT
      vs.
    FRANCIS M. WRIGHT, unknown heirs of JAMES FARRINGTON, deceased, and unknown heirs of JULIMA BACON, deceased
    The residence of defendants is unknown
    Must appear before 4th Monday in December 1889
    CONLEY & SAWYER, attorneys for plaintiff
    Filed November 12, 1889
                            A.R. HOPKINS, Clerk

Notice of Application for Liquor License
    WILLIAM J. BROPHY – Clinton

Administrator's Sale of Real Estate
    Estate of JOSEPH HOLTZ, deceased
    Sale to be held Saturday, December 14, 1889
    Sale on premises in Eugene
        Lot 19 in Eugene
        Out lot 6 in Eugene
                            H.H. CONLEY, Administrator

Administrator's Sale of Real Estate
    Estate of ADALINE V. JONES, deceased
    Sale to be held Saturday, December 14, 1889
    Sale to be held on premises in Perrysville
        S ½ Lot 36 in Perrysville
        21 feet off N side of Lot 37 in Perrysville
                            B.O. CARPENTER, Administrator

Notice to Non-Residents
> DAVID HANDLEY & SALINA W. HANDLEY
> Vs.
> MARY WRIGHT, WILLIAM CHUNN, STEPHEN CHUNN, ALICE CHUNN, MARTHA E. WILSON, JOHN CHUNN, GEORGE E. CHUNN, FRANK CHUNN, CHARLES CHUNN, ALICE WHITSEL, CATHERINE McWETHY, JOSEPHINE HARRISON, ANNIE TAYLOR, FRANCIS M. WRIGHT, unknown heirs of JAMES FARRINGTON
> Defendants STEPHEN CHUNN, MARTHA E. WILSON, CATHERINE McWITHY, and unknown heirs of JAMES FARRINGTON, deceased, are not residents of Indiana
> Must appear before 4th Monday in December 1889
> CONLEY & SAWYER, attorneys for plaintiff
> Filed November 12, 1889
>
> A.R. HOPKINS, Clerk

Wednesday, November 20, 1889

Serious Accident
On last Wednesday afternoon, a number of our citizens were at the Newport flouring mills, to inspect the running of the beautiful machinery. Among the visitors was JACOB WIMSETT, an old farmer, aged 63 years, who resides 2 miles south of town on the Opedee Road. He was examining the mill very closely, and when he came to where the steel rolls were, he raised the lid and stuck in his right hand to grab up some of the brand, and in an instant the rolls which revolve at lightning speed, caught his hand and ground his four fingers off up to the palm of his hand before he could release himself. The fingers were ground finer than gold dust flour, only the tendons being left which were not as large as fiddle strings. He was brought to Dr. HALL's office where Dr. HALL and Dr. WALLACE amputated his hand about an inch and a half above the knuckles.

Fodder Shock Nubbins
Dana News
Born – last Saturday morning, a big girl baby to STEVE CLARK and his wife.

FISH McROBERTS has bought GEORGE ELDER's farm, west of Bono. It is a fine tract of land 211 acres.

The birth of a big girl baby, to Marshall STOKES and wife should have been recorded last week, having arrived Tuesday, November 5th, 1889.

Died, at her home at Bono on Friday, November 8th, 1889, Mrs. ZERILDA MACK, in her 68th year. She was the widow of CEPHUS MACK. This old couple was about the first near Bono, and owned nearly all of the land at one time. For four or five years before her death, Mrs. MACK had been a helpless invalid. Rev. J.E. WRIGHT conducted the funeral services which took place on Saturday.

From Quaker Hill
Mrs. MARTHA CROSS, nee WALTHALL, arrived from Iowa to attend the funeral of her brother.

Death
During the past 12 weeks, the family and friends have watched and waited with a sad foreboding, the silent work of disease as it wound its icy bands around the faithful friend SMITH WALTHALL, who departed this life, November 13, 1889, aged 18 years. While young in years and full of life and love and hope, he longed to live. Religious services were conducted at Hopewell Church by JAMES P. HAWORTH, after which the remains were laid to rest in the beautiful burying ground so near his home.

Helt Township Items
BOB BALES has moved to Jonestown and is the proprietor of the Jonestown mills.

HENRY KENT moved to St. Marys, where he intends to make his home in the future.

A.L. CHURCH and wife celebrated the 10th anniversary of their married life on November 13th, and to say that they got lots of tinware and had a good time would be putting it mild.

In 21 years from last Thursday, DICK CHURCH will have another son old enough to vote the Republican ticket.

Mrs. NANCY TUTTLE, of Hutchinson, KS, is back here visiting her mother, SUSAN JAMES.

Home News
WILLIAM A. JAMES, of Hillsdale, has been granted an increase in pension.

CALE WATERMAN, of Lodi, Parke County, gave us a pleasant call on Friday last.

HARRY B. RHOADS, of Greencastle, was over to Waveland last week, to visit his parents.

WILLIAM WALKER, of Wabash, paid his sweetheart, Miss MATTIE DONDELL, a teacher in the Newport high schools, a visit on Sunday last.

FRANK H. MUNSON, of Opedee, has bought JOHN L. PETERS' city restaurant at Cayuga, and moved up there last week. He is going to run a bakery in connection with the restaurant.

Twins
The wife of ROBERT A. HART, residing 2 miles northwest of town, gave birth to 2 fine looking boys on last Sunday night.

Another Failure
It is currently reported that EMMET LANG, a dry goods merchant of Dana, has failed, and his creditors have taken charge of the stock. Mr. LANG is a clever and accommodating gentleman, and we are sorry of his misfortune.

Notice to Non-Residents
    AMOS J. BETSON
    Vs.
    Unknown heirs of ISAAC RAMSEY, deceased, ERI DAVIS, JOHN DAVIS, RILEY DAVIS & LUCINDA FRINGER
    Complaint No. 3209
    Residence of defendants is unknown
    Must appear before 4th Monday in December
    Filed November 18, 1889
                        A.R. HOPKINS, Clerk

Death
SMITH WALTHALL, son of WILLIAM B. WALTHALL, was born October 15, 1871, at Quaker Hill, where he lived and died November 13th, 1889, after a protracted illness of typhoid fever. A father, 6 brothers, and 4 sisters mourn his death.

Wednesday, November 27, 1889

Fodder Shock Nubbins
Congratulations to STEWART WISHARD, of Toronto. It is a boy and arrived last Saturday.

The infant child of Mr. and Mrs. ALBERT AYE died on last Monday evening, and was interred at Cedar Corner Cemetery Tuesday evening.

Death
Mrs. WILLIAM CAMPBELL, of Clinton, who has been in poor health for some time, dropped dead on last Thursday evening from heart disease. The deceased was a member of the Presbyterian Church, and a most estimable lady. She was 52 years of age. The funeral took place on Friday and was very largely attended. Rev. HOOK, of Clinton, and Father GRIFFITH, of Montezuma, performed the last sad rites.

Pumpkin Vine News
Clinton Argus
Mrs. MARY McCARTY, of Helt Township, mother of BAT McCARTY, died at her home, Wednesday. Mrs. McCARTY was a native of Ireland and was so old that the family had lost the record, but she was said to be past 90. The remains were taken to Armiesburg for interment.

Home News
Mrs. WILSON HASTY, of Chillicothe, IL, is here visiting her parents, Marshal BOB WHITE and family.

Miss MARY HOLLINGSWORTH went over to Chrisman, IL, yesterday on a short visit to her sister, Mrs. ELIZA GILBERT.

Mrs. SAMUEL E. KAUFMAN, of Dana, accompanied by Mrs. LAURA AIKMAN, paid the editor's family a visit on Sunday last.

J.C. JACKSON, of Hillsdale, has sold his stock of dry goods, groceries, notions, etc., of that place, to JOHN S. HOUCHIN.

ORA DeLOSS DAVIS is going up to Lafayette today, to visit his cousin, Miss ALLIE KOONSE, and eat Thanksgiving turkey tomorrow.

Married
By Rev. W.A. SMITH, on the 17th, at the residence of the bride's mother, Mr. FRANK LEWSADER and Miss ROSELLA JOHNSON, all of Fountain County.

Accident
On last Saturday afternoon, OWEN FULK, a middle aged man of Opedee, who is married, concluded he would take a little hunt, and on his return home in the evening, he met a neighbor in a two horse wagon, and stopped to chat with him for a moment. He had a double-barreled, muzzle loader, shotgun, and set the breech of the gun on the hub of the wheel. It slipped off and fell, striking the hammers against the iron band of the hub, discharging both barrels, striking his right hand and tearing it all to pieces. Dr. M.L. HALL and Dr. JAMES WALLACE were sent for and amputated his hand about three or four inches above the wrist joint. He is reported to be getting along nicely. The accident is an unfortunate affair for him, as he has no education, and cannot earn a living by any business occupation. The county will have to provide for him.

Death
Miss HATTIE RAMSEY, daughter of WILLIS and SARAH RAMSEY, departed this life on last Wednesday morning. She was 17 years of age, was very well respected, and loved by all. She had been sick for about 6 months. She leaves a father, mother, brothers, sisters, and many friends to mourn her loss. She was a granddaughter of Mrs. HARRIET RODGERS. The funeral services were held on Friday at Union Chapel, by Rev. SHIRES. The remains were carried to the Atherton Cemetery.

Chicken Gravy Club
On last Friday night, the "Chicken Gravy Club" of this place, composed of some of our most estimable ladies, gave Mrs. JAMES HASTY a happy surprise. It was her 42nd birthday, and the Gravy Club thought it would help her celebrate the event.

Surprise
On November 22, 1889, the family and friends of the widow CLEARWATERS, aged 77 years, living 4 ½ miles southwest of Newport, made a birthday surprise for her, and in order to make the surprise complete, they sent her to WILLIAM HOLLINGSWORTH's, and all the family from a distance, being notified, came together at the appointed time. Rev. J.A. CLEARWATERS, from Greencastle, RICHARD A. CLEARWATERS from Newton, IL, and R.H. CLEARWATERS of Hutchinson, KS, and all of the family living in the community, consisting of 5 sons and 2 daughters, and a number of grandchildren and great-grandchildren, and about 30 of the neighbors, gathered. When all was ready, they sent for her. All was in readiness, and everyone had a wonderful time.

Real Estate Transfers
>JOHN H. BOGART et ux to JOSEPH ZELANKA
>Lot 8 in Bogart's second addition to Clinton
>$65

>EMMET B. LANG to THOMAS J. LANG
>Lots 11 & 12 in Dana
>$600

>WILLIAM RHEUBY, Sheriff, to H.H. CONLEY
>80 acres in Helt Township
>$874.43

>WILLIAM S. PONTON to POLLY PONTON
>96 acres in Helt Township
>14 lots in Alta
>$10

>ALBERT FRAZIER to MELVIN FRAZIER
>52 acres in Vermillion Township
>$2000

Wednesday, December 4, 1889

Fodder Shock Nubbins
Dana News
JIM RALSTON is a high stepper this morning (Wednesday). A big girl arrived last night at his house.

Clinton Echoes
Mrs. CLARA MALLORY, neé SMITH, of Veedersburg, visited her parents at this place last week.

LARZ and ARTHUR WHITCOMB and WILLIS HANDLEY of DePauw University, and SEYMOUR MATTHEWS of the Polytechnic came home on a short vacation last Thursday.

CHARLES CURTIS and family, of Georgetown, IL, moved to Clinton last week and CHARLES has gone to work for the Norton Coal Co.

Married
At the residence of the bride's parents on Tuesday evening of last week, ANDREW JACKSON SMITH, of PA, and Mrs. ANNIE EADS, of Clinton, Rev. HOOK officiating. Mr. SMITH left for the oil regions yesterday, and will be absent this winter, after which they will remove to Pennsylvania.

About a year ago, FRED MOORE, a night operator at this place, was called away and on leaving left his best girl in the care of his friend, A.N. TURSHER, the popular young agent on the C. & E.I. Railway. On last Thursday evening, Mr. TURSHER and the young lady – Miss SADIE DOWDY, one of Clinton's favorite belles, were united in marriage by Rev. HOOK at the residence of the bride's mother on West Mulberry Street.

Marriage
Mr. GRANT OVERPECK and Miss RHODA COUGILL, one of the most amiable young ladies in Helt Township, were united in marriage at the residence of N.T. LEITON Tuesday night.

Bucktown Items
KATE BLEVINS is teaching school up at Owl Creek.

Strange Case
On last Friday morning about 9 o'clock, WILLIAM JONES, residing 6 miles west of here on the gravel road, suddenly became deaf, blind, and crazy. He continued in that condition until last Sunday, when his hearing, eyesight, and senses came to him. He is 70 years of age, and the doctors cannot account for this. It is thought it may have been an attack of apoplexy. He is quite wealthy, being worth at least 30 or 40 thousand dollars.

Stricken
At about 10 o'clock on last Thursday night, J.W. McCONNELL, an old and respected citizen, of this place, aged 73 years, had a light stroke of paralysis. It is on his right side, and he is gradually getting a little worse instead of better. His daughter, LAURA McCONNELL, who is an employee of the Soldiers' Home at Knightstown, was telegraphed of the sad condition of her father, and immediately left for home, arriving here on the midnight train Friday night. Mr. McCONNELL is being kindly cared for by his son WILLIAM McCONNELL and daughter LAURA.

Home News
ELMA VAN ALLEN, daughter of Pastor VAN ALLEN, is seriously afflicted with a cankered sore mouth.

SAM D. COLLETT, of the Polytechnic Institute, Terre Haute, came home last week to eat Thanksgiving turkey.

PAUL RHOADS, of Wabash College, came home last week to eat Thanksgiving turkey with his parents.

Mrs. L.C. PARKS, a former resident of this place, is clerking in a dry goods store in Terre Haute.

Miss BUN NIXON, who is attending Coats' College at Terre Haute, came home last week, accompanied by a young lady friend, to spend Thanksgiving here.

Miss BELLE ROGERS, a teacher in the Rockville schools, a very estimable and highly respected young lady, died of quick consumption on Friday of last week
Montezuma Reporter

Dr. M.L. HALL, who is seriously afflicted with piles, had Dr. WALLACE perform a surgical operation upon him one day last week, and he is now unable to leave the room.

The Board of County Commissioners met in regular session on Monday last. PHILO CURTIS, the new member took the oath of office and a position on the Board, which is now constituted of the following gentlemen: F.M. RILEY of Highland Township, GEORGE F. HAWORTH of Vermillion Township, and PHILO CURTIS of Clinton Township. Mr. RILEY was elected President of the Board.

Death

Died at her quiet home in Bono, November 8th, in the 68th year of her age, Mrs. ZERILDA MACK, the wife of CEPHUS MACK, who died some 4 years ago at Summit Grove. Mrs. MACK, whose maiden name was JORDAN, was the last but 2 of 14 children – one brother, WILLIAM JORDAN of Kansas, and a sister Mrs. RUSSELL, near Dana. She leaves 7 children – 4 sons and 3 daughters – and a host of friends to mourn her loss. She was a faithful Christian, a tender mother and a steadfast friend, who had been well tested in all the changes in the lot of common life, but ever manifested that spirit which leads mortals to that home beyond the skies. She was a Christian at church and at home, a Christian in health and in sickness. Even through long and trying sickness, her kindness was ever manifest, and to those whom she was the greatest charge, most deeply mourn her loss, and feel the need of her consolation. The funeral services were conducted by Brother WRIGHT of Dana, and her remains laid to rest in the Helt's Prairie Cemetery by the side of her husbands.

Marriage Licenses issued for the month of November 1889
- ISRAEL NEWPORT and REBECCA E. LANCASTER
- JAMES T. GRIFFITH and SARAH S. HUTCHINSON
- BYRD C. MONROE and LOIS M. MACK
- ANTHONY N. TURSHER and SADIE M. DOWDY
- ELMER G. OVERPECK and RHODA A. COUGILL
- ANDREW H. SMITH and ANNIE EADS
- FRANKLIN J. DUNLAP and JENNIE SPARKS
- ISAAC DAVIS and MARTHA E. KING

Pension

Mrs. MARY A. WANN, who resides near Howard, Parke County, made a big haul. She was over here on Friday last executing a voucher for $2000 pension money; $1057 was pension due her husband, who died in 1881, and the balance of $1003, the amount due her up to the present time.

Liquor Licenses Granted

SAM HAIN	Perrysville
JACOB I. MARTIN	Gessie
JOE LOWE	Cayuga
RICHARD T. MITCHELL	Newport
PAT FLYNN	Hillsdale
LAWRENCE MONAGHAN	Dana
WILLIAM BROPHY	Clinton

Noitce of Final Settlement of Estate
Estate of SAMUEL C. JOHNSON, deceased
Filed December 2, 1889

A.R. HOPKINS, Clerk

Real Estate Transfers
JOHN S. GRONDYKE to JOHN W. DAVIS
Lots 33 & 34 in Cayuga
$335

ELIZABETH I. DICKASON etal to SAMUEL R. ROYSE
Out lot 20 in Perrysville
$75

JOSEPH F. SMITH et ux to ANDREW R. MARLATT
Part of out lot 24 & 25 in Perrysville
$250

R.E. WHITLOCK and GRACE H. WHITLOCK to MARTHA M. WHITLOCK
Lots 27 & 28 in Fisher's addition to Dana
$1

JOHN H. BOGART to E.G. OVERPECK
137 ½ acres in Helt Township
$5100

HENRY H. TATE to GEORGE H. McNEILL
Out lot in Perrysville
$135

Obituary
ALEXANDER E. DUNLAP was born in Maryland, near Baltimore, February 7th, 1813, and died November 28th, 1889, of consumption of the bowels, with which he was a sufferer since last spring. He leaves a wife and 5 children to mourn his loss. He was the 7th son of a family of 13 children, all of whom are laid to rest. His mother died when he was 3 years old, after which he was in the care of his sister, Mrs. SARAH MOORE and husband, who brought him to Columbus, OH, remaining there until 1833, when they came to Vermillion County, IN. He was married in 1839 to Miss MARGARET FOSSELMAN with whom he has lived for 50 years, and had no deaths in the family until his spirit took its flight. The evening before his death, he preached temperance until he was entirely exhausted, and asked to be placed in his armchair. He then fell asleep and was aroused at midnight when he told them to let him alone, that he was resting so easy and was aroused no more. He was a noble father, a kind husband, and ever ready and willing to do something for his family and friends.

Wednesday, December 11, 1889

County Hotel
Superintendent JOE CONRAD, of the county poor asylum, who has taken care of the unfortunate poor of this county for several years, will be succeeded by GEORGE SHORT on the first of next March, who is an orphan, and at one time an inmate of the house he has chosen to superintend. He was taken from the poor house when a small boy and raised by CHARLEY POTTS, who gave him a good country school education. He agrees to take care of the poor for $400 per year, which will be a saving of $200 a year to the taxpayers.

Fodder Shock Nubbins
Dana News
JOHN ALLEN of Washington, IN, nephew of G.W. ALLEN, visited relatives at this place last week.

NORM CURTIS, of Oakland, IL, visited with his uncle ANDY CURTIS and GRANT DAVIS last Saturday and Sunday.

Montezuma News
JAMES QUINLAN and JAMES RAIRDON, Sr. were granted liquor licenses yesterday by the county commissioners.

Death

At 12:45 on last Friday morning, November 6, 1889, the spirit of JEFF DAVIS winged its way to the world beyond. He died at New Orleans, where he had been moved a few days previous to his death.

Allowances by Board of Commissioners for December 1889

S.J. HALL, roads	1.50
J.E. ELLIS, roads	1.50
THOMAS PATRICK, roads	1.50
HENRY DICKERSON, roads	1.50
E.L. HIBERLY, roads	.50
WILLIAM RHEUBY, roads	7.50
C.W. BROWN, books and stationary	73.75
W.B. BURFORD, books and stationary	139.13
S.B. DAVIS, poor	255.00
G.O. NEWTON, poor	276.68
W.K. McNEILL, poor	250.00
E.H. McDANIEL, poor	139.53
SOL WEATHERWAX, poor	161.03
HENRY NEBEKER, poor	37.25
ERASTUS MACK, poor	25.00
ELMER E. SMITH, poor	25.00
J.A. BARNES, poor	25.00
M.L. HALL, poor	56.25
R.W. STEPHENS, insurance	176.50
THOMAS CUSHMAN, insurance	87.50
H.S. CADY, bridges	35.33
W.K. McNEILL, bridges	375.00
GEORGE W. BRINDLEY, coal	35.10
A.R. HOPKINS, county offices	10.70
JOE CONRAD, poor asylum	476.46
M.L. HALL, Board of Health	48.50
M.G. RHOADS, attorney	125.00
W.F. KERNS, courts	7.00
PHILO CURTIS, courts	21.00
G.F. HAWORTH, courts	24.50
F.M. RILEY, courts	21.00
WILLIAM RHEUBY, criminals	210.00
W.M. HAMILTON, fees & salary	544.94
W.F. THORNTON, public buildings	22.00
JOHN MILLER, public buildings	8.00
FRED RUSH, bridges	26.00
S.B. DAVIS, printing	33.36
DAVID AGGRA, janitor	50.00
G.W. DEALAND, county superintendent	265.75
W.B. HOOD, gravel roads	3173.33
	2120.00
	516.33
	1047.72
	1624.60
	60.00
	1065.98
	530.78
	1639.63
	1652.63
	603.00

Death
Mrs. MAGGIE SIMPSON HOLTZ, of Cayuga, died of quick consumption after an illness of only a few days, on last Wednesday, December 4, 1889, at 4 o'clock in the afternoon, aged 37 years. Her marriage, from some cause, did not seem to be a happy one. At the time of her death, her husband was in some western state. Shortly before she died, someone asked her if she wanted to see him, and she said "Don't mention him to me." She leaves a bright and pretty little baby, aged 13 months, which will be kindly cared for by her folks. MAGGIE had many warm friends in Newport who deeply regret her sad death. There was not a more generous or better hearted woman ever lived than the deceased. Everybody loved and respected her, and deeply sympathize with the relatives in her untimely death. The funeral occurred on last Thursday afternoon, and was very largely attended, the remains being interred in the Opedee Cemetery.

Cayuga Clatter
WILLIAM HEIBREDER has rented the butcher shop of W.W. PORTER. He will continue to do business at Porter's old stand.

W.P. BROWN is building a butcher shop south of the Clover Leaf Railroad.

Home News
WILLIAM M. MITCHELL, of Clinton, an old 18th boy, has been granted an increase in pension.

STEVE GALLAHER, of Terre Haute, has moved up here and is tending bar for DICK MITCHELL.

JOHN W. AYE, of Hillsdale, has been granted a pension of $6 per month. He gets $150 arrears.

BEN G. SOUDERS, of Hillsdale, whose claim for pension under J.C. BLACK was rejected, came to us last July and placed his case in our hands. We made out the necessary papers to have his case re-opened, and forwarded additional evidence, and last week received notice that his pension had been granted at the rate of $2 per month from April 23, 1885.

Marriage
A marriage license was taken out on last Monday for WILLIAM CHUMLEA, of Illinois, and Miss IMOGENE COLLINS, of Perrysville. Mr. CHUMLEA is a telegraph operator and Miss COLLINS is a most excellent lady and a good fiddler.

Real Estate Transfers
BEN HARRISON et ux to BENJAMIN F. HARRISON
51.8 acres in Clinton
$500

CHARLES PAYTON and ARTHUR PAYTON, trustees of the U.B. Church to
ANDREW J. BURK
5/8 acre in Helt Township
$50

GEORGE ELDER et ux to CLARA A. McROBERTS
241 2/3 acres in Helt Township
$9600

CHARLES F. BASSETT et ux to SAMUEL R. JAMES
13 acres in Helt Township
$350

JACOB B. JULIAN to MARY J. DOWNEY etal
231.16 acres in Helt Township
$?

Wednesday, December 18, 1889

Marriage
AUGUSTUS FORD and ROSANNA GERTRUDE AMMERMAN, of Dana, Vermillion County, IN, arrived in the city last evening on the 7:30 train, and were driven from the depot to HENRY SEEKAMP's Hotel. They then dispatched to Magistrate B.F. CAMP to come to the hotel to join their hearts and hands. Upon the Squire's arrival he found that the couple had forgotten to provide themselves with the essential legal document. Deputy County Clerk C.D. GOEPER was then summoned and returned with the Magistrate to the hotel. Here it was found that another barrier would have to be surmounted before their happiness was complete. The young lady being only 18 years of age, the law was evaded by the formal appointment of HENRY SEEKAMP, the host, as guardian of the young lady, with AUGUSTUS FORD, the groom, as his bondsman. Mr. SEEKAMP gave his consent, supplemented by his blessings. Love has triumphed over difficulties. The bride and groom are first cousins, and they could not be married under the Indiana law. They will return to their home this morning.
                Louisville Commercial, December 10

Sheriff's Sale
 JOHN WHITCOMB vs. FRANK REEDER & LUCINDA REEDER
 $150
 Sale to be Saturday, January 11, 1890
 Sale to be held at courthouse between 10 and 4
  N 1/3 Lot 6 Block 3, in Clinton
 CONLEY & SAWYER, attorneys for plaintiff
 Filed December 18, 1889
                WILLIAM RHEUBY, Sheriff

Home News
CHARLES H. FITHIAN, of Knox County, was killed one night last week by the limb of a falling tree, while he and his son and another party were out coon hunting.

GOULD RHEUBY, son of the old sheriff, who is teaching school in Highland Township, came down here on Saturday to spend Sunday with his parents.

MONROE G. HOSFORD, of Eugene, has been appointed administrator of the estate of Mrs. MAGGIE B. HOLTZ, deceased.

JOSHUA N. DAVIS has been appointed administrator of the estate of GEORGE W. VANDEVENDER, deceased.

JIM CAMPBELL, an old 14th regiment, Indiana, was up here last week visiting JOE FOOS and family.

Mrs. BELL KERDOLFF, who has been on the sick list for a long time, has gone to Terre Haute to be treated in a hospital in that city.

Miss GERTIE TROWBRIDGE, of Plymouth, this state, sister-in-law of Pastor GEE, is here on a visit, and will remain during the winter.

HARRY E. JAMES, who has been an operator on the Missouri Pacific Railway at Lincoln, NE, for the past 5 years, arrived at Hillsdale one day last week on a short visit to his parents, WILLIAM A. JAMES and family.

Grand Army Officers
Shiloh Post No. 49, Grand Army of the Republic of this place, met Friday night and elected the following officers for the ensuing year:

Commander	THOMAS J. NICHOLS
Senior Vice Commander	JERRY BULGER
Junior Vice Commander	ISAIAH HATON
Quarter Master	JOHN RICHARDSON
Surgeon	Z.P. THORNTON
Chaplain	Rev. R.B. VAN ALLEN
Officer of the Day	ROBERT J. HASTY
Outside Guard	M.B. CARTER
Delegate to State encampment	DANIEL WILLIAMS
Alternate delegate	GEORGE JONES

Death
Mrs. SAMUEL LANE of Alta, died at the home of her son-in-law, WILLIAM HARRISON, one mile north of Summit Grove. The funeral was held at Salem Wednesday, and the remains were interred in the Salem Cemetery.

Death
Mrs. WILLIAM CHUNN died at her home 5 miles southwest of this place Sunday, December 9th, of lung fever. The funeral ceremony was conducted Monday. The interment took place in the Shepherd Cemetery.

Pumpkin Vine News
Clinton
Miss ANNA FULTON of Camargo, IL, is in the city visiting her friend, Miss SARAH DOWNING.

Married
By Rev. W.A. SMITH, on the 11th instant, at the residence of the bride's parents, Mr. WILLIAM D. CHUMLEA of St. Francisville, IL, and Miss IMOGENE R. COLLINS of Perrysville. Mr. CHUMLEA is a telegraph operator and a young man of good habits, and Miss COLLINS is one of Perrysville's most estimable young ladies. They will make their home in St. Francisville.

Married
Capt. JOHN T. CAMPBELL left for New York City where he will attend the marriage of his daughter EVA to GUSTAVE A. PETERSON on next Sunday evening, December 15th. Mr. PETERSON was born in Stockholm, Sweden, and has been in the country about 18 months. Miss EVA is well known here, and went to New York some months ago to study painting and has since been on the stage.

                             Rockville Republican

Real Estate Transfers
  WARREN S. RAYNES et ux to JOHN McMILLEN
  30 acres in Clinton Township
  $150

  JACOB C. FONCANNON etal to JACOB E. FONCANNON
  21.40 acres in Helt Township
  Love and affection and $1

  JOHN W. DINWIDDIE et ux to MARTHA J. BRIGHT
  Out lot in Clinton
  $250

M.J. BRIGHT to JOHN and ANN COOK
Out lot in Clinton
$300

CATHERINE PEARMAN etal to JOHN W. BLAKESLEY
70 acres in Helt Township
$2400

L.A. WICK to AMANDA C. HENDERSON
Lot 6, Block 3, in Clinton
$115

Fodder Shock Nubbins
Dana News
Mr. HUGH MILLER and sister MARY MILLER of Des Moines, IA, visited with J.W. REDMAN's Tuesday. They are cousins to Mrs. REDMAN.

Wednesday, December 25, 1889

Haloes From the Hill
B.S. BOTHWELL and daughter BESSIE, left Tuesday night for Clay City, IL, to spend the holidays with his relatives and children.

WILLIAM HENDERSON and family have been living for some time near Decatur, AL. He was in very poor health when he left here last summer, and has gradually grown worse ever since. His brother JOHN HENDERSON left last Thursday to visit him, but it is thought that he cannot long survive.

Cayuga Chatter
D.L. PETERS is counter hopping for H.A. STURM.

Notice of Administration
    Estate of ALEXANDER E. DUNLAP, deceased
    Filed December 17, 1889
                                        JOHN D. COLLETT, Administrator

Home News
Mrs. McCLELLAN, an old and respected lady of Eugene, died on last Thursday evening, after an illness of one week. Her funeral took place on Friday last.

STEVE JENKS Jr., and GRACE AIKMAN, both of Bono, were united in wedlock by Rev. JOHN A. MAST on last Sunday evening. Both are less than 18 years of age.

PAUL RHOADS, of Wabash College, has returned home to spend the holidays with his parents and the young friends.

L.J. PLACE, who is digging a well on his farm a short distance west of the fairground, struck a seven foot vein of fine coal, at a depth of 100 feet, a few days ago. The well is not much over a quarter of a mile from the C. & E.I. Railway.

Mr. EBERSOLE, of Ohio, and Miss VISTA MYERS, residing two miles south of town, were united in wedlock on last Sunday evening, Rev. J.W. PARRETT performing the ceremony.

GEORGE W. BRINDLEY, of Opedee, has been granted a pension.

Dr. JAMES A. BARNES, of Gessie, has been granted a re-issue of his pension.

Miss CLARA MYERS, who is attending school at Urbana, IL, is at home to spend the holidays.

GEORGE WELSHAN and family, of Streator, IL, are here visiting JOHN HASTY and family.

OLIVER P. LAYMAN, the deaf and dumb man of Howard, Parke County, was in town on Saturday.

PATRICK BREEN, residing 12 miles west of here, received a telegram on last Saturday noon that his only sister, who resides at Terre Haute, was lying at the point of death. He came down here and took the 9 o'clock train that evening for that city.

DAVE COSLET, an old 18th Indiana boy, who now resides near Tuscola, IL, was over here on Wednesday last, and gave us a very pleasant call. It was the first time we had met during the last 12 years. He does not now look like the sprightly youth he was when he enlisted in Company C of the 18th Indiana in 1861. He was then a beardless boy, only 18 years of age. Now his whole face is covered with a heavy growth of beard, and he has the appearance of a man who has passed his best day.

Obituary
ANN McGINNIS, born October 21, 1809, in Butler County, OH, came to Indiana in 1823, settled one mile and a half south of Rockville, Parke County. She moved from there to Eugene in 1847. She was married in 1841 to THOMAS McCLELLAN, who died in 1850. Five children were born to them, of whom only two are living. She was converted and united with the church at the age of 18, and remained a faithful member until her death. Her death occurred on Thursday last, and the funeral on Friday afternoon, Rev. F.M. GEE, pastor of the M.E. Church, performing the last sad rites.

NAME INDEX

Adam, Mary J. 66
Adams, A.J. 171
Adams, Bob 10
Adams, Dave 82
Adams, Eva 171
Adams, Gracie 46
Adams, John 37, 42, 136
Adams, John Quincy 113
Adams, Mart 33, 42
Adams, Mrs. A.J. 171
Adams, Mrs. John 66
Adams, Mrs. Taylor 76
Adams, Robert 12, 113
Adams, Taylor 79, 161
Aggra, David 81, 119, 170, 204
Aggra, Jennie H. 119
Aikman 27, 49, 55, 62, 67, 74, 94, 98, 103, 133, 154, 186
Aikman, Adaline 93
Aikman, B.S. 54, 76, 84, 125
Aikman, Barton S. 53, 174, 188
Aikman, Barton Scott 168, 172
Aikman, Clara 133, 138
Aikman, E. 24
Aikman, E.A. 34, 39
Aikman, Ed 5, 48, 49, 64, 84, 175
Aikman, Ed A. 58, 173
Aikman, Ed E. 140
Aikman, Emma V. 26
Aikman, Etta 181
Aikman, Franklin 167, 170
Aikman, Grace 208
Aikman, H. 86
Aikman, Harry 13, 66
Aikman, John B. 66
Aikman, L. 35
Aikman, L.H. 2, 11, 178, 179
Aikman, Laura 195, 199
Aikman, M. 86
Aikman, Mrs. Ed 5, 48
Aikman, Mrs. William 176
Aikman, Peter 61, 177
Aikman, Roy 103
Aikman, S. 36, 87, 194
Aikman, S.S. 124
Aikman, Sam 16, 111
Aikman, Samuel 50
Aikman, Scott 11, 24, 166, 168
Aikman, Tom 24
Aldrich, Amanda E. 170
Aldridge, C.A. 37
Aldridge, Carry 37
Aldridge, James 178
Aldridge, John E. 92
Aldridge, Julius 145, 163
Aldridge, Mary 26
Alexander, Angeline 195
Alexander, Charley 15

Alexander, Herold 61
Alexander, Jennie 61, 64
Allen, Allie M. 34
Allen, G.W. 203
Allen, George 96
Allen, Grace 120, 144
Allen, John 203
Allen, Lige 162
Allen, Louis C. 56
Allen, Mrs. George W. 58
Allen, Mrs. Lige 162
Allen, Mrs. W. 181
Allen, Tom 96
Allen, W.Y. 46
Ally, William 154
Ambrose, Isaac 119
Ammerman, Fred 90
Ammerman, James 77, 90
Ammerman, John 90
Ammerman, Rosanna Gertrude 206
Ammerman, Theopolis 90
Andbow, July 155
Anderson, Albert 139
Anderson, Claude 47
Anderson, Daniel 139
Anderson, Dunk 18, 55, 65
Anderson, Grace 76
Anderson, Henry H. 196
Anderson, Jennie A. 15
Anderson, John S. 168
Anderson, Lawrence 47
Anderson, N.C. 86, 134
Anderson, Platt Z. 15
Andrews, Elsie 26, 165, 173
Andrews, I.L. 34
Andrews, Jasper 173
Andrews, Ollie 57
Andrews, S.E. 134
Andrews, W.J. 117
Andrews, W.P. 134
Andrews, William 71
Anstead, Emmet 99
Antrum, Joseph S. 76, 78
Archie, Jennie 48
Armour, Thompson 40
Arnold, Blanche 60
Arrasmith, Alva 54, 103, 116
Arrasmith, Clarence 34, 39
Arrasmith, Elizabeth 180
Arrasmith, Frank 95, 105
Arrasmith, J.W. 42
Arrasmith, James 11
Arrasmith, James A. 101
Arrasmith, John Wesley 40
Arrasmith, Levi 111
Arrasmith, Mrs. 84
Arrasmith, Mrs. Alva 64
Arrasmith, Thomas T. 116

Arrasmith, W.C. 112, 119
Asbury, E. 101
Asbury, George W. 15
Asbury, James 36, 52
Asbury, John 40
Ashby, Florence 164
Aston, Perry 4
Aston, Ura 119
Aston, W.P. 10
Atherton, George 68, 71, 92, 121
Atherton, Sarah J. 68
Austin, F.N. 3, 62, 88
Austin, J.L. 75
Axton, Catherine 167, 171
Axton, Henry 41
Axton, Henry H. 40
Axton, Mrs. Henry H. 43
Aye, Albert 194, 199
Aye, Henry H. 135
Aye, John W. 205
Aye, Mrs. Albert 194, 199
Ayers, Charity 8
Ayers, Oscar 141
Ayres, Charley 9
Babcock, Henry 96
Bacon, Julima 196
Bailey, Bruce 56, 107
Bailey, Ella 171
Bailey, Maggie 26
Bailey, Minnie 167
Bailey, Minnie B. 174
Bailey, R.B. 34
Bailey, William W. 146
Baker 170
Bales, Bob 198
Bales, Cale 18
Bales, Caleb 177
Bales, Carrie 26
Bales, D.C. 33
Bales, Dewit C. 37
Bales, Effie 26
Bales, Emma 18
Bales, Esther H. 76
Bales, Frank 120, 176
Bales, Idora 71
Bales, Mrs. Caleb 76, 167
Bales, Myrt 147
Bales, Myrtle 26
Bales, Sarah 50, 145
Bales, William 76, 79
Bales, William F. 176, 178
Ballah, Lydia 191
Barker, David 104
Barker, Huldah E. 131
Barker, Joe 46
Barker, John 44
Barker, John G. 46, 53, 131
Barker, Kitty A. 104
Barnes, J.A. 169, 204

Barnes, James 88
Barnes, James A. 209
Barnes, James T. Sr. 141
Barnes, Mrs. James 88
Barnhardt, Levina 174
Barnhart, D.A. 58
Barnhart, Mary 111
Barnhart, Myrtle 103
Barnhart, Osa 103
Barns, Charles 124
Barr, Emma 189
Barrett, John 56
Barris, Joseph 146
Barron, Harriet 87
Basinger, Tom 155
Bassett, Charles F. 205
Bates, Elizabeth 31
Bates, Emily 31
Bates, G.W. 21
Bates, John 31
Bates, Thomas 31
Baum, Adam P. 48
Baum, Patsey 48
Beard, Fred 33
Beard, J.W. 122
Beard, James 195
Beard, John 1
Beard, John W. 188
Beard, Mrs. John 1
Beaumont, Adaline 131
Beck, A.J. 153
Beck, Andrew J. 175
Beckman, Alice 40, 167, 169
Bell 3, 62, 88
Bell, Catherine 188
Bell, D.W. 61
Bell, Henry 49
Bell, James A. 11, 41
Bell, John 177
Bell, Joseph 124
Bell, L.H. 178
Bell, Susie 11
Bell, T.W. 28
Bell, William 28
Bell, William P. 110, 193
Bell, Wils 28
Bells 1
Bellus, Lee 191
Benefiel, Ruth 2
Bennett, J.A. 113
Bennett, James 25, 27
Bennett, L.R. 55
Bennett, Lee J. 188, 193
Bennett, William C. 25, 140
Benson, E.M. 117
Benson, Gertie 117
Benson, Gertrude 169
Benson, H.H. 169
Benson, Henry 117
Benton, Lida 131
Berry, Charley 27
Bertolett, J.R. 100

Betson, A. 179
Betson, Amos J. 198
Betson, Arthur 112
Betson, Frank 3
Betson, Ham 112, 150
Betson, Hamilton 32, 70
Betson, Mrs. Amos 181
Bidwell, Elias 116
Bidwell, Emma 116
Bigney, Stephen 42
Bilsland, J.E. 3, 36, 62, 88
Bilsland, John 16, 17, 18, 20, 60, 166
Bilsland, John E. 20
Bilsland, Mr. 188
Bilsland, Mrs. J.E. 172
Bilsland, Mrs. John 69
Bindley, E.H. 39
Bines, John 21
Bines, Mary L. 21
Bines, William M. 21
Bipus, Phillip 88
Bish, William 108
Bishop, F.M. 158
Bishop, George R. 93
Bishop, Lewis L. 28, 30
Black, General 76
Black, J.C. 205
Black, Joe 77
Blackmore, Emma 43
Bladsel, Miss 58
Blair, Henry 155, 172
Blair, Mrs. Henry 172
Blakesley, John 162, 175, 186
Blakesley, John W. 208
Blanchard, Ben 30, 77
Blanchard, Mrs. Benjamin 79
Blasdale, Jennie 166
Blevins, Kate 201
Blink, Frank 141
Blithe, Mrs. 135
Blithe, Mrs. M. 135
Blunk, Frank 38, 58, 115
Blunk, Ollie 10
Blunk, Thomas J. 41
Blunt, James 177
Blyth, Mrs. 149
Bogart, Dr. 108
Bogart, J.H. 21, 36, 87, 112, 113, 122
Bogart, John 47
Bogart, John H. 143, 146, 191, 195, 200, 203
Bogart, S.A. 85
Bogart, Silas 47
Bollis, Daniel W. 8
Bond, George 54
Bond, Gertrude 53, 54
Bond, Mrs. George 54
Bond, Rev. 19, 53
Boren, Catherine 129
Boren, Rosalie 26

Boren, Rose 103
Boren, William S. 190
Borgman, Frank 17
Borgman, Frank J. 89
Borgman, John 89
Borin, Mary E. 23
Borris, Edith 54
Bost, Lizzie 82, 175
Bost, Mrs. Jacob 46
Bothwell, B.S. 60, 63, 151, 165, 208
Bothwell, Mr. 80
Bothwell, Mrs. B.S. 151
Bowen, J.F. 134
Bowen, John 48
Bowen, William R. 190
Bowerman, Sarah J. 106
Bowers, Rev. 161
Bowers, S. 26, 83
Bowers, Samuel 11
Bowman, E.N. 177
Bowman, Mrs. E.N. 181, 182, 183
Bowman, N. 183
Boyd, Alice M. 91
Bozarth, James M. 8
Bracken, John W. 62, 70, 104, 193
Bracken, Josephine 62, 70, 104
Bracken, Mrs. Deloss 64
Brake, John J. 147
Brazil, Jim 79
Breen, Patrick 209
Breidenback, Ferdinand 192
Brener, Joseph 50
Brewer, David 172, 174
Bright, A.S. 67
Bright, Jane A. 16
Bright, M.J. 208
Bright, Martha J. 207
Bright, Mrs. Billy 1
Briles 97
Briles, Charles F. 191
Briles, Emery 33, 88, 132, 134, 153
Brindley, Andy 61
Brindley, Coroner 23, 66, 80, 116, 150, 184
Brindley, Frank 22
Brindley, G.W. 180
Brindley, George W. 179, 180, 204, 208
Brindley, John 24, 111
Brindley, Lou 4
Brindley, Lucy 15, 36
Brindley, Mrs. Thomas 5
Brindley, Thomas 68, 96, 137
Brindley, William 61
Brock, Annie 176, 193
Brock, James 7
Brock, Mary E. 190
Brokaw, A.C. 22

Brokaw, A.C. Jr. 78
Brokaw, Charley 115
Brookbank, Charley 64
Brookbank, J.W. 26, 137
Brookbank, John W. 55
Brooks, Sarah E. 135
Brooks, T.J. 49
Brophy, William 202
Brophy, William J. 72, 92, 155, 164, 196
Brown, A.V. 50, 99
Brown, Anna 26
Brown, C.W. 81, 118, 170, 204
Brown, Charles 1
Brown, David 7, 92
Brown, E.B. 19, 61, 73, 78, 173, 179, 187
Brown, Ed 84
Brown, Edna 4, 34, 39, 165
Brown, J.S. 5, 7, 14
Brown, Jacob 41
Brown, Jacob A. 71
Brown, John 187
Brown, John D. 105
Brown, John S. 117
Brown, Lucinda 96
Brown, Lucinda E. 98
Brown, Mina 62
Brown, Miss Willie 72
Brown, O.P. 166
Brown, Orpha 195
Brown, Rachel 19
Brown, Samuel 40
Brown, Sevree 99, 104
Brown, Stephen 24
Brown, Steve 23, 144
Brown, W.P. 205
Brown, William 119
Brown, William S. 124, 194
Brownbaugh, R.F. 155
Bruce, Viola 104
Bruner, David 42
Brush, Dock 111
Buffey, Samuel 70, 104
Buffey, Sarah 104
Buffey, Sarah C. 70
Bulger, Jerry 207
Bullington, India 133, 138
Bullock, H.W. 152
Bumberger, Mr. 43
Bumgardner, Cora M. 148
Burford, W.B. 204
Burford, William B. 81, 118, 170
Burgess, Nona 131
Burgess, Sarah A. 196
Burk, Andrew J. 205
Burke, Minnie 135
Burnett, James F. 50
Burnett, James F. Jr. 85
Burns, Ed 42
Burns, Ed H. 33, 52

Burns, Ellen 68
Burns, Joe 189
Burns, Joseph 12, 140
Burns, Robert 68
Burroughs, Frank 26
Burson, Mrs. 30
Burt, Miss 63
Burton, Belle 26
Bush, Amanda 141
Bush, Marion 26
Butler, John 15, 31
Butler, Lewis 15, 31
Butler, W.F. 125
Butler, William 31
Butts, A.L. 1
Butts, Mary 164
Butts, Mr. 1
Byers, Frank R. 154
Byers, Michael 154
Cade, John 2, 62, 88, 159
Cady, Ella 15
Cady, H.S. 81, 118, 204
Cady, L.M. 60
Cady, Lina 80
Cady, Linn 64
Cady, Lou 4, 84, 165
Cady, Lou E. 39
Cady, Olin M. 165
Cain, Elizabeth 10
Cain, Fred 10, 119
Cale, W.H. 90
Callornce, Mr. 67
Camer, Sally 49
Camp, B.F. 206
Campbell, Anna B. 160
Campbell, Bell 117
Campbell, Eva 160, 207
Campbell, Frank 47, 80
Campbell, George W. 43
Campbell, Jim 206
Campbell, John T. 207
Campbell, Leonard 26
Campbell, Lillie 160
Campbell, Mrs. William 199
Canaday, William A. 8, 93
Cannon, Anna E. 189
Cannon, Dr. 189
Carico, Mrs. Armanta 7, 12
Carithers, Charles L. 171
Carlin, Thomas 134, 152
Carmine, W.T. 51
Carpenter, B.O. 58, 144, 196
Carpenter, Benjamin O. 129, 146
Carpenter, Bertha 80
Carpenter, L.D. 71
Carpenter, Martin 92
Carpenter, Mood 16
Carpenter, O.C. 80
Carpenter, Rebecca 71
Carpenter, Solomon 107, 122
Carr, John F. 193
Carr, Mary E. 113, 193

Carroll, Thomas 21
Carson, John T. 164
Carter, C.H. 101
Carter, George H. 51
Carter, Grace 48, 84
Carter, Joe 49, 67
Carter, M.B. 34, 121, 207
Carter, Melville B. 10, 96
Carter, Mrs. George H. 51
Carter, Mrs. M.B. 134
Carter, Rosa 187, 193
Caruthers, J.J. 135
Casebeer, A.B. 170
Casebeer, H. 34
Casebeer, Hezekiah 189
Casey, Deacon 55
Casey, Mont 37
Casey, Mrs. Michael 103
Castle, John 167
Castle, M.H. 35
Castle, Sarah 125
Castle, Zera 178
Cates 2, 83, 118
Cates, Joseph 170
Caywood, William 54, 59, 76
Chadd, Mary 49, 59, 195
Chaney, John C. 147
Chapman, Nora 187, 193
Chase, Alice 130
Chase, Henry 130
Chase, Margaret 8
Chase, Mrs. 130
Cheesewright, Annie 103
Chenoweth, Hiram 50, 146, 192
Chenoweth, Lemon 50
Chenoweth, Miss M.M. 151
Chipps 178
Chipps, Alfred 91
Chipps, James 105, 118, 143
Chipps, Jimmy 26
Chipps, Lura 34, 39
Chipps, Mary 11, 84, 166, 168, 172
Chipps, Mary B. 174
Chipps, Willis 84
Chisler, Cora 163
Chisler, Kitty 163
Chumlea, William 205
Chumlea, William D. 207
Chunn, Alice 3, 139, 197
Chunn, Anna 104
Chunn, Charles 197
Chunn, Frank 197
Chunn, George E. 197
Chunn, Joe 67, 75
Chunn, John 197
Chunn, Joseph 139, 143
Chunn, Mrs. William 207
Chunn, Stephen 197
Chunn, William 50, 197
Church, A.L. 198
Church, Dick 9, 198

Church, Link 76, 187
Claphan W.E. 166
Clark, Emma 185
Clark, Eva 133, 138
Clark, James 36
Clark, Jno. 112
Clark, Martha 31
Clark, Mr. 80
Clark, Mrs. Tom 166
Clark, O.T. 60
Clark, Owen T. 77, 165
Clark, Santa 15
Clark, Steve 2, 197
Clark, W.V. 18
Clark, William V. 15
Clawson, Isaac 50
Claypool, H.R. 25
Claypool, Mary 25
Clearwaters, Emma 15
Clearwaters, Glen 15
Clearwaters, Hettie 15
Clearwaters, J.A. 200
Clearwaters, Lon 110
Clearwaters, Mary E. 15
Clearwaters, Mrs. 200
Clearwaters, Mrs. Hardesty 28
Clearwaters, R.H. 200
Clearwaters, Richard A. 200
Clearwaters, William A. 111
Clearwaters, William Alonzo 111
Clem, Bell 175
Clendening, Levi 49
Cleveland, President 107
Clifton, Lucy 152
Clines, Isaac T. 187
Clouser, Fred 104
Clouser, George 168
Clover, Mrs. William 85
Clover, William 85
Clowser, Mrs. William 58
Coates, Dora 73
Cockrum, Newton 97
Coffeen, H.A. 36
Coffeen, Henry A. 8
Coffen, William 26
Coffin, Belle W. 185
Coffin, M.W. 3, 61, 135
Coffin, Milt 105
Coffin, Posmaster 157
Coffin, R.A. 185
Coffin, S.W. 111, 179, 180, 185
Coffin, W.T. 3, 112
Coffman, Samuel R. 189
Coffman, W.N. 56, 66, 163
Coil, Lorie E. 34
Cole, Mrs. Bill 47
Cole, Phila 92
Cole, Susan M. 34
Coleman, John W. 9
Coleman, M.G. 9, 171
Colfax, Schuyler 12

Coll, Leorie 39
Collett, Joe 111
Collett, John 44
Collett, John D. 131, 177, 208
Collett, Joseph 194
Collett, Josephus 92
Collett, Mrs. S.S. 181
Collett, Mrs. Stephen S. 14
Collett, Ollie 181
Collett, Sam 57
Collett, Sam D. 49, 98, 128, 201
Collett, Stephen S. 166
Collett, William 112, 196
Collin, Milton 49
Collins, Imo 110
Collins, Imogene 163, 205
Collins, Imogene R. 207
Collins, Nathan 175
Collins, Zadah 81, 110
Combs, M.A. 125
Comingore, H.S. 180
Comingore, Hugh S. 50
Compton, Catherine 8
Compton, J.F. 101
Compton, John F. 70
Compton, L.H. 92
Compton, Mrs. John F. 109
Compton, Roscoe M. 34
Conklin, Clark 144
Conley 12, 14, 44, 48, 50, 68, 73, 75, 77, 126, 154, 156, 192, 196, 197
Conley, Elijah P. 70, 128
Conley, Elijan M. 59
Conley, H. 2
Conley, H.H. 2, 58, 83, 132, 179, 196, 200
Conley, Hugh H. 98
Conley, James 52, 94
Conley, Jerry 42, 163
Conley, Mrs. 58
Conley, Paul 119
Conley, Phebe 59
Conley, William 59
Conner, A.J. 13
Conner, Allie 16
Conner, Alma Josephine 13
Conner, Clara B. 193
Conner, Frank M. 189
Conner, Kate 193
Conner, Mrs. A.J. 13
Conner, Z.R. 194
Connor, Annie 68
Connor, Thomas 68
Conoly, James 67
Conover, Mary 165
Conrad, Joe 45, 64, 128, 203, 204
Conrad, Joseph 81, 119, 144, 170
Conrad, Minerva 64
Conrad, Superintendent 65

Cook, Ann 208
Cook, Flora 46
Cook, J.F. 110, 123
Cook, Joe 177
Cook, Joseph F. 123, 141
Cook, Will 117
Cook, William 113
Cook, William C. 167, 171
Coonce, Joseph T. 102, 111
Coonse, Jesse 22
Cooper, Charles 146
Cooper, Dr. 72
Cooper, John 20, 93
Cooper, Sarah J. 20
Corbin, Kate 140
Corbin, Mrs. J.A. 52
Corbridge, Thomas 7, 12
Corder, Wesley 41
Cordrey, Nathan A. 175
Coslet, Dave 209
Cossey, Mrs. 82
Cossey, Peter 34, 175
Cottrell, Charles 137
Cougill, Rhoda 201
Cougill, Rhoda A. 202
Covington, Levi 137
Cox, Ida 137
Cox, J.M. 179
Cox, Mary 164
Crabb, Elizabeth J. 162
Crabb, Emma 85
Crabb, G.A. 187
Crabb, George A. 69, 145
Crabb, Mary 48
Crabb, Mrs. G.A. 187
Crabb, Walter 47
Crabb, William 85
Crabb, Winfield S. 145
Craft, A.H. 49
Craft, Aaron H. 136, 150, 155
Craft, Arminda E. 155
Craig, Bob 52
Craig, D. 100
Craig, James 40
Craig, R.A. 43
Craig, R.J. 99
Craig, Sarah E. 155
Crane 86
Crane, Alice 51, 191
Crane, Bell 116, 120
Crane, Edna 120, 191
Crane, Erastus K. 87
Crane, James 116, 120
Crane, James C. 149
Crane, John 4, 61
Crane, Mrs. James 81
Crane, Rat 33, 46
Crane, Tottie 108
Craner, Ozro 89
Creviston, Adelia 133
Creviston, William W. 133, 146
Crippen, Peter 50, 91, 94, 98

Crocket, Allen S. 8, 93
Crockett, Mrs. 54
Crompton, John 85
Crompton, Mrs. John 72
Cross, Carrie 10
Cross, J.W. 45
Cross, Josie M. 119
Cross, Lora 104
Cross, Martha 197
Cross, Mrs. John W. 45
Crumley, Claude 29
Crumley, Ida 29, 121
Crumley, Myrtle 29
Culp, Bettie 159
Cumby, Emma 7
Cumby, Henry 7
Cummings, Charles W. 165
Cummings, J.B. 165
Cummings, James 156
Cummings, Mattie 156
Cummings, Rachel 156
Cummings, Rev. 166, 185
Cummins, Malinda 27
Cunningham, Charles 103
Cunningham, Clara S. 34
Cunningham, Ed 150
Curtice, Irvin 67
Curtice, L.O. 67
Curtis, Andrew 69
Curtis, Andy 203
Curtis, Charles 119, 200
Curtis, John B. 74, 104
Curtis, Minnie M. 74, 104
Curtis, Mr. 67
Curtis, Norm 203
Curtis, Philo 68, 168, 195, 202, 204
Cushman, Mr. 140
Cushman, Thomas 2, 50, 62, 88, 109, 122, 170, 204
Daily, Catherine 77, 91
Daily, John T. 77
Dallas, Caroline 187
Dallas, S.H. 28, 34, 80, 130
Dallas, Spencer H. 116, 126
Dallas, Tip 155, 181
Dallas, W.H. 180
Daniels, Henry 76
Darby 178
Darby, Ernest 4
Darby, John A. 5, 14, 20, 27, 29, 30, 67, 68, 77
Darby, Mrs. John 181
Darby, Sheriff 18, 55, 65
Darling, Rufus 154
Darling, Susan 154
Darnall, Mrs. William 108, 116
Darnall, Mrs. William H. 20
Darnall, William 18, 108, 173
Darnall, William H. 148, 165, 175
Darrah, Horace L. 79

Darrah, Lou 185
Darrah, Mrs. Lou 160
David, Elmer E. 34
Davidson, Ben 137
Davidson, Jane 130
Davidson, Samuel 84
Daviess, Lydia M. 106
Davis 31
Davis Silas 111
Davis, Blanche 129
Davis, C.S. 13, 18, 62, 110, 127, 154
Davis, Cora 188, 193
Davis, D.T. 77
Davis, E.E. 26, 63, 81, 87, 100, 117, 166
Davis, E.F. 119, 130, 189
Davis, Edward E. 114, 155
Davis, Elisha 189
Davis, Elizabeth 104
Davis, Elmer 64
Davis, Elmer E. 60, 152, 165
Davis, Evan 149
Davis, F.M. 80, 179
Davis, Farmer 129
Davis, Flora 108, 109
Davis, Francis M. 175
Davis, Fred 32, 34, 39
Davis, George 175
Davis, Grant 23, 24, 97, 203
Davis, Hattie 119
Davis, Homer D. 112
Davis, Howard 102
Davis, I.M. 34
Davis, Ida 196
Davis, Isaac 202
Davis, J.N. 37, 118
Davis, Jeff 204
Davis, Joe 14
Davis, John 47
Davis, John G. 117
Davis, John W. 202
Davis, Joseph 145
Davis, Joshua 108
Davis, Joshua N. 79, 206
Davis, Laura 114, 117
Davis, Lem 189
Davis, Luella 102
Davis, M.B. 5
Davis, Maggie 46, 94
Davis, Mary 10, 13
Davis, Mary S. 87, 159
Davis, Mattie 156
Davis, Mr. 38, 46, 77, 80
Davis, Mrs. 77
Davis, Mrs. C.S. 46
Davis, Mrs. Ol 138
Davis, Mrs. R.A. 109
Davis, Nellie 46
Davis, O.P. 43, 52, 100, 138
Davis, Ol 45, 129
Davis, Oliver L. 129

Davis, Oliver P. 117
Davis, Ollie 117
Davis, Omer 124
Davis, Ora 4
Davis, Ora DeLoss 44, 199
Davis, Paul 10, 13, 102
Davis, Paul Wilfred 13
Davis, Postmaster 125
Davis, R.A. 109
Davis, Ren M. 10
Davis, Robert 50
Davis, Rowena 164
Davis, S.B. 2, 81, 118, 119, 169, 170, 204
Davis, Sammy 32, 109
Davis, Samuel 79
Davis, Samuel B. 145
Davis, Sarah C. 181, 183
Davis, Silas 191
Davis, T.C. 151
Davis, Thomas 114, 124, 151, 163
Davis, Thomas C. 168
Davis, Tom 186
Dawson, Charles 42, 158, 161
Dawson, Charley H. 40
Day, J.W. 67
De Haven, Malissa 18
De Haven, William 35
Dealand, G.W. 81, 204
Dealand, George 170
Dealand, George W. 26, 96, 119
Deardolff, Benjamin 52, 120
Deardorff, Benjamin F. Jr. 126
Deardorff, Benjamin F. Sr. 126
Deardorff, Benjamin Jr. 133
Deardorff, Benjamin Sr. 133, 134
DeHart, Mr. 150
DeHaven, Charley 43
DeHaven, Perry 178
DeHaven, Sammy 117
Dennis, H.G. 111
Denton, Sarah 65
Depuy, Alfred 126
Depuy, Clara 124
Derby, Horace G. 26
Derr, Mary Ann 47
Derthich, Otis 52
Devins, Dave 17
DeVoss, Elizabeth Caroline 112
DeVoss, Solomon 109, 111
Dice, Sophia 122
Dickason, Burton Jay 19
Dickason, Elizabeth I. 203
Dickason, John 50
Dickason, Josie 19
Dickason, L.T. 196
Dickason, Miss E. 88
Dickason, Robert 134
Dicken, Andy 158
Dicken, Anna 153

Dicken, Frank 88
Dicken, Jerome 135
Dicken, Jerome B. 41
Dicken, Jerry 132, 134
Dicken, Mrs. 153
Dicken, Sarah E. 158
Dicken, William R. 42
Dickerson, Henry 204
Dickerson, Serena J. 70
Dickinson, Clinton W. 75
Dickson, Ellen 147
Dies, A.S. 113
Dies, H.C. 113
Dillman, L. 24
Dillow 112
Dillow, Cofra 52
Dillow, Eliza 32
Dillow, Joseph 169
Dillow, Liza 159, 181
Dillow, Mrs. Henry 166
Dillow, Mrs. Liza 184
Dinsmore, D.B. 11
Dinsmore, David B. 146
Dinwiddie, John 93
Dinwiddie, John W. 73, 207
Dixon, James M. 40
Dixon, Mr. 177, 178
Dixon, Solomon 54
Dixon, Thomas E. 40
Dole, William P. 174
Domis, Anton 155
Donaldson, Judge 166
Donaldson, W.C. 189
Dondell, Mattie 198
Doss, B.F. 168
Doss, William 45
Doty, James 63
Doughty, Albert J. 174
Douglas, David 92
Douglas, George T. 57
Douglass Kersey 141
Douglass, Belle 15
Douglass, Dave 141
Douglass, Florence 193
Douglass, George 15
Douglass, Oscar 141
Douglass, Sylvester 86
Douglass, Vincent 41
Douley, John 124
Dove, M.L. 183
Dowdell, Gertie 47, 127
Dowdell, Jacob 27, 42, 76
Dowdell, Maria 76
Dowdell, Mary 119
Dowdell, Mrs. Jacob 88, 109
Dowdy, Amanda 37
Dowdy, Amon 92, 147, 154
Dowdy, Capt. 26
Dowdy, Ida 167
Dowdy, Mariah C. 154
Dowdy, Mollie 128
Dowdy, Sadie 201

Dowdy, Sadie M. 202
Dowell, Mattie 166
Dowers, Asa 194
Dowers, James 56
Dowers, Lucinda 123
Downey, Mary J. 206
Downey, Mrs. Will 166
Downey, William 85
Downing, Daniel 41
Downing, Decatur 63
Downing, Eliza 165
Downing, Eliza A. 143
Downing, Mrs. Decatur 73
Downing, Nancy 59
Downing, Sarah 16, 207
Downs, Cy 94
Drake, Leonidas 155
Drollinger, Hiram 112
Dudley, F.A. 99
Dudley, H.B. 100, 141
Duffer, Elizabeth 8
Dugan, Maria 28
Dugger, Lula 26
Dugger, Mrs. S.C. 62
Dugger, William S. 26
Dukes, Thomas B. 91
Duncan, Dave 28
Duncan, Mrs. 114
Duncan, Mrs. W.A. 14
Duncan, Sib 120
Duncan, W.A. 144
Dungan, Margaret 28
Dunlap, Alex 36, 127
Dunlap, Alexander 4
Dunlap, Alexander E. 203, 208
Dunlap, Charles 178, 180
Dunlap, E.H. 2
Dunlap, Emma 182, 183
Dunlap, Franklin J. 202
Dunlap, J.P. 2
Dunlap, Miss 131
Dunlap, Mr. 131
Dunlap, Mrs. 131
Dunlap, Sarah 130
Dunlap, Van 150
Dunlap. Mrs. E. 181
Dunn, Sarah 64
Durham, J.B. 141
Durham, Mrs. J.B. 141
Durham, T.W. 141
Durham, Thomas W. 65
Dutton, Henry C. 125
Dutton, Jennie M. 72
Duzan, Alma 175
Duzan, Belle 10
Duzan, Fred 175, 176
Duzan, Frederick 10
Duzan, James 46, 50
Duzan, Maria 105, 109, 111
Dye, Laura 163
Dye, Laura E. 164
Eads, Annie 137, 201, 202

Earles, Abner 79
Earles, Jennie 124
Earles, Mary J. 124
Earley, John 27
Eaton, Glendora 124
Eaton, Henry C. 69
Ebersole, Mr. 208
Edmonds, Ed 61
Edmonds, Edmond Jr. 12, 106
Edmonds, Jesse 22, 28
Edmonds, Lacie 61
Edmonds, Maggie 88
Edmonds, Mrs. Ed 61
Edmonston, L.T. 35
Edmonston, Lee 42
Edmonston, Malissa 42
Edmonston, W.E. 186
Edmonston, William 35, 42
Edwards, Annie M. 164
Edwards, Diana 14
Edwards, Etta 40, 72, 73
Edwards, Frank 1
Edwards, George W. 3, 62, 73
Edwards, Louisa 53, 70, 104
Edwards, William H. 53, 70, 104
Eels, E.M. 10
Eggleston, Henry H. 40, 42
Eggleston, J.L. 112
Eggleston, John L. 4, 117, 132, 159
Eggleston, Margaret 181
Eggleston, Mrs. J.L. 156
Eggleston, Mrs. John L. 45, 159
Eggleston, Mrs. S.B. 186
Eggleston, Mrs. Seldon 171
Eggleston, Naomi 63
Eggleston, Naomi C. 193
Eggleston, Naomi E. 58
Eggleston, S.B. 60, 161, 163, 173, 186, 187
Eggleston, Seldon 161, 175
Eggleston, Seldon B. 132, 166, 184
Eggleston, Stant 161, 175
Eggleston, Stanton 68, 177
Eggleston, William 106, 187
Elberson, Art G. 35
Elberson, C.M. 35
Elberson, James B. 35
Elder, George 197, 205
Elder, Mattie 182
Elder, Susan P. 182
Elder, Susan R. 183
Elliott, John 38
Ellis, B.F. 28, 99
Ellis, Benjamin F. 71
Ellis, J.E. 204
Ellis, James 151
Ellis, John 154
Ellis, Jonathan 91
Ellis, Nancy 151
Ellis, Rebecca R. 99

Ellis, Tom 102, 153
Emerson, Hester A.B. 146
Emerson, William H. 146
Emley, Mose J. 41
English, J.G. 196
English, John 11
English, Sarah J. 146
Ennis, Mary 165
Evans, Alena 124
Evans, Judge 162
Evans, Ned J. 41
Ewing, Sarah G. 1
Farr, Mary E. 106
Farrington, James 196, 197
Farrington, Ward 21
Farris, Charles 190, 193
Fennimore, Peirson 169
Ferguson, Amanda 146
Ferguson, Mary A. 46, 146, 147
Ferguson, William T. 41, 46
Fillinger, Mary 59
Fillinger, Mattie 25
Fillinger, Mrs. J.B. 58
Fillinger, Sarah M. 89
Finnel, James R. 37
Finnell, J.R. 3, 62
Finnell, James R. 154
Finnell, S.R. 89
Finney, D.W. 124, 125, 160, 180, 181, 183
Finney, Daniel W. 70, 191
Finney, David 160
Finney, Mrs. D.W. 180
Finney, Will 191
Finney, William 26
Finney, Willie 165
Fischer, Mrs. Charles 144
Fisher, George 185
Fisher, Sibbell J. 182
Fithian, Charles H. 206
Fitzgerald, Maurice 3
Flaid, Charley 37
Flanders, C.S. 26, 33
Flanders, Ella 23
Flanders, Mr. 63
Flaugher, Dr. 67
Flaugher, E.A. 3, 81, 88, 118
Fleener, Mart 170
Fleming, Nancy 103
Fleshman, Amos 15
Fleshman, John W. 15
Floyd, John 42
Floyd, William F. 42
Flynn, Joseph 6
Flynn, Mrs. Pat 19, 154
Flynn, Pat 202
Flynn, Patrick 6, 72, 190
Foley, Tom 30
Folger 83, 180, 181
Folger, A.M. 14, 90
Folger, E.C. 136
Folger, Mrs. A.M. 90, 167

Folger, Uriah 92, 136
Folsom, Lulu 155
Foltz, Jefferson 75
Foncannon, A. 177, 178
Foncannon, Albert 23, 89, 178
Foncannon, Emma F.A. 134
Foncannon, Frank 133
Foncannon, George 46
Foncannon, George W. 152
Foncannon, J. Edwin 61
Foncannon, J.C. 133
Foncannon, Jacob 61, 77
Foncannon, Jacob C. 207
Foncannon, Jacob E. 207
Foncannon, John A. 102
Foncannon, Mr. 61
Foncannon, Mrs. 61
Foncannon, Mrs. J.C. 133
Foncannon, Raymond 177
Foncannon, Ruth 147
Foos, Almetta 148, 155
Foos, Bertha 34, 39
Foos, Joe 206
Foos, Martha 159
Foos, Valentine 159
Ford, Albert 48, 71
Ford, Augustus 206
Ford, Eliza A. 48, 69
Ford, George 11, 76, 97, 172, 176
Ford, Jane 21
Ford, Mattie 97
Fortner, A.G. 64, 78
Fortner, Albert G. 76, 78
Fortner, Buck 26
Fortner, El 102
Fortner, Ella M. 51
Fortner, Frank 150, 155
Fortner, Hannah 119
Fortner, James C. 147
Fortner, Jonas 51, 70
Fortner, Jonas C. 191
Fortner, William P. 76, 78
Fosselman, Margaret 203
Foster, R.B. 18
Foster, Robert 175
Fouts, Martha 146
Fowler, W.S. 22
Fowler, William 69
Fox, Anna 82
Fox, Elisa J. 93
Fox, John 128
Fox, John L. 141, 156
Frazer, Amanda 181
Frazier, Albert 200
Frazier, Felix 158
Frazier, Florella D. 111
Frazier, Inez 75, 108
Frazier, Melvin 200
Frazier, Miss 110
Frazier, Mrs. William 45
Frazier, William 158

Freeman, Mrs. E.E. 183, 184
French, Fred G. 155
French, Gus D. 149
French, Joe 97
French, William 18
Fringer, Herod 42
Frist, Abbie 121
Frist, Bennie 29
Frist, Elija 97
Frist, J. 42
Frist, J.N. 100
Frist, Manie E. 34
Frist, Mr. 94
Frost 23
Fry, John D. 76
Fry, T.A. 30
Fulk, Owen 199
Fulton, Anna 16, 207
Fulton, Mrs. O.P. 188
Fulton, O.P. 188
Fultz, Billy 28
Fultz, Clara B. 91
Fultz, Henry 91
Fultz, Jacob 55
Fultz, Nancy 55, 62
Fulwider, W.E. 186
Funkhouser, Bessie 10
Funkhouser, D.Y. 10, 17, 78, 134
Funkhouser, Elizabeth 10
Funkhouser, Ettie 10
Funkhouser, Frank 153
Fyffe, Rev. 169
Gabriel 70
Gadd, Lucy 169
Gadd, Lucy M. 174
Gallaher, Rev. 131
Gallaher, S.D. 101
Gallaher, Steve 131, 205
Galloway 97
Galloway, Flora 126
Galloway, Grant 38
Galloway, J.W. 97
Galloway, Jesse 38
Galloway, John 38, 81, 94
Galloway, John W. 126, 173
Galloway, Mrs. Glant 62
Galloway, Mrs. William 88
Galloway, Mrs. Z.T. 195
Galloway, William 88
Galloway, Z.T. 165
Galloway, Zach 38
Galloway, Zach T. 38
Gardner, Charles 160
Gardner, Sophia 96
Garlinghouse, James 124
Garlinghouse, Jessie E. 143, 148
Garlinghouse, Ves 124
Garrett, Joe 193, 195
Gasaway, Mary A. 8
Gasman, Mr. 85
Gebhart, Abraham 124

Gebhart, Eliz. 136
Gebhart, Freddie 168
Gebhart, Levi 193
Gebhart, Mary 193
Gebhart, Perry 40
Gee, Elder 171
Gee, F.M. 171, 184, 193, 209
Gee, Pastor 206
Gee, Rev. 185
Geer, John 50, 70, 104
Geer, Mary A. 50, 70, 104
Gentry, Grace 152
Gerard, Stephen 115
Gessie, R.J. 50, 109, 132
Gessie, Robert J. 171
Gibbens, E.C. 37
Gibbens, John 41
Gibbens, Mrs. John G. 28
Gibbons, Boone 84
Gibbons, Mrs. John 57
Gibbons, William 131
Gibson 6, 30, 31, 50, 53
Gibson, Anna 47
Gibson, Bob 42
Gibson, Jesse 99
Gibson, John 108
Gibson, Mary 171, 186
Gibson, Minas T. 93
Gibson, O.B. 35
Gibson, Oscar B. 6, 30, 83
Gibson, W. 123
Gibson, William 42, 108, 129
Gilbert, Eliza 199
Gilchrist 94
Gillespie 92
Gillespie, Kate 18
Gilmore, Charles M. 124
Gilmore, John 46
Gilmore, Mary A. 71
Gilmore, R.F. 41
Gish, Mrs. A. 56
Gleason, William 15
Glindmeier, Christian 175
Glines, Isaac T. 193
Glover, Maggie 67
Goddard, Leonard G. 40
Godfrey, Mrs. Samuel 72
Godfrey, Samuel 72
Goeper, C.D. 206
Goff, Clarinda 63
Goff, David 73
Goff, George W. 71, 73
Goff, Mary 168
Goff, Philander 51
Goff, William 34
Goldsberry, Dr. 39, 41
Goldsberry, Lolly 41
Good, Lucy 193
Goodner, Joseph P. 91
Gosnell, Albert 34
Gosnell, Clarence 71, 172
Gosnell, Mary 172

Gosnell, Mr. 64, 80
Gosnell, Mrs. Clarence 172
Gosnell, Stella 15
Gosnell, W.B. 15, 60, 165
Gosnell, Willard 127
Gouty, David Henry 25
Gouty, Katie 25
Gouty, Thomas 15
Graves, Rosetta 109
Graves, Rosetta A. 111
Gray, Charles 39
Gray, Charles R. 10, 34
Gray, D.R. 5, 10, 105, 157
Gray, E.O. 10
Gray, Gov. 108
Gray, Matthew A. 86, 104
Gray, Nettie G. 104
Green, Franklin 48
Green, Lewis A. 67
Green, Myrtle 48
Green, Otha 48
Greenhill, Mattie 140, 148
Greer, Anna E. 7
Gregg, Robert 98
Gregg, Sarah 98
Gregory, Anna M. 21
Gregory, H.K. 21
Gregory, J.C. 186
Greiner, D.C. 144
Griffis, Vina 193
Griffith, Father 199
Griffith, James 23
Griffith, M.L. 51, 73
Griffith, Rev. 68
Griffith, Thomas 57, 61, 172
Grimes, Anna 51
Grimes, Bell 51
Grimes, Ethel 51
Grimes, H.L. 23, 51
Grimes, H.S. 64
Grimes, M.B. 51
Grimes, Morgan B. 64
Grimes, Ruth M. 56
Griswold, J.N. 139
Groendyke, J.S. 11
Groendyke, Samuel 11
Grondyke, J.S. 102
Grondyke, John S. 136, 202
Groves, Beulah 4
Groves, Fred P. 55
Groves, John 116
Groves, John B. 4
Groves, John W. 55
Groves, Johnny 158
Groves, Julius 116
Groves, Julius C. 126
Groves, Laura 126
Groves, Mary E. 55
Groves, William 116, 126
Groves, William C. 121
Grow, Miss P.C. 67
Grubb, John 119, 148, 155

Grubb, Mrs. P.W. 18
Grubb, Ol 74
Grubb, Oliver 119
Grubb, Oliver P. 11
Grubb, P.W. 18, 84
Grubb, Sylvester 110
Grumbly, J.B. 57
Guilliams, Clari 15
Guilliams, W.H. 123, 124
Habeck, Richard 29
Hacker, Charles 83, 119
Hacker, Charley 47, 79, 137
Hacker, Maggie 119
Hacker, Mrs. Charles 53
Hacker, Mrs. Fred 148
Hacker, William 148
Hackett, Anna 173
Hacklethorne, James L. 196
Hackney, R.A. 34
Hadley 163
Hadley, Levi 177
Hager, C. 134
Hager, E.J. 134
Hahna, Elnora B. 147
Hail, S.J. 43
Hain, Louisa 177
Hain, Sam 202
Hain, Samuel 190
Hain, William 177
Hains, Sarah R. 125
Haley, John 59, 73
Hall 118
Hall, Allen 42
Hall, Dr. 51, 197
Hall, Effie 90, 97
Hall, John 41, 56, 90
Hall, M.L. 81, 118, 169, 170, 199, 201, 204
Hall, Maggie 138
Hall, Melvin L. 126
Hall, S.J. 80, 125, 204
Hall, Sam J. 112
Hall, Silas M. 34
Haller, Mrs. Charles 165
Halt, Katy 30
Hamilton, C.W. 111
Hamilton, Mary P.1 36
Hamilton, W.M. 118, 170, 204
Hamilton, William 40
Hamilton, William M. 68, 82, 96
Hammersley, George 29
Hammond 186
Hammond, Branson 47
Hammond, H. 100
Hammond, H.B. 100
Hammond, Henry B. 36, 154
Hammond, Jerry 70
Hammond, Marcus 70
Hammons, Rev. 38
Hancock, S.P. 42
Handley, David 197

Handley, Rev. 130, 139, 149, 162, 167, 173
Handley, Salina W. 197
Handley, Willis 167, 200
Hane, Julia A. 193
Haney, John 135
Haney, Mrs. 135
Hann, Allie 60
Hann, J.E. 99
Hann, Joe 51, 148
Hann, Joseph 53, 87, 145
Hann, Mrs. Joe 3, 51
Hanna, H.C. 179
Hanna, John 17
Hanna, Mrs. J.J. 141
Hannah, H.C. 15
Hannah, William P. 80
Hannahs, Dick 39
Hannum, Harriet E. 124
Hansicker, Ellen 135
Hanson, Joseph 15, 155
Hanson, Mrs. Joseph 72
Hanson, Mrs. Peterson 48
Hanson, Nelson 86
Hanson, Peterson 48
Hanum, Harriet E. 131
Hanum, Hattie 10
Hardin, Mark 19
Harding, A.G. 177
Harding, Joe 160
Harding, Marcus 132
Hargrave, Mrs. Marion 30
Hargrave, R. 151
Harlan, El 179, 180
Harlan, Eli 46
Harlan, James 10, 178
Harlan, Mrs. James 10, 181
Harlan, Thomas 4
Harlan, Tom 179
Harmeson, Albert F. 143
Harney, James 185
Harper, Anderson 55
Harper, Austey F. 14
Harper, Cora 128
Harper, Douglas 20
Harper, George 148
Harper, George A. 140
Harper, J.M. 88, 97
Harper, Mrs. J.B. 21
Harrier, Phillip 40
Harrington, Carrie M. 34
Harrington, Clyde 29
Harrington, Gertie 29, 121
Harrington, Madge 29, 121
Harrington, May 29
Harrington, Mrs. 114
Harrington, Nina 29
Harrington, Stephen 115
Harrington, U. 29
Harris, James 162
Harris, Martin 103
Harris, Mary 119

Harris, Milton 139
Harris, Minton 119
Harris, Quince 25
Harris, Samuel 50
Harrison 40
Harrison, Alex 97
Harrison, Annie 10
Harrison, Belle 5
Harrison, Ben 161, 164, 205
Harrison, Benjamin 16
Harrison, Benjamin F. 205
Harrison, Benny 105
Harrison, Bruce 104
Harrison, C.P. 164
Harrison, Dan 105
Harrison, Ella 63
Harrison, General 54
Harrison, Georgie 63
Harrison, J.C. 40, 153, 170
Harrison, John 4, 119
Harrison, Josephine 197
Harrison, Marsh 60
Harrison, Marshall 63
Harrison, May 148
Harrison, McCage 41
Harrison, Nellie 119
Harrison, Thomas 50
Harrison, Thomas H. 50
Harrison, William 207
Harrison, William Henry 50, 52
Harshorn, O.H. 118
Hart, Robert A. 198
Hart, Vina 179, 181, 182
Harter, Charles H. 165
Hartley, E.W. 75
Hartman, John W. 78
Harvey, B.W. 178
Harvey, Frank 179
Harvey, George 75
Harvey, Homer H. 156
Harvey, Ida 156
Harvey, J.T. 110
Harvey, Minta 132
Harvey, Mrs. Cad 60, 68
Harvey, W.F. 85
Haskell, Etta 76
Haskell, W.P. 170
Haskell, William 62
Hasty, Elizabeth 32
Hasty, Frank 88
Hasty, Henry 31
Hasty, John 6, 19, 25, 50, 91, 195, 209
Hasty, Mahlon 22, 25
Hasty, Mrs. Henry 22
Hasty, Mrs. James 200
Hasty, Mrs. John 29, 46, 64
Hasty, Mrs. Wilson 199
Hasty, Robert J. 207
Hasty, Wilson 13
Hathaway, Willie 2
Haton, Isaiah 207

Hattrey, Harvey 192
Hattrey, Rebecca J. 192
Haughney, T.P. 165
Havens, Net 44
Havens, Will 17
Hawkins, Coe 49
Hawkins, Cora 21
Hawkins, Ellen 146, 192
Hawkins, Nancy 113
Hawkins, R.T. 76
Hawkins, Richard 10
Haworth, G.F. 169, 204
Haworth, George 96
Haworth, George F. 69, 119, 202
Haworth, James 38, 151
Haworth, James P. 197
Haworth, John 34, 141
Haworth, Lucy 26
Haworth, Myra 26, 46, 66, 194
Haworth, Richard 141
Haworth, T.J. 181
Haworth, Will 194
Haws, Matthew 172, 174
Hayes, Nancy 95
Hays, J.F. 122
Hays, J.M. 93
Hays, James M. 69
Hays, John F. 92
Hays, Louis M. 73
Hays, Milt 13, 51, 117, 139
Hays, Mr. 180
Hays, W.A. 93, 122
Hays, William 122
Hays, William A. 71, 134
Hays, William F. 122, 124
Hays, William L. 33, 42, 122
Hayward, Frank 73
Hayward, Roxana 73
Hazelet, Mary M. 34
Heaps, George 6
Hearn, J.H. 128
Heaton, E.M. 57
Hedgecock, Sarah 28
Hedges, Charles 65
Hedges, Mrs. 143
Hedges, S.P. 112
Heffleman, F.H. 104
Heffleman, Frost 96
Heffleman, Frost H. 76
Hegarty, Ed 140
Hegarty, James 51
Hegarty, Kate 18
Hegarty, M. 81, 118, 170
Hegarty, Maurice 18, 51, 70, 74, 140
Hegarty, Mrs. Maurice 85, 87, 131, 175
Hegarty, Nellie 87
Hegarty, Willie 175
Heibreder, Gotlieb 132
Heibreder, William 205
Helt, Alvin 29, 121

Helt, Betsey 121
Helt, Catherine A. 32, 39
Helt, Charley 114
Helt, E.E. 47
Helt, F.M. 87
Helt, Lizzie 29
Helt, Nancy 32
Helt, Ray 29, 121
Helt, Sant 29, 121
Helt, Thomas 8
Henderson, A.C. 194
Henderson, Albert 96, 98
Henderson, Amanda C. 208
Henderson, Dr. 110
Henderson, J.T. 107, 118
Henderson, James T. 81
Henderson, John 136, 151, 154, 177, 189, 208
Henderson, Mrs. John 189
Henderson, Nancy E. 82
Henderson, Thomas 34
Henderson, William 208
Henderson, William E. 150
Henderson, William F. 149, 189
Hendricks, W.J. 113
Hendrix, W.J. 124
Hendrix, William 110
Henry, James 97
Henry, John 173
Henry, Mrs. James 173
Henry, William 132
Hensley, William R. 193
Henson, Elmer 119
Henson, Ida 119, 140
Henson, J.P. 5
Henson, John 76, 126
Henson, John H. 29
Henson, John P. 30, 109, 141, 157, 158, 161, 166
Henson, Mary E. 126
Henson, Mrs. Elmer 115
Henson, Mrs. John 43
Henson, Mrs. John P. 44
Henson, Mrs. W.P. 88
Henson, Perry 106
Henson, Roswell 157
Henson, W.P. 2, 5, 44, 76, 106, 109, 143
Herbert, W.J. 40, 50
Hess, Emma 180
Hester, Martha 151
Hester, Thomas 151
Hiberly, E.L. 34, 113, 204
Hiberly, Ernest 178, 193
Hiberly, Fred 193
Hiberly, Grandma 193
Hicklan, Emma 8
Hicks, Frank 188
Hicks, George C. 26
Hiddle, Christopher 48
Hiddle, Mary 48
Higgins, J.J. 103

Higgins, Mrs. 114
Higgins, Mrs. Trap 152
Higgins, Trap 152
Highfill, Col. 103
Highfill, John R. 75
Hill, Mrs. William 137
Hiller, Mary 119
Hilon, Celesta 193
Hines, Anna 68
Hines, David 196
Hines, Elizabeth 178, 179, 181
Hines, George 41
Hines, George W. 3
Hines, Josie 74
Hines, Mary E. 99
Hines, Thomas 132
Hinton, Asa 124
Hise 139
Hise, Cornelius 69
Hise, Louis G. 57
Hite, Elizabeth 194
Hobart, Almira 55
Hobbs, Barnabas C. 90
Hogue, Ellen 164
Hogue, Lydia 99
Hogue, Lydia A. 104
Hold, Dave 11
Hold, Scott 164
Holder, Amos 139
Holder, Bertie May 139
Holder, Flora 139
Holder, Frank 139
Holland, Curt 139
Hollensby, George 30
Hollingsworth, Allen 187, 193
Hollingsworth, Billy 128
Hollingsworth, Caley 131
Hollingsworth, E. 100
Hollingsworth, Earl 119
Hollingsworth, Eber 50
Hollingsworth, Elizabeth 138
Hollingsworth, Emma 110, 111
Hollingsworth, Henry 41, 42
Hollingsworth, J. 101
Hollingsworth, Joel 149
Hollingsworth, John R. 76
Hollingsworth, Joseph M. 174
Hollingsworth, Lida B. 12
Hollingsworth, Lizzie 15
Hollingsworth, Mary 161, 199
Hollingsworth, Milton 15
Hollingsworth, Mina 10
Hollingsworth, Morton 19, 127
Hollingsworth, Mrs. Henry 40
Hollingsworth, Patience 101, 174
Hollingsworth, Peggy 84, 99, 101
Hollingsworth, R. 101
Hollingsworth, Rebecca 42, 158
Hollingsworth, Samuel C. 7, 12, 57

Hollingsworth, Sarah 57
Hollingsworth, Silas 47, 84, 94, 101, 106
Hollingsworth, Simeon 144, 148
Hollingsworth, William 200
Hollingsworth, William R. 149
Holmes, A.V. 19, 132
Holmes, Harriet Utter 132
Holtz, Bob 90, 121
Holtz, James T. 126
Holtz, Jim 121
Holtz, Joseph 93, 126, 196
Holtz, Maggie B. 206
Holtz, Maggie Simpson 205
Holtz, Margaret 112
Holtz, Mrs. James 169
Holtz, Robert J. 28, 67, 126, 131
Holycross, Amos 90
Hood, Amos 50
Hood, J.M. 62
Hood, James T. 168
Hood, Mrs. Sam 108
Hood, Mrs. T.S. 58
Hood, Polk 24, 33, 168
Hood, Rev. 44
Hood, Sam 108
Hood, T.C. 10, 14, 170
Hood, T.S. 10, 167
Hood, Thomas S. 50
Hood, W.B. 118, 204
Hood, William B. 12, 30, 68, 83, 96, 118
Hood, William H. 77, 83, 106
Hook, Rev. 66, 78, 164, 199, 201
Hooker, C.C. 177
Hooker, Charley 120
Hoon, C.L. 151
Hooper, William 84, 113
Hooten, C.B. 112
Hopkins, A.R. 3, 6, 12, 15, 17, 20, 31, 39, 48, 50, 53, 55, 62, 65, 73, 74, 75, 78, 82, 87, 96, 103, 104, 106, 111, 126, 133, 148, 156, 166, 174, 175, 191, 192, 193, 196, 197, 202, 204
Hopkins, Ann 165
Hopkins, Ann J. 27
Hopkins, Clerk 98
Hopkins, D.S. 5, 81
Hopkins, David S. 27, 98
Hopkins, Emma 123, 124
Hopkins, Ester C. 119
Hopkins, Jane 181, 182
Hopkins, Joe 39, 79
Hopkins, Joseph M. 76
Hopkins, Maggie 4, 60, 80, 84, 165
Hopkins, Mrs. D.S. 5, 48
Hopkins, Mrs. J.M. 147
Hopkins, Mrs. Joseph M. 76
Hopkins, Riley 107
Hopkins, Zula 5, 48, 76, 182

Hopp, Blanche 60
Horn, Lulu 189
Horney, John 155
Hosford 1, 3, 62, 88
Hosford, Billy 28, 117
Hosford, H.H. 15
Hosford, Julia B. 106, 146
Hosford, M.G. 11, 102
Hosford, Monroe G. 206
Hoss, Nelson, 47
Houchin, H. 139
Houchin, J.S. 86, 135, 186
Houchin, Jesse 29
Houchin, John S. 86, 146, 186, 199
Housand, William 62
Hout, William 111
Howard, Ellen 103
Howard, Ida 97, 104
Howard, Sarah B. 79
Howe, Benjamin S. 104
Howell, Laura B. 150, 155
Howlett, George W. 51
Howlett, Mrs. George W. 51
Howminski, Mary 26
Hudson, John 137
Hudson, R.N. 160
Hudson, Robert N. 163
Huey, Roy 26
Hughes, A.R. 164
Hughes, Charles 163
Hughes, Charles G. 164
Hughes, Ehud 191
Hughes, James W. 82, 141
Hughes, John 15
Hughes, Morris 7, 9
Hughes, Silas 156, 196
Hughes, William 191
Hull, Mrs. John 66
Humphries, Mary J. 134, 148
Humrickhouse, Isabel 79
Hunm, Mrs. 107
Hunt, Annie 73
Hunt, Charles 73
Hunt, Charley 165
Hunt, Edmond 73, 87
Hunt, Fred 26
Hunt, Harvey 50, 73, 87
Hunt, J.P. 185
Hunt, James D. 26
Hunt, John F. 138
Hunt, Mrs. J.P. 185
Hunt, Steve 85
Hunter, J.D. 121
Hunter, James T. 26
Hunter, Park 49
Hunter, William P. 131
Hupp, Blanche 80, 85, 137
Hupp, Rate 74
Hutchinson, Mrs. William 172
Hutchinson, William 172
Hutson, M.J. 35, 36

Hybarger, Ellen F. 106
Iles, J.H. 11
Iles, James B. 172
Iles, Miss 191
Ingam, Susan 161
Ingram, America 1
Ingram, Andrew J. 159
Ingram, James 19
Ingram, Mrs. 18
Ingram, Mrs. Charley 19
Ingram, Sylvestor 188
Ingram, Wake 161
Ingram, William 14
Innis, Mrs. O.J. 126
Insley, Mrs. 79
Irwin, Jane 40
Isinbuger, Nancy J. 97
Isrig, William E. 141
Jackson, Andrew 53
Jackson, Andy 104
Jackson, Becky, 42
Jackson, Celia 20
Jackson, Charles 177, 178
Jackson, Charles S. 137
Jackson, Claude 50
Jackson, E.Y. 144
Jackson, E.Y. Jr. 195
Jackson, Edward Y. 71
Jackson, J.C. 2, 3, 62, 83, 88, 170, 199
Jackson, Joe 46, 133
Jackson, Jos. 128
Jackson, Joseph A. 137
Jackson, Mary Jane 162
Jackson, Matt 13
Jackson, Mother 105
Jackson, Mrs. 162
Jackson, Sam 46
Jackson, Samuel 44
Jackson, Whit 133
Jackson, William 39, 42, 43
Jacobs, Elder 172
Jacobs, Pet 182
Jaggers, Robert 48
James, Anna 168
James, Annie R. 71
James, Betsy 40, 136
James, C. 34
James, Carrie 105
James, Charles 124
James, Collon D. 13
James, Crews 94
James, Dulin 163
James, E.D. 152
James, Edmund 151
James, Elva 29, 144
James, Eva 29, 121
James, F.M. 152
James, Frank M. 77
James, Fred 144
James, Gertie 29, 121
James, Harry E. 206

James, Hatton 26
James, Joe 94
James, Joseph 32
James, Lily 20
James, Maria 61, 64
James, Matilda 24
James, Maurice 105
James, Mother 40
James, Ollie 29, 144
James, Poe 29
James, Ray 29, 121
James, Roy 29
James, Sam 24
James, Samuel R. 205
James, Susan 198
James, Susie 29, 121
James, White 43
James, William 111
James, William A. 198, 206
James, Willie 155
James, Wright 168
James, Z.D. 38, 168
James, Zachariah 40
James, Zachariah D. 75
James, Zoote 33
Jamieson, Ella 129
Jaques, F.E. 190
Jarrell, Charles A. 33
Jarvis 98
Jarvis, Elder 28
Jarvis, J.W. 10, 133
Jarvis, John W. 86, 98, 122, 146
Jeffries, Laura J. 134
Jenks, Alma 1
Jenks, August 70
Jenks, Henry 170
Jenks, Mamie 26
Jenks, Stephen 15, 70
Jenks, Steve Jr. 208
Jewell, W.S. 46
Johns, Alonzo 99
Johns, Susan 53
Johns, T.B. 30
Johns, William 137
Johnson, A.J. 114
Johnson, A.W. 168
Johnson, Albert W. 92
Johnson, Ann 28
Johnson, Anna Mary 34
Johnson, August 169
Johnson, D.C. 20, 37
Johnson, David B. 192
Johnson, E.E. 171
Johnson, Editor 45
Johnson, Elizabeth 92
Johnson, Helen B. 192
Johnson, J.C. 28
Johnson, J.W. 85
Johnson, James F. 132
Johnson, John 16
Johnson, John H. 19
Johnson, Laura 124

Johnson, Lora 45, 58
Johnson, Ora 143
Johnson, Presley 42
Johnson, Rosella 199
Johnson, Samuel C. 114, 202
Johnson, Sarah 28, 194
Johnson, Solon 110, 113
Johnson, W.H. 28
Johnson, William H. 8, 56, 92
Johnson, William R. 52, 60
Johnston, Erin 188
Johnston, Flora 67
Johnston, J.E. 188
Johnstone, Mr. 43
Jones, Adaline V. 131, 144, 196
Jones, Alta 46
Jones, C. Winfred 67
Jones, Charlotte L. 152
Jones, Dave 76, 78
Jones, David 78
Jones, Delilah 191
Jones, E.A. 41
Jones, E.E. 44
Jones, Edward J. 91, 104
Jones, Elmer 191
Jones, Emily 191
Jones, Frank 82
Jones, George 207
Jones, Harmon 39
Jones, Harry 17
Jones, J.N. 131
Jones, J.W. 123, 125
Jones, James 32, 191
Jones, John 96
Jones, Joseph 17, 96
Jones, Lacie 191
Jones, Laura A. 191
Jones, Louisa 48
Jones, Martin 61
Jones, Mary L.E. 40
Jones, Mattie 114
Jones, Mrs. William M. 166
Jones, Nellie 49
Jones, Nelson 17
Jones, Ora 191
Jones, Perry 41
Jones, R.O. 152
Jones, Rosa 191
Jones, Seth 160
Jones, Sexton 119
Jones, Silas 48, 70, 147, 162, 185, 191
Jones, Sile 157
Jones, Solomon 20
Jones, Voorhees 51
Jones, W.M. 44
Jones, William 122, 201
Jordan, H. 100
Jordan, Ike 179
Jordan, Isaac 177
Jordan, John 156
Jordan, William 202

Jordan, Zerilda 202
Julian, Jacob B. 206
Jump 31
Jump, Joshua 141
Jump, Judge 14
Jump, Mrs. 64
Junkins, Rev. 38
Kaufman 169
Kaufman, Jesse 71, 110, 123, 131, 159, 162
Kaufman, Mrs. James 151
Kaufman, Mrs. S.E. 59
Kaufman, Mrs. Samuel E. 199
Kaufman, S.E. 16, 25, 97, 113
Kaufman, Samuel 154
Kaufman, Samuel R. 193
Kearns, Professor 138
Kearns, Ulysses G. 174
Kearns, W.A. 40, 137
Kearns, William 105
Keily, Martin 85
Keily, Mrs. John 131
Kelley, Ella 181, 182, 183
Kelp, Mrs. William 79
Kelsh, John 2
Keltz, William F. 104
Kemp, J.C. 16, 152
Kenover, Mary E. 174
Kent, Henry 198
Kerdolff 112
Kerdolff, Amanda 10
Kerdolff, Bell 159, 206
Kerdolff, John 10, 51
Kerdolff, John H. 51, 147
Kerdolff, Kate 51
Kerdolff, Mrs. John 10
Kern, Agnes L. 187, 193
Kern, John A. 135
Kerns, Dewie 6
Kerns, Eva G. 51
Kerns, John 38
Kerns, Oscar 15, 170
Kerns, W.A. 34
Kerns, W.F. 81, 119, 170, 204
Kerns, William F. 51, 96
Kerr, Sterling 26
Kespler, Ann P. 147
Kespler, Conrad 35
Kespler, Freddie 55
Kespler, George 55
Kespler, George A. 35
Keyes, C.F. 9
Keyes, Jane 37
Keyes, Mrs. 33
Keyes, Sallie L. 44
Keys, O.M., 16
Kibby, Isaac 105, 147, 162
Kibby, Thomas A. 105, 162
Kibby, Thomas A. Sr. 50
Kibby, Tom 104, 105
Kibley, Emma 159
Kiger, Ed 42

Kiger, John 34, 164
Kiger, Nathan 90
Kiger, S.B. 123
Kildow, Adam H. 93
Kilgore, H.M. 87
Kilgore, R.M. 87
Kimber, A.M. 97
Kinderman, Alex 169
Kinderman, Alexander 174
Kinderman, Dr. 11, 67
King, Catherine 32
King, Dan 25
King, H.D. 65
King, M. 123
King, Martha E. 202
King, Melvina 194
Kintz, Frank 67, 69
Kintz, George 67
Kintz, Henry J. 67
Kintz, Margaret 67, 69
Kintz, William O. 67, 69
Klein, Solomon 71
Knight, Emma 149
Knight, Emma E. 155
Knight, J.J. 137
Knight, James 52
Knight, James J. 140
Knight, John L. 174
Knight, Oliver 159
Knight, Oliver H. 77
Knight, Orie 66
Knowles, Charles B. 159
Knowles, J.A. 34
Knowles, J.E. 85
Knowles, James E. 146, 159
Konkle, John 147, 165
Konkle, Lucinda 165
Koonse, Allie 2, 15, 45, 199
Koonse, Allie V. 10
Kritzenger 23
Kritzenger, Alfred H. 24
Kritzenger, Alfred Harry 23
Krout, Rebecca N. 106
Kunkle, Henry 145
Kunkle, Mary A. 101
Lacey, Bertha J. 26
Lacey, Cora 26
Lacey, Rosa 174
Ladd, Maggie 99, 104
Laeff, W.H. 139
Lafferty, Frank 15
Lake 61
Lake, Carrie L. 34
Lake, Casper 110
Lake, Chester 11
Lake, Jasper H. 58
Lake, John 110
Lake, Joseph 124
Lamb, Elias 50, 62, 157, 160, 171
Lamb, Frank 66
Lamb, I.B. 41

Lamb, Irvin 66
Lamb, Joseph 13
Lamb, Lista 171
Lamb, Mattie 11
Lamb, Mrs. Elias 14, 108
Lamb, Mrs. Irvin 42, 56, 143, 187
Lancaster, Katie 30
Lancaster, Rebecca E. 202
Lancey, William K. 60
Landers, Minnie 75
Landers, Rosa 24
Lane, Fred 124
Lane, Hubert 124
Lane, Mrs. Samuel 207
Lang, Ben 28
Lang, Emmet 89, 198
Lang, Emmet B. 152, 200
Lang, Thomas J. 200
Langer, Omer 60
Langley, Mrs. 102
Langley, Sarah M. 111
Langston, Frank 3, 62, 89
Langston, Minerva 9
Langston, Samantha 60
Langtry, Lily 168
Larr, David M. 155
Lashley, Daniel 115, 136, 152
Lashley, John H. 115
Lawson, Mrs. James 18
Layman, Oliver P. 23, 209
Leach, George 15
Leatherman, Abe 12
Leatherman, Elizabeth 132
Lebo, Miss 44
Lee, Charles 25
Lee, Emily 77
Lee, John 77
Lee, Martha E. 8
Lee, Maude ? 61
Lee, William 7
Leechman, John 144
Leeds, E.W. 83
Leiton, N.T. 201
Lenover, John 67
Lenton, D.B. 77
Lewellen, George 5
Lewis, Addie A. 4
Lewis, Americus 103
Lewis, Cassie 32
Lewis, Charles H. 103
Lewis, Emma 103
Lewis, Frank 103
Lewis, Isaac 103
Lewis, James 169
Lewis, James J. 50, 75, 79, 83
Lewis, John 103
Lewis, John F. 103
Lewis, Joshua 32, 57, 71, 103
Lewis, Maggie 194
Lewis, Mary 133, 146
Lewis, Mary Ann 194

Lewis, Meredith 79, 83, 103
Lewis, Mrs. James 169
Lewis, Seward 71
Lewsader, Frank 199
Light, Maggie 65
Linch, A.D. 35
Linch, R. 35
Lincoln, President 174
Lindley, Mrs. Charles 189
Lindsey, Bell 82
Lindsey, Fred 167
Lindsey, John 130
Lindsey, John L. 21
Lindsey, Jones 117, 129
Lindsey, Joseph 65, 69
Lindsey, Lee 48
Lindsey, Ol 50, 117
Linebarger, Andrew 166
Link, Mrs. George 83
Link, S.P. 147
Lippingood, Dr. 141
Liston, H.C. 124
Liston, Rev. 184
Little, Bob 49
Little, C.H. 21
Little, Dave 49, 59
Little, Eunice 60, 64, 80
Little, R.P. 80
Littlepage, Adam B. 131, 166
Littlepage, Mrs. Adam 49
Littlepage, Mrs. Adam B. 14, 57
Livengood, Dr. 80
Lloyd, Jno. 123
Lloyd, Lucinda 112, 123
Logan, John A. 56
Lohrmann, Katy 165
Lonbarger, John 76, 91
Long, John 18, 47
Long, Joseph 119
Long, William 18
Loomis, E.C. 83, 110
Lough, George M. 186
Love, A.C. 15
Lowe, Harry 2
Lowe, Joe 202
Lowerman, Charley 55
Lowry, Eliphaz 117
Lowry, O.B. 87
Lowry, Sallie 159
Lucas, James 87
Luce, J.O. 100
Luke, Nettie 191
Lunger, Marie 47
Lunger, Omer 28, 101, 105, 109, 111
Lusadder, Nellie 102, 104
Lynch, John 47
Lytle, Matthew 5, 10, 126
Lytle, Minnie R. 10
Lytle, Mrs. M. 5
Lytle, Mrs. Matthew 176
Mack, A.L. 161

Mack, Alonzo L. 162
Mack, Annie G. 34
Mack, Cephus 197, 202
Mack, Daniel 145
Mack, Daniel V. 174
Mack, David 32
Mack, E. 169
Mack, Erastus 81, 118, 204
Mack, Gilbert L. 44, 124
Mack, Joe L. 121
Mack, Lois M. 202
Mack, Mrs. Gil 21
Mack, Mrs. Spencer 57
Mack, Napoleon B. 47
Mack, Rebecca 44
Mack, Spencer 57
Mack, Zerilda 197, 202
Maffett, I.M. 2
Magee, Bell 53
Magers, Gertie 166
Maglossen, Georgie 18
Mahan, Emma M. 69
Mallory, Clara 200
Mallory, Ed 6
Malone 146, 188
Malone, A.W. 34
Malone, Amassa 119
Malone, Bird 103
Malone, Dick 151
Malone, Eva 165
Malone, F. 186
Malone, Florence 47
Malone, Frank 176, 193
Malone, Harry C. 111
Malone, Hugh 119
Malone, James 11, 81, 102
Malone, Jim 28
Malone, John 103, 111
Malone, Nellie 133, 138
Malone, Richard 50, 119
Malone, Sam 79, 113, 176
Malone, Samuel G. 8, 119
Malone, William 119
Manges, Mrs. John 184
Mann, Frank 187
Mann, Mrs. 173
Mann, Mrs. Frank 187
Mann, Win 187
Manning, John 27, 92, 98
Manning, Rose 27
Marble, Jacob 52
Marble, Mrs. Jacob 28
Marble, Susan A. 52
Markle, H. 181, 182, 183
Markle, Sallie 181
Marlatt, Andrew R. 203
Marlow, Austin 77
Marris, Amanda 6
Marshall, Clara 183
Martin, Frank E. 8
Martin, J.B. 29
Martin, Jacob I. 190, 202

Martin, John B. 6
Martin, Mrs. R.S. 89
Martin, R.S. 9, 10, 11, 13, 15, 22, 24, 29, 56, 63, 64, 65, 66, 69, 75, 76, 78, 79, 98, 109, 111, 117, 132, 135, 138, 140, 143, 167
Martin, William G. 63
Mason, Anna 119
Mason, Frank 145
Mason, William 145
Mast, John 85
Mast, Johnny 23
Mater, Harriet 45
Mater, Ira 19, 45, 149, 156, 168
Mater, John 45
Mater, Mary 45
Mater, Rev. 19, 56, 58, 60, 99, 143, 176, 187
Matthews, Claude 23, 36
Matthews, Seymour 200
Matthews, William 187, 193
Maxfield, William 71
Maxwell 192
Maxwell, Joseph 41
Maxwell, Matilda 96, 104
May, Minna C. 11
May, W.T. 11
McBeth, David 37, 99, 140, 185
McBeth, Mabel 34
McBroom, Emily 193
McCabe, Dr. 141
McCarty, Bat 62, 199
McCarty, Mary 199
McCauliff, William 115
McClellan, Mrs. 208
McClellan, Thomas 209
McClellan, William 7
McConnell, Archie 4, 162
McConnell, Etta 4
McConnell, J.W. 3, 201
McConnell, Joseph W. 68, 158
McConnell, Laura 13, 64, 201
McConnell, William 201
McCormack, Charles 147
McCormack, E.G. 99, 179
McCormack, Edwin G. 147
McCormack, Mary 26
McCormack, Smith 99, 141, 147
McCowan, Edward A. 63
McCowan, Squire 154
McCowen, Minnie 124
McCown, E.F. 88
McCullough, Mary 26
McCune, Henry C. 93
McDaniel, E.H. 81, 100, 118, 169, 170, 204
McDaniel, Eli 29, 35
McDaniel, Eli H. 87
McDaniel, Laura 56
McDaniel, Rev. 52, 56
McDonald, Alf 96, 107
McDonald, Alfred 188

McDonald, D. 125
McDonald, Marion 41, 140
McDonald, Mattie 140
McDougall, Cadi 104
McDowell, Carrie 121, 129
McDowell, Edward 174
McFadden, Ed 119
McGinnis, Ann 209
McGoon, Mary 153
McGwiggins, Mrs. Peter 55
McIntyre, Levi 163
McKee, F.D. 100, 101
McKee, G.D. 136
McKee, J.D. 87
McKee, John 113
McKee, Sam 189
McKee, T.D. 35, 111, 112, 113, 195
McKee, Thomas 152
McKee, Thomas D. 123
McKeen, Dr. 72
McKeen, Samuel G. 72
McKneill, W.K. 193
McKnight, Jennie 4
McKnight, L.A. 160
McKnight, Mrs. Thomas 56
McKnight, Tom 39, 62, 106
McKouse, Isaac 193
McLaughlin, Georgia 19
McLaughlin, J. 122
McLaughlin, James 50, 74
McLaughlin, Jane 39, 161
McLaughlin, Mary 101
McLean, William E. 186
McMasters, Omar 7
McMechen, Caldie 183
McMendenhall, Mr. 178
McMillen, Cora A. 113
McMillen, John 108, 207
McMullen, Albert 177, 178
McMurtry, William 177
McNeil, J.B. 54
McNeill, George H. 50, 94, 98, 203
McNeill, John B. 70
McNeill, John R. 50
McNeill, W.K. 81, 118, 169, 170, 204
McNulty, Frank 118
McRoberts, Alda 63
McRoberts, Clara 36
McRoberts, Clara A. 205
McRoberts, Fish 197
McRoberts, John 66
McRoberts, Lizzie 190, 193
McWethy, Catherine 197
McWethy, Link 89
McWethy, Mrs. Link 89
Meadows, Willis 69
Mendenhall, J.W. 179
Mendenhall, Jane 181, 182, 183
Mercer, Sarah A. 71

Meredith, Brother 163
Meredith, Rev. 102, 136, 164
Merriman, Bruce 178
Merriman, Jonathan 15, 186
Merriwether, Si 177
Metcalf, John Q. 129
Metzger, David 71
Metzger, Grace 34
Metzger, Jonas 16
Metzger, Mary 16
Miles, Benjamin 23
Miller, Augustus 15
Miller, Augustus O. 190
Miller, Austin 153
Miller, Daniel 85
Miller, Elnora A. 34
Miller, Frank B. 62
Miller, Hugh 208
Miller, Jacob 50
Miller, James H. 47
Miller, John 81, 118, 119, 122, 170, 204
Miller, L. 165
Miller, Mary 159, 208
Miller, Mr. 158
Miller, Mrs. J.T.H. 182, 183
Miller, Samantha 191
Miller, Sarah 15
Miller, Stephen 8, 175
Miller, Steve 57
Millikin, Billy 28
Millikin, Grandma 12
Millikin, Hattie 12
Millikin, Mrs. Stephen 9
Millikin, O.W. 12
Millikin, Otis W. 70
Millikin, Porter 2, 87
Millikin, Scott 12
Millikin, W.S. 8, 12
Millikin, Will 169
Millikin, Willie 12
Mills, Abraham 62
Mills, J.M. 111
Mills, Mr. 63
Mitchell, Alice 47
Mitchell, Carrie 181
Mitchell, Dick 166, 205
Mitchell, Grace 2
Mitchell, James N. 14
Mitchell, Joe 2
Mitchell, L.R. 157
Mitchell, Mrs. L.R. 157
Mitchell, Reese 95
Mitchell, Reese D. 109
Mitchell, Richard T. 161, 190, 202
Mitchell, Thomas J. Sr. 50
Mitchell, William 51
Mitchell, William M. 205
Moffatt, R.D. 50, 122
Moffatt, Robert D. 109
Moffatt, Tom 159

Moffatt, Walter E. 109
Monaghan, Lawrence 202
Monroe, Byrd C. 202
Moore, Addie 174
Moore, Alice 172
Moore, Allie 174
Moore, Elizabeth 147
Moore, Fred 201
Moore, Joseph 127, 130
Moore, Marietta 164
Moore, Sallie 80
Moore, Samuel 71, 177
Moore, Sarah 70, 130, 135, 203
Moore, Sarah E. 127
Moore, W.J. 103
Moorhead, Dr. 46
Morehead, Joe 168, 178, 182
Morehead, Mary 181
Morehead, Reta 72, 168, 181
Morehead, Zan 187
Morehouse, Dr. 80, 187
Morey, Mrs. 114
Morey, S.J. 194
Morey, Sallie 128
Morey, Sally 130
Morey, W.L. 21
Morgan, Charles 92
Morgan, L.A. 68
Morgan, Lewis A. 69
Morgan, Mr. 187
Morgan, Mrs. 187
Morgan, O.P. 152
Morgan, Oliver P. 159
Morgan, Perry 84, 147
Morgan, Sarah A. 123
Morgan, W.T. 100
Morris, Charles 135
Morris, Samuel 49
Morris, Sarah 92
Morris, William 170
Morrison, Adaline 193
Morrison, Billy 107
Morrison, Mrs. William 49
Morrison, William 87, 97
Morrison, William F. 104
Mosbarger, D. 123
Mosewell, John 155
Moudy, Peter S. 125
Moudy, Robert B. 70
Muller, Mrs. 163
Muller, Peter J. 163
Munson, F.H. 32
Munson, Frank H. 198
Murry, E.R. 185
Musser, Rev. 166
Myers 125
Myers, Clara 2, 82, 141, 168, 209
Myers, Emily 151
Myers, Eva 97
Myers, George 119
Myers, J.H. 43

Myers, Jacob 21, 43, 136
Myers, Jane 28
Myers, Levi 151
Myers, Mollie M. 124
Myers, Mrs. T.B. 110
Myers, Mrs. William C. 195
Myers, Q.A. 60, 166
Myers, Quincy 4, 34, 39, 80, 84, 161
Myers, Quincy A. 76
Myers, R.H. 106, 189
Myers, Robert 28
Myers, Sam 1, 43
Myers, Spencer 28
Myers, T.B. 110
Myers, Thomas 165
Myers, Vista 208
Myers, W.C. 94
Myers, William 51, 178
Myers, William C. 79
Nason, George 67
Nation, Rilla S.D. 174
Naylor, Mrs. 172
Naylor, W.L. 106
Nebeker, A. 86
Nebeker, Dr. 150, 162
Nebeker, E.H. 76
Nebeker, Henry 86, 118, 146, 149, 169, 204
Nebeker, Mrs. 153
Neel, Charles S. 123
Neel, E.E. 27, 165
Neel, Edward E. 60
Neel, George M. 66
Neel, J.W. 139
Neel, John W. 100, 104
Neel, Martha J. 100
Neel, Mary J. 104, 122, 123
Neel, Mr. 80
Neel, Susana 122
Neel, William S. 26
Neff, Susan 146
Nelson, H.C. 177, 178
Nelson, Laura 26
Nelson, Mrs. J.L. 160
Nelson, Mrs. R.S. 24
Nesbitt, Mrs. R.C. 157
Nesbitt, R.C. 157
Nevins, Charley 164
Nevins, Joe 52
Nevins, Oscar F. 27
Newell, Cora L. 166
Newell, J.T. 40
Newell, John T. 175
Newell, Lafayette 77
Newell, Lafe 45, 52, 59
Newell, Mrs. Lafe 59
Newell, Sallie 59
Newhouse, Fin D. 115
Newlin, Della 25
Newlin, Lafayette 166
Newlin, Samuel 189

Newman, Joe 67
Newport, Israel 202
Newport, Peter 24
Newton, Dr. 38
Newton, G.O. 30, 81, 118, 169, 170, 204
Niccum, William 50
Nicholas, J.H. 170
Nicholas, Mahala 95
Nicholas, William 95
Nichols, A. 101
Nichols, Albert H. 190
Nichols, Ann 122
Nichols, Brenton 193
Nichols, Henry C. 155
Nichols, J.M. 44, 115, 140
Nichols, James Madison 149
Nichols, Jane 193
Nichols, Madison 106, 109, 148, 149
Nichols, Maria 102, 111
Nichols, Mrs. 18, 163
Nichols, Mrs. J.M. 155
Nichols, Mrs. Oscar 193
Nichols, Omer 54, 103
Nichols, Oscar 141
Nichols, R.E. 76
Nichols, Robert E. 155
Nichols, Sallie 155
Nichols, Sarah 103
Nichols, Sophia 15
Nichols, T.J. 84, 102
Nichols, Thomas J. 51, 76, 78, 83, 207
Nichols, William 50
Nier, Alf 177, 178
Nixon 2, 83, 118
Nixon, Bun 201
Nixon, Henry V. 186
Nixon, Ida 20, 74
Nixon, Marshal 52
Nixon, Mary F. 132
Nixon, Mrs. Marshal 52
Nixon, Mrs. R.H. 74
Nixon, Mrs. Robert 32
Nixon, R.H. 20, 32, 74, 81, 112, 113, 117, 137, 170
Nixon, Robert 20, 32, 38, 60
Nixon, Robert H. 68, 71
Nixon, Sarah P. 38
Nixon, Virgil 52
Nolan, A. 85
Nolan, Alfred 167
Nolan, Monroe 113
Norman, Allie 162
Norman, Anna 162
Norris 98
Norris, Bob 66
Norris, Eva 16
Norris, George P. 100
Norris, John 35, 98, 100, 192
Norris, L.C. 58

Norris, Lewis 16, 128, 162
Norris, Sarah E. 192
Norris, William A. 71
Norton, Cornelius H. 53, 145
Nourse, E.B. 50
Nourse, Eunice 149
Nowling, Sarah 125
Noyes, Jason 42
Odekirk, S.V. 41
Odell, Edward 120
Odell, Flora 159
Odell, George W. 60, 116, 120
Odell, Otis 120
Odell, Otis M. 158
Olney, Bessie 77, 182
Orr 156
Orr, J.M. 156
Orr, James M. 186
Orth, William 147
Osborn, Charley 47
Osborn, H. 11
Osborn, Hester 67
Osborn, James 94, 140, 141
Osborn, Jim 88
Osborn, John 96
Osmon, J.B. 40, 84, 88, 115
Overpeck, E.G. 203
Overpeck, Ella 22
Overpeck, Elmer G. 202
Overpeck, Grant 201
Overpeck, Maggie 22
Overpeck, Mattie 29
Overpeck, Mrs. Perry 22
Overpeck, Perry 22
Owens, Amelia 132
Owens, Jack 42
Oxford, Ed 124
Oxford, Edmund R. 168, 174
Paine, Mary 71
Palmer, C.C. 153
Palmer, Eli 41
Palmer, Taylor 31
Parke, Mrs. Shelby F. 54
Parke, Shelby 57, 59
Parke, Shelby F. 54, 65, 69
Parker, Emily S. 98, 104
Parker, Richard 164
Parks, C.M. 62
Parks, Mrs. L.C. 201
Parrett, Bob 140
Parrett, Charles 80
Parrett, Charley 153
Parrett, Ella 5, 86, 134, 149
Parrett, Eva 149, 157
Parrett, J.W. 35, 36, 50, 86, 157, 184, 208
Parrett, John W. 13, 32, 54, 59, 102, 129, 156, 176
Parrett, L. 183
Parrett, Mary 157
Parrett, Mrs. Robert 10
Parrett, R.A. 2, 48, 68, 148, 157

Parrett, Rev. 166
Parrett, Robert A. 83, 189
Parrett, Robert V. 96
Parrett, Watson 161
Parrett, William 111, 157
Parrett, William F. 149
Patrick, Hiram 79, 81
Patrick, Martin 112
Patrick, Thomas 196, 204
Patrick, Vara 4, 5, 39
Patrick, Vara A. 34
Patterson, Edward C. 74
Patterson, George 118
Patterson, Hattie B. 58
Patterson, Mr. 6
Patterson, Mrs. T.A. 118
Patterson, Pene 33, 40, 43
Patterson, Sarah E. 93
Patterson, T.A. 118
Patton, Barney 1
Patton, Mrs. B.F. 137
Patton, Mrs. Barney 1
Patton, Rachel J. 8
Pauley, John 190
Pauley, Susan A. 124
Pauley, W.B. 191
Pauley, W.B. 87, 113
Pauley, William 53
Pauley, William B. 86
Paxton, Harvey H. 58
Payne, Able W. 193
Payne, Elizabeth 193
Payne, Harriet 193
Payne, Jim 16
Payton, Arthur 121, 205
Payton, Charles 205
Payton, Dick 47
Payton, Eliza 192
Payton, Ella E. 121, 124
Payton, Harvey H. 175
Payton, Hattie M. 193
Payton, John 128, 190, 192
Payton, Johnny 115
Payton, Ollie 164
Pearman, Adam 141
Pearman, Catherine 208
Pearman, David 159
Pearman, Oscar 141
Pearman, William 48
Pearson, Daniel J. 55
Peeler, J.F. 18, 150
Peeler, John 10
Peer 26
Peer, D. 113
Peer, Ira 150, 151, 165
Peer, J.L. 83, 151
Peer, Mrs. William 103
Peer, William 84, 103, 122
Pegg, James 146
Penn, George 93
Perkins, P.D. 30
Perrant, Elizabeth 48

Perrin, Ed 130
Perrin, Ettie B. 196
Perrin, Hyde 93
Perrin, J.W. 168
Perrin, James B. 17
Perrin, Mrs. Otis 135
Perrin, Ote 195
Perrin, Susan 92
Peters, Charles 26
Peters, D.L. 208
Peters, F.F. 139
Peters, Frank 194
Peters, H.O. 11, 110, 113, 166
Peters, John L. 198
Peters, Mrs. H.O. 97
Peterson, Gustave A. 207
Pettinger, William 147
Petty, Ann 7
Petty, James 41
Petty, Malinda 7, 91
Petty, Martin 5, 112
Peyton, Dr. 59
Peyton, Ella 129
Peyton, H.H. 54, 65
Peyton, Harvey H. 129
Peyton, Henry H. 129
Peyton, James 99
Peyton, John C. 99
Peyton, Lola 129
Phelps, E.P. 41
Phenegar, Hattie 74, 143
Phenegar, Hattie E. 78
Phillips, Phoebe 150, 155
Pickes, J. 99
Pierce, Harrison 8
Pierce, Pearl 3
Pierce, Thomas 41
Pike, Lydia 166
Pinegar, Alice 22
Pinson, Maggie 153
Pinson, William 80
Piper, Mrs. 3
Pixley 83
Pixley, H.D. 2
Place, Ada 181, 183
Place, Ada May 119
Place, Ernest 28
Place, L.J. 4, 36, 156, 170, 180, 181, 208
Place, Mrs. L.J. 193
Place, Mrs. Lee J. 131
Place, W.M. 155
Place, Walter 84
Place, Walter J. 42, 50
Place, Walter Jr. 44
Platt, Allen 49
Poland, Dr. 55
Pollard 132
Pontoon, Oliver 188
Pontoon, Polly 200
Pontoon, William S. 188, 200
Poor, William 145

Poore, Andrew 15
Porter, Essie 10
Porter, Hattie 119
Porter, Hettie 48, 53, 54, 164
Porter, John 48, 167
Porter, John C. 55, 70, 99, 102, 104, 145
Porter, John R. 145
Porter, John W. 48
Porter, Mary E. 87
Porter, Mary L. 21
Porter, Minnie 48
Porter, Mrs. Isaac 12
Porter, Richard 138
Porter, Robert K. 51
Porter, Ruth 138, 140
Porter, Ruth S. 149
Porter, W.L. 81, 118
Porter, W.W. 48, 99, 111, 205
Porter, William 119
Porter, William E. 124
Porter, William I. 21, 138
Porter, William L. 126
Porter, Worth W. 70, 145
Porter, Zoe 48
Porter, Zoe M. 55
Post, M. 118
Potter, Effie 29
Potter, Emma 56
Potter, John 29
Potter, Levi 124
Potter, Priscilla 8, 101
Potter, Rosa 29
Potter, Washington 102
Potts, Charles P. 175
Potts, Charley 137, 203
Potts, Ella 15
Potts, Nellie 15
Powers, Mr. 114
Powers, Mrs. William 189
Powers, William 189
Prater, Isaac 122
Prentiss, George D. 127
Price, Huldah A. 168, 174
Priest, George L. 112
Pringle, D.E. 183
Pringle, Mrs. D.E. 183, 184
Pritchard, Elias 115, 194
Pritchard, Mrs. Elias 47
Puett 163
Puett, George 103
Puffer, Reuben 190
Pugh, Edwin R. 38
Pugh, Monroe 38, 178
Pugh, Mrs. E.R. 24
Purcell, Ida 18
Purky 156
Purky, L.F. 156
Puttmann, John J. 67
Pyle, A. 186
Quick, Mary E. 174
Quick, May 37, 107

Quinlan, Indiana 161
Quinlan, James 141, 146, 161, 186, 203
Rabb, Joe 46
Rabb, Smith 3, 9, 62, 88
Radloff, Helena 29
Ragsdale, William 15
Rainbole, Emma L. 103
Rairdon, James Sr. 203
Rairdon, Mrs. James 152
Ralph 83, 180, 181
Ralph, A.J. 18
Ralph, Mrs. A.J. 18
Ralston, Charles 11
Ralston, Henry 50, 78
Ralston, Jim 200
Ramey, Mr. 150
Ramsey, Hattie 199
Ramsey, Isaac 198
Ramsey, Lucinda A. 124
Ramsey, Sarah 199
Ramsey, Willis 199
Randall, Bertha J. 5
Randall, George 52
Randall, J. 99
Randall, M. 186
Randall, M.H. 101
Randall, Morris H. 121, 124
Randolph, F.E. 83
Randolph, H.C. 11
Ranger, Ad 85
Ranger, D.A. 79
Rankin, Prof. 16
Raynes, Warren S. 207
Read, Oliver L. 139
Red, Elizabeth 48
Redman, J.W. 3, 56, 77, 208
Redman, Mrs. J.W. 208
Redman, Undertaker 14, 31, 185
Reed, Alfred M. 48, 69
Reed, Charles 48
Reed, Charles S. 48
Reed, Charlie 150
Reed, D.A. 38, 39, 150
Reed, David A. 39
Reed, Edward 106
Reed, Eliza 48
Reed, Lewis 72
Reed, Mary 137
Reed, Mrs. D.A. 150
Reed, Mrs. Frank 185
Reed, Mrs. William 23
Reed, Sampson, 146
Reed, William 128, 180
Reeder, Albert 22
Reeder, Frank 137, 192, 206
Reeder, Frank L. 53, 70, 71, 133, 155, 164, 195
Reeder, Laura 137
Reeder, Lucinda 192, 206
Reeder, Marion 71, 75
Reeder, Mrs. Frank 137

Reeder, William A. 75
Reeder, William B. 71
Refit, Mary 82
Reid, James 135
Remley, Daniel A. 174
Remley, Jacob 40, 41
Remley, John W. 185
Remley, Sarah 104
Remley, Sarah R. 98
Renicks, Norbin 78
Reynolds, Rebecca 123
Rheuby, Elizabeth 119
Rheuby, Gould 206
Rheuby, Gould G. 26, 119
Rheuby, Grace 119, 171
Rheuby, Sheriff 157
Rheuby, William 68, 77, 81, 94, 96, 98, 118, 119, 126, 136, 154, 170, 192, 200, 204, 206
Rhoads 27, 49, 55, 62, 67, 74, 94, 98, 103, 133, 154
Rhoads, Charles 39
Rhoads, George 33
Rhoads, H.B. 57
Rhoads, Harry B. 22, 39, 56, 127, 128, 158, 198
Rhoads, M.G. 2, 5, 58, 66, 81, 101, 104, 119, 128, 140, 149, 170, 204
Rhoads, Madie 10
Rhoads, Martin 121
Rhoads, Martin G. 33
Rhoads, Mrs. M.G. 47, 109, 181
Rhoads, Paul 4, 201, 208
Rhoads, Sarah 33
Rhoads, Will 154
Rhodenbaugh, George H. 78
Rhodenbaugh, George W. 76, 78
Rhodenbaugh, Pete 187
Rice, Fracie M. 165
Rice, Frances 26, 80
Rice, Isaac 178
Rice, Mary F. 60
Rice, William Y. 153
Richard, Rose 174
Richards, Flora 119
Richards, John 119
Richardson, Anna 4, 5, 165
Richardson, Billy 66
Richardson, Ella 4, 84, 184
Richardson, Frank C. 195
Richardson, John 2, 25, 78, 81, 118, 207
Richardson, Mrs. John 177
Richardson, Sarah 48
Richardson, William 39, 69, 144
Richardson, William E. 34
Richardson, Willie 4
Riddle, Mrs. M.M. 77
Ridgely, Henderson 98, 104
Rightsell, George 164

Riley, F.M. 81, 119, 170, 202, 204
Riley, Frank 96
Riley, Frank M. 141
Riley, John 68
Riley, Mary 68
Ripetoe, Rev. 68
Rittenhouse, George 53
Rittenhouse, Sam 172
Rittenhouse, William 106
Rivers, James 36
Roach, L. 11
Roach, William 194
Roach, William H. 69
Robanon, Lula 131
Robb, Martha 36
Robbins, Isa 82
Robbins, John 167
Robert, Mrs. John 130
Roberts, Arthur 133, 138
Roberts, Jim 11, 21
Roberts, John 130
Robertson, James A. 75
Robinson, B.C. 35
Robinson, D.D. 35
Robinson, Daisy 40, 42
Robinson, Harry W. 146
Robison, Daisy 137
Robison, Daisy E. 171
Robison, Ida 141
Robison, Jessie A. 171
Robison, Sophia 161
Rodgers, Elizabeth 194
Rodgers, Harriet 199
Rogers, Belle 201
Rogers, Isaac 107
Rogers, James 39
Rogers, John O. 39
Rogers, Joshua 39, 90
Rogers, Leonard 93
Rogers, Margaret 90
Rogers, Mrs. Isaac 107
Rogers, Susan A. 52
Roll, B.J., 35
Ross, Anna 170
Ross, Rose A. 174
Ross, Thompson 45
Rouse, Mack 193
Rowland, Alice 22
Rowland, Edith 58
Rowland, Mary A. 180, 181, 182, 183
Rowland, Miss 25
Royes, Mary 73
Royse, Samuel R. 203
Rucker, R.M. 51
Rudy, Martin B. 147
Rudy, Milo J. 135
Ruhl, Grace 111
Rumisel, J.H. 4
Runyan, Charles D. 134
Runyan, D.C. 124

Runyan, Daniel R. Sr. 50
Runyan, Ella J. 74
Runyan, J.P. 134
Runyan, James 50, 145
Runyan, Jesse 97, 124, 152
Runyan, John 134
Runyan, Phoebe 134
Rush, Fred 2, 26, 89, 118, 204
Rush, James 139
Rush, Mark 6, 139
Rush, Prof. 13
Rusk, Michael 98, 104
Rusmisel, Rev. 176
Russell 77
Russell, A.E. 15
Russell, Bill 27
Russell, Harriet 45
Russell, John 45
Russell, Mollie 15
Russell, Mrs. 202
Russell, William 36, 190
Russell, William Jr. 174
Russell, William Sr. 36, 174
Rutherford, Bayless 162, 164
Ryan, Jesse 92
Ryce, Frances 64
Sabin, Joe 20
Sabins, Amanda 45
Sager, Bud 187
Sagers, I. 131
Saltsgaver, C. 37
Saltsgaver, W.H. 159
Salyards, Carrie 26
Sam, Uncle 192
Sam, Uncle 28, 109
Samuel 146
Sanderford, Ervan 103
Sanders, C.M. 125
Sanders, Charles 73
Sanders, Charley 82
Sanders, David 73
Sanders, Emaline 6, 29
Sanders, Ezra 6, 29
Sanders, Harry 73
Sanders, Harry E. 129
Sanders, J.A. 135
Sanders, Len 45
Sanders, Leonard 45
Sanders, Link 180
Sanders, Loretta 73
Sanders, Mrs. 11
Sanders, Mrs. Sam 151
Sanders, Sam 78
Sanders, William 73, 125, 129
Sankey, Freeman 25
Saunders, Mag 48
Sawyer 12, 14, 44, 48, 50, 68, 73, 75, 77, 126, 154, 156, 192, 196, 197
Sawyer, J.C. 2, 28, 35, 83, 84, 86, 112, 125, 132
Sawyer, James C. 98, 192

Sawyer, Jimmie 26
Sawyer, John P. 75
Sawyers, William 56
Sayre, I.D. 177, 178
Schloss, Phil 72
Schroeder, Will 62
Schweizer, Mrs. William F. 186
Schweizer, William F. 49
Schwiezer, Pet 63, 143, 171
Schwiezer, William F. 186
Sconce, Elizabeth 188
Sconce, Mrs. 188
Scooler, Lawrence 140
Scott, Billy 49
Scott, Dollie 72, 137
Scott, Jennie 60
Scott, Matthew 173
Scott, Matthew W. 112, 143
Scott, Minerva 93
Scott, Minerva C. 188
Scott, Miss 44
Scott, William 49
Scott, Winfield S. 69
Searey, Maggie 75
Sears, Claude 4, 39
Sears, Claude M. 34
Sears, Daniel 30, 31
Sears, George H. 9
Sears, Jack 30, 120
Sears, Jacob 9
Sears, Jake 31
Sears, R.B. 9, 31
Sears, Senator 3, 13
Secrist, William 82
Sedgewick, Lottie 189
Seeds, John P. 71
Seeds, Ora M. 71
Seekamp, Henry 206
Selch, Charles D. 143
Selch, Charles E. 148
Self, John 11
Sewell, William J. 129
Sexton, Abel 5, 95
Shaffer, Henry 97, 141
Shannon, Emma F. 102, 155
Sharp, Bill 160
Sharp, Otho 160
Sharp, W.C. 81, 118
Sharp, William 189
Shaw 15
Shaw, Charles 56, 153
Shaw, Elias G. 14
Shaw, Lizzie 2
Shaw, Mrs. Charles 153
Shaw, Simeon 40
Sheeley, G.W. 65
Shelato, Grace 57
Shelato, Inez 171
Shelato, Mrs. William 171
Shelato, W.M. 81
Shelato, William 78, 171
Shelato, William M. 57, 119

Shelby, J. 67
Shepard, Grace 194
Shepard, Hiram 36, 126, 152, 192
Shepard, Lewis 5, 118, 138, 149, 179
Sheperd, James N. 92
Sheperd, Quinton 69
Shepherd, Harry 16
Shepherd, Mrs. 193
Shepherd, Mrs. Henry 187
Shepherdson, Frank 103
Shepherdson, Mrs. Frank 103
Shew, Aurilla B. 104
Shew, Coney 127
Shew, Lewis 121
Sheward, Charles C. 6, 30
Sheward, James 93, 112
Sheward, William L. 6, 30
Shewmaker, John 93
Shields, Mrs. N. 139
Shipman, Ozias 85
Shires, Rev. 199
Shirk, Dave 47
Shirk, David 25
Shirk, George E. 25
Shirk, J.M. 177, 178, 185
Shirkie 80
Shirkie, Jennie 34
Shoaf, Solomon 125
Shoe, I. 67
Shoe, Lewis 174
Shores, F.M. 100
Short, Albert 99, 104
Short, George 203
Shorter, James 88
Shorter, William 12
Shute, Daniel 95
Shute, Ephraim 95, 101, 122
Shute, Mrs. David 135
Shute, Mrs. Joseph 135
Shute, Richard 95
Sidebottom, Aaron 25
Sidebottom, Aaron S. 92
Siders, Isaac 192
Siders, Thomas 192
Sidwell 4
Sigler, Mrs. S.W. 166
Simpson, Bruce 1
Simpson, C.W. 112
Simpson, Charles W. 32, 106, 132
Simpson, Mary 101
Sims, Abraham 144
Sims, Abram 193
Sims, Elizabeth 7
Sims, Joseph V. 104
Sims, Lewis 7
Sims, O.B. 152
Singleton, Jasper 111
Singleton, Jasper A. 193
Skeen, T.D. 54

Skidmore, Emma 48
Skidmore, Fidelia 64
Skidmore, Frank 22
Skidmore, Henry 137
Skidmore, Jasper F. 48
Skidmore, Joe 22
Skidmore, John 22
Skidmore, Mrs. William 64
Skidmore, Robert 155
Skidmore, W.H. 101, 112, 113
Skidmore, Wilbert 22
Skidmore, William 64, 84
Skinner, Lewis 6, 29
Skinner, Lewis S. 136
Skinner, Norman C. 193
Slater, Frank 72
Slater, James 128
Slater, Martha J. 94
Slater, Melissa 128
Slater, Mrs. 23
Slater, Mrs. Frank 72
Slater, Mrs. William 107
Slater, Panzy 72
Slater, Wiley G. 92, 94
Slater, William 42
Slaughter, Dr. 38
Slaughter, R. 34, 35
Sleeth, O.P. 60
Small, Dr. 177
Small, Mrs. 177
Smith, Abbie 48
Smith, Amassa 164
Smith, Andrew H. 202
Smith, Andrew Jackson 201
Smith, Bertie 160
Smith, Charles 191
Smith, Clara 6, 200
Smith, D.G. 75
Smith, E.E. 169
Smith, Ed 98
Smith, Elmer S. 204
Smith, Frank S. 55
Smith, Grandmother 6
Smith, Henry 124
Smith, J. Mart 103
Smith, J.F. 177
Smith, J.L. 170
Smith, James B. 124
Smith, John F. 51
Smith, John H. 145
Smith, John L. 177
Smith, Joseph F. 203
Smith, Laura 115
Smith, Lochie 15
Smith, Mary 48
Smith, Mary W. 55
Smith, Massa 89
Smith, Mrs. 114
Smith, Mrs. A. 162
Smith, Mrs. Dr. 172
Smith, Nat 115
Smith, O.J. 95

Smith, Sam 21
Smith, Sarah C. 154
Smith, Sarah J. 141
Smith, Susan 26
Smith, Thomas H. 51
Smith, W.A. 17, 22, 32, 39, 40, 44, 51, 72, 74, 82, 91, 102, 131, 199, 207
Smith, William 41
Smith, William A. 51
Smith, William P. 23, 51
Smock, Randolph 146
Snider, Parley 141
Snyder, A.M. 172
Snyder, George W. 101
Snyder, L. 101
Snyder, Michael 131
Soliday, Grace 133, 138
Soliday, William 110
Sollars, Dan 28
Sollars, Daniel L. 14
Sollars, Della 10
Sollars, John 10
Sollars, Martha J. 152
Sollars, Mrs. N. 10
Sollars, William 10
Songer, Frank 84
Songer, Samantha 45
Sorg, J.F. 36
Souders, Ben G. 205
Southward, Bernie 29
Southward, Burt 125
Southward, Elizabeth 162
Southward, Eura 161
Southward, Huron 39
Southward, Minnie 29, 121
Southward, Mrs. 21
Sparks, Alice 69
Sparks, George 43
Sparks, J.N. 179
Sparks, Jennie 202
Sparks, Joseph 69
Sparks, Sarah 122
Spellman, Clara 15
Spellman, Ernest 15
Spence, Mrs. J.N. 182, 183
Spencer, James E. 111
Spicer, B.F. 135
Spotswood, Mrs. E.T. 22
Sprague, George 58
Sprague, H.D. 11, 102, 112
Sprague, Harry 58
Sprague, Harry J. 100
Sprague, Henry D. 53, 155, 164
Sprouls, Lillie 171
Spry, David 50, 129
Staats, Bell F. 181, 182
Staats, Fred 122
Staats, Fred A. 152
Staats, Frederick 150
Staats, Harry 150

Staats, Joe 16, 133, 136, 158, 164
Staats, John 23, 47, 52
Staats, Joseph 52
Staats, Mrs. Harry 150
Staats, Phoebe 150
Staats, Sarah 136
Stadler, Carrie 45
Stadler, L.C. 75
Stadler, Mrs. Dr. 45
Stahl, John R. 2, 24, 26, 28, 170
Stanfield, Sarah 31
Stanley, Frank 51
Stanley, Lizzie 61
Stanley, Sue 183
Stanley, W.P. 61
Stark, Jasper N. 193
Stark, Monroe 106
Stark, Mrs. C.M. 64
Stark, T.J. 51
Stark, Thomas J. 53, 155, 164
Starry 177
Statler, James C. 24
Stearns, Hattie 131, 155
Steavers, Agnes 88
Steele, Widow 42
Steely, Mark 90
Steen, E.D. 87
Stephens, Alice M. 5
Stephens, Bertie 4, 5
Stephens, J.S. 56
Stephens, P. 34
Stephens, Pailo 34
Stephens, R.E. 78, 170
Stephens, R.W. 2, 183, 204
Stephens, Thomas W. 5, 7
Stephenson, Nettie 185
Sterling, Lizzie 165
Stevens, E. 74
Stevens, Elhanan 24, 51, 78, 143, 147
Stevens, Hattie 147
Stevens, Hattie A. 143
Stevens, Mary L. 73
Stevens, Wat 67, 73
Stevenson, Phila A. 164
Stewart, Charles 76
Stewart, Charley 91
Stewart, Dora 110, 111
Stewart, Ed 12
Stewart, Flora 139
Stewart, Frank 12
Stewart, James 12
Stewart, John F. 12, 30, 42, 65
Stewart, M.A. 36
Stewart, Manford E. 170
Stewart, Mary 12
Stewart, Mary A. 37
Stewart, Mrs. Charles 182
Stillar, Mary 166
Stokes, Lucy R. 10
Stokes, Marshall 197

Stokes, R. 179
Stokes, R.B. 165
Stokes, Susie 10
Stokesberry, Al 114
Stokesberry, Bernard 133
Stokesberry, Eva 26
Stokesberry, M.J. 140
Stokesberry, O.S. 1
Stokesberry, William 159
Stone, Lucretia 133
Stonebreaker, Israel 193
Storey, Hamilton L. 70
Stout, Clifford K. 147
Straight, Frank 124
Strain 15
Strain, Daniel E. 159
Strain, George 29
Strain, Isaac 100
Strain, Isaac H. 4, 107
Strain, John 49
Strain, John A. 100
Strain, Joseph 163
Strange, John 151
Straughn, John W. 92
Strauser, Anna 64
Streetmocker, Peter 17
Stultz, Charles A. 124
Stultz, Solomon 3
Sturm, Foxy 191
Sturm, G.W. 26
Sturm, H.A. 208
Sturm, Mrs. M.R. 183
Stutler, Charles J. 103
Stutler, James C. 14
Stutsman, Lewis 163
Stutsman, Nancy J. 155
Sullivan, Clara 166
Sullivan, J.M. 125
Swaim, Belle 2
Swaim, Cora 185
Swaim, David 177, 178
Swaim, Jemima 191
Swaim, Joseph 185
Swaim, Lafayette 146
Swaim, Moses 146
Swaim, W.P. 126
Swaim, William 191
Swain, J.R. 2, 10, 44, 48, 183
Swain, M.S. 10
Swain, Morrey 4, 39
Swain, Mrs. S.A. 10
Swain, Sanford M. 34
Swank, Elizabeth 151
Swem, Eliza 195
Sweringen, W.W. 151
Swift, Rebecca 123
Swindell, W.J. 123
Swindell, William 16, 102, 113, 167, 170
Swindell, William J. 190
Swisher, Rebecca 37
Swisher, Wesley 51

Switzer, Joseph 36
Switzer, Leonard H. 193
Switzer, Minnie 166
Switzer, William 36
Sykes, Anul 13
Sykes, Ella 189, 193
Sykes, James W. 75, 172
Tanner, Commissioner 158
Tarrence, Anna 171
Tarrence, Ed 158
Tarrence, Ella 61
Tarrence, William G. 51
Tate, Charles R. 170
Tate, Hannah 47
Tate, Henry 129
Tate, Henry H. 203
Tate, John 51
Tate, S.B. 39
Tate, William H. 65, 102, 104, 161
Tatinan, William 145
Taylor, Annie 197
Taylor, C.M. 125
Taylor, Carrie M. 123, 190
Taylor, Ed 136
Taylor, Fred 13
Taylor, J.M., 83
Taylor, J.N. 35
Taylor, Levi 104
Taylor, Mary 33
Taylor, Rev. 127
Taylor, Samuel N. 8
Taylor, Sanford 69
Taylor, Sant 33
Taylor, Silas 90
Taylor, W.M. 122
Teegarden, Jerusha 194
Temple, Carl 12, 14, 160
Temple, George 165
Terry, L.M. 128
Terry, Mrs. G.W. 107
Thomas, Charles G. 141
Thomas, Charley 28, 134
Thomas, Clay E. 141
Thomas, Dan 154
Thomas, E.A. 34
Thomas, Ed W. 41
Thomas, Eli 40
Thomas, J.B. 177, 178, 179
Thomas, John 19
Thomas, L.D. 34, 194, 196
Thomas, Leslie D. 132
Thomas, Margaret J. 122
Thomas, Mrs. Dan 154
Thomas, Mrs. Norbin 90
Thomas, Paris 28
Thomas, Stephen A.D. 5
Thomas, Steve 82
Thomas, Tom 28
Thomas, Warren 40, 41
Thomasmyer, Elizabeth 184
Thomasmyer, Henry 37, 184

Thomasmyer, Mrs. Henry 158, 174, 175
Thompson, Abigail 141
Thompson, Abner 188
Thompson, Alice 91, 104, 124
Thompson, Bert 124
Thompson, Cora 169
Thompson, Della 188
Thompson, E. 125
Thompson, Ed 133
Thompson, Eddie 138
Thompson, Esq. 2, 24, 47, 58, 105
Thompson, J.F. 151
Thompson, Martha J. 132
Thompson, Moses 173
Thompson, Mrs. R.J. 76
Thompson, Porter 156
Thompson, Sarah J. 70
Thompson, W.S. 180
Thompson, Wallace 93
Thorne, F.P. 86, 100
Thorne, Hattie 160
Thorne, John J. 78
Thorne, L.W. 86
Thorne, Lou 185
Thorne, Rev. 158
Thorne, U.E. 86
Thornton 170
Thornton, Bell 2, 159
Thornton, Carrie 84
Thornton, Charley 4, 84
Thornton, Emma 49, 61
Thornton, Mrs. 84
Thornton, Postmaster 195
Thornton, W.F. 204
Thornton, William F. 4, 77, 105, 135, 137
Thornton, Z.P. 2, 78, 102, 105, 207
Thrift, Frank 153
Tiffany, Ed 170
Tillotson, Demetrus 167
Tillotson, G.B. 170
Tillotson, Rebecca 194
Tincher, W.L. 123
Todd, Christia A. 87
Todd, Mrs. T.S. 114
Todd, S.K. 11
Todd, T.S. 114
Toler, John 21
Tomlin, J.H. 137
Tomlin, Professor 138
Tompkins, J. 21
Toops, William 37
Tosser, Harvey 193
Towel, Julia 176
Towel, W.C. 106
Towle, Julia 120
Traphagan, Marcellus 104
Traphagan, Susan 104
Trimble, Mrs. J. 24
Trosper, Mahala 91
Trowbridge, Gertie 206
Truitt, A.W. 86
Truitt, Florence 31, 32
Truitt, G.F. 181
Truitt, Samuel 41
Truman, Ernest 174, 176
Truse, William 80
Tucker, M.J. 42, 167
Tucker, Morgan J. 37, 134, 175
Turner, Frank 6, 39, 74, 76, 78, 94, 95, 110, 140
Turpening, Harriet 9
Tursher, A.N. 40, 201
Tursher, Anthony N. 202
Tutt, Edah 113
Tutt, James 81, 143
Tutt, James C. 128, 156
Tutt, Jimmy 152
Tutt, John C. 52
Tutt, Malinda 52
Tutt, N.M. 102, 179
Tutt, Nathan M. 58
Tuttle, Nancy 198
Tweedy, Cora 133, 138
Underwood, Mary A. 19
Underwood, Tilman 60
Underwood, Tom 12
Utter, Richard R. 42
Valentine, Hannah 31, 44, 104
Valentine, William A. 104
Valentine, William H. 31, 44
Van Allen, Bob 19, 72
Van Allen, Elma 107, 201
Van Allen, James 1
Van Allen, Pastor 107, 201
Van Allen, Perry 72, 159, 174
Van Allen, R.B. 9, 21, 22, 25, 31, 40, 51, 53, 57, 60, 61, 63, 78, 79, 90, 99, 102, 105, 109, 110, 119, 120, 121, 127, 135, 138, 144, 148, 149, 151, 154, 162, 164, 187, 188, 193, 195, 207
Van Allen, Rev. 5
Van Allen, Roy 102
Van Houten, Emmet 43
Van Houten, Rev. 55
Vance, Mrs. C.W. 182, 183, 184
Vandevender, George W. 176, 190, 206
Vandevender, John 81, 195
Vandevender, Mary 182
Vanduyn, Ella 93
Vanduyn, John Sr. 52
Vangilder, James 122
Vanhuss, Mr. 107
Vanleer, Ella 50, 68, 104
Vanleer, Ellen 70
Vanleer, Henry 50, 70, 104
Vannest, Jane 105
Vannest, Taylor 18, 20
Vansickle, E. 135
Vansickle, E.A. 62
Vansickle, Ed 3, 20, 157, 169
Vanvleit, Charles 179, 180
Vanvlejt, Charley 105
Varner, J.C. 178
Varner, J.D. 178, 179
Vaughn, Harve 44
Vaughn, James 8
Vaughn, James H. 173
Vaughn, Jessie 188
Vaughn, William 133
Vest, Eli 60
Vestal, Laura A. 104
Victor, Tom 62
Virgin, W. 123
Volkill, Angeline 71, 73
Volkill, Henry 73
Wade, Henry E. 70
Wade, John 88, 162
Wade, Thomas V. 162
Waggoner, Daniel 106
Waggoner, Henry 8, 71, 106
Waggoner, Isaac 77, 83, 106
Waggoner, Mary J. 106, 146
Waggoner, Samuel 146
Walden, Mr. 48
Walker, Barbara 28
Walker, Charles P. 27
Walker, Harrison 141
Walker, Mrs. 27
Walker, Mrs. W.C. 131
Walker, Ruth Ruby 141
Walker, William 198
Wallace 118
Wallace, Dr. 197, 201
Wallace, James 199
Wallace, Joseph 40, 41
Walls, Mrs. 116
Walraven, Elials 196
Walraven, Mrs. 11
Walraven, R.W. 56
Walter, John F. 171
Walthall 33
Walthall, Allen 108, 161
Walthall, Allen J. 38
Walthall, D.B. 161
Walthall, David 54
Walthall, Frank 162
Walthall, Lydia 60, 80, 174
Walthall, Martha 197
Walthall, Media 26
Walthall, Mrs. William B. 160
Walthall, Sarah 60, 64, 80, 165
Walthall, Smith 197
Walthall, Thomas B. 186
Walthall, W.B. 186
Walthall, William 34
Walthall, William B. 52, 160, 198
Walther, Henry 33
Wann, John 91
Wann, Mary A. 202

Wannamaker, Postmaster 130
Wantling, Mrs. Tom 11
Ward 6, 30, 31, 50, 53
Ward, C.W. 98
Ward, Charles W. 6, 30, 43, 69, 83, 145
Ward, James 149
Ward, Mrs. C.W. 11, 64
Warren, Susan F. 192
Washburn, Anna 74
Washburn, Col. 162
Washburn, H.G. 86
Washburn, Harlow 139
Washburn, R.H. 96, 105, 139
Washburn, Serena 74
Washburn, Serena J. 86
Washburn, William O. 28, 96
Waterman, Cale 198
Watkins, Dr. 38, 72
Watson, A.M. 178
Watson, Catherine 104
Watson, Clint 33
Watson, D.C. 36, 93
Watson, D.W. 118
Watson, David 137
Watson, Dewit 104
Watson, Edward L. 140
Watson, Ella 19
Watson, G.L. 11
Watson, George L. 102
Watson, Henry 157
Watson, Mrs. 154
Watson, Nancy 19
Watson, Tom 177
Watt, Samuel 51
Weatherwax, Sol 81, 118, 169, 170, 204
Weatherwax, Trustee 161
Webb, Joseph 41
Weber William 138
Weber, Carrie 127
Weber, Mrs. 27
Webster, August L. 71
Webster, John L. 188
Webster, John W. 69, 145
Webster, Lewis 26
Webster, Mary H. 69, 145
Webster, Stephen 51
Weiler, John 31
Weir, Jake 54
Welch, J.M. 177
Welch, Mrs. C.S. 141
Welhaus, Alice 6, 46
Wellman, John 80
Wells 26
Wells, Frank 139
Wells, George 93
Wells, Horace 107, 180
Wells, Mary 138
Wells, Melvin H. 174
Welshan, George 209
Welshan, S.P. 88

West, T.J., 35
West, Thomas J. 102
Westan, Mr. 40
Westbrook, Levi M. 87
Westdahl, John 43
Westdahl, Mrs. Pene 171
Westfall, P.S. 90
Westfall, Perry S. 95
Wetherspoon, Elizabeth 172, 174
Wheeler, Al 163
Wheeler, Al C. 161
Wheeler, Albert 4
Wheeler, E.D. 176
Wheeler, Elvin 51
Wheeler, Hal 163
Wheeler, Harriet 10
Wheeler, Hattie 182
Wheeler, Len 105
Wheeler, Leonard 10
Wheeler, Mrs. L.M. 181
Whetsel, Harry D. 124
Whipple 94
Whipple, Frank 126
Whipple, J.E. 35, 38, 58, 64, 94
Whipple, L.R. 1
Whipple, Sarah 35
Whipple, W.P. 94
Whitcomb, Arthur 167, 200
Whitcomb, Charles 55, 134, 147
Whitcomb, Clara 147
Whitcomb, Derexa 34
Whitcomb, Emeline 147
Whitcomb, Harry 28
Whitcomb, John 85, 99, 103, 141, 147, 154, 155, 175, 192, 206
Whitcomb, Larz 167, 200
Whitcomb, M.S. 85
Whitcomb, Mary S. 28
Whitcomb, Mrs. John 103
Whitcomb, Mrs. John R. 14
Whitcomb, Nema 133
Whitcomb, Nettie 138
Whitcomb, Sue 73
White, Alex 56
White, Ared F. 58
White, Bettie 48
White, Bob 199
White, C.M. 82
White, Charley 89
White, Cliffie 26
White, Clifton 180
White, Cora 17
White, Elizabeth J. 162
White, Ernest 14
White, Eva 162
White, Fanny 58
White, Florence 108
White, Grace G. 174, 176
White, H.A. 47
White, Harry 29, 121

White, J.D. 155
White, Jacob 188
White, James A. Sr. 89
White, James, 13
White, Joe 56
White, Judge 37
White, Lucy 84, 119
White, Max 29, 121
White, Mrs. Alex 175
White, Mrs. James 13, 162
White, Mrs. W.H. 141
White, Okie 29, 89, 121
White, Orsen 97
White, Pearl 29, 89, 121
White, Pick 89
White, Rea 147
White, Robert 17
White, Sarah 123, 186
White, Sarah A. 122
White, W.P. 88
White, Warren P. 89
White, William 14
Whiteside 1
Whitlock, B.E. 178
Whitlock, Grace 144, 164
Whitlock, Grace H. 203
Whitlock, Martha M. 203
Whitlock, Mr. 140
Whitlock, Mrs. Jacob 1
Whitlock, Mrs. Matt 164
Whitlock, R.E. 26, 33, 40, 137, 203
Whitney, Riley 6, 19
Whitsel, Alice 197
Whitson, Gertrude 32
Whitson, Oliver 6
Whittaker, Charley 73
Wick, A. 36
Wick, L.A. 208
Wick, Lucy Ann 143
Wick, Marion 164
Wick, Morton 143
Wickens, James 123
Wicks, Mort 89
Widner, Jeff 66
Wieler, Laura 31
Wigley, Orpha 194
Wigley, William 194
Wiles, Frank 128
Wiley, Charles B. 82
Wiley, G. 17
Wiley, Mr. 95
Wiley, Rev. 19, 75
Wilfong, George 40, 41
Wilkins, Dora 85
Wilkins, Elizabeth 104
Willey, Mrs. N.N. 64
Williams, Capt. 114
Williams, Daniel 207
Williams, Joe 30
Williams, Lyman B. 149
Williams, Mary 131

Williams, Philip T. 49
Williams, Rev. 32
Williams, Tice 167
Williams, Tice W. 174
Williamson, Anna 84
Williamson, Miss 58
Willis, A.B. 121
Wilson 86
Wilson, A.L. 35
Wilson, Abe 31
Wilson, Carrie 153
Wilson, Cora 21
Wilson, Elias 15
Wilson, Israel 193
Wilson, James 135
Wilson, Jesse T.S. 155
Wilson, John T. 178
Wilson, Martha E. 197
Wilson, Rosa 31
Wiltermood 15, 43
Wiltermood, Albert B. 128
Wiltermood, Alwida 128
Wiltermood, Anna 119
Wiltermood, Attorney 116
Wiltermood, Charles W. 63
Wiltermood, Charley 4, 60
Wiltermood, Ethel Madaline 128
Wiltermood, Frank 102
Wiltermood, Henry 121
Wiltermood, J. 113
Wiltermood, J.F. 87, 100
Wiltermood, John A. 43, 190
Wiltermood, Martha 92
Wiltermood, Mrs. Charley 19
Wimsett, Andy 64
Wimsett, Dick 26, 31
Wimsett, Ella 148
Wimsett, Jacob 178, 180, 197
Wimsett, Lou 148
Wimsett, Mrs. Dick 19
Wise, Allie 15
Wise, Dan 14
Wise, Daniel 180
Wise, James 14
Wise, Mary E. 119, 124
Wiseman, May 148
Wishard, Esq. 129, 173
Wishard, James 130
Wishard, James L. 4
Wishard, Justice 104
Wishard, Laura 129
Wishard, Mrs. 24
Wishard, S.E. 18, 83
Wishard, Samuel E. 174
Wishard, Stewart 198
Wishard, Sue 114, 130
Wittenburg, G.D. 11
Wolf, Charley 72
Wolf, David 72
Wolf, Lon 72
Wolf, Mrs. C.A. 30
Wolfe, Charles 150
Wolfe, David J. 132
Wood, A. 151
Wood, Hiram 25
Wood, Israel 138, 139, 141
Wood, Rebecca J. 165
Wood, William 100, 141, 156
Woodard, Alice 102, 104
Woodgate, John 107
Woodgate, Mrs. John 107
Woodmanse, L.D. 51
Woodward, Jacob 47
Woodward, James 137
Woody, Mr. 185
Woolen, Guy 65
Wooster, Hattie M. 163
Wooster, Mrs. William 158
Wooster, William 57
Wright, Bertha 26, 182
Wright, Brother 202
Wright, Charley 148
Wright, Dave 16
Wright, David L. 147
Wright, F.M. 58
Wright, Francis M. 196, 197
Wright, J.E. 33, 56, 63, 85, 88, 97, 128, 136, 172, 183, 189, 190, 197
Wright, Jacob 71, 104
Wright, James M. 195
Wright, John 50, 80, 88, 108, 113, 176, 186, 190
Wright, Johnny 165
Wright, Lucian 79
Wright, Lula 27
Wright, Martin L. 10, 12, 146
Wright, Mary 197
Wright, Mr. 58
Wright, Mrs. Robert 9
Wright, Myrtle 133, 138
Wright, Nannie 17
Wright, Nettie M. 58
Wright, Peter L. 12
Wright, Rev. 64, 84
Wright, Robert 9, 20, 71, 138
Wright, Sarah M. 71, 104
Wright, Ulysses G. 190
Wright, William 17, 43, 156, 165, 168, 178, 196
Wright, William L. 167
Wright, William P. 9, 27, 83, 138, 184
Wrightmier, Bell 146
Wrightmier, Richard 146
Wrork, Owen, 65
York, J.P. 10
York, Mrs. J.P. 89
York, Travis P. 146
Young, Agnes 119
Young, Edward H. 175
Young, Henry 22, 27, 41
Young, Mrs. Squire 19
Young, Sarah 28, 119
Young, Squire 92
Younger, Bob 168
Yount, Jacob 40
Yount, Mrs. A.J. 66
Yount, W.H. 127
Yount, William H. 117
Zelanka, Joseph 200
Zener, Adam 112
Zook, Mrs. S.C. 140
Zook, Peter 63, 115
Zook, Rev. 63, 140
Zook, S.C. 115

www.ingramcontent.com/pod-product-compliance
Lightning Source LLC
Chambersburg PA
CBHW081146230426
43664CB00018B/2828